Strategy in the American Independence

This book explores the strategies pursued by the Colonies and the other combatants in the American War for Independence, placing the conflict in its proper global context.

Many do not realize the extent to which the 1775 colonial rebellion against British rule escalated into a global conflict. Collectively, this volume examines the strategies pursued by the American Colonies, Great Britain, France, Spain and Holland, and the League of Armed Neutrality, placing the military, naval and diplomatic elements of the struggle in their proper global context. Moreover, assessing how each nation prosecuted their respective wars provides lessons for current students of strategic studies and military and naval history.

This book will be of great interest to students of strategic studies, American history, Military History and political science in general.

Donald Stoker is Professor of Strategy and Policy for the U.S. Naval War College's Monterey Program in Monterey, California. He joined the Strategy and Policy faculty in 1999 and has taught both in Monterey and Newport.

Kenneth J. Hagan, Professor Emeritus, the U.S. Naval Academy, is currently Professor of Strategy and Policy for the U.S. Naval War College's Monterey Program.

Michael T. McMaster is a Professor at the U.S. Naval War College in Monterey. He is a retired U.S. Navy Commander.

Cass military studies

Intelligence Activities in Ancient Rome
Trust in the gods, but verify
Rose Mary Sheldon

Clausewitz and African War
Politics and strategy in Liberia and Somalia
Isabelle Duyvesteyn

Strategy and Politics in the Middle East, 1954–60
Defending the northern tier
Michael Cohen

The Cuban Intervention in Angola, 1965–1991
From Che Guevara to Cuito Cuanavale
Edward George

Military Leadership in the British Civil Wars, 1642–1651
'The genius of this age'
Stanley Carpenter

Israel's Reprisal Policy, 1953–1956
The dynamics of military retaliation
Ze'ev Drory

Bosnia and Herzegovina in the Second World War
Enver Redzic

Leaders in War
West Point remembers the 1991 Gulf War
Edited by Frederick Kagan and Christian Kubik

Khedive Ismail's Army
John Dunn

Yugoslav Military Industry 1918–1991
Amadeo Watkins

Corporal Hitler and the Great War 1914–1918
The list regiment
John Williams

Rostóv in the Russian Civil War, 1917–1920
The key to victory
Brian Murphy

The Tet Effect, Intelligence and the Public Perception of War
Jake Blood

The US Military Profession into the 21st Century
War, peace and politics
Edited by Sam C. Sarkesian and Robert E. Connor, Jr.

Civil–Military Relations in Europe
Learning from crisis and institutional change
Edited by Hans Born, Marina Caparini, Karl Haltiner and Jürgen Kuhlmann

Strategic Culture and Ways of War
Lawrence Sondhaus

Military Unionism in the Post Cold War Era
A future reality?
Edited by Richard Bartle and Lindy Heinecken

Warriors and Politicians
U.S. civil–military relations under stress
Charles A. Stevenson

Military Honour and the Conduct of War
From Ancient Greece to Iraq
Paul Robinson

Military Industry and Regional Defense Policy
India, Iraq and Israel
Timothy D. Hoyt

Managing Defence in a Democracy
Edited by Laura R. Cleary and Teri McConville

Gender and the Military
Women in the armed forces of western democracies
Helena Carreiras

Social Sciences and the Military
An interdisciplinary overview
Edited by Giuseppe Caforio

Cultural Diversity in the Armed Forces
An international comparison
Edited by Joseph Soeters and Jan van der Meulen

Railways and the Russo-Japanese War
Transporting war
Felix Patrikeeff and Harold Shukman

War and Media Operations
The US military and the press from Vietnam to Iraq
Thomas Rid

Ancient China on Postmodern War
Enduring ideas from the Chinese strategic tradition
Thomas Kane

Special Forces, Terrorism and Strategy
Warfare by other means
Alasdair Finlan

Imperial Defence, 1856–1956
The old world order
Greg Kennedy

Civil–Military Cooperation in Post-Conflict Operations
Emerging theory and practice
Christopher Ankersen

Military Advising and Assistance
From mercenaries to privatization, 1815–2007
Donald Stoker

Private Military and Security Companies
Ethics, policies and civil–military relations
Edited by Andrew Alexandra, Deane-Peter Baker and Marina Caparini

Military Cooperation in Multinational Peace Operations
Managing cultural diversity and crisis response
Edited by Joseph Soeters and Philippe Manigart

The Military and Domestic Politics
A concordance theory of civil–military relations
Rebecca L. Schiff

Conscription in the Napoleonic Era
A revolution in military affairs?
Edited by Donald Stoker, Frederick C. Schneid and Harold D. Blanton

Modernity, the Media and the Military
The creation of national mythologies on the Western Front 1914–1918
John F. Williams

American Soldiers in Iraq
McSoldiers or innovative professionals?
Morten Ender

Complex Peace Operations and Civil–Military Relations
Winning the peace
Robert Egnell

Strategy in the American War of Independence
A global approach
Edited by Donald Stoker, Kenneth J. Hagan and Michael T. McMaster

Strategy in the American War of Independence
A global approach

Edited by Donald Stoker,
Kenneth J. Hagan and
Michael T. McMaster

Taylor & Francis Group

LONDON AND NEW YORK

First published 2010
by Routledge
2 Park Square, Milton Park, Abingdon, Oxfordshire OX14 4RN

Simultaneously published in the USA and Canada
by Routledge
711 Third Avenue, New York, NY 10017

Routledge is an imprint of the Taylor & Francis Group, an informa business

First issued in paperback 2011

© 2010 Selection and editorial matter, Donald Stoker, Kenneth J. Hagan and Michael T. McMaster; individual chapters, the contributors

Typeset in Times by Wearset Ltd, Boldon, Tyne and Wear

All rights reserved. No part of this book may be reprinted or reproduced or utilized in any form or by any electronic, mechanical, or other means, now known or hereafter invented, including photocopying and recording, or in any information storage or retrieval system, without permission in writing from the publishers.

British Library Cataloguing in Publication Data
A catalogue record for this book is available from the British Library

Library of Congress Cataloging in Publication Data
A catalog record for this book has been requested

ISBN13: 978-0-415-36734-9 (hbk)
ISBN13: 978-0-415-69568-8 (pbk)
ISBN13: 978-0-203-01970-2 (ebk)

For our wives
Carol
Vera
Laura

And to Lady Rose

Contents

List of illustrations — xi
About the editors — xii
List of contributors — xiv
Preface — xvii

Introduction — 1
ERIC J. GROVE

1 **Colonial military strategy** — 5
DONALD STOKER AND MICHAEL W. JONES

2 **The birth of American naval strategy** — 35
KENNETH J. HAGAN

3 **British military strategy** — 58
JEREMY BLACK

4 **British naval strategy: war on a global scale** — 73
JOHN REEVE

5 **The King's Friends: Loyalists in British strategy** — 100
RICARDO A. HERRERA

6 **Ambivalent allies: strategy and the Native Americans** — 120
KARIM M. TIRO

7 **French strategy and the American Revolution: a reappraisal** — 141
JAMES PRITCHARD

8	**Spanish policy and strategy** THOMAS E. CHÁVEZ	163
9	**Dutch maritime strategy** VICTOR ENTHOVEN	176
10	**The League of Armed Neutrality, 1780–83** LEOS MÜLLER	202

Select bibliography   221
Index   237

Illustrations

Tables

9.1	Disposition of Dutch navy ships, fall 1780	187
9.2	Armament of the largest Royal Navy and Dutch navy ships, 1781	188
9.3	Number of Dutch navy ships, October 1782	189
10.1	Scandinavian voyages beyond Cape Finisterre, according to passports issued in 1776–85	216

Appendices

9.1	Shipbuilding funds allocated for the Dutch navy, 1771–80	196–7

About the editors

Donald Stoker, PhD, is Professor of Strategy and Policy at the U.S. Naval War College in Monterey, California. He is the author of *Britain, France, and the Naval Arms Trade in the Baltic, 1919–1939: Grand Strategy and Failure* (Frank Cass, 2003), and the co-editor (with Jonathan Grant) of *Girding for Battle: The Arms Trade in a Global Perspective, 1815–1940* (Praeger, 2003). He also edited *From Mercenaries to Privatization: The Evolution of Military Advising and Assistance, 1815–2007* (Routledge, 2008), and is a co-editor (with Frederick Schneid and Harold Blanton) of *Conscription in the Napoleonic Era: A Revolution in Military Affairs?* (Routledge, 2009). He is currently writing a book on Civil War strategy for Oxford University Press.

Kenneth J. Hagan, PhD, is Professor of Strategy and Policy at the U.S. Naval War College in Monterey, California, and Professor and Museum Director Emeritus at the U.S. Naval Academy. He wrote *American Gunboat Diplomacy and the Old Navy, 1877–1889* (Greenwood, 1973) and *This People's Navy: The Making of American Sea Power* (Free Press, 1991), and *Unintended Consequences: The United States at War* (Reaktion, 2007), co-authored with Professor Ian J. Bickerton of the University of New South Wales. Recently he published the anthology, *In Peace and War: Interpretations of American Naval History, 30th Anniversary Edition* (Greenwood, 2008), co-edited with Michael McMaster. He is a co-author of the seventh edition of *American Foreign Relations: A History*, 2 vols. (Boston: Wadsworth, 2010). Ken is a retired Captain in the U.S. Naval Reserve. For over 30 years he has served as academic advisor and curriculum director of the Sea Power Course of the national college-level Naval ROTC program.

Michael T. McMaster is Professor of Joint Maritime Operations at the U.S. Naval War College in Monterey, California. He is a graduate of the University of New Mexico and the Naval Postgraduate School. He served 22 years in the U.S. Navy as a Surface Warfare Officer and is a retired Commander. In 2006 and 2007, he jointly presented papers (with Kenneth Hagan) on the history of U.S. naval strategy at Sea Power Conferences of the Royal Australian Navy. He is co-author of "The United States Navy Since President Ronald Reagan," in *Sea Power: Challenges Old and New* (Halstead, 2006) and a contributor and associate editor for the Thirtieth-Anniversary Edition of *In Peace and War: Interpretations of American Naval History* (Greenwood, 2008). He annually contributes to the curriculum review of the Sea Power Course of the national college-level Naval ROTC program. In September 2009, Mike and Ken Hagan presented a paper on Admiral William S. Sims and the Anglo-American Naval Alliance at the Fifth Conference of the International Society for First World War Studies, Imperial War Museum, London.

Contributors

Jeremy Black, MBE, is a British historian and Professor of History at the University of Exeter. He is a senior fellow at the Center for the Study of America and the West at the Foreign Policy Research Institute. He is the author of over 70 books, especially on eighteenth-century British politics and international relations. He graduated from Queens' College, Cambridge, with a starred first and then did postgraduate work at St John's and Merton at Oxford, and taught at Durham University as a professor before moving to Exeter in 1996. He has lectured extensively in Australia, Canada, Denmark, France, Germany, Italy and the U.S., and was awarded an MBE for services to stamp design. He has also recently been involved with the Oxford Discovery Program on the Transatlantic Crossing of the Queen Mary 2 where he delivered a series of four lectures. His most recent publications include: *Eighteenth Century Britain, 1688–1783* (Palgrave, 2008) and *George III: America's Last King* (Yale, 2007).

Thomas E. Chávez is a historian with a PhD from the University of New Mexico. He recently retired as the Executive Director of the National Hispanic Culture Center in Albuquerque. Before that he was director of the Palace of the Governors in Santa Fe, New Mexico for 21 years. He has published numerous book reviews, articles and books, and wrote a monthly article for *The Santa Fe New Mexican*. Currently, he is helping the Museum of Spanish Colonial Art raise an endowment. His published books are: *Conflict and Acculturation: Manuel Alvarez's 1841 Memorial* (Museum of New Mexico Press, 1989), *Manuel Alvarez, 1794–1856: A Southwestern Biography* (University Press of Colorado, 1990), *In Quest for Quivera: Spanish Exploration on the Plains, 1540–1821* (Southwest Parks and Monuments Association, 1992), *An Illustrated History of New Mexico* (University Press of Colorado, 1992), *Spain and the Independence of the United States: An Intrinsic Gift* (University of New Mexico Press, 2002), *España y la Independencia de Estados Unidos* (Taurus, 2006), *Wake For A Fat Vicar: Padre Juan Felipe Ortiz, Archbishop Lamy and the New Mexican Catholic Church in the Middle of the Nineteenth Century*, co-authored with Fray Angélico Chávez (LPD Press, 2004) and *New Mexico: Past and Future* (University of New Mexico Press, 2006).

Victor Enthoven, PhD, is associate professor at the Netherlands Defense Academy and senior researcher at the Free University Amsterdam. He was trained as a maritime historian at Leiden University. In 2003 he published, in conjunction with Johannes Postma, the edited volume *Riches from Atlantic Commerce: Dutch Transatlantic Trade and Shipping, 1585–1817* (Brill, 2003).

Eric J. Grove, PhD, has been Professor of Naval History and Director of the Centre for International Security and War Studies at the University of Salford in Greater Manchester since 2005. After studying at Aberdeen University and King's College, London, Dr. Grove began his teaching career as a civilian lecturer at the Royal Naval College, Dartmouth. He has been professionally associated with the Council for Arms Control, the Royal Naval College Greenwich, the University of Cambridge, the Foundation for International Security, and the University of Hull where in 1993 he became Reader in Politics and International Studies and Director of the Centre for Security Studies. He is Vice President of the Society for Nautical Research, a Member of the Council of the Navy Records Society and a Fellow of the Royal Historical Society. A partial list of his books includes *Vanguard to Trident: British Naval Policy since World War II* (Naval Institute Press, 1987), *The Future of Sea Power* (Routledge, 1990), *Sea Battles Close-Up: The Age of Nelson* (Ian Allan, 1996), *Fleet to Fleet Encounters: Tsushima, Jutland, Philippine Sea* (Arms and Armour, 1991), *The Price of Disobedience: The Battle of the River Plate Reconsidered* (Naval Institute Press, 2000) and *The Royal Navy Since 1815: A New Short History* (Palgrave Macmillan, 2005).

Ricardo A. Herrera, PhD, is a historian on the Staff Ride Team, Combat Studies Institute, United States Army Combined Arms Center, at Fort Leavenworth, Kansas. A graduate of Marquette University and the University of California at Los Angeles, Herrera has been a department chair and director of honors. Herrera also served as an Armor and Cavalry officer.

Michael W. Jones is Professor of Strategy and Policy at the U.S. Naval War College in Monterey, California. He earned his PhD from Florida State University where he specialized in the French Revolution and Napoleonic history. His minor fields include American military history, nineteenth- and twentieth-century Europe and Latin America. His previous teaching assignments have been at Florida State University and Southeastern Louisiana University. He has published several articles on Napoleonic diplomacy and is the author of "The Philippines: Striking into Emptiness (1944–1945)," in *Amphibious Assault: Manoeuvre from the Sea* (Crown, 2005; Seafarer Books, 2007). In 2003 he received a direct commission as an intelligence officer in the United States Navy Reserve and currently serves at the Naval Strike and Warfare Center in Fallon, Nevada.

Leos Müller, PhD, is Associate Professor in the Department of History at Uppsala University. He is the author of *The Merchant Houses of Stockholm, c. 1650–1800: A Comparative Study of Early Modern Entrepreneurial*

Behaviour (Uppsala, 1998), and *Consuls, Corsairs, and Commerce: The Swedish Consular Service and Long-Distance Shipping, 1720–1815* (Uppsala, 2004). He has published a number of articles on trade and the maritime history of early modern Sweden. He is currently working on a book on Sweden's neutrality and shipping industry in the eighteenth century.

James Pritchard is Professor Emeritus of History at Queen's University, Canada. He is the author of *Louis XV's Navy: A Study of Organization and Administration* (McGill-Queen's University Press, 1985), *Anatomy of a Naval Disaster: The French 1746 Expedition to North America* (McGill-Queen's University Press, 1995) and *In Search of Empire: The French in the Americas* (Cambridge University Press, 2004), which have received prizes in the United States and Canada. He is currently writing a history of the Canadian shipbuilding industry during the World War II.

John Reeve, PhD, is Senior Lecturer and Osborne Fellow in Naval History at the University of New South Wales, Australian Defence Force Academy, and a Fellow of the Royal Historical Society. A graduate of Melbourne and Cambridge Universities, his publications include *Charles I and the Road to Personal Rule* (Cambridge University Press, 1989) and (co-edited) *The Face of Naval Battle: The Human Experience of Modern War at Sea* (Allen & Unwin, 2003).

Karim M. Tiro is Associate Professor of History at Xavier University. He is co-editor of *Along the Hudson and Mohawk: The 1790 Journey of Count Paolo Andreani* (University of Pennsylvania Press, 2006). His articles have appeared in the *Journal of the Early Republic, American Indian Law Review* and *American Quarterly*.

Preface

Long ago, John Adams prophesied that when the history of the American War of Independence was written, it would mythologize George Washington and Benjamin Franklin above all others. He fantasized that Americans would come to believe God struck Franklin's kite with lightning and the electrical charge zipped down the string to the ground causing a violent explosion. From the billowing smoke emerged a fully uniformed General George Washington, who would single-handedly win the war. Adams fretted that his own very substantial contribution to American independence and liberty would be largely overlooked.

As Eric Grove's engaging description of his own first encounters with American students in the 1980s makes clear, Adams was not too far from the mark. Most military histories of the war treat it almost exclusively as an Anglo-American affair, a struggle between a virtuous David and an overwhelmingly oppressive Goliath, the outcome of which was decided by the genius of George Washington. A half-century ago, the British historian Marcus Cunliffe set out to correct this misapprehension in his brilliantly inquiring book, *George Washington: Man and Monument*, but in the end he pretty much conceded failure in the valiant attempt to show that Washington had feet of clay. The present volume revives the question about Washington's primacy in determining the outcome of the war and in doing so it assails the notion of the exclusively bilateral nature of the conflict.

Our concept in proposing the book to the editors at Routledge was to produce a study that convincingly demonstrates the global and multilateral aspects of the war, principally from the strategic perspective. In compiling a list of entities involved in the war at this level we have focused mostly on nation-states, but we have included some groups not considered states in the eighteenth-century sense, notably the Native Americans and the Loyalists. We may have erred by omission, perhaps especially by not including the African-American slaves, and we regret this; but they did not constitute an element possessing the opportunity or organization to make strategic decisions. As Douglas R. Egerton demonstrates in *Death or Liberty: African Americans and Revolutionary America*, and Simon Schama in *Rough Crossings: Britain, the Slaves, and the American Revolution*, slaves and black freedmen, like many others in the colonial world, were swept into the maelstrom on both sides. Our concern is with the identifiable power centers that shaped strategies for coping with the war in North America and its fallout.

It is our hope that this book will contribute to the broadening of conceptual horizons by showing that from the moment of its inception in July 1776 the United States has been inescapably enmeshed in the military and diplomatic affairs of the rest of the world. Presidents George Washington, John Adams and Thomas Jefferson warned and fought against the dangers of this entanglement, but the history of their own War of Independence shows that escape is impossible. The only realistic option is to maximize the opportunities presented by the interrelationships for the benefit of the nation – and of its allies.

Donald Stoker
Kenneth J. Hagan
Michael T. McMaster
Monterey, California

Introduction

Eric J. Grove

Just after starting my most enjoyable exchange posting from the Royal Naval College Dartmouth to the U.S. Naval Academy in 1980–81, I had to teach a session on the War of American Independence or "The Revolution," as I found Americans called it. This opportunity coincided with a fascinating visit to a local high school where I was asked to say a few words. As a strong believer in questioning students' assumptions (the role of a civilian lecturer in a military academy, as I was told by my first Director of Studies, the late Harry Stewart), I gave both audiences a strong justification of the British position in that conflict, from the point of view of the assailed great power. In the aftermath of the Vietnam War, and in the context of the Iranian hostage crisis of 1979–81, my perspective struck a dissonant chord with many members of my audiences, although one midshipman who later failed her examinations said in justification of her poor history results that she had been mixed up as to who were "us" and who "them." Clearly my strategy had worked, perhaps too well in this case. One of the high-school students who later served me in a restaurant exclaimed: "Gee, you're the professor who told us how the British were right in the Revolution!" I seemed at least to have broadened her perspective a little.

As the following chapters make clear, the war of 1775–83 was a truly global conflict where the political rather than the military dimensions of strategy were never more important. The falling out of Great Britain with a significant proportion of the inhabitants of the 13 North American colonies had major international repercussions. France was determined to bring Britain down a peg or two in order to make her a less overbearing companion in the system of European great powers. Spain wanted to do something to reverse the steady expansion of the British Empire at her expense, and notably – but far from exclusively – achieve the return of Gibraltar and Minorca to Spanish control. Both countries supported the American rebels from the start, if at first carefully and covertly in order to avoid unnecessary conflict with the world's greatest individual global power.

The international nature of the contemporary global maritime trading system meant that other nations were also eventually pulled in or forced to take up officially neutral positions. The Netherlands was dragged, somewhat reluctantly, into war with Britain because of its interests in providing channels of trade with the rebellious colonies. Denmark and Sweden, together with Russia, declared themselves "Armed Neutrals" to safeguard their shipping. Russia in addition had its own continental interests to pursue, and Prussia and Austria – unlike in the previous wars of the mid-eighteenth century – kept their contemporary squabble, the War of the Bavarian Succession of 1778–79, disentangled from the maritime struggles for global empire. Canada, as the elder William Pitt had boasted, might have been conquered on European battlefields in the previous war of 1756–63, but in this new conflict the 13 American colonies were not going to be retained because of actions in Germany.

There has been a tendency to criticize Lord North's government for not having a continental dimension to its strategy to deter France from coming to the aid of the rebels or, if that failed, to decisively weaken France's overseas war effort. I was one of those naval historians of the Cold War era brought up by Professor Brian Ranft of the Royal Naval College Greenwich to note well that Britain's only significant defeat in the last three centuries was in the war in which Britain lacked a continental dimension to its strategy. More recently the pendulum of opinion has begun to swing the opposite way. As Jeremy Black argues in the following pages, Britain as a status quo power had, on balance, no need to risk the perils of continental embroilment any more. She needed to concentrate her military expenditures and strategy directly to pacify America and hang on to Gibraltar. In a subsequent chapter, John Reeve quotes Professor Nicholas Rodger's assertion that the French navy's weaknesses were not contingent upon a diversion of resources to the army. They were intrinsic to French naval strategy. Nevertheless, one should not throw out the baby with the bathwater. Le Comte de Vergennes, the most important French minister guiding his country's destiny in the war, was only too quick to do his best to prevent the "Potato War" over Bavaria from getting out of hand. France's unique opportunity to concentrate on the sea and land dimensions of a truly maritime strategy was too good an opportunity to be thrown away.

Britain was also unfortunate that the Marine Royale was in pretty good shape in 1775 to pursue its country's maritime ambitions. Its gunnery was much improved, although it was still not up to the standards of the ever-improving British. It is true that the newly professionalized French gunners knew their weaknesses as well as their strengths and, as at the battle of the Saints, would take refuge below rather than face more powerful ships in close-range combat. Nevertheless, one gets the impression in this war that the clear British naval superiority, so well displayed in the later stages of the Seven Years' War and against the navy of Napoleon beginning in 1798, was at its lowest level in relative terms in the 1770s and 1780s. French admirals might sensibly continue to place the attainment of wider objectives before battle for its own sake; by doing so, they achieved perhaps the most decisive result in the French Navy's history, the battle of the Virginia Capes, the immediate prelude to Yorktown. Here and elsewhere, British admirals probably had more reason than at other periods not to take too many risks with their opponents, and this must account at least in part for the uncharacteristic timidity shown by British naval commanders for most of the war. Even the conflict's greatest British victory at sea, that of Rodney at the

Saints in April 1782, was most likely a result of contingency as much as intention.

Spain's navy gave the allies numerical superiority over their British enemy, but there was one weakness that had not been attended to by the Continental maritime powers. The British naval obsession with cleanliness had a key operational purpose, the ability to deploy fleets with healthy crews, in a modern sense, keeping the ships' mechanisms in working order. It was rampant illness, coupled with the brilliant "fleet-in-being" strategy adopted by the British, that defeated the great Franco-Spanish expedition of 1779 to capture the Isle of Wight so it could be exchanged for Gibraltar after the war.

In his study of Spanish policy and strategy in Chapter 8, Thomas Chávez demonstrates how, despite such reverses, the Spanish record in the war is remarkably positive. Not least of the contributions was the synergy with the French that led to Yorktown. The allies had been planning a descent on Jamaica but, when news came in of the decisive opportunity offered by Cornwallis' predicament, the allied leadership decided to take advantage of it. The Spanish would look after the Caribbean; de Grasse would go to Chesapeake Bay. This movement of ships and men had to be paid for in theater, and Chávez documents how Spanish resourcefulness provided the funds. The American historical debt to Spain is thus almost as great as the one owed to France.

The British surrender at Yorktown in October 1781 was clearly the major turning point in the American victory. Again, it and the covering battle of the Virginia Capes were not the only factors in the outcome of the war. As Ricardo A. Herrera shows later in Chapter 5, Cornwallis' stand at Yorktown came at the end of a failed campaign where the Loyalists, upon whom Britain's hopes in its southern strategy rested, had demonstrated their inability to play their part in the overly ambitious British plans. The Loyalists receive too little attention in accounts of the war. Their potential was greater than the jaundiced British commanders later believed, as Donald Stoker and Michael W. Jones point out in the opening chapter on American military strategy in the war. They also clearly demonstrate how Nathanael Greene's masterly Fabian strategy of preserving his "army-in-being" was another key factor in forcing Cornwallis northwards to his ultimate surrender.

As long as the rebels could keep their forces in the field, the British could not win. One is drawn to the conclusion that perhaps the greatest British missed opportunity of the war was the Howe brothers' failure to smash Washington's army after the masterly amphibious beginning to the New York campaign in 1776. To be sure, Washington's skill in keeping his forces from being prematurely crushed was a factor. Probably more important, however, was the Howe brothers' reluctance to seek a military solution, a cautiousness rooted in their own Whiggish anti-Lord North political positions and in their interpretation of their instructions to achieve a negotiated peace. Like many Britons, they failed to pay sufficient regard to the colonial fixation with independence as the Americans' minimum, non-negotiable political objective. Once the opportunity was missed decisively to remake the political context by clear military success, the stage was set for the ultimate failure of pacification and the loss of the 13 colonies.

The battles that actually reset the agenda were Saratoga in 1777 and Yorktown in 1781, not for their direct military significance but for their political results. The first brought in France, and thus later Spain, although the strategic connection from Madrid to the rebellious colonists ran firmly through Paris. The latter led to the fall of the North government in March 1782 and the advent of the Rockingham Cabinet, which was committed to peace negotiations. As Jeremy Black points out in Chapter 3, the center of gravity of the overall war had moved firmly to the Caribbean by then. Rodney's victory in the fleet action of the Saints resulted from an opportunity to stress the traditional British naval virtue of superiority in firepower. By then, Britain had also corrected the quantitative naval balance. With the overall strategic position thus redressed, Britain was ready for a compromise eighteenth-century peace in which, as John Reeve points out, she retained the main strategic benefits of 1763: Gibraltar, Canada, India and the important parts of the West Indies. The British calculated that the new confederation of former colonies might well not be a permanent friend of France and Spain, and in this they were proved to be correct.

This book, given its wide-ranging approach, has allowed an international group of experts to provide a number of interlocking perspectives on a very complex global conflict. Not all the chapters agree with each other in every detail, but this adds to, rather than detracts from, the collection's value. One cannot but read it as a whole without acquiring valuable new insights, be they on the broader significance of the raiding activities of John Paul Jones or the tangled attitudes of the Native Americans, who were natural allies of neither side and had important interests of their own. Reading it will also mean that one cannot ever again take a simplistic view of this most multifaceted conflict. It has certainly made me think again. The book also has another utility in present times. It clearly demonstrates that in any era the pacification of a hostile, unwelcoming country can be more difficult than it promises to be at first sight. This strategic reality was underscored a generation ago in Vietnam, and it has been dramatically illustrated once again at the beginning of the twenty-first century. Contemporary politicians and strategists in Washington and London therefore have much to learn from contemplating this book's re-examination of the War of American Independence.

1 Colonial military strategy

Donald Stoker and Michael W. Jones[1]

The development and implementation of a successful military strategy proved critical to the colonial achievement of independence. The American colonies emerged victorious not merely as a result of the mistakes of their enemy (which indeed helped), nor just because of the French and Spanish intervention (though this proved indispensable). America won its war by developing suitable and effective strategic responses to the situation at hand.

A strategy founded upon weakness – and a clear objective

British errors and foreign assistance do not in themselves trump the basic weaknesses of the colonial strategic and military situation. The rebelling Americans were an isolated lot, on the ragged edge of the Western, industrializing world, lacking in industry (other than distilleries, a possible center of gravity neglected by the British), divided in loyalties and bereft of any formal army. Their only military force was a militia of infinite utility but dubious quality. Despite all of these limitations, they emerged victorious against the greatest power of the age.

One thing that contributed decisively to this outcome was the great clarity of vision that the political and military leadership developed in regard to how they defined victory: independence. It took more than a year for the Revolutionaries to reach this consensus, but once they did, and actually declared independence in July 1776, they possessed a clear objective for which to fight, and upon which to hang their military and diplomatic efforts, something that aligns with the advice of the Prussian military theorist Carl von Clausewitz.

The nature of the war

The outbreak of fighting at Lexington and Concord in April 1775 provided early clues as to the military nature of this war. The irregular warfare pursued by the Americans against the British troops marching back to Boston provided the first glimpse of one approach to warfighting that remained a constant throughout the struggle. Although spontaneous and poorly directed at first, irregular warfare became a key element of colonial warfighting, one George Washington eventually integrated into his strategy for fighting the war.

The British seizure of Boston's Bunker and Breeds Hills on 18 June 1775 demonstrate a second element of the war's nature. Here, the British carried the day, driving the Americans from their fixed positions, defeating the enemy in a traditional military manner.[2] Generally, when the colonials faced the British on the field in a traditional fight, they lost. But the British always paid a price in casualties – a cost they could not afford to pay. Their manpower limits increased their susceptibility to an attritional strategy. Eventually, both of these sides of the military struggle worked against them.

Colonial strategy – the first phase: aggression and consolidation

With Boston besieged by an army that arose spontaneously from the population of the 13 colonies, the Continental Congress searched for a general to lead it. On 16 June 1775, the Congress informed George Washington that they had picked him. Washington was 43, Virginia gentry, a planter, surveyor, politician, militia officer and veteran of the French and Indian War (1756–63), a man who from his youth had been ambitious for military glory. The choice was partly political, an effort to weld the southern states closer to the United Colonies. He was also not really qualified for the job, but neither was anyone else, even though he was the only delegate at the Congress who showed up in uniform.[3]

Washington took the post when it was offered to him, but though he must have wanted the job, or something similar to it, he approached it trembling. He told Patrick Henry: "From the day I enter upon the command of the American armies, I date my fall and the ruin of my reputation."[4] Washington was always an optimist.

When Washington arrived outside Boston on 2 July 1775, he inherited a Sisyphean task: build an army from nothing in the face of a skilled opponent. He proceeded to do this twice during the nearly year-long siege because the short enlistment period of the first members of this new Continental Army meant that most of them went home on New Year's Day 1776.[5]

Washington's realization that not much militarily was going to happen at Boston led him to recruit privateers to raid British transports. The first sailed in September 1775; others followed in October. Their primary task: seize the ships bringing fresh provisions from Nova Scotia and Canada to the British troops in Boston. But no one would be displeased if they took any other British ship, especially if it carried arms or powder, both of which the Americans desperately needed.[6]

The Congress, though restrained at first, quickly developed an aggressive streak in regard to Canada. The most ambitious American leaders saw it as a potential fourteenth colony and determined to have it from the beginning. By early June 1775, Congress had information from Canada "that the French are not unfriendly" to the American cause. Plus, the Americans had the perfect jumping-off point for an invasion: Fort Ticonderoga, which they had seized in the opening days of the struggle. Congress passed resolutions on 27 June 1775 that boiled down to calling on Major General Phillip Schuyler, the American commander at Ticonderoga, to drive the British out of Canada – if he found it feasible – and if the Indians and Canadians did not object. This was a change. Previously, on 1 June, Congress forbade any troops from entering Canada. Receipt of a letter detailing British Governor General Sir Guy Carleton's boat-building efforts at St. John (Jean), 15 miles to the east of Montreal, and that the Caughnawaga Indians had decided to fight for King George, changed the congressional minds.[7]

Washington soon became a supporter of Congress' campaign against Canada. On 20 August 1775, he proposed supplementing it with what became Benedict Arnold's expedition up the Kennebec River to Quebec. To Washington, this would divert Carleton from the primary American offensive.[8]

The command of the other prong of the offensive devolved upon the very capable Brigadier General Richard Montgomery, who departed Ticonderoga for Montreal in September at the head of 1,000 men. He took the city's surrender on 13 November. On New Year's Eve, the Americans attacked Quebec in the midst of a blinding snowstorm. The operation proved a debacle. Montgomery was killed, Arnold wounded. Defeat, though, did not end the colonists' Canadian ambitions.[9]

Washington looked beyond just the capture of Quebec, and even of Canada itself. He looked for a way to win the war, to remove the burden of the army's support upon his country "by some decisive Stroke."[10] But his immediate concern remained Boston.

Washington found the British in Boston strongly entrenched and protected by the guns of their fleet, not a situation to his liking, but one he could do little about, though he would certainly try. Congress had instructed him to expel the British from Boston and as he built, and then built again, an American army, he and his subordinates considered a number of risky schemes for attacking the city, something Washington dearly wanted to do. Fortunately for the American cause, his generals talked him out of them. But the right plan eventually emerged: they would place guns on Dorchester Heights, thus threatening the entire garrison, and the British ships in the harbor. Hastily, on 17 March the British sailed from the city, bound for Nova Scotia.[11]

Colonial strategy – the second phase: the war of posts

While still embroiled in the siege of Boston, Washington worried about Britain's intentions. In January of 1776 he looked down from the heights around Boston to see the British fitting-out their fleet for an imminent departure. But where were they going? To Washington, the lateness of the season meant that the British could only conduct operations south of Boston. The previous October, he received intelligence from Britain insisting upon future British operations aimed at New York City and the Hudson River. Washington well knew the Loyalist proclivities of the residents of New York and Long Island, and the strategic importance of the great city at the mouth of the Hudson. In his mind, this fleet *had* to be destined for New York or Long Island. Washington believed it was critically important to keep the British from gaining control of New York City and the Hudson River, thus giving them "command of the Country, and the Communication with Canada." Hence, after discussions with the Congress, Washington dispatched Major General Charles Lee to New York to raise volunteers to prepare the city and the Hudson River's fortifications for defense, and to disarm any enemies of the cause.[12]

Meanwhile, Congress reorganized the American army command system. It divided the middle colonies into two departments, the Middle, comprising New England, New York, New Jersey, Delaware, Pennsylvania and Maryland; and the Southern, consisting of Virginia, the Carolinas and Georgia.[13]

By the time May became June, Washington believed the British would make their major pushes for 1776 in Canada and New York. He began sending detachments to New York City before the British evacuated Boston, and came himself with the bulk of the army in April 1776. Worse, he thought the Americans unprepared to meet them in manpower and arms.[14] In July he wrote that the British intended to concentrate on "the state of New York, to penetrate into it by way of the Lakes and the North [Hudson] River & to unite their attacks."[15] Operationally, he was not so sure how they would go about it. But to meet them, he insisted, "I think it is necessary to exert our every nerve, and by defeating their views this Campaign be enabled to meet them with double advantage the next, should they think proper to pursue their unwarrantable measures."[16] Significantly, Washington drew a firm connection between the success of operations in Canada and of his forces in New York. He viewed the theater of war in a strategic sense, as a whole, one supported by multiple operational campaigns.

Washington did express at least some confidence in facing the enemy, and hoped that if his forces were not victorious at least the British would suffer more than they could bear, and raise the cost of their victory beyond their ability to pay:

> I trust through divine favor and our own exertions they will be disappointed in their views, and at all events any Advantages they may gain will cost them very dear. If our Troops will behave well, which I hope will be the case, having every thing to contend for that Freemen hold dear, they will have to wade through much blood & Slaughter before they can carry any part of our Works, If they carry 'em at all, and at best be in possession of a melancholy and mournfull victory.[17]

Washington hoped to bleed the British in New York as the Americans had at Bunker Hill. He decided to fight from a series of fixed positions, sapping the strength of the British in each fight. Later, Washington referred to this as a "War of Posts." From the Americans' perspective, this made sense. They could not stand against the British and their German mercenaries in the open field, but they believed that behind fortifications they stood a decent chance.[18] The problem with this approach was the underlying and dubious assumption that the British would fight in New York as they had at Bunker Hill.

Washington was very aware of the tenuous position his army occupied in New York. Washington assigned three divisions to defend New York City and Manhattan Island's southern tip. A forth division held northern Manhattan, anchoring its defense at Fort Washington. The fifth and final division guarded the eastern heights of Long Island, including the Brooklyn Heights, which dominated New York City. British ships completely cut his communications via water between his position in New York City and Albany to the north. Plus, he expected even *more* British forces to arrive and soon he had intelligence that the British army in America by the end of July was to be 50,000 men. General Sir William Howe would eventually command 32,000 troops in New York. Washington initially opposed him with 19,000, though August found him with 28,000.[19] Despite this, he elected to stay, and the obvious question is, "Why?"

Part of why must have been his conclusion that the British intended to make New York a theater of decision. The arrival of General Sir Henry Clinton's forces from the failed British campaign against South Carolina fed his conviction. He made note of this, and the information he had of British intentions to supplement Howe's army with another 11,000 men from Newfoundland any day. "An attack is now therefore to be expected which will Probably decide the Fate of America," Washington wrote on 7 August 1776. But he did not believe the fight for the area around New York City was the only one coming. Washington was firmly convinced, particularly because of what was going on in northern New York state, that "Our Enemies seem determined to push US on All Quarters. It is Nothing but what We may expect." Washington believed much was at stake, writing that if the Americans proved successful in the coming contest, it "will put us on such a footing as to bid defiance to the utmost malice of the British Nation and those in alliance with her."[20]

But the area around New York City was where the fight was directly his, and where he believed the heaviest blow would fall. His intelligence put the anticipated British numbers facing him at 30,000. His own returns put American strength, including sick and furloughed, at 20,537. Moreover, in his mind, the British *had* to act here: "The disgrace of the British army to the southward, and the season being far advanced will make them exert every nerve against us in this Quarter." To not do all that they could, he noted, would be "tempting Providence." Washington believed British action became inevitable when the anticipated forces from Newfoundland arrived.[21]

The American commander-in-chief continued to lack optimism about a future positive result in New York. One is hesitant to call it fatalism because Washington was not the type; stark acceptance of the realities of his situation is perhaps the best description. In early August 1776, in their posts on New York, Long Island, Governor's Island, and Paulus Hook, the Americans had 17,225 men. But, "Our posts too are too much divided having Waters between many of them and some distant from Others Fifteen Miles. These circumstances sufficiently distressing of themselves, are much aggravated by the Sickness that prevails through the Army." He listed over 3,600 sick, present and not. Despite these omens, he would fight:[22]

> Under every disadvantage my utmost exertions shall be employed to bring about the great end we have in view, and so far as I can Judge from the professions and apparent disposition of my Troops, I shall have their Support. The Superiority of the Enemy and the expected Attack, do not seem to have depressed their Spirits. These considerations lead me to think, that though the Appeal may not terminate so happily in our favor as I could wish, that yet they will not succeed in their views without considerable loss. Any advantage they may get, I trust will cost them dear.[23]

But if he did not think he could win in New York, why did he fight there? Washington realized his tactical and operational positions planted the seeds of potential disaster, and that the enemy had superior numbers. Yet, he fought. Was it just to hurt the British, initiating the blood-letting he seemed to believe so necessary to winning the war? Or was it his impression that the pivotal hour had arrived? Or was it the strategic concerns he had earlier identified that made holding New York so vital to the American cause? It was probably all three.

On 21 August 1776, Washington reported intelligence that the British were finally "upon the point of striking the long expected Stroke," possibly attacking up the Hudson River and some of the "lower posts." The British landed troops at Gravesend Bay on Long Island the next day. The British commander, General Howe, then proceeded to attack Washington's strategy. Howe refused to blissfully march into the teeth of the American fortifications. He fought a deliberate, cautious campaign in New York City and its environs, one that preserved his forces because he refused to frontally assault Washington's strong points and generally took them by turning the colonial flanks or using his supporting naval forces to land behind American positions. Meanwhile, his consistent battlefield success decimated the colonials in the form of desertions, prisoners taken and battlefield casualties.[24] But he failed in his most important task: he did not destroy Washington's army because he did not properly pursue.

Although Howe did not destroy the colonial forces, by the end of August 1776 he had taken their posts and broken their morale. The militia proved particularly despondent, and left in large numbers, sometimes by regiments and, Washington wrote, "their example has Infected another part of the Army." This collapsing militia support strengthened Washington's conviction that the colonials needed a regular army and fed his conviction of the futility of relying on the militia for defense. Contradicting some of his earlier impressions, Washington told John Hancock, the president of Congress, "Till of late I had no doubt in my own mind of defending this place nor should I have yet If the Men would do their duty, but this I despair of." Washington promised to do all he could, but he also seemed to be preparing Hancock for coming disaster: "Every power I possess shall be exerted to serve the Cause, & my first wish is, that whatever may be the event, the Congress will do me the Justice to think so."[25]

The critical shift

By the summer of 1777, Washington had a clear view of how to counter the British foe: "My design is to collect all the force that can possible [sic] be drawn from other quarters to this post," he wrote from his camp in New Jersey,

> so as to reduce the security of this army to the greatest certainty possible, and to be in a condition of embracing any fair opportunity, that may offer, to make an attack on advantageous terms – In the mean time I intend by light Bodies of militia, seconded and incouraged by a few Continental Troops, to harass and diminish their number by continual Skirmishes.[26]

Concentrate. Protect his army. Fight only when things suited him. And wear down the enemy with militia supported by Continentals. The war had solidly entered its Fabian phase. But how had it come to this?

On 8 September 1776, Washington had assessed for his superiors his army's situation and the enemy's intent:

> It is now extremely obvious, from all Intelligence, from their movements, and every other circumstance, that having landed their whole Army on Long Island (except about 4,000, on Staten Island) they mean to enclose us on the Island of New York by taking post in our Rear, while the shipping effectually secure the Front, and thus either by cutting off our communication with the Country, oblige us to fight them on their own Terms, or surrender at discretion, or by a brilliant Stroke, endeavour to cut this Army in pieces and secure the Collection of Arms and Stores which they well know we shall not be soon able to replace.[27]

The question he put to a council of his generals the day before was: what should they do about it? Washington's answer to this included an explanation of the previous colonial failure:

> In deliberating on this Question it was impossible to forget, that History, our own experience, the advice of our ablest Friends in Europe, the fears of the Enemy, and even the Declarations of Congress demonstrate, that on our Side the War should be defensive. It has even been called a War of Posts. That we should on all Occasions avoid a general Action, or put anything to Risque, unless compelled by a necessity, into which we ought never to be drawn.[28]

Washington concluded that the idea of basing American strategy on fighting from fortified positions as they had done in New York was dead, killed by Howe's success and American failure to hold such posts.

In many respects, the initial colonial military response made sense: it sought to reduce the detrimental effects of American weaknesses, i.e., their military inferiority, while trying to minimize the great military superiority of the British army. But there were several problems with this strategy that help to explain why it failed. The first boils down to scriptwriting, in that the success of the strategy depended upon the enemy doing *exactly* as the Americans wanted. When the British refused to cooperate, the strategy was well on the way to failure. Second, the "War of Posts" was a strategy of tactics, meaning, it banked upon tactical successes to deliver operational as well as strategic dividends. Historically, it has proven very difficult to achieve one's desired end-state by dependence upon tactical success. The Germans counted on their Storm Troop tactics to deliver victory in 1918. Tactically, and even operationally, the Germans scored great successes, penetrating the Allied defenses, but this tactical effort did not produce the desired strategic result: victory. The Germans dwelt upon tactical issues, but failed to give sufficient thought to what they should do *after* they penetrated the Allied trench lines. The U.S. failure in Vietnam also suffered from the "tacticization of strategy." General William Westmoreland's war of "search and destroy" produced a stream of tactical successes against the North Vietnamese army and guerrillas, but abandoned to the enemy control of the object of the war: the people of South Vietnam. A final weakness, though a smaller one in the colonial approach, was that it surrendered the initiative to the enemy, something one does not want to do. The defense is indeed easier to pursue, at all levels of war, but it can give the enemy the opportunity to dictate much of the shape of the war, as well as its momentum. The choice of a defensive war, though, especially considering the colonial military weaknesses, is understandable.

The discussion of how next to fight the war included a vigorous debate over whether or not to try to hold New York City. In his contribution to this discussion, Major General Nathanael Greene, one of Washington's most trusted subordinates, began a line of thought that became one of the underpinnings of American strategy:

> The City and Island of New York are no objects for us; we are not to bring them in Competition with the General Interest of America. Part of the army already has met with a defeat; the Coungry [sic] is struck with a pannick; any Cappital loss at this time may ruin the cause. Tis our business to study to avoid any considerable misfortune, and to take post where the Enemy will be obliged to fight us and not we them.[29]

In this last sentence of the lapsed Quaker from Rhode Island we find the beginnings of the Fabian approach in American military thinking: fight where advantageous; avoid a decisive defeat that would fatally wound the cause. Such was Greene's view.

Washington valued Greene's advice, as well as that of other subordinates, and the combination of disaster, confidence in Greene's advice and desperation coalesced to create a new approach for fighting the war. In early September 1776, as the good campaigning weather of summer began fading into autumn, Washington wrote from New York City:

I am sensible a retreating Army is incircled [sic] with difficulties, that the declining an Engagement subjects a General to reproach and that the Common cause may be in some measure affected by the discouragements which it throws over the minds of many; nor am I insensible of the contrary effects, if a brilliant stroke could be made with any Probability of success, especially after our loss upon Long Island: but when the fate of America may be at stake on the Issue; when the Wisdom of cooler moments and experienced Men have decided that we should protract the War if Possible; I cannot think it safe or wise to adopt a different System, when the season for Action draws so near a close.[30]

Here is notification of one of the key decisions of the conflict: Washington's decision to seek its protraction rather than its quick end. To do this, the colonials would pursue a Fabian strategy.

What, though, is meant by "Fabian strategy?" The best place to start is with Fabius himself, Fabius Maximus Cunctator, or Fabius Maximus, "the Delayer." During Hannibal's invasion of Italy, unable to stand toe-to-toe with the Carthaginians in the field with any chance of success, the Roman general Fabius simply refused to do so. Fabius kept his forces in the hills to thwart Hannibal's cavalry superiority. He refused to fight a major battle with Hannibal because of the high risks of defeat and the terrible cost of failure. But he also refused to leave the enemy undisturbed and picked at them with small detachments and raids. He sought to wear down their strength and also to prevent them from recruiting from their conquered regions. Liddell Hart described the Roman strategy well:

Hovering in the enemy's neighbourhood, cutting off stragglers and foraging parties, preventing them from gaining any permanent base, Fabius remained an elusive shadow on the horizon, dimming the glamour of Hannibal's triumphal progress. Thus Fabius, by his immunity from defeat, thwarted the effect of Hannibal's previous victories upon the minds of Rome's Italian allies and checked them from changing sides.[31]

This is not an easy approach to warfighting to take. The success of Fabius' strategy demanded the cooperation of other military commanders, as well as the "persistent support of the senate and the people." His strategy had the potential to strain the fibers of the state because it needed that most irreplaceable and precious of commodities – time. J.E.A. Crake made an observation on Fabius' struggle that applies equally to Washington's: "Nothing makes greater demands on loyalty and morale than a plea for patience, a promise of a long war, and a failure to strike back while a foreign army occupies territory of your friends and threatens your own."[32]

Although the Americans apparently decided at their 7 September 1776 council to adopt a Fabian approach to the war, both Washington, who made the ultimate decision, and Greene, who certainly had a say, did not sufficiently subdue their natural eagerness and aggressiveness and put the Fabian strategy into immediate practice. The first example was their hemming and hawing over whether or not to defend New York City during the second week of September 1776.[33] This was followed by the back and forth about defending Manhattan Island's Fort Washington on the banks of the Hudson. Believing the position impregnable, Greene saw in holding it a chance to successfully bleed the British à la the "War of Posts." Retreating from his own advice, Greene prevailed in the argument over whether or not Fort Washington should be abandoned and the Americans chose to fight for it, suffering one of their worst defeats of the war, including the loss of 2,900 men taken as prisoners.[34] Thomas Mifflin, one of the generals present at the critical 7 September meeting, bitterly wrote that the colonials should have "adhered to the Fabian plan" instead of reinforcing Fort Washington.[35]

Despite their losses and defeats, the American efforts in New York had produced some beneficial effect on the American war effort. At the end of October, before the disaster at Fort Washington, Washington wrote:

> We have, I think, by one Manouvre and another, and with a parcel of – but it is best to say nothing about them – Mixed, & ungovernable Troops, spun the Campaign out to this time without coming to any decisive Action, or without letting Genl How [sic] obtain any advantage which, in my opinion, can contribute much to the completion of the business he is come upon, or to the Honour and glory of the British Arms, and those of their Auxilaries [sic] – Our numbers from the Beginning have been disjointed and confused, and much less than were apprehended. [sic] had we ever hazarded a general Action with them therefore, unless it had been in our Works at New York, or Harlem heights, we undoubtedly should have risked a good cause upon a very unfavorable Issue.[36]

Tench Tilghman, Washington's secretary, offered his own assessment: "I think ... we have done greatly in stopping the career of Monsr Howe with the finest army that ever appeared in America, opposed to as bad a one as ever appeared in any part of the Globe."[37]

Executing the Fabian war: the third phase

In November and December 1776, the remnants of Washington's army retreated across New Jersey and into Pennsylvania. Washington, beaten, but not defeated, looked for opportunities to strike back. He also harassed the enemy with militia, issuing in mid-December orders to various commanders to use detachments, if they could, to harass the enemy whenever possible. He also pushed his regular commanders to gather their troops, as well as information on the enemy, in the hopes of doing something to recover their fortunes. The partisan war was about to heat-up.[38]

Washington and his generals possessed great familiarity with the military manuals of the day that dealt with partisan warfare, or as it was also called,

Petite Guerre ("Little War"). For example, Washington recommended Capitaine de Jeney's *The Partisan: or, The Art of Making War in Detachment*, to a fellow officer.[39]

Washington first suggested this mode of warfare at a war council in July 1776, proposing a "Partizan Party" for operations against the British on Staten Island.[40] It became a key element of how Washington fought the war, one often overlooked in studies of the war in the northern colonies. The Americans would use detachments of regular troops, as well as militia units, to constantly harass the British, ambush their messengers and foraging parties, and attack their supply lines, thus tying down their manpower and depleting their resources. Indeed, this type of fighting not only supported the Fabian approach because it concentrated on whittling away the enemy's strength, it was an element of how the ancient Fabius fought his war. It should not, though, be confused with modern-day theory on guerrilla warfare, though their tactical activities were in some respects quite similar. Modern guerrilla warfare theory views the guerrilla fighters as the beginning, core elements of a resistance that then evolves into a regular army that can contest the enemy head on. Military leaders of Washington's day saw their "partisans" as supplements to their formal armies.

Facing the utter dissolution of his army because of its expiring enlistments, Washington famously struck back at Trenton and Princeton in December 1776. Washington's offensive with his regular forces was not all he planned. He had pulled together what militia he could and made sure they had orders to prosecute partisan warfare against the British. Moreover, his victory at Trenton had a landslide effect. Congress voted to give him the extraordinary powers he had requested over military matters. In his reply, he promised that since they had given them as "the last Resort for the preservation" of their liberties, he would lay them aside as soon as their "Liberties are firmly established." In the campaign that followed, Washington was at his best. Using his tiny regular army, and intense partisan activity, the colonials recovered almost all of New Jersey, Howe's command only retaining Brunswick and Amboy on the New Jersey coast.[41]

By the end of February 1777, Washington recognized that the nature of the military struggle was shifting yet again: "I do not apprehend however that this Petit Guerre will be continued long." Anticipating the return of more formal forms of warfare, he wrote, "I think matters will be transacted upon a larger Scale." Washington believed the British would soon break out of their post at Brunswick, toward where, he had ideas, but remained uncertain.[42]

After wintering at Morristown in early 1777, Washington prepared to take the field again. Now, though, he and his commanders had bought wholeheartedly into the Fabian idea. The campaign he waged in the spring and summer of 1777 resembles, operationally and strategically, that of Fabius. Strategically, the colonials faced an aggressive and more skilful opponent. The fate of the Patriot cause rested partly on the performance of subordinate commanders on far-flung fields. And the longer the war went on, the more the patience and support of the people would be tested – and erode.

Operationally, Washington decided he could not force the British from New Jersey, but adopted a plan authored by Nathanael Greene to pin them in their posts by occupying various critical points. The bulk of the army stayed with Washington in Morristown while detachments occupied key positions from Morristown into the very teeth of the British. These included Chatham Turkey (now New Providence), Basking Ridge, Boundbrook, Quibbletown (now New Market), Millstone, Newark, Springfield and some advanced posts commanded by Greene near the British camps at New Brunswick and Amboy.[43]

By mid-June 1777, Washington thought he had a clear understanding of the enemy's options, while identifying their key problem. He believed that the British intended to try to inflict "a severe blow" on his army and seize Philadelphia, the accomplishment of the second necessitating the achievement of the first. He also accurately noted the importance of the continued preservation of his army, writing that "while we have a respectable force in the field, every acquisition of territory they may make will be precarious and perhaps, burthensome."[44] As long as the Americans kept an army in the field, this limited Britain's military options, and made it difficult for them to maintain control over any areas they occupied.

While the Americans watched Howe in the summer of 1777, Alexander Hamilton, Washington's aide, penned what must not only be the best analysis of the American Fabian strategy, but also its best defense:

> I know the comments that some people will make on our Fabian conduct. It will be imputed either to cowardice or weakness: But the more discerning, I trust, will not find it difficult to conceive that it proceeds from the truest policy, and is an argument neither of the one nor the other. The liberties of America are an infinite stake. We should not play a desperate game for it or put it upon the issue of a single cast of the die. The loss of one general engagement may effectually ruin us, and it would certainly be folly to hazard it, unless our resources for keeping an army were to end, and some decisive blow was absolutely necessary; or unless our strength was so great as to give certainty of success. Neither is the case. America can in all probability maintain its army for years, and our numbers though such as should make us intirely [sic] sanguine.... It is therefore Howe's business to make the most of his present strength, and as he is not numerous enough to conquer and garrison as he goes, his only hope lies in fighting us and giving a general defeat in one blow.... Their affairs will be growing worse – our's [sic] better; – so that delay will ruin them. It will serve to perplex and fret them, and precipitate them into measures, that we can turn to good account. Our business then is to avoid a General engagement and waste the enemy away by constantly goading their sides, in a desultory teazing way.[45]

Hamilton penned his explanation in late June 1777. When Howe began his summer campaign, Washington refused to come down from the heights to face him. Here was Fabian war in practice: Washington avoided battle, except on his terms, and generally kept to the hills around Boundbrook, New Jersey. If Howe did move against him, and it became necessary to retreat, Washington had everything prepared to do so. Meanwhile, he bled the British with detachments and militia waging *Petite Guerre*. Howe withdrew back to New Brunswick, unwilling to risk a fight on such disadvantageous ground. Finally, Howe, unable to bring Washington to battle, decided that staying in New Jersey served no purpose and decamped for Staten Island.[46]

The colonial decision to protract the war paid dividends elsewhere in 1777. As in 1776, the British aimed to sever the northern colonies by controlling the Hudson River and Lakes George and Champlain. Determining exactly how the enemy planned to do this remained the problem for Washington. He suspected that Major General John Burgoyne, advancing from Canada, would try to make a junction with an advance by Howe from New York, but he was not sure. Because of this, he did not want to send his entire army to Ticonderoga, but detached elements and ordered them supplemented with militia. Washington feared that the drive from the Canada toward Ticonderoga was a feint to draw off his army and that if he took the bait he would leave Philadelphia open to attack by Howe, which, as he suspected, was the general's real objective. So Washington moved his army back to Morristown, New Jersey, a position that allowed him to watch Howe's forces in New York while protecting his own, and held it ready to move when the enemy's plans became clear.[47] Again, he modeled himself on Fabius.

Washington's "shyness," as Hamilton put it, served to "precipitate" Howe "into measures, that we can turn to good account." Washington's preservation of his army, his ability to hang on Howe's heels and strike British detachments, made it impossible for Howe to safely move overland on Philadelphia during Britain's 1777 campaign. Howe chose another route, via the sea, one that took far too long. His troops entered Philadelphia on 26 September after defeating Washington at Brandywine. By now, winter threatened, and the end of the campaign season found Howe still in Philadelphia, instead, as he had planned, marching to help General John Burgoyne.[48] In New York, on the far-flung fields of Freeman's Farm and Bemis Heights, Washington's subordinates delivered one of the key colonial victories of the war, one that precipitated French and Spanish entry on the colonial side, and changed the nature of the war – in the Americans' favor.

Although defeated at Brandywine in September and Germantown in October, Washington preserved his army, thus maintaining the colonial ability to continue prosecuting the war. He had not waged a perfect campaign, considering Howe's successes, but he was learning. The next year, he would do even better. His forces harassed the British when they withdrew from Philadelphia in the summer of 1778, fighting them to a standstill at Monmouth on 28 June. Washington struck when the odds favored him, gaining an advantage while weakening the opponent, but also preserving his own strength.[49]

The war in the North continued, but its intensity diminished. After 1778, even with French help, American poverty limited the Continental Army's offensive operations. The expansion of the war into a global conflict, and Britain's subsequent emphasis on operations in the southern colonies, also helped produce what was largely a stalemate in the North from 1779 to 1781.

The war in the South

Washington's Fabian strategy of avoiding major engagements and making surprise hit-and-run raids in the middle colonies so thoroughly frustrated the British that in 1779 they embarked on an invasion of the southern colonies where they hoped to gain Loyalist support in establishing a base for future operations.[50] In February 1780, Major General Benjamin Lincoln decided to fight for Charleston rather than to abandon it, a misguided attempt to resurrect Washington's earlier strategy of fighting from fixed defensive positions, the discarded "war of posts." Lincoln ineptly defended Charleston and on 12 May 1780, capitulated to General Henry Clinton, the third largest surrender of American forces after Harpers Ferry in 1862 and Bataan in 1942. Over 5,000 Americans were removed from the defense of the South because Lincoln failed to understand the Fabian strategy in which he had participated while he was under Washington's command.[51]

On 29 May, shortly after the fall of Charleston, Lieutenant Colonel Banastre Tarleton and Loyalists under his command encountered a local American militia contingent of roughly 400 men at Waxhaws, South Carolina. After Tarleton deceptively offered the American commander terms of surrender, he attacked and routed the American militia. The slaughter that ensued became symbolic of the war that was unfolding. Colonel Tarleton blamed his men's behavior on "vindictive asperity," a trivial statement given how badly the bloodshed undermined Britain's control of the countryside.[52] But Tarleton was not being honest. He freely admitted in his memoirs that "terror" was part of his operating procedure in the lead-up to the battle of Camden. He described his movements on the Black River as purposely designed "to punish the inhabitants ... for their late breach of paroles and perfidious revolt," and he considered his acts as "a necessary service ... to strike terror into the inhabitants" in order to protect British communications in South Carolina.[53] For the British army, Tarleton's victory seemed to herald an approaching end to organized American resistance. Confident that South Carolina was again effectively in the possession of the Crown, General Clinton sailed for New York on 5 June leaving Lieutenant General Charles Cornwallis in command of about 8,000 British soldiers.

Watching from afar, the members of the Continental Congress were as dispirited as the British were elated. On 13 June, they replaced the thoroughly discredited Lincoln with Major General Horatio Gates, who took command of the southern army on 25 July. As the hero of Saratoga, Gates seemingly possessed the credentials for independent command. However, he failed to understand that the British possessed a clear advantage in tactical skill if he accepted battle. Whereas the Fabian Washington had carefully husbanded his forces, and refused to engage in battle unless he had maximized his advantage and minimized the danger of losing his army, Gates would rush into a decisive engagement with a poorly trained army lacking intelligence on the enemy.[54] The result was Cornwallis' destruction of Gates' Continental Army at the battle of Camden on 16 August 1780. This defeat temporarily removed the American threat of conventional arms south of Virginia. It also led to the replacement of Gates with Major General Nathanael Greene, formerly Washington's quartermaster general.

Without the threat of an enemy field force, the British seemed to possess a critical advantage in waging counterinsurgency: the ability to disperse and hunt down the partisans. The collapse of organized resistance by the Continental Army likewise allowed the British to hold forts throughout the interior of South Carolina, from the coast to Fort Ninety-Six on the Saluda River. However, the British methodology, exemplified by Tarleton's behavior, increasingly infuriated the southern population, generating recruits to the Patriot cause and swelling the numbers of partisans.

British reports noted worrisome resistance to the re-establishment of British rule in many frontier settlements in the Carolinas. For example, Brigadier General Thomas Sumter was maneuvering a dangerous element of 1,500 militia along the Catawba River in north-central South Carolina. The apprehensive Cornwallis also realized that despite tangibly rising Loyalist support, the Patriots had the clear military advantage of intimidation that necessitated constant protection of anyone publicly avowing loyalty to England.[55] Lord Francis Hastings Rawdon noted after Camden that "not a single man, however, attempted to improve the favorable moment or obeyed that summons for which they had before been so impatient."[56] This deplorable state of affairs ran contrary to earlier inflated British assessments. Cornwallis' angry impotence spilled over in a letter to a subordinate: "I cannot defend every man's house from being plundered and I must say that when I see a whole settlement running away from twenty or thirty robbers, I think they deserve to be robbed."[57]

Although they lacked strategic cohesion, the Patriot forces soon proved a serious threat to British plans. On South Carolina's western frontier, 700 partisans led by Colonel Elijah Clarke attacked the town of Augusta, Georgia, from 14–18 September 1780. The British reacted by assembling Cherokee allies, Loyalists and a relief column from Fort Ninety-Six. The partisans broke off the attack. However, this incident illustrated that fighting on the frontier favored the Patriots owing to the distances of the country, the speed of American movements on horseback, and the British difficulty in gathering intelligence. These advantages, and Cornwallis' failure to keep his forces in mutual support of one another, handed the Americans a bloody and overwhelming victory at King's Mountain, 7 October 1780, perhaps the most important battle of the entire Southern campaign.[58]

The British defeat shook Loyalist faith in British arms and ended Cornwallis' attempt to invade North Carolina to raise Loyalist militia. With his left flank gone and the countryside depleted of supplies, he could not risk the destruction of his lines of communications with British posts in South Carolina. He retreated from North Carolina to regroup his army within the security of his string of forts.[59] King's Mountain had reversed the tide of war in the South, but it remained for a reformed Continental Army finally to drive Cornwallis and his army entirely out of the Carolinas.

The rebuilding of the southern army and the redesigning of its strategy fell to Nathanael Greene, who had assumed command in early December 1780. Despite the enormous logistical and manpower deficiencies Greene encountered, he quickly seized the strategic initiative.[60] Greene was steeped in the experience of executing a Fabian strategy and possessed a masterful grasp of logistics owing to his former position as Washington's quartermaster general.[61] Instinctively, he grasped the nature of the war in the South as a mix of the conventional, partisan and civil. Although his men were in wretched condition and outnumbered, Greene exhibited an equanimity that resonated throughout his correspondence with politicians, subordinate officers and in the field. General Greene's operational plans were a product of his efforts to establish a base of operations, the weakness of his forces and the relative strength of Cornwallis' army. Greene instructed the North Carolina Board of War to build a few supply depots in the western portion of the state because he envisioned this region as the most likely route of invasion. He correctly surmised that Cornwallis would not invade the central portion of North Carolina for fear of exposing his operational flanks. Nor could the British be opposed on the coast owing to their command of the sea. Therefore, the western portion of North Carolina was the best place to mount a defense. His real fear was that Cornwallis would conduct a strategic defense using his line of forts along South Carolina's rivers. With his forces lacking the heavy artillery and manpower necessary to besiege them, Greene knew they would be impregnable.[62] Fortunately for him and for the American cause, Greene's fears would not come to pass because his initial operational moves led Cornwallis to overreact by invading North Carolina.

While Greene reorganized his small band of "starving and naked men," he incorporated the partisans into his operational plans. Greene instructed Brigadier General Francis Marion:

> Until a more permanent Army can be collected than is in the Field at present we must endeavor to keep up a "Partizan" War and preserve the Tide of Sentiment among the people as much as possible in our favor.

He praised the attention Marion paid to tactical security by continually moving his forces to elude British patrols. Greene would embrace this expedient on the operational level. He also urged Marion to gather intelligence. Taking a page from George Washington's use of intelligence, Greene asked Marion to send him as much information on the British order of battle as possible. He even advised Marion on how the spy should conduct himself.[63] Greene's orders to Marion illustrated his efforts to utilize all assets available to defeat Cornwallis. He used the partisans to the best of their ability, without forcing them to fight in a manner inconsistent with their training and fragile moral.

Colonel Thomas Polk, Gates' superintending commissary general, stated that General Greene had demonstrated a better grasp of the army's supply shortages in one night of conversation than Gates ever had.⁶⁴ The devastation of previous campaigns, North Carolina's sparse population and the poverty of the Continental Congress left the southern army bereft of supplies. Greene could not remedy all problems immediately, but he quickly solved the ones in his control. He instructed Baron Friedrich Wilhelm von Steuben, the Inspector General commanding in Virginia, to "examine all public works and stores" in Virginia.⁶⁵ Next, he ordered a survey of North Carolina's rivers and roads. Greene then specified the building of shallow draft boats to move goods and men.⁶⁶ Under General Gates flour had been carted 60 miles by wagon. Greene used more reliable and faster river traffic to shorten the route to 30 miles.⁶⁷

Given the limited resources of North Carolina, he also set the framework for a practice of calibrated requisition and destruction, but he did not conduct a scorched earth strategy. Throughout the campaign he attempted to seize goods from an area for his own use – when it did not turn local inhabitants against the Patriots – and to deny the British access to badly needed resources. He even resorted to dismantling mills so they could be reassembled later. If American forces lacked the logistical means to transport the resources, his last resort was to order them destroyed. He advised Governor Abner Nash to seize all goods on the coast that would be valuable to the enemy, in particular, horses, cattle and rum.⁶⁸ All of these measures were aimed at crippling British movements and, in turn, limiting their control of the people. Greene's far-sighted attention to detail would save the Continental Army within the next two months.

Greene understood that the underpinnings of military success relied upon the political support of the southern states and their militias. As such he maintained a steady correspondence with the governors of North Carolina and Virginia. He explained to both that, "In all governments much depends upon opinion – in modern terms, the 'support of the people' – but more in this than almost any other from the circumstances of the currency and the division of sentiment amongst the inhabitants." To maintain the people's "opinion," he believed it was incumbent to protect both their liberties and property. However, it would be a defense tempered with not risking the entire army for a parcel of territory.⁶⁹

Greene's concern for the support of the people led him to caution the governors on the necessity of restraining the militias. Astutely, he declared the militia a "great bulwark of civil liberty [that] promises security and independence to this country." But in the same sentence he advised Governor Thomas Jefferson of Virginia to use them as an auxiliary to forestall laying waste to the countryside's resources and overtaxing the treasury.⁷⁰ Here was the key to the best use of militia, an undisciplined and poorly trained body whose members undermined the people's support whenever they wantonly stripped the country bare. The militia was only to be called out to counter an immediate threat from the enemy.⁷¹ Later in the campaign, Greene would have to remind his subordinates of the militia's proper use. He wrote militia general Andrew Pickens, "I am sorry the militia desert you, but it is the practice of all militia. All you have to do is to make the most of those remaining with you."⁷² Greene recognized that improper use of militia was counterproductive, doing more harm to a state's financial and material resources than the British army. It was a lesson he had learned while serving with Washington and which was reinforced by what he witnessed upon his arrival in North Carolina.

After establishing his logistical base and coordinating with the partisans, Greene began operations against the British. Unable to feed a concentrated southern army and looking to harass British communications, Greene broke with the military axiom of keeping forces united. He divided the army into multiple contingents that would cooperate with partisans and militia. Brigadier General Daniel Morgan, commanding the light troops, was dispatched to conduct limited attacks on the British in the vicinity of Fort Ninety-Six, while Greene shifted his main body to Cheraw Hill along the Pedee River in north-central South Carolina.

Much has been attributed to Greene's strategic "genius" concerning the division of his forces in the face of a numerically and qualitatively superior enemy, and for the most part it seems warranted. Sending Morgan to operate on the west side of the Catawba River, he derived many advantages. From his position Morgan could threaten the flank of any attack on Greene's forces. He could harass the enemy, collect intelligence and encourage the people to join the cause. He also planned to strip bare the land between Camden and Cheraw to limit Cornwallis' logistical reach in the north-central region of South Carolina. Greene's decision displayed an immediate grasp of his weaknesses and the determination to act in spite of them.[73] These actions were characteristic of Greene's entire Southern campaign. He denied the enemy resources, limited their mobility while increasing his own and constantly wore down Cornwallis' forces to lead the British general into making mistakes.

It is illustrative to examine Greene's other options in order to understand the significance of his strategic choices. The army he inherited was destitute of supplies in a country picked clean by the militia. It was significantly inferior in numbers to the British army. Given this desolate state of affairs and the inability to supply the army in North Carolina, Greene could have withdrawn to the safety of Virginia. With North Carolina acting as a buffer state, Greene could have reconstituted his army in relative safety from a quick British strike. However, moving so far from South Carolina would have eliminated the opportunity to harass the British posts in cooperation with the partisans, and may have emboldened Loyalists to join the British in greater numbers. Greene's decision to operate in the northern portion of South Carolina gave the American army operational security, because it could retreat into the relative sanctuary of North Carolina, and the opportunity for limited offensives to harass British lines of communication. Lastly, Greene's choice would place Cornwallis on the horns of an operational dilemma that would become a strategic disaster. To ignore Greene's forces and hunker down in the line of British forts would cede the countryside to the Americans. If he attacked, Greene could force the British army to overextend its limited logistics in a pursuit through North Carolina.

Greene did not have long to wait for a British reaction that would be extremely dangerous in the short run but ultimately would play perfectly into

American hands. In a testament to Greene's extraordinary understanding of the nature of the war, his most capable subordinate, Daniel Morgan, failed to grasp the significance of his role in harassing Fort Ninety-Six. On the other hand, Cornwallis immediately understood that Morgan could isolate the fort and possibly sever communications with his Cherokee allies. Morgan expressed to Greene his frustration in simply operating on the west side of the Catawba River. In fact, three weeks before he destroyed Tarleton's army at Cowpens, Morgan stated, "When I have collected my expected force I shall be at a loss how to act."[74] Morgan even petitioned for permission to invade Georgia. Meanwhile, Cornwallis was reacting to Morgan's force by dividing his own army and ordering Tarleton to drive him off. "If Morgan is ... anywhere within your reach," Cornwallis wrote Tarleton, "I should wish you to push him to the utmost.... Ninety-Six is of so much consequence, that no time is to be lost."[75] The operations that Greene had set in motion would result in a British disaster.

The American victory at Cowpens on 17 January 1781 resulted in 929 British casualties out of a force of 1,100 and raised Patriot spirits in the South. Nevertheless, it is telling to review Greene's correspondence with Morgan two days after the battle, while he was still ignorant of events. Greene insisted that the army's survival was more important than holding territory:

> It is not my wish you should come to action unless you have a manifest superiority and a moral certainty of succeeding. Put nothing to the hazard, a retreat may be disagreeable but not disgraceful. Regard not the opinion of the day. It is not our business to risk too much.[76]

Greene was treating his dispersed forces as an army-in-being, a term strategists generally apply to fleets. Simply maintaining such a force compels the opponent to face a strategic dilemma. It represents an entity that can strike at any time or withdraw into a sanctuary to mount a constant threat. Greene's alternative was brashly to seek a decisive battle, which would most likely result in defeat. The nature of the war in the South necessitated avoidance of battle in the short term, until Greene could acquire sufficient reinforcements and until peripheral operations reduced Cornwallis' strength. While his conduct seemed to mirror a Fabian strategy, it was much more complicated. He would preserve his army-in-being, raid British outposts and lines of communication, denude the countryside of resources and seek to win the "hearts and minds" of locals; he also would fight battles, whether from a tactically defensive or offensive position, the moment he believed doing so served his purpose. He was, in fact, the most aggressive American commander in the war, but his aggressiveness was always tempered by cautious calculation.

The fear Greene expressed in his letter would seem to challenge Morgan's decision to stand and fight, but juxtaposed, they clarify his strategic goals. Battle was the most certain means of destroying the British army and returning the South to American control. Yet his subordinates needed to understand that it should be avoided unless success or a means of escape were virtually assured.

Despite Greene's fear of a general engagement in late 1780, the trust he placed in his subordinate bore fruit at the battle of Cowpens on 17 January 1781. Morgan baited Tarleton into a frontal assault that destroyed his entire force, "the best troops of the army," as Cornwallis referred to them. By risking battle, Morgan had shifted the momentum of the campaign.[77] Now Cornwallis, reinforced with Major General Alexander Leslie's 1,500 men, was determined to redress the verdict of Cowpens. He destroyed all gear considered unessential to pursue Morgan's contingent.[78]

In the famous Chase to the Dan River, Greene's foresight of placing boats on "four wheels ... to be moved with little more difficulty than a loaded wagon" proved essential to the army's survival.[79] Greene had not only devised the operations and strategy of an army-in-being, he had created the logistical means to ensure the strategy could be carried out. Morgan soon provided intelligence of Cornwallis' offensive, and Greene attempted to fall back and pull together his forces to give battle at an advantageous position in North Carolina. In the midst of these endeavors, he learned of Cornwallis' decision to burn his baggage train. Greene now grasped the invaluable opportunity to overextend the British army.[80] "I am not without hopes of ruining Lord Cornwallis if he persists in his mad scheme of pushing through the country," Greene wrote.[81]

The Chase to the Dan River in February 1781 was not a pell-mell route of the American forces; rather, it was a calibrated retreat with Colonel Otho Williams, who replaced the sick Morgan, conducting a rearguard delay of the British army long enough to remove precious supply magazines and the main body of the American forces.[82] Although circumstances dictated a retreat, Greene saw the possibility of decisively engaging Cornwallis, whose desperation caused him to march northward in the hopes of trapping and destroying the American field army. If the British army passed its culminating point of attack and the militia heeded his summons, Greene would turn and fight from a position of strength. It was the militia's failure to organize that forced Greene to continue retreating.[83]

If Greene could preserve his army in the chase, he had reason to surmise Cornwallis' gamble might leave the British vulnerable to a counterattack because its strength had diminished relative to the growing American force falling back on its base of supply and recruits.[84] Greene was reversing Clausewitz's statement: "The natural goal of all campaign plans therefore is the turning point at which the attack becomes the defense."[85] The American was seeking the point at which to transform his defense into the final winning offensive. Greene began to realize that Cornwallis was surpassing his culminating point of attack even as the American army temporarily conceded North Carolina to the British.[86] After crossing the Dan River on 14 February 1781, Greene positioned his army at Halifax Court House, near the North Carolina–Virginia border, perhaps to tempt the British army into further pursuit.[87]

Greene astutely expected Cornwallis to fall back on Hillsborough, North Carolina, for supplies, and to recruit Loyalists. With Virginia and North Carolina militia flocking to his army, Greene now prepared to go on the long-deferred offensive. He would return to North Carolina to seek a battle and deny Cornwallis the critical time he needed to regroup.⁸⁸ "The moment the enemy moves towards Hillsborough I shall fall into their rear," he wrote.⁸⁹ Cornwallis acted as Greene expected; Greene gave chase. Cornwallis hoped to establish a base of operations at Hillsborough and open a line of communication to Cross Creek, in the direction of Wilmington on the coast.⁹⁰ Given time, Cornwallis may have been successful in reconstituting his worn-out forces. But Greene's counteroffensive had the desired effect. The gathering Loyalists were shattered at the battle known as Pyle's Massacre, 24 February 1781, denying Cornwallis local manpower and supplies and thereby enhancing his desperation to seek battle.⁹¹

The balance of power had shifted temporarily and both belligerents realized it. Cornwallis could not obtain supplies from the North Carolina countryside without the American army attacking his divided forces. If Cornwallis retreated to South Carolina, Greene could fall upon his exhausted and hungry men. Retreat would also mean losing the support of the remaining Loyalists. Greene had forced Cornwallis into seeking a battle. Cornwallis wrote: "It would be impossible to succeed in that great object of our arduous campaign, the calling forth of the numerous loyalists of North Carolina, whilst a doubt remained on their minds of the superiority of our arms."⁹²

Greene suddenly found his army in a strong operational position that could have significant strategic implications. Cornwallis had to strike; therefore, Greene could accept battle or again retreat. If he stood his ground and fought, Cornwallis would be forced to take the disadvantageous position of tactical offense. A battle at this point meant Greene had everything to gain and little to lose. Victory could be a southern Saratoga. Defeat would not have jeopardized Greene's forces because he was willing to sacrifice the militia and could extricate his regular troops from the battlefield. Moreover, an indecisive tactical victory or defeat would play to American strengths. Greene would retain sufficient numbers to hold North Carolina while heavy British losses would cause Cornwallis to fall back on the coast to avoid encirclement. Therefore, he went hunting for Cornwallis' army. Tarleton summed up one aspect of Greene's strategic and operational advantage best: "A defeat of the British would have been attended with the total destruction of Earl Cornwallis' infantry whilst a [British] victory could produce no very decisive consequences against the Americans."⁹³

Barring the complete destruction of Greene's army, a near impossibility, the strategic and operational verdict of Guilford Courthouse, 15 March 1781, was a foregone conclusion. Cornwallis retained the field of battle but owing to his tactical offensive against Greene's strong defensive position, his army was shattered. The British lost one-quarter to one-third of their ranks in casualties as compared to one-twentieth of the American force. Cornwallis knew that a second battle would spell doom and fell back to Wilmington on the coast.⁹⁴ At this critical junction, Cornwallis could either return to South Carolina or invade Virginia. He chose the latter course in the belief that securing Virginia would end the struggle in the South. But the invasion led to his defeat at Yorktown, 19 October 1781, a strategic disaster that perfectly complemented Burgoyne's surrender at Saratoga in 1777. The former had brought the French into the war; the latter removed the British from it.

After Cornwallis moved into Virginia, Greene faced two choices. He could pursue Cornwallis to check his campaign in Virginia, or return to South Carolina to roll back the British interior positions. Greene wisely chose the latter course and marched on Camden. The strategic stage was now set for the collapse of British control in South Carolina and Georgia. Tarleton later wrote, "The wisdom and vigor of the American operations not only deranged all the designs of Cornwallis at Wilmington, but threatened severe consequences to the British forces in South Carolina."[95] Receiving word of Greene's march, Cornwallis feared becoming the pursued if he moved south. Owing to his lack of boats, he could be trapped by Greene between the numerous southern rivers. Once again Greene's logistical foresight provided mobility to the American army that the British lacked.[96] Backed into the North Carolina coast, Cornwallis could not risk a march through North Carolina for fear of being encircled, much as Burgoyne had been forced to surrender at Saratoga. Greene also believed the British grip on South Carolina was tenuous:

> The enemy [Cornwallis] will be obliged to follow us or give up their posts in that state. If the former takes place it will draw the war out of this state [North Carolina] and give it an opportunity to raise its proportion of men. If they leave their posts to fall they must lose more there than they can gain here.[97]

Although the British outposts would be without a primary field force to protect their line of communications, with roughly 8,000 men scattered throughout both states they still outnumbered Greene's forces. With militia enlistments expiring, Greene's army quickly dwindled to roughly 2,000 combatants.[98] His advantage would lie in American dominance of the countryside and the dispersed British forces.

Although much of the ensuing campaign would unfold as Greene predicted, upon reaching the British fort at Camden he discovered the fortifications were strong and the garrison numerous and well supplied.

> The enemy has got a firmer footing in the southern states than is generally expected. Camden, Ninety-Six, and Augusta cover all the fertile parts of South Carolina and Georgia, and they are laying waste the country above them, which will effectually secure those posts, as no army can be subsisted in the neighborhood to operate against them.[99]

If the British exercised caution and remained in their forts, his efforts would be undone, but once again Greene's actions precipitated a British mistake. Greene camped just outside of Camden in a defensive position to use his army as bait. Lord Rawdon, the acting British commander in South Carolina, unwittingly played into American hands when he led a sortie against the strong position

Greene had chosen. The ensuing battle of Hobkirk's Hill, 25 April 1781, once again left the British in possession of the field but it was also a testament to Greene's skill. He had exercised operational security to protect against a sudden British strike, and he withdrew the army in such good order that Lord Rawdon could not derive any advantage. After a short retreat, Greene returned to the offensive. By keeping his army intact, Greene continued the execution of his fundamental strategy of maintaining an army-in-being, even writing, "This little repulse will make no alteration in our general plan of operation."[100] The British commanders failed to understand that the quest for a decisive battle hastened their self-destruction.

With Cornwallis' field force gone, and the British tied to their forts by Greene's army-in-being, the American general was able to unleash his partisan bands to further isolate the British posts. He divided South Carolina between Thomas Sumter and Francis Marion.[101] As the battle of Hobkirk's Hill was taking place, Marion, in conjunction with Colonel Henry Lee, harassed British communications with Charleston by taking Fort Watson on the Santee River.[102] Although the partisan raiders were unable to hold the fort, they dismantled its fortifications and cowered Loyalists in the vicinity, thereby denying the position to the British. The partisans then rolled up the small but critical British forts in the interior of South Carolina and forced the British to abandon Georgetown on the coast.[103] Greene recognized the contribution of his partisan leaders and praised Marion; "To fight the enemy with a prospect of victory is nothing; but to fight with intrepidity under the constant impression of a defeat, and inspire irregular troops to do it is a talent peculiar to yourself."[104]

At this juncture, an American victory appeared inevitable, but looks were deceiving. The remaining British forces contracted their front into a pocket around Charleston, Savannah and Fort Ninety-Six.[105] From his distant vantage point in Virginia, Cornwallis tried to put the best light on this situation by blaming the perfidy of the Loyalists:

> The perpetual instances of the weakness and treachery of our friends in South Carolina, and the impossibility of getting any military assistance from them, make the possession of any part of the country of very little use, except in supplying provisions for Charleston.[106]

However, Cornwallis' use of the words "weakness" and "treachery" ring hollow when weighed against the difficulty Greene encountered with Loyalist forces that continued the fight. "In collecting provisions and forage we are obliged to send the same guards and escorts," Greene wrote, "as if the country was avowedly our enemy's."[107] When Greene besieged Fort Ninety-Six, June 1781, the Americans had to counter 500 Tory militia harassing their lines of communication.[108] The Loyalist guerrillas and militia in conjunction with Lord Rawdon's 2,000 reinforcements caused Greene to abandon the siege.[109] In typical Greene fashion, he recognized that this British force was too dangerous to fight in an open battle but too small to drive his army from the state. He planned to hover on Rawdon's flanks to prevent plundering and to seize opportunities when they arose, as Washington had done in the North.[110]

Upon arriving at Ninety-Six, Rawdon sought a decisive battle with Greene's army. Once again the slippery American general eluded his foe owing to tactical skill and having stripped the countryside to eliminate succor for the British army. Greene effectively conducted a strategy of calibrated destruction by ordering the dismantling of all mills along his army's path. He could then rebuild the mills for his anticipated return to besiege Ninety-Six.[111] With Greene out of reach, and orders from Cornwallis to abandon Ninety-Six, a position he earlier deemed so important that its defense led Tarleton into the disastrous battle of Cowpens, Rawdon split his army and returned to Charleston.[112] Receiving intelligence on Rawdon's action, Greene saw opportunity. Despite having a larger army in theater, a British commander was giving him another chance to force a decisive battle by destroying a contingent of his force. Ordering Lee to prevent a junction of other British forces with Rawdon's troops, Greene attempted to pull together every able-bodied man in the region.[113] Patriot forces decimated Rawdon's foraging parties while Greene assembled 2,000 men. Although Rawdon managed to save himself owing to a good choice of defensible ground and the timely junction of his forces, Greene demonstrated a tenacious determination to take advantage of any opportunity and neuter British control of South Carolina everywhere outside the environs of Charleston.[114]

With Greene's forces harassing all British troops outside Charleston's fortifications, Lord Nisbet Balfour, commandant at Charleston, informed Major General Henry Clinton that the British campaign in South Carolina had reached its nadir.[115] What is most interesting regarding Balfour's comment is that simultaneously Greene was writing Thomas McKean, the President of the Continental Congress, that the British numbered 4,000 infantry, 400 cavalry and 1,000 Loyalist militia. These numbers dwarfed the manpower Greene could bring to bear and did not include Loyalist guerrillas and British allied Indians.[116] Nevertheless, Greene's unrelenting offensive created the perception that British arms were overmatched. The British confined themselves to Charleston, and their operations south of Virginia were effectively over.

At Yorktown, on 19 October 1781, Lord Cornwallis' surrender of his army to the Franco-American armies of George Washington and Comte de Rochambeau formally sealed the fate of Britain's Southern campaign and in effect ended the war by precipitating the fall of the ministry of Lord North the following March. The hapless British contracted their front by evacuating troops from North Carolina and sending them to Charleston. With Greene incapable of besieging Charleston, a strategic stalemate ensued in which both sides waited for an end to the war.

The British failure in the Southern campaign has often been attributed to inflated assessments of Loyalist support, born of frustration with the northern strategies of 1776 and 1777.[117] Yet the evidence suggests the British estimations were correct. The southern colonies had a sizable Loyalist population from which to build a base of operations. General Greene wrote:

> The more I enquire into the natural strength of North and South Carolina, either to form, or support an Army, the more I am persuaded they have been greatly overrated. More of the inhabitants appear in the King's interest than in ours.... The militia in our interest can do little more than keep Tories in subjection, and in many places not that.[118]

With over 10,000 well-trained and equipped soldiers, and a large indigenous support base, the British conquered two states and initially destroyed an American army. After the collapse of Patriot resistance in South Carolina, the British raised over 4,000 Loyalist militia.[119] Yet they were unable to consolidate their grip on the South because of the tenacity of Patriot partisans and the Continental Congress' wise decision to appoint Nathanael Greene as the Southern commander in 1780.

General Greene assumed command facing enormous strategic odds and prevailed in little over a year. His victory was due to a combination of factors, including his detailed attention to logistics, intelligence and the terrain. He used the militia and partisans in a manner consistent with their strengths and weaknesses. When his forces were weak, he avoided Cornwallis' strength, his army, and attacked his weakness, control of the country. He preserved his own force as an army-in-being while conducting a raiding strategy against the British forts. Although his methodology was reminiscent of the Fabian strategy Washington executed in the North, he conducted it in a more aggressive manner than his superior. Greene's forces maintained an operational tempo that was unmatched in earlier campaigns. In avoiding battle he caused the enemy to overextend his forces. The American army's constant activity baited Tarleton into a trap at Cowpens, induced Cornwallis to overextend his logistical lines during the chase to the Dan River, and provoked Lord Rawdon to impale the British army at Hobkirk's Hill. Even with the numerous Loyalist guerrillas and militias, Greene's operations convinced the British leaders that the people had abandoned them. Perhaps this was his most successful achievement. Unable to coordinate his strategy with the locals, Cornwallis effectively abandoned British posts in Georgia and South Carolina, as well as the Loyalists, so he could chase the American army into North Carolina. Greene's campaign was so successful that even the Cherokee Indians were aware of their British ally's failure and sought to negotiate peace.[120] Greene's strategy and operations drove Cornwallis into the fortuitous but fatal trap in Virginia, protected North Carolina's integrity, and returned two states to the Patriot cause in the face of a better-armed, better-trained and larger enemy army. Greene achieved this strategic victory with an American army that by August of 1781 was "as ragged as wolves."[121]

Conclusion

The American Fabian strategy, combined with the waging of partisan war, helped keep an American army in the field and the colonial cause alive. The decision to implement such an approach to the struggle proved a critical shift that allowed the colonists to make effective use of their scant resources, and contributed to Britain's growing frustration with their American war, as well as their eventual disillusionment. Washington, once he adopted this course, adhered to it for the rest of the struggle. In the South, Nathanael Greene adapted Washington's strategy to his aggressive leadership. Inheriting a strategic situation that could only be labeled as bordering on collapse, Greene brought an energetic cohesiveness to Patriot efforts. Greene's command provided direction to the partisans and merged their operations with those of the regular army and militia. With an army that he described as literally naked, Greene seized the initiative and never relinquished it. His attention to logistics, and the demonstration of the possibility of snatching victory from the jaws of defeat, reinvigorated the morale of his army and pro-Patriot Southerners. Like Washington, Greene yearned for a decisive battle but possessed an intrinsic understanding of the nature of the war that gave him the patience to wait for the right moment to engage his opponents.

Washington and Greene understood that success in the American Revolution depended on preserving the Patriot center of gravity, the army – in the North and in the South – and demonstrating success through incremental victories that in turn fed the colonials' ability to preserve their army. Conversely, they had to convince King George's government that the cost of retaining the colonies was beyond their value to the British Empire. Despite numerous tactical defeats and the temporary loss of whole states, the colonials stayed in the war. The battle of Yorktown in October 1781 was the culminating point of six years of a successful strategy that helped the Americans to achieve their primary policy objective of a free and independent nation.

Notes

1 This chapter could not have been written without the generous support of a grant from the Society of the Cincinnati Library, Washington, D.C.
  In direct quotations, the original spelling and punctuation have been retained.
2 Robert Middlekauff, *The Glorious Cause: The American Revolution, 1763–1789*, revised edn. (Oxford and New York: Oxford University Press, 2005), pp. 287–98.
3 Catherine Drinker Bowen, *John Adams and the American Revolution* (Boston: Little Brown and Co., 1950), pp. 529, 533; Joseph J. Ellis, *His Excellency: George Washington* (New York: Vintage/Random House, 2004), p. 68.
4 Quoted in Victor Brooks and Robert Hohwald, *How America Fought its Wars: Military Strategy from the American Revolution to the Civil War* (Conshohocken: Combined Books, 1999), p. 40.
5 Edward G. Lengel, *Washington: A Military Life* (New York: Random House, 2005), pp. 93, 105–6; Philander D. Chase *et al.*, eds., *The Papers of George Washington, Revolutionary War Series* (Charlottesville and London: University Press of Virginia, 2002) (hereafter *PWR*), 3:3–4, fn. 1.
6 Washington to Broughton, 2 Sept. 1775, *PWR*, 1:398–400; Washington to J.A. Washington, 13 Oct. 1775, *PWR*, 2:160–2; Washington to Hancock, 12 Oct. 1775, *PWR*, 2:146–8; Instructions to Captains Nicholson Broughton and John Selman, 16 Oct. 1775, *PWR*, 2:179–80; Washington to Arnold, 5 Dec. 1775, *PWR*, 2:493–4; Washington to Ramsey, 4–11 Dec. 1775, *PWR*, 2:488–9.
7 Maurice Matloff, ed., *American Military History* (Washington, D.C.: Office of the Chief of Military History, United States Army, 1969), p. 50; John Adams to James

Warren, 7 June 1775, in *Warren–Adams Letters, Being Chiefly a Correspondence Among John Adams, Samuel Adams and James Warren* (Boston: The Massachusetts Historical Society, 1917), 1:52–3; Washington to Hancock, 28 June 1775, *PWR*, 1:42–3, 43, fn. 1.

8 Washington to Schuyler, 20 Aug. 1775, *PWR*, 1:331–3.
9 *PWR*, 2:396–7, fn. 1; Matloff, *American Military History*, p. 50; Middlekauff, *The Glorious Cause*, p. 313. See the additional correspondence in *PWR*, vol. 3, for colonial ambitions toward Canada.
10 Washington to Hancock, 21 Sept. 1775, *PWR*, 2:24–30.
11 Instructions from the Continental Congress, 22 June 1775, *PWR*, 1:21–2; various correspondence, *PWR*, vols. 1 and 2; Middlekauff, *The Glorious Cause*, pp. 314–17.
12 Washington to Trumbull, 7 Jan. 1776, *PWR*, 3:51–2; Washington to Lee, 8 Jan. 1776, *PWR*, 3:53–4; Hancock to Washington, 5 Oct. 1775, *PWR*, 2:108–10; Washington to Hancock, 4 Jan. 1776, *PWR*, 3:18–20, 20, fn. 2; John Adams to Washington, 6 Jan. 1776, *PWR*, 3:36–8. Lee never took up the command as Congress ordered him south, Lee to Washington, 3 Mar. 1776, *PWR*, 3:404–5, 405, fn. 1.
13 Hancock to Washington, 6 Mar. 1776, *PWR*, 3:415–6.
14 Washington to J.A. Washington, 31 May–4 June, *PWR*, 4:411–13; Washington to Arnold, 3 Apr. 1776, *PWR*, 4:21–2; see also Washington to Schuyler, 3 Apr. 1776, *PWR*, 4:28–9; John Ferling, *Almost A Miracle: The American Victory in the War of Independence* (Oxford and New York: Oxford University Press, 2007), p. 123.
15 Washington to Ward, 9 July 1776, *PWR*, 5:254–6.
16 Washington to Trumbull, 9 July 1776, *PWR*, 5:253–4.
17 Washington to Hancock, 10 July 1776, *PWR*, 5:258–60.
18 On the influence of Bunker Hill on colonial strategy, see Ellis, *His Excellency*, p. 77, and Lengel, *Washington*, p. 105.
19 Washington to J.A. Washington, 22 July 1776, in John C. Fitzpatrick, ed., *The Writings of George Washington* (Washington, D.C.: GPO, 1937) (hereafter *WW*), 5:325–7; *PWR*, 5:495–6, fn. 1; Craig L. Symonds, *A Battlefield Atlas of the American Revolution* (Mount Pleasant: Nautical & Aviation Publishing, 1986), p. 27.
20 Washington to Root, 7 Aug. 1776, *PWR*, 5:610–11; Washington to Schuyler, 7 Aug. 1776, *PWR*, 5:611–14; Washington to Trumbull, 18 Aug. 1776, *PWR* 6:70–1.
21 Washington to Trumbull, 7 Aug. 1776, *PWR*, 5:615–16, 516. fn. 1.
22 Washington to Hancock, 8 Aug. 1776, *PWR*, 5:625–8.
23 Ibid.
24 Washington to Heath, 21 Aug. 1776, *PWR*, 6:98; Washington to Trumbull, 24 Aug. 1776, *PWR*, 6:123–4, 124, fn. 1. For an overview of the New York campaign, see Ira D. Gruber, *The Howe Brothers and the American Revolution* (Chapel Hill: University of North Carolina Press, 1972), pp. 88–136, and Russell Weigley, *The American Way of War: A History of United States Military Strategy and Policy* (Bloomington: Indiana University Press, 1977), pp. 8–11.
25 Washington to Hancock, 2 Sept. 1776, *PWR*, 6:199–201.
26 Washington to Arnold, 17 June 1777, *PWR*, 10:58–60.
27 Washington to Hancock, 8 Sept. 1776, *PWR*, 6:248–52; *WW*, 6:27, fn. 27.
28 Washington to Hancock, 8 Sept. 1776, *PWR*, 6:248–52.
29 Greene to Washington, 5 Sept. 1776, in Richard K. Showman, *et al.*, eds., *The Papers of Nathanael Greene* (Chapel Hill: University of North Carolina Press, 1976), 1:294–5.
30 Washington to Hancock, 8 Sept. 1776, *PWR*, 6:248–52; *WW*, 6:27, fn. 27.
31 Sir Basil Liddell Hart, *Strategy*, 2nd edn. (New York: Meridian, 1991), pp. 26–7.
32 J.E.A. Crake, "Roman Politics from 215 to 209 B.C.," *Phoenix*, 17, 2 (Summer 1963): 126.
33 Certain General Officers, 11 Sept. 1776, *PWR*, 6:279, 280, fn. 2; Washington to Hancock, 11 Sept. 1776, *PWR*, 6:280–1; Council of War, 12 Sept. 1776, *PWR*,

6:288–9, 289, fn. 4; Washington to Hancock, 14 Sept. 1776, *PWR*, 6:308–9; Mark M. Boatner, III, *Encyclopedia of the American Revolution* (New York: David McKay, 1966), p. 386.

34 Washington to J.A. Washington, 6–19 Nov. 1776, *PWR*, 7:102–5; Washington to Hancock, 6 Nov. 1776, *PWR*, 7:96–8; Washington to Greene, 8 Nov. 1776, *PWR*, 7:115–16, 161–2, fn. 1; Washington to Hancock, 16 Nov. 1776, *PWR*, 7:162–5, 165, fn. 4, 168–9, fn. 9, 105–6, fn. 10; Ferling, *Almost a Miracle*, pp. 151–3.

35 Mifflin to Morris, 21 Nov. 1776, *Collections of the New York Historical Society for the Year 1778* (New York: New York Historical Society, 1879), pp. 404–5. This is the earliest direct mention of colonial Fabian strategy that we have found. See also Theodore Thayer, *Nathanael Greene: Strategist of the American Revolution* (New York: Twayne Publishers, 1960), p. 124.

36 *PWR*, 7:1–3, fn. 1; Washington to J.A. Washington, 6–19 Nov. 1776, *PWR*, 7:102–5.

37 Tilghman quoted in *PWR*, 7:105, fn. 2.

38 Washington to Hancock, 1 Dec. 1776, *PWR*, 7:245; Washington to Hancock, 5 Dec. 1776, *PWR*, 7:262–4; Washington to Heath, 18 Dec. 1776, *PWR*, 7:366–7; Washington to Lincoln, 18 Dec. 1776, *PWR*, 7:367–8; Washington to Maxwell, 21 Dec. 1776, *WW*, 6:414–16; Washington to Heath, 14 Dec. 1776, *PWR*, 7:334; Washington to Lord Stirling, 14 Dec. 1776, *PWR*, 7:339.

39 Washington to Woodford, 10 Nov. 1775, *PWR*, 2:346–7, 2:347, fn. 3: Capitaine de Jeney, *The Partisan: or, The Art of Making War in Detachment*, J. Berkenhout, trans. (London, 1760). On Washington and the irregular war in the north, see Mark V. Kwasny, *Washington's Partisan War, 1775–1783* (Kent: Kent State University Press, 1996).

40 Council of War, 12 July 1776, *PWR*, 5:280.

41 *PWR*, 7:197, fn.2; Washington to Cadwalader, 24, 25 Dec. 1776, *PWR*, 7:425, 439, 425, fn. 1; Executive Committee of the Continental Congress to Washington, 31 Dec. 1776 and 1 Jan. 1777, *PWR*, 7:495, 499–500. For Washington's instructions to use militia as irregulars, see also Washington to Heath, 28 Dec. 1776, *PWR*, 7:468. For this campaign, especially the irregular elements, see David Hackett Fischer, *Washington's Crossing* (Oxford: Oxford University Press, 2004), pp. 346–62.

42 Washington to Schuyler, 23 Feb. 1777, *PWR*, 8:433–4.

43 Thayer, *Greene*, pp. 156–7.

44 Washington to Arnold, 17 June 1777, *PWR*, 10:58–60.

45 Hamilton to Livingston, 28 June 1777, in Harold C. Syrett, *et al.*, eds., *The Papers of Alexander Hamilton* (New York and London: Columbia University Press, 1961), 1:274–7.

46 Thayer, *Greene*, p. 173; Gruber, *The Howe Brothers*, pp. 228–9.

47 Washington to Schuyler, 2 July 1777, *PWR*, 10:170–2; Washington to Rutledge, 5 July 1777, *PWR*, 10:198–9.

48 Piers Mackesy, *War for America, 1775–1783* (Lincoln and London: University of Nebraska Press, 1992), pp. 121–3, 129.

49 Symonds, *Atlas*, pp. 57, 65.

50 Simpson to Germain, 28 Aug. 1779, cited in Alan Valentine, *Lord George Germain* (Oxford: Clarendon Press: 1962), p. 367.

51 Banastre Tarleton, *A History of the Campaigns of 1780 and 1781* (New York: New York Times, 1967), p. 23.

52 Tarleton to Cornwallis, 30 May 1780, *Campaigns*, p. 45.

53 Tarleton, *Campaigns*, pp. 100–1.

54 George Marshall, *Memoir of Brigadier-General John Dagworthy of the Revolutionary War* (Wilmington: Historical Society of Delaware, 1895), pp. 43–6.

55 Cornwallis to Clinton, 30 June 1780, cited in Tarleton, *Campaigns*, p. 117.

56 Lord Rawdon to Clinton, 29 Oct. 1780, in Derek Ross, ed., *Correspondence of Charles, first Marquis Cornwallis* (London: J. Murray, 1859), pp. 62–3.

57 Cornwallis to Kirkland, 13 Nov. 1780, Cornwallis, *Correspondence*, p. 70.
58 Dawson to Sumner, 10 Oct. 1780, Tarleton, *Campaigns*, pp. 161–5, 195.
59 Tarleton, *Campaigns*, p. 166.
60 Greene to Huntington, 28 Dec. 1780, *Greene Papers*, 7:7.
61 Edward McCrady, *The History of South Carolina in the Revolution, 1780–1783* (London: Macmillan Company, 1902), pp. 14–15.
62 Greene to the North Carolina Board of War, 7 Dec. 1780, *Greene Papers*, 6:548.
63 Greene to Jefferson, 6 Dec. 1780, *Greene Papers*, 6:530. Greene had to send forces home for lack of clothing. Marion to Greene, 4 Dec. 1780, *Greene Papers*, 6:520.
64 Greene to Polk, 9 Dec. 1780, *Greene Papers*, 6:559.
65 Greene to Steuben, 20 Nov. 1780, *Greene Papers*, 6:496.
66 Greene to Stevens, 1 Dec. 1780, *Greene Papers*, 6:513. See also Carrington to Greene, 6 Dec. 1780, *Greene Papers*, 6:537. Provides an update on American efforts to acquire boats to ford North Carolina's numerous rivers. Greene to Long, 15 Dec. 1780, *Greene Papers*, 6:578.
67 Thayer, *Greene*, p. 289.
68 Greene to Nash, 15 Dec. 1780, *Greene Papers*, 6:578–9.
69 Greene to Nash, 6 Dec. 1780, *Greene Papers*, 6:533.
70 Greene to Jefferson, 20 Nov. 1780, *Greene Papers*, 6:491–2.
71 Greene to Steuben, 27 Nov. 1780, *Greene Papers*, 6:506.
72 Greene to Pickens, 21 Feb. 1781, *Greene Papers*, 7:327.
73 Greene to Morgan, 16 Dec. 1780, *Greene Papers*, 6:589–90. See also Greene to Huntington, 28 Dec. 1780, ibid., 7:8 and Thayer, *Greene*, p. 299.
74 Morgan to Greene, 31 Dec. 1780, *Greene Papers*, 7:31.
75 Cornwallis to Tarleton, 1 Jan. 1780, Tarleton, *Campaigns*, p. 210; Morgan to Greene, 31 Dec. 1780, *Greene Papers*, 7:30.
76 Greene to Morgan, 19 Jan. 1781, *Greene Papers*, 7:146–7.
77 William Duane, ed., *Extracts from the Diary of Christopher Marshall, During the American Revolution, 1774–1781* (Albany: Joel Munsell, 1877), pp. 268–9.
78 Cornwallis, *Correspondence*, p. 84.
79 Greene to Morgan, 19 Jan. 1781, *Greene Papers*, 7:147.
80 Morgan to Greene, 29 Jan. 1781, *Greene Papers*, 7:215. See also Greene to Colonel William Campbell, 30 Jan. 1781, *Greene Papers*, 7:218–19.
81 Greene to Huger, 30 Jan. 1780, *Greene Papers*, 7: 220.
82 Greene to Washington, 15 Feb. 1781, *Greene Papers*, 7:293.
83 Greene to Huntington, 31 Jan. 1780, *Greene Papers*, 7:225–6.
84 Greene to Marion, 16 Feb. 1781, *Greene Papers*, 7:297.
85 Carl von Clausewitz, *On War*, Michael Howard and Peter Paret, eds. and trans. (Princeton: Princeton University Press, 1984), p. 570.
86 Greene to Nash, 9 Feb. 1781, *Greene Papers*, 7:263.
87 Greene to Clay, 17 Feb. 1781, *Greene Papers*, 7:300.
88 Greene to Steuben, 1 Mar. 1781, *Greene Papers*, 8:375–6.
89 Greene to Nash, 17 Feb. 1781, *Greene Papers*, 7:302–3; Greene to North Carolina Legislature, 15 Feb. 1781, *Greene Papers*, 7:291.
90 Cornwallis to Rawdon, 21 Feb. 1781, Cornwallis, *Correspondence*, p. 85.
91 Thayer, *Greene*, p. 323.
92 Cornwallis, *Correspondence*, p. 267.
93 Tarleton, *Campaigns*, p. 277.
94 Thayer, *Greene*, p. 333.
95 Tarleton, *Campaigns*, pp. 282–3.
96 Thayer, *Greene*, p. 335.
97 Greene to Washington, 29 Mar. 1781, *Greene Papers*, 8:481.
98 Greene to Nash, 29 Mar. 1781, *Greene Papers*, 8:480.
99 Greene to Huntington, 22 Apr. 1781, *Greene Papers*, 8:130.

100 Greene to Huntington, 27 Apr. 1781, *Greene Papers*, 8:157.
101 Greene to Thomas Sumter, 23 Apr. 1781, *Greene Papers*, 8:136.
102 Marion to Greene, 23 Apr. 1781, *Greene Papers*, 8:139–41.
103 Thayer, *Greene*, pp. 351–3. See also Marion to Greene, 29 May 1781, *Greene Papers*, 8:329. See also Pendleton to Read, 21 May 1781, *Greene Papers*, 8:291.
104 Greene to Marion, 24 Apr. 1781, *Greene Papers*, 8:144.
105 Greene to Huntington, 9 June 1781, *Greene Papers*, 8:364.
106 Cornwallis to Rawdon, 20 May 1781, Cornwallis, *Correspondence*, p. 99.
107 Greene to Reed, 4 May 1781, *Greene Papers*, 8:200.
108 Thayer, *Greene*, p. 357.
109 Sumter to Greene, 17 June 1781, *Greene Papers*, 8:408. See also Greene to Huntington, 20 June 1781, *Greene Papers*, 8:419.
110 Greene to Pickens, 19 June 1781, *Greene Papers*, 8:415.
111 Greene to McKean, 17 July 1781, *Greene Papers*, 9:28.
112 Cornwallis to Clinton, 20 May 1781, Cornwallis, *Correspondence*, p. 100.
113 Greene to Lee, 4 July 1781, *Greene Papers*, 8:489.
114 Greene to McKean, 17 July 1781, *Greene Papers*, 9:29–30.
115 Thayer, *Greene*, p. 365.
116 Greene to McKean, 26 July 1781, *Greene Papers*, 9:85.
117 Middlekauff, *The Glorious Cause*, p. 440.
118 Greene to Huntington, 22 Apr. 1781, *Greene Papers*, 9:130.
119 Boatner, *Encyclopedia*, p. 56.
120 Lanier to Greene, 27 May 1781, *Greene Papers*, 8:317.
121 Henry Lee, *Memoirs of the War in the Southern Department of the United States* (New York: University Publishing Company, 1869), p. 572.

2 The birth of American naval strategy

Kenneth J. Hagan

In 1890, slightly over a century after the American War of Independence, the iconic American naval strategist Captain Alfred Thayer Mahan published his strategy-altering classic, *The Influence of Sea Power upon History, 1660–1783*.[1] Masquerading as a narrative of naval history in the age of sail, the book was intended to stimulate the transformation of U.S. naval strategy from one of a numerically small navy relying on coastal defense and commerce-raiding, or *guerre de course*, into one of a large fleet of battleships seeking engagement with enemy battle fleets with the purpose of annihilating the opponent and winning command of the seas. Given this intent, it is not surprising that the bulk of Mahan's book was devoted to descriptions and analyses of fleet engagements between the British Royal Navy and its oceanic enemies: the French, Spanish and Dutch. Even so, it is remarkable that in his first path-breaking book Mahan, an officer in the United States Navy teaching at the U.S. Naval War College, largely ignored the strategies and operations of his predecessors during the war that gave birth to the nation under whose flag he was serving. In doing so, he cast into oblivion the birth of a tradition that had guided the United States in peace and in war for more than a century. The discarded tradition accommodated American maritime inferiority vis-à-vis the great powers of Europe, especially Britain; it was non-doctrinaire and highly utilitarian; it capitalized on the opportunities of the moment; and it repudiated the emulation of nations that built great and costly fleets only to send them into mortal combat. Unlike Mahan, the founding fathers of early American naval strategy did not labor under the illusion that navies could single-handedly win wars.[2]

The American naval strategy terminated by Mahan and his numerous apostles in and out of uniform had its beginnings in the Second Continental Congress, which convened in Philadelphia in May 1775. That year the American colonists had begun armed resistance against imperial Britain, but they had not yet reached the point of declaring their political independence. They retained the chimerical hope that they could underscore their determination to win redress for grievances real and imagined that they had suffered under the Crown as a consequence of the colonial and British victory over the French in the Seven Years' War (1756–63). Committed to eliminating what they saw as oppressive taxation, unreasonable interference with their maritime trade and an unconscionable absence of representation in Parliament, they had almost accidentally initiated armed resistance with the "Minute Men's" attacks on a British army column at Lexington and Concord on 19 April 1775. Two months later, on 15 June, the Congress appointed George Washington commander-in-chief of the nascent Continental Army; two days later – before Washington arrived in Boston – the battle of Bunker Hill took place. That battle showed the British how deadly earnest the Americans could be, but Congress was not yet determined upon independence and therefore sent the so-called "Olive Branch Petition" to London proclaiming the colonists' fidelity to the Crown and petitioning King George III to eliminate the measures they found unreasonable and oppressive.

While the King was rejecting the petition, Congress was busily devising a national naval strategy. The immediate stimulus came from a petition of the Rhode Island state legislature proposing the formation of a national navy. On 13 October 1775, Congress authorized the fitting out "with all possible dispatch" of two ten-gun cruisers to attack British transports burdened with "warlike stores and other supplies for our enemies."[3] To oversee the construction and deployment of the raiders, a three-man naval committee was appointed on the same day. As unprepossessing as they were, these congressional initiatives established what would become the most fundamental element of the American naval strategy during the eighteenth and nineteenth centuries: attacking the oceanic transports of the enemy.

After providing for *guerre de course*, Congress quickly intensified its creation of a national naval strategy. On 30 October 1775, it approved two additional vessels "to be employed ... for the protection and defense of the United Colonies."[4] This was an enlargement of the mission to include coastal defense, another hallmark of pre-Mahanian American naval strategy. The inter-colonial national legislature also added four congressmen to the Naval Committee, the most vigorous of whom was John Adams of Massachusetts, a revolutionary patriot only slightly less radical than his cousin Samuel. Three days later, on 2 November, Congress appropriated $100,000 for more ships. The Committee immediately purchased eight merchant vessels and began converting them into warships mounting between eight and 24 guns each.[5] Their mission was straightforward: interdict British logistical lines by attacking supply ships, bring them into port and distribute the cargoes to George Washington's army.

On 9 November, Congress was stung by news of the King's rejection of the Olive Branch Petition. It swiftly passed three complementary measures defining a national maritime strategy. On 10 November, it authorized two "battalions of American Marines," the rudimentary but not humble precursor of today's United States Marine Corps.[6] The purpose of the Continental Marines was to assist sailors in landing on enemy coastal enclaves to harass the people and capture supplies and weapons useful to Washington's troops. A second measure passed on 25 November gave statutory authorization to the practice of privateering, a form of legalized piracy by which privately owned and very lightly armed vessels swooped down upon isolated British merchantmen and hauled their victims into port where prize courts condemned them and enriched the owners and crews of the privateers.

This kind of *guerre de course* carried the potential of great profitability and little personal risk, so it was widely embraced by the mercantile classes of the Atlantic seaboard. In the course of the war, Congress issued letters of marque – the documents that made privateering a legitimate act of war – to more than 2,000 vessels that took an estimated 600 prizes, approximately three times the number taken by ships of the Continental Navy. Popular and effective in the American War of Independence, privateering has been described as "quite literally, a license to steal."[7] A favorite strategy of weaker naval powers, it remained an American mainstay until the mid-1850s, when it was outlawed by the major European powers. Privateers by no means won the American War of Independence, but together with the Continental Navy's *guerre de course* they provoked the Lloyd's of London insurance company to double the rates for covering maritime shipping, a tangible annoyance for merchants with influence in the Parliament. Their will to continue the war diminished as their profits from shipping declined.

The final congressional naval measure of November 1775 was passage on the 28th of the "Rules for the Regulation of the Navy of the United Colonies of North-America." This governing document of 44 articles gave the lie to the colonists' contention that they were still loyal subjects regretfully resisting the Parliament's incursions upon their rights as Englishmen. Written by John Adams, the document constituted a statement of national sovereignty whose intent was to encourage enlistments by promising sailors a kind of shipboard due process. As the preamble made clear, the Rules were being "Established for Preserving their Rights and Defending their Liberties, and for Encouraging all those who Feel for their Country, to enter into its service in that way in which they can be most Useful."[8] The authority of ships' commanders to inflict corporal punishment was strictly defined and limited, procedural guidelines for courts martial were established and review by higher authority was dictated for convictions involving the death sentence. The Rules governed the American navy until superseded by "An Act for the Government of the Navy of the United States," passed in March 1799 during the presidency of John Adams. These two measures alone should earn Adams recognition as the statesman most responsible for the shape of the early American navy.

The passage of the Rules and Regulations brought the Naval Committee's work to an end. Congress abolished it in order to broaden the political base of the navy, and between 11 and 14 December a permanent Marine Committee was established with representatives from each of the 13 colonies. The new committee's broad charter included overseeing the administration of the Continental Navy, recommending construction of additional vessels and directing the deployment of warships. Immediately, on 22 December 1775, the Marine Committee persuaded Congress to authorize construction of 13 frigates in seven different colonies at an average cost of $66,666 each. The broad dissemination of contracts for construction was intended to maximize the effective use of scarce raw materials and skilled labor, and to win local support for the navy. In the latter regard, the measure initiated the permanent American practice of spreading appropriations throughout as many congressional districts as possible for the political benefit of the people's elected representatives.

As a shaper of naval strategy, the act failed in the short run. Only seven of the 13 planned frigates ever got to sea, and all were lost during the war. They succumbed to the overwhelming might and widespread dispersion of the Royal Navy and to the British army's invasion of their home ports, notably Philadelphia in 1777 and Charleston, South Carolina, in 1780. Historian Craig Symonds has noted that "the tragic history of those vessels emphasizes the difficulty of attempting to create a navy in the midst of a war without a mature naval industry."[9] To this perceptive admonition a caveat must be entered: by authorizing vessels suitable for challenging all but the largest warships of European navies, the Congress had planted a seed for a naval strategy of bold single-ship combat and coastal assault that would flower magnificently in the wars against France (1798–1800), the Barbary powers of North Africa (1801–07) and England (1812–15).

In 1776 the Marine Committee's direction of naval operations did not fare any better than its construction policy. The legislators were worried that Loyalist raids being made on Patriots' estates in the Chesapeake Bay by sailors under the command of the former royal governor, Lord Dunmore, would undermine Virginia's enthusiasm for armed resistance, so they appointed a brother of one of the Marine Committee's members to rid the Chesapeake of the annoyance. Congress commissioned Esek Hopkins as a commodore in the Continental Navy and "commander in chief of the fleet,"[10] and assigned eight small warships to him. On 5 January 1776, the congressmen ordered Hopkins to set sail from Philadelphia in order to assess the strength of Lord Dunmore's forces and destroy them if "you find that they are not greatly superior to your own."[11] Temperamentally disinclined to risk his ships in a fight with vessels of the Royal Navy, and rightly fearing the hazardous winter waters off Cape Hatteras, Hopkins bypassed the cold mouth of the Chesapeake by at least 100 miles and headed for the balmier climes of the Bahamas. On 3 March he landed about 300 sailors and marines who, covered by the guns of the commander-in-chief's *Providence*, 12, and *Wasp*, 8, stormed two forts and occupied New Providence Island. In their first amphibious operation, the marines captured 73 cannons, numerous mortars and a stockpile of munitions, all of which they embarked for conveyance to Washington's Continental Army.

The trip home proved undesirably eventful. On 6 April, off the coast of Rhode Island, the American squadron fell upon the 20-gun British brig *Glasgow*. They engaged her, and in response she disabled the *Cabot*, 14. Hopkins gave chase, lost his prey and limped into New London, Connecticut. Ten Americans had died and 14 were wounded; British casualties were one killed and three injured. The southern colonies felt abandoned by Hopkins, and the value of the captured matériel was insufficient to overcome congressional disgust with a commodore who disregarded his orders and fought with less than heroic distinction.

More fundamentally, by not entering the Chesapeake to challenge Dunmore, Hopkins had undercut what would become a standard component of American naval strategy: to fight the enemy whenever he was not overwhelmingly superior in numbers or firepower. This was precisely what Oliver Hazard Perry did on Lake Erie in the War of 1812, earning immortality in U.S. naval annals. But the maladroit Hopkins proved unable even to get his ships to sea again, in part because the New England seafarers preferred the profits of privateering to the rigors of naval service. Congress censured Hopkins in August 1776 and finally dismissed him from the service in January 1778, "an ordinary man who had the misfortune to live in extraordinary times."[12] The gallant twentieth-century submariner and naval historian Captain Edward L. Beach has written a more comprehensive epitaph: "All in all, the Continental Congress and the thirteen colonies had very little to show for their initial efforts to create a viable navy."[13]

As the congressional navy was floundering at sea, George Washington, who had taken command of the Continental Army besieging Boston on 3 July 1775, was running his own naval war. It began with the transformation of a 78-ton fishing schooner, the *Hannah*, into a commerce-raider, whose sole purpose was to capture supplies for his army. The *Hannah* soon ran aground and her short-lived career disappointed Washington, but the strategy of commerce-raiding was the only blue-water one available to him. Facing a dozen British warships in Boston Harbor, the frustrated general respected the Royal Navy's dominance and understood that the Americans could not challenge its local and regional command of the sea. The most he could do on salt water was to capitalize on the American penchant for attacking enemy transports. He chartered 11 small ships, one of which, the schooner *Lee*, captured the British brig *Nancy* in November. The victim was laden with 2,500 muskets, some cannon and 30 tons of shot. This was the kind of haul Washington sought, and he petitioned Congress to authorize prize courts so seizures could be judicially legitimized. His focus was absolutely clear: "The Design," he admonished his commanders, "is to intercept the Enemy's supplies, not to look for the Enemy's Armed Vessels."[14] They evidently understood his intent; the general's 11 nautical commerce-raiders captured 55 prizes before the British evacuated Boston on 17 March 1776.

The British withdrawal was prompted by the return in January of Colonel Henry Knox, whom Washington had ordered to strip all arms from Fort Ticonderoga, at the south end of Lake Champlain. The cannons Knox seized at Ticonderoga and dragged over the snow and ice gave the Americans an umbrella of fire while building reinforcements in Boston. This development caused Major General Sir William Howe, who was more desirous of reconciling with the Americans than slaughtering them, to embark his army and hundreds of nervous Loyalists onto naval warships and transports and set sail for the large British base in Halifax, Nova Scotia, where he would regroup. Washington had intelligence indicating that Howe's ultimate destination was New York City; in March and April, he headed overland to the city with his army to prepare for an enemy assault.

On 2 July 1776, a large British fleet and 10,000 soldiers descended upon him; ten days later Lord Richard Howe – the general's brother – appeared with more warships and 150 transports. A series of frontal battles ensued, punctuated by the regular arrival from the sea of British reinforcements. Washington's determination to wage classical warfare was demolished by large numbers of casualties, the offshore bombardment from Royal Navy warships and the seemingly endless offloading of additional British troops. He grasped the strategic reality: "The amazing advantage the Enemy derive from their Ships and the Command of the Water, keeps us in a State of constant perplexity and the most anxious conjecture."[15] The mobility and firepower exhibited by the Royal Navy was quantitatively and qualitatively superior to anything the Americans could hope to replicate by themselves, and it demonstrates the fatuousness of applying the Mahanian critique to the Continental Navy.

Realizing he must save his army as a Clausewitzian center of gravity in what was now a war for independence, General Washington overcame his own reluctance to retreat.[16] With General Howe in hot pursuit, the American commander-in-chief moved northward and then fled as quickly as possible into encampments in Pennsylvania and New Jersey. His hallmark thereafter became the preservation of his army as a symbol of national existence and the execution of surprise raids such as those on Trenton and Princeton in the winter of 1776–77.

While still in Boston, Washington had endorsed a plan hatched by Congress to invade Canada and attack Quebec. The purpose was to win Canadians to the American cause and make impossible a British movement on the St. Lawrence River and south on the Richelieu River toward Lake Champlain. He offered the command to an operationally gifted officer, Benedict Arnold. With about 600 men, Brigadier General Arnold made an arduous overland march to the St. Lawrence, where he was joined by 300 soldiers under Brigadier General Richard Montgomery. The forces jointly assaulted Quebec in December 1775 with disastrous results for themselves. Montgomery was killed. Arnold was wounded but nonetheless maintained a siege until British reinforcements arrived in the spring and took the offensive, at which point he led his men in retreat up the St. Lawrence to its juncture with the Richelieu River. He ascended the river to the southern tip of Lake Champlain, at Crown Point, where he was met by Major General Horatio Gates and 3,500 men. They had been rushed there by a Congress sensibly fearing a British invasion that would split the ardently rebellious New England colonies from the other nine in what would be a prelude to British suppression of the most fundamental supporters of the Revolution. If that happened, the war would be lost.

The enemy force commanded by Major General Sir Guy Carleton numbered 11,000 men, and they began moving up the Richelieu in June 1776. Realizing that the key to further movement southward was absolute control of the lake, Carleton halted at St. Johns, where the river drained the lake. A naval race ensued. Carleton brought a ship-rigged vessel in sections from the St. Lawrence to Champlain and reassembled it. He constructed two schooners of 12 and 14 guns each, a seven-gun gondola, 20 gunboats and a huge flat-bottomed vessel, the aptly named *Thunderer*, which accommodated a crew of 300 and mounted several heavy, 24-pound cannons. He had every reason to expect a sweep of the lake when he resumed his naval advance in October, but he could not guess at the energy, innovativeness and operational skills of Benedict Arnold.

Besotted by an egomania that ultimately would undo him, Arnold was gifted with strategic and tactical insight, exemplary leadership skills and a first-rate administrative imagination.[17] Fully grasping the mortal strategic threat facing Gates and the American cause, Arnold set up camp at the southern extreme of Lake Champlain, some 50 miles below Carleton. He began to build a navy by offering skilled workers "five dollars a day in coin, all the food a man could eat, and a cow as a bonus."[18] The lure drew hundreds of carpenters and shipwrights to Arnold's sylvan yard, and in a frenzy they outpaced the world's master builders at the north end of the lake. The lucid American military historian Geoffrey Perret evokes the evolving scene:

> Strange fleets arose. Lake Champlain is shallow. The vessels Arnold and Carleton constructed appeared to be warships above the waterline, but were like flat-bottomed scows below. Without a stiff wind from behind they could hardly move.[19]

On 24 August, Arnold sailed into Lake Champlain "with eleven instant warships looking for battle."[20] Carleton would not be ready to set sail for nearly two more months, a delay that cost him dearly. In the critical interim, Arnold drilled his men on the tactics of shallow-draft naval warfare and laid his plans for the coming encounter. On 11 October his lookouts spotted the British squadron heading south. He took up a position in the lee of the heavily forested Valcour Island, midway up the western shore of Champlain. The wind was blowing from the north, and the British had already passed by before sighting Arnold's anchored flotilla. To reach their enemy the British had to come about and beat to windward. *Thunderer* failed the test, and Carleton's other vessels were hard-pressed to close on Arnold. "Even so," Craig Symonds records, "the superior fire-power of the ship-rigged *Inflexible* overpowered the American vessels, though darkness fell before the British could complete their victory."[21] Blessed by a thick early morning fog, Arnold glided along the shallow waters of the forested coastline, past the waiting British. With dawn, they took up a hot pursuit and in two days forced Arnold to beach his craft one-by-one, until he reached Crown Point with only five of the 16 vessels with which he had begun to fight.

Arnold's campaign was viewed by his American compatriots as another defeat and a setback for their cause. In fact, however, it must be properly interpreted as a classic tactical defeat that produced a strategic victory. By the time that Carleton's navy defeated Arnold on the fringe of the great inland lake the season for fighting was well advanced. The cautious British general decided that winter was too near to permit him to collect his forces and continue the march to the south. He headed back toward Canada to await spring, giving Gates and other leaders of the American forces time to prepare for the next round. It came not on the lake but on the land. In the summer of 1777, Carleton's replacement, Major General John Burgoyne, marched south along the Richelieu and Lake Champlain expecting to rendezvous with William Howe's army coming up the Hudson River from New York City, but Howe had decided instead to attack and occupy Philadelphia, the congressional seat. Burgoyne was left to his own devices in the middle of the woods, far from his base of supply and without any hope of reinforcement from New York. Harassed by the Americans' guerrilla warfare and defeated in the battles of Freeman's Farm (19 September) and Bemis Heights (7 October), Bourgoyne retreated to Saratoga. There, on 17 October 1777, he surrendered his army of nearly 6,000 men.

Burgoyne's unprecedented capitulation to Horatio Gates helped to induce monarchical France to ally with the Revolutionaries, fundamentally altering the war's military balance. It was an unexpected vindication for Arnold, who unwittingly had established a basic permanent principle of American naval strategy: to steadfastly resist every British attempt to win command of the major lakes on or near the northern American border. In the War of 1812 this resistance was achieved by Oliver Hazard Perry on Lake Erie, Isaac Chauncey on Ontario and Thomas Macdonough on Champlain. The tactical disposition adopted by Macdonough replicated Arnold's, and the shallow-draft vessels employed by all three officers were as freshly built from green timber as his had been. His brown-water naval strategy for defense of the great northern lakes only became obsolete when Great Britain and the United States ceased to regard one another as potential enemies in the gradual Anglo-American reconciliation of the late nineteenth and early twentieth centuries.

In 1777, reconciliation with London was far from the minds of congressmen. In late September they had fled Philadelphia as General Sir William Howe prepared to enter the nominal national capital after defeating Washington's army at Brandywine Creek. The war was at best a stalemate, and the Americans were single-handedly fighting the world's greatest sea power. If it really wished to do so, the Royal Navy could interdict what few maritime lines of supply the Americans had; it could drive their pitifully few frigates from the sea; it could deprive their privateers of booty; it could attack and torch American coastal cities with impunity; and it could move armies of Red Coats from point-to-point anywhere on the seaboard. For the congressmen contemplating this very grim situation, news of Burgoyne's surrender at Saratoga came as a stroke of lightning. It galvanized them into renewed efforts to win overt support from France, which was always desirous of striking back at the British for the humiliating defeat endured in the Seven Years' War (1756–63).

Since March 1776, the French government had been giving clandestine aid to the Americans through a dummy company organized by Pierre-Augustin Caron de Beaumarchais, a polymath, inventor, spy and author of two comedies that became operas, *The Barber of Seville* and *The Marriage of Figaro*. But transoceanic shipments of muskets and cannons could run afoul of predatory ships of the Royal Navy and, short of formal diplomatic recognition and a military alliance with the United States, the French navy could do nothing to help the Americans at sea. The Declaration of Independence of July 1776 made an alliance between two countries legally possible, and Congress sent Benjamin Franklin to Paris in the late fall of that year with instructions to see if one could be arranged. He took the French royal court by storm, enthralling noblemen and ladies alike with his brilliance and faux air of a genial frontiersman. But the sophisticated and cagy foreign minister, Comte de Vergennes, would not commit the monarchy of Louis XVI to a major war until given a sign that the Americans could militarily defeat a strong British force. That was precisely what they had done at Saratoga, as Franklin explained to Vergennes.

The American also warned the French minister that a pending English offer of reconciliation short of independence was gaining appeal among his war-weary countrymen. The offer could be vitiated by conclusion of Franco-American treaties of commerce and military alliance, but time was running out. Vergennes was persuaded, and on 6 February 1778, he and Franklin signed two treaties, one of which bound the United States not to make peace with England until authorized to do so by France. This full-fledged military alliance opened the floodgates of aid to Washington's army, and on the high seas it offered the Royal Navy a challenge from a navy that was its numerical match, or nearly so, in ships-of-the-line.

In April 1779, Spain allied with France, presenting Whitehall with the nightmarish challenge of fighting two major European navies at once. In a little over a year's time, the American War of Independence had mutated into a global war in which the European navies were fighting for command of the seas and for acquisition of colonial possessions everywhere from the West Indies through the Mediterranean to the Indian Ocean. North America had become a backwater in this now monumental contest, one that would drag on until 1783, a year after the English granted the Americans their independence in a secretly negotiated bilateral treaty.

This worldwide naval confrontation mesmerized Alfred Thayer Mahan in 1890, but in 1778 his predecessors were fixated only on what the French navy could do for them in North American waters. The definitive and war-winning answer would be given at Yorktown, Virginia, in October 1781, but in the meantime the French navy offered only limited direct help. Aside from anticipation of a major act of intervention, therefore, the situation in the American theater remained largely as Washington had described it in July 1777: the Royal Navy's command of the sea guaranteed perpetual anxiety on the part of American military leaders. It remained for them to devise their own strategies of naval warfare while waiting for a decisive intervention by the French, something that conceivably might never come from a power seeking colonial aggrandizement wherever the British appeared vulnerable.

The Americans continued their strategy of commerce-raiding with privateers and whatever warships the Continental Navy could get to sea, but between 1779 and 1780 they added to their repertoire an audacious new component, what in the twenty-first century would be called the "projection of force." For the modern U.S. Navy this means deploying warships and amphibious forces thousands of miles from continental North America. The reach of the directors of naval strategy in the War for Independence was usually more modestly confined to their own Atlantic seaboard, and even here the strategy was largely ineffective because, once alerted, the Royal Navy could smugly overwhelm the American invaders regardless of the ongoing oceanic war with the French navy. This was the case with both the Penobscot expedition of July 1779 and the defensive sortie into Charleston harbor in the spring of 1780.

In 1779, Penobscot Bay lay within the boundaries of Massachusetts and the Massachusetts General Court became irritated when the British established a haven for Loyalist refugees at Castine, a town covering a spit of land within the bay.[22] The insult was compounded by the British military occupation of the town and construction of a small fort nearby. Massachusetts decided to commit its entire state navy, the brigantines *Active* and *Tyrannicide*, to an expedition that would liberate the citizens of Castine. Neighboring New Hampshire ordered its only fighting vessel, the *Hampden*, to join the force. This was an unusual demonstration of solidarity because state navies rarely operated outside local waters, and they almost never cooperated with one another.

The purpose of a state's navy in the American War of Independence was the coastal defense of that state, yet no state possessed enough resources to construct a force that could survive a serious encounter with even a small squadron of the Royal Navy. But the expedition of 1779 had fired the people's imaginations, and Massachusetts convinced the owners of 16 privateers to go along, promising the capitalists indemnification for any losses they might suffer and a fair share of any prize money that might be gained. Finally, Massachusetts persuaded the Congress to attach three Continental Navy ships to the flotilla, frigate *Warren*, sloop *Providence* and brig *Diligent*. The 22 fighting vessels were augmented by 18 transports armed with 1,000 Massachusetts militiamen whose purpose was to forcibly expel the British from Penobscot Bay.

The rather considerable armada sortied on 24 July 1779. It was commanded by Commodore Dudley Saltonstall of Boston, a privateer in the Seven Years' War and commander of the flagship *Alfred* during the Hopkins' expedition to the Bahamas. Governmental hierarchy and the preponderance of the Continental Navy's detachment dictated that the expedition should be commanded overall by an officer of the national navy, but Saltonstall's authority was not absolute. The militia fell under the control of Brigadier Solomon Lovell, who was seconded by Paul Revere as chief of artillery. The separate jurisdictions of the components of the flotilla destroyed the chain of command and guaranteed discord. Saltonstall's predicament was irremediable: "he could not exercise effective control over his disparate naval forces, and worse, he could not issue orders to the Massachusetts militia under BGEN Solomon Lovell."[23] The two commanders could not agree on an operational plan. The military officer wanted the navy to attack three British naval sloops anchored in the bay; the commodore wanted the American troops to purge the small fort of its British regulars.

The division within the American high command contributed to a lackluster performance of both militiamen and sailors, and the inevitable outcome came with merciful alacrity. On 11 August, when confronted by 50 British regulars who ventured out from the fort to engage them, the militiamen fled. Saltonstall meanwhile was preparing a naval attack when the Royal Navy arrived in awe-inspiring force: one ship-of-the-line, three frigates and three sloops. Hopelessly outgunned, Saltonstall and his sailors raced upriver, grounded their ships as the water's flow progressively narrowed and fled into the forest. The crew of the *Warren* burned their frigate to prevent her from being added to the British naval order of battle. Every American armed ship and transport was lost in the debacle.

Saltonstall returned home to face a court martial, censure and dismissal from the service. He thoroughly deserved his fate for not exerting effective command, but "the mixed bag of national, state, and private vessels that made up his 'fleet' had handicapped him throughout the campaign."[24] In this regard, Saltonstall and Lovell had set a precedent of sorts, even if it was an ominous one. Throughout American naval history the effectiveness of amphibious operations has been diminished by the rivalry and contentiousness dividing the senior naval and military officers conducting the campaigns. This was notoriously the case with the rancorous dispute between Rear Admiral David Dixon Porter and Major General Benjamin Butler during the Union assault on Fort Fisher, North Carolina, in early 1865. In the twentieth century, the cancerous phenomenon was so evident during the invasion of Guadalcanal in August 1942 that 60 years later there still existed a palpable Marine Corps resentment toward the U.S. Navy for allegedly having withheld full air support after the initial landings.

Regardless of his limitations as a fighting commander, Saltonstall had been met by a superior British naval force, a fate that also befell Commodore Abraham Whipple when he attempted to assist in the defense of Charleston, South Carolina, in 1780. Unable or unwilling to capture the foxy George Washington and his evasive army, and facing an expanding war with France and her allies, the British in late 1779 resolved upon a new strategy for breaking the Revolutionaries' will to fight. They would dismember the American confederation by detaching the southern block of states. Transported on ships escorted by the Royal Navy, British soldiers would invade the Carolinas and Georgia, capitalize on what London perceived to be vigorous Loyalist support, re-establish sovereignty over the extreme South and then recapture Virginia for the Crown. The endeavor ultimately was doomed by the brutality British troops showed toward the local population, the resourcefulness of American irregulars and mountain men and the operational genius of General Nathanael Greene; but it began auspiciously in early 1780.

Sailing from New York on 26 December 1779, Vice Admiral Marriot Arbuthnot commanded a fleet of five ships-of-the-line, seven frigates, and two sloops escorting 90 transports and 8,500 men under the command of General Sir Henry Clinton. The general had made a stab at Charleston once before, in 1776, and had been repulsed by the stout walls of Fort Moultrie, at the entrance to Charleston harbor. Made wiser by his defeat, Clinton in 1780 eschewed a frontal assault on the fort, opting instead to march around the city of Charleston and lay siege to it from the rear. Arbuthnot's task was simply to close off the entrance to the harbor with a close-in blockade, but on 8 April he slipped seven of his frigates past Fort Moultrie and anchored just off the city with their guns pointing landward.

Among those caught in the harbor was Commodore Abraham Whipple of Rhode Island. Like Saltonstall, in 1776 he had commanded one of Hopkins' ships, the *Columbus*, but unlike Saltonstall he was a fine tactician and hard fighter. At one point very early in the war an irate British captain had threatened to hang him for having burned "His Majesty's vessel, the *Gaspee*," to which chilling threat Whipple responded, "Always catch a man before you hang him."[25] Now, in 1780, he faced the impossible mission of assisting Major General Benjamin Lincoln and perhaps 5,500 soldiers and militiamen in defending Charleston against an enemy with a growing regular army already nearly twice the size of the Americans' amateur force, not to mention a naval fleet strong enough to defeat a substantial European battle fleet. Whipple calculated the odds and acted sensibly. He removed his ships' guns and whatever else might be useful in the defense of the city, scuttled the vessels as an impediment to the Royal Navy's movement past the city and up the Cooper River and ordered his sailors to join the forces defending the city.

After giving fair warning in a classical eighteenth-century manner, Clinton on 9 May laid on a terrifying all-night bombardment of Charleston. The chastened city fathers begged Lincoln to save their city by surrendering, which he did on 12 May 1780. The British offensive would now move inland and continue for over a year, until Nathanael Greene drove Lieutenant General Lord Charles Cornwallis into Virginia and toward what the British general hoped would be the security of the Royal Navy off Yorktown. Whipple and his officers, meanwhile, were treated as prisoners of war by the British, who had captured them in Charleston.

The commodore's role in the 1780 battle for that city has been less emphasized than General Lincoln's surrender, which "remains to this day the third largest U.S. military capitulation in history behind Bataan in World War II and Harpers Ferry in the Civil War."[26] Nonetheless, when combined with Hopkins' defeat in 1776 and Saltonstall's collapse in 1779, Whipple's catastrophe served as a strategic and operational admonition to the post-Revolutionary War American navy not to engage fleets – or even squadrons – of the Royal Navy. This precaution governed U.S. naval strategy on the Atlantic during the War of 1812, as a result of which operationally dispersed American frigates fighting singly or in pairs defeated several British counterparts and earned the grudging respect of the Royal Navy's officers. Had the Americans concentrated their frigates into a fleet in that war they easily could have lost them all in one large engagement and, in defeat, exposed the United States coastline to perpetual blockade and incessant raids from the sea.[27]

Raiding the enemy's coast was a strategy perfected by the Continental Navy's most audacious officer, John Paul Jones, who was also a master of *guerre de course*. Born in Scotland in 1747, and already a merchant shipmaster by the age of 21, Jones volunteered to fight against Britain at the time Congress was authorizing the first ships of the American navy. He was commissioned as the senior lieutenant of the Continental Navy in December 1775, and he first served aboard Esek Hopkins's flagship, the 24-gun sloop *Alfred*, in the expedition to the

Bahamas of early 1776. In May of that year he was given command of the 12-gun sloop *Providence* and cruised about North American waters convoying merchantmen from port to port. His success, although not in any way spectacular, earned him a commission as a captain in the Continental Navy on 8 August 1776.

Now began Jones' meteoric rise to fame. Preying lethally between the Delaware Capes and Nova Scotia from August to October 1776, *Providence* took 16 prizes. Only through her skipper's gifted ship-handling did she escape the claws of a 28-gun British frigate, *Solebay*. Back in Providence, Rhode Island, Jones accepted command of the larger *Alfred* and in company with *Providence* sailed on 1 November with orders to raid Cape Breton, Nova Scotia. *Providence* started taking on water and turned back on 13 November, but Jones continued unfazed into enemy waters. By the time of his return to Boston on 18 December, he had twice raided and burned buildings in Nova Scotia and seized or destroyed nine ships, including the ten-gun *John*. The captured transport *Mellish* yielded 10,000 suits of uniforms and 150 prisoners. This combination of coastal raids and maritime prize-taking, supplemented with his energetic and self-aggrandizing lobbying of congressmen, led Jones to his next major command, the 18-gun sloop-of-war *Ranger*. As her captain, he would carry his methods of warfare into England's home waters and onto her coasts.

A bold strategist of offensive warfare, in January 1777 Jones proposed cruising along the west coast of Africa where he would pillage unprotected British colonial trading posts and grab transports of the British East India Company. But his plans were twice reshaped by Congress, partially under the influence of Robert Morris, a representative from Pennsylvania with a keen interest in the Continental Navy. On 1 February, Morris outlined to Jones the strategic rationale for carrying naval warfare to the enemy.

> It has long been clear to me that our infant fleet cannot protect our own Coasts; and that the only effectual relief it can afford to us is to attack the enemy's defenseless places and thereby oblige them to station more of their Ships in their own countries, or to keep them employed in following ours, [and] either way we are relieved so far as they do it.[28]

As a means of drawing the Royal Navy away from America's Atlantic shores, Morris favored sending Jones with five ships to capture Pensacola, Florida, to lurk about the mouth of the Mississippi River in search of "booty," and to strike at the numerous British possessions in the Caribbean and West Indies. It was apparent to the Marine Committee that the Continental Navy was too small and fragile for such a broad expansion of the war. The governing body instead opted for single-ship incursions into British home waters, an audacious but geographically highly focused thrust at the enemy's heart. The first officer to execute the strategy was Lambert Wickes, whose 18-gun brig *Reprisal* had carried Benjamin Franklin to France to join two other American diplomatic commissioners in November 1776.[29] Freed of his passenger, Wickes in January 1777 began a five-month rampage of prize-taking in the English Channel and Irish Sea, causing London sternly to protest "neutral" France's violation of its obligations not to harbor warships or privateers of belligerents, especially ones the English considered rebels. By May, Wickes and his fellow raider, Gustavus Connyngham of the ten-gun lugger *Surprize*, were grounded by the apprehensive French authorities.

Meanwhile, as mentioned earlier, Jones had wrested from Congress the command of *Ranger*, which was under construction at Portsmouth, New Hampshire. It took him the summer and autumn of 1777 to ready his ship for sea, but when *Ranger* sailed for Europe on 1 November, Jones knew of General John Burgoyne's surrender at Saratoga two weeks earlier. *Ranger*'s arrival in France coincided propitiously with the strategically incalculable consequence of that surrender: the signature of the Franco-American Treaty of Alliance by Franklin and Vergennes on 6 February 1778. Eight days later, Jones brought *Ranger* into Quiberon Bay on France's Biscay coast, where he received from a French flagship the first official salute to the American flag from a foreign nation.

With a base of operations now legally possible, and in fact established, Jones headed across the English Channel and into the Irish Sea, a confined oceanic lake where no enemy of England had dared show its flag for over a century. Between 14 February and 8 May he landed a party at Whitehaven, spiked the defending guns and roamed around in search of the Earl of Selkirk, whom he hoped to capture and exchange for American prisoners of war. To the earl's good fortune, he was nowhere to be found, so Jones re-embarked his men and headed up into the North Channel. There he met, engaged, defeated and took as a prize the *Drake*, a Royal Navy 20-gun sloop-of-war. Flushed with victory, he returned to Brest, France, proclaiming that he had demonstrated to the British that "not all their boasted navy can protect their own coast, and that the scene of distress which they have occasioned in America may soon be brought home to their own shores."[30] The spirit was ardent, the wherewithal nearly non-existent.

After dispatching *Ranger* to the United States with her exhausted and restive crew, Jones stayed on in France while Benjamin Franklin struggled to find him a new ship. It was not an easy matter, in part because war now existed between France and England. Seaworthy warships were in high demand by the French navy, and only leftovers could be spared for the Americans. As a result, Jones was left ashore to chafe at his enforced idleness throughout the remainder of 1778, the year in which French admirals were aggressively carrying the maritime war into the English Channel and as far west as Newport, Rhode Island.[31] Finally, on 7 February 1779, the French government donated to Jones an old East Indiaman, *Le Duc de Duras*, "a broad-beamed hermaphrodite vessel designed to carry cargo as well as fight."[32] In the course of the next several months Jones converted the hog into the semblance of a frigate and renamed her *Bonhomme Richard*, the pen name of his patron and the negotiator of the alliance that had made it possible for Jones and other ships of the Continental Navy to operate out of French ports.[33]

The summer of outfitting *Bonhomme Richard* brought strategic chaos. Jones wished to reprise the coastal raids he had made with *Ranger*, believing them to be the most efficient strategy he could employ to weaken the British will for continuing the war. The French presented objections. For a while, the Marquis de Lafayette indicated he intended to sail with Jones and several other American ships in an amphibious assault upon Liverpool. That plan collapsed when the French decided on an extremely complex and ambitious operation involving their battle fleet and that of Spain, which formally declared war against England on 21 June 1779. The allies' goal was to establish Franco-Spanish command of the English Channel, one feature of which was the destruction of the English fleet anchored at Spithead.[34] Jones was to lead a diversionary raid against Scotland or northern England, but he failed to organize his part of the operation in time to be of use.

A strong French fleet had sailed from Brest on 3 June, and when combined with a Spanish armada it promised to overwhelm the Royal Navy's much smaller and less heavily armed fleet. Shielded by westerly winds and shrouding fog, the British admiral, Sir Charles Hardy, delayed engagement as long as possible. He was providentially saved by a debilitating and mortal illness that swept the lower decks of the French and Spanish fleets, forcing their retreat to home ports in early September 1779.

While disease was incapacitating his allies and driving them from the fight, Jones at last went to sea under the burden of yet another set of orders from the French: to raid the enemy's commerce. He had objected because he thought that raiding the English coast was a more direct means of warfare. He preferred national victory over the private profits of prize-taking, and he protested to Franklin to no avail. America's senior representative in Europe told him simply that since the French were "at the Chief expense, I think they have the best right to direct."[35] Undercut by his allies, Jones prepared a commerce-raiding expedition while still hoping to land at least twice on the coasts of Scotland and England.

Jones' frustrations were exponentially increased by the additional requirement that he sail in company with the new American-built 36-gun frigate *Alliance* and three French ships: the 32-gun frigate *Pallas*, the 18-gun cutter *Le Cerf* and the 12-gun corvette *La Vengeance*. The French captains thought themselves in every way superior to Jones; this conceit especially characterized the French commander of *Alliance*, Pierre Landais, who in addition was psychologically unstable. On 14 August 1779, this group of naval potentates sailed from L'Orient with seven ships. After reaching the waters west of Ireland they headed north toward Scotland, east into the North Sea and southward along the east coasts of Scotland and England. Along the way they took a dozen prizes, mostly in the passage between the Orkney and Shetland Islands.

On 23 September 1779, with only *Bonhomme Richard*, *Alliance* and *Pallas*, Jones met destiny head-on, in the North Sea, off Flamborough Head, Yorkshire. Quite unexpectedly, his small squadron of prize-takers ran into a British convoy of 41 ships homeward-bound from the Baltic. Two warships were escorting the transports. One was formidable: HMS *Serapis*, a spanking-new two-decked "fifth rate" ship nominally mounting 44 guns but at that moment glowering with 50. The other chaperone, the 20-gun sloop-of-war *Countess of Scarborough*, could be managed, as was demonstrated by her surrender to the *Pallas* after an hour's struggle. *Bonhomme Richard*, "rotten, unhandy and slow," should have been quickly demolished by *Serapis*, but Jones was willing to fight to the death.[36] He lashed his ship to his opponent's, and for three or four hours the two warhorses fired broadsides and everything imaginable at one another. In the midst of the bloody melee the British captain shouted an invitation to surrender. Jones is alleged to have retorted, "I have not yet begun to fight."[37] Finally, with his mainmast tottering and a serious fire about to engulf his wrecked frigate, Captain Richard Pearson of the Royal Navy surrendered to Captain John Paul Jones of the Continental Navy.

The flames aboard *Serapis* were extinguished, but *Bonhomme Richard* was fatally wounded and sank on 25 September. Deeply saddened by his ship's loss and equally elated by his victory over the British frigate, Jones took his prize and prisoners to Texel in the United Netherlands, which was not a formal ally of the United States.[38] He had lost 150 men killed and wounded out of a crew of 322; Pearson lost 170 of 325. Landais, on the *Alliance*, had inexplicably fired his cannon at both ships before withdrawing; he would ultimately be stripped of his naval commission.

Captain Pearson fared surprisingly well. He was knighted by George III for saving the convoy. The knighthood demonstrated that the protection of maritime commerce was more important than individual victories or defeats, and it buttressed the argument for *guerre de course* as a wise strategy for weaker naval powers such as the United States in the age of sail.

Jones's shining glory soon darkened. He was awarded the French Order of Military Merit and presented with a court-sword by Louis XVI. Congress cast a gold medal of him in 1781 and gave him command of *America*, a ship-of-the-line that was under construction but which saw no action before being given to the French at war's end. Without a war, without a ship, without prospects, Jones drifted off into the Russian navy and ended up destitute in Paris, where he died in 1792. His status as a widely recognized American hero had to await the twentieth century, when Theodore Roosevelt and other prominent navalists would bring his body to Annapolis, Maryland. It rests there today in a solitary sarcophagus beneath the Naval Academy Chapel. Commodore Dudley W. Knox, an 1896 graduate of that institution who became one of the twentieth century's foremost U.S. naval strategists, composed the navy's simple, brief eulogy of restoration for Jones and his victory: "This brilliant affair was the most notable enterprise of the Continental Navy whose activities were thereafter diminished."[39]

In the final analysis, Jones's contribution was not that of a strategist; it was that of a classic naval warrior. His commerce-raiding lit a beacon for Raphael Semmes in the Civil War. His incursions on the enemy's coast set a precedent for Stephen Decatur in 1804, John Sloat in 1846 and David G. Farragut in 1864. His classic single-ship duel beckoned to Thomas Truxtun of *Constellation*

The birth of American naval strategy 51

(1800), Isaac Hull of *Constitution* (1812) and the commanders of *Monitor* and *Virginia* in 1862.

At a more mundane level, the success of *Bonhomme Richard* was owed as much to France as to Jones. Benjamin Franklin's treaty of alliance with Vergennes had generated the financial backing necessary to convert and man the frigate, and the pact opened the ports from which Jones operated. All other commanding officers of the Continental Navy and all American privateers operating in European waters after February 1778 made use of French harbors. This convenient availability of repairs, food, water and sailors' liberty permitted the American commerce-raiders to outrage British merchants with attacks upon shipping in England's home waters, and to hit their pocketbooks by driving up insurance rates. But the far more crucial role of France in the naval strategy and operations of the American War of Independence was the global one performed by its navy.

The Franco-Spanish challenge to English security and control of the Channel that had failed in 1779 was a fairly minor episode in the globalized naval warfare that followed France's alliance with the Americans. From 1778 until 1783, with or without their continental European allies, the French continually contested British naval dominance in the English Channel, the Mediterranean, the Indian Ocean and, most importantly, the West Indies. The first fleet action in European waters came early in the Anglo-French war, on 27 July 1778, 100 miles west of Ushant, an island at the mouth of the English Channel. Of equal strength at 30 ships each, two English and French battle fleets fought violently for several hours with neither side scoring a clear victory. Alfred T. Mahan, who reserved his highest praise for battles of annihilation, rated the battle of Ushant as "wholly indecisive in its results."[40] On the other hand, Ushant did maintain the status quo in the Channel, leaving England reasonably free from the threat of invasion and therefore able to fight France and her allies elsewhere.

The struggle in the Mediterranean took the form of a futile three-year siege of Gibraltar by the French and Spanish navies. At the end of the siege, England retained possession of the vital choke point controlling the western entrance to the otherwise land-locked maritime body.

The protagonists in the naval face-off in the Indian Ocean had as their objective the political dominance of India, and the five battles fought by Admirals Edward Hughes and Pierre André de Suffren Saint-Tropez in 1782–83 put France in position to dispossess the British.[41] The historic opportunity was lost only when Hughes and Suffren quit fighting upon learning of the provisional Anglo-French-Spanish peace treaties of early 1783.

The strategic and operational situation in the West Indies was more complex. It consisted of battles for naval supremacy, raids on enemy colonies and convoys and opportunistic French sorties to North America in support of the ever-struggling Revolutionaries. The first large expedition to the north was undertaken in 1779 by Vice Admiral Jean-Baptiste-Charles-Henri-Hector, Comte d'Estaing. Hoping to invade British-occupied Savannah, he brought 20 ships-of-the-line and 3,000 troops in transports to Georgia. His coordination with

Washington was imperfect, in part because the general was fixated on attacking the British in New York City. D'Estaing himself was anxious to return to France, as he had been ordered to do, and yet he wanted to aid the Americans. On 9 October 1779, in concert with a contingent of the Continental Army, the French admiral initiated an assault on the besieged city. The well-fortified British army repulsed the invaders; d'Estaing was seriously wounded and sailed for France. He had had the right strategic concept, but successful operational implementation eluded him. Two years would elapse before a similar move in Yorktown, Virginia, would be crowned with victory.

With d'Estaing out of the picture, George Washington was left in New Jersey, fuming about how badly he wanted a continuous French naval presence in North American waters. In July 1780 he made his case to Lieutenant General Comte de Rochambeau, who had just arrived in Newport with an army of 6,000 men: "In any operation, and under all circumstances, a decisive naval superiority is to be considered as a fundamental principle, and the basis upon which every hope of success must ultimately depend."[42]

Washington knew full well that naval superiority could not even be attempted by the Continental Navy. He must also have understood that French naval predominance in North American waters could only be temporary and geographically limited, as had been the case during d'Estaing's incursion into Georgia. In fact, the French fleet associated with Rochambeau in Newport was blockaded by the Royal Navy until the summer of 1781. Only then did Rochambeau march to join Washington, who still favored an attack on New York City.

The objective, however, was changed by information that a French fleet escaping the hurricane season was headed up from the West Indies, and by Rochambeau's insistence that the combined operation must be directed toward the vicinity of Yorktown, Virginia, where American troops commanded by the Marquis de Lafayette were battling soldiers of Benedict Arnold, now a brigadier general in the British army. Also present and threatening were the substantial remnants of the army that General Lord Charles Cornwallis had brought from his defeats at the hands of Nathanael Greene in the Carolinas. Under orders from General Sir Henry Clinton, the British commander-in-chief in New York, Cornwallis was establishing a defensive position on the Virginia Peninsula for the purpose of sheltering ships of the Royal Navy. Perhaps this was a prudent stratagem if absolutely certain of the presence of the Royal Navy, but by moving his army onto a narrow peninsula Cornwallis trapped himself in a box from which he could not escape when confronted by the combined armies of Rochambeau and Washington on the landward side, and by the French navy just offshore.

The initiator of the battle that won the American War of Independence was Rear Admiral François J.P. Comte de Grasse who decided to capitalize on the coming hurricane season in the West Indies and head for the Chesapeake Bay to see what mischief he could accomplish. He wrote George Washington of his plans on 5 August in a letter the American commander-in-chief received at his headquarters in the Hudson River highlands on 14 August. Still preferring to attack the British stronghold in New York City, Washington realized that he lacked the numbers of men to do so, even if he combined his army with Rochambeau's, which at the time was garrisoned in Newport, Rhode Island. The French and American generals agreed that Cornwallis' army now presented the best potentially vulnerable center of gravity. They began a march toward Yorktown after Washington had left a decoy force of 2,500 soldiers seeming to threaten an assault on Staten Island as a means of keeping the British focused on the defense of New York.

While Rochambeau and Washington were rushing their combined armies to the Chesapeake, events at sea moved with great rapidity. De Grasse arrived at the Chesapeake on 30 August and anchored in Lynnhaven Bay, just inside Cape Henry and across from Yorktown, in order to disembark 2,500 French troops as reinforcements for Lafayette. Six days later, on 5 September, 19 British ships-of-the-line commanded by Rear Admiral Thomas Graves, who was seconded by Rear Admiral Sir Samuel Hood, arrived from New York. Hood had been pursuing de Grasse from the West Indies and had reached New York on 28 August without having found him. Fully grasping the seriousness of the situation Cornwallis must be facing, he convinced Graves of the danger and they had rushed to sea on 1 September and headed to the Chesapeake. As Graves and Hood arrived offshore, de Grasse was still disembarking troops and replenishing his shipboard supplies. Meanwhile, another French fleet commanded by Comte de Barras de Saint Laurent was heading from Newport to the Chesapeake. De Barras' eight ships-of-the-line were escorting 18 transports burdened with munitions and siege cannon for the combined armies. De Grasse faced a dilemma:

> In sailing out he ran a double risk – of being defeated, and of having the British slip into the Bay behind him. On the other hand, remaining in the Bay would sentence de Barras to almost certain capture on his arrival, with the loss of all the French siege artillery and munitions. Weighing these alternatives, de Grasse decided to leave the Bay for battle.[43]

The battle of the Virginia Capes between the fleets of de Grasse and Graves lasted from about 3:45 p.m. until about 6:30 p.m. on 5 September. At its end, neither fleet had been decisively beaten. Anticipating a renewal of fighting, de Grasse and Graves maneuvered for advantage for several days, but although de Grasse gained the windward gauge – a great advantage in the age of sail because it made it possible to descend upon the enemy at the moment of one's choice – the French admiral chose not to fight. His objective was to hold the Chesapeake, not to annihilate the British fleet. Thus, on 11 September, he returned to Cape Henry, where to his great joy he found de Barras with the munitions and cannon for the armies. Of equal importance, with Barras' warships added to de Grasse's, the Frenchman now commanded 36 ships-of-the-line to Graves's 19. The order of battle had shifted completely and decisively in favor of the French. Graves on 13 September decided to return to New York to regroup and reconsider.

Between 14–26 September, Washington and Rochambeau arrived and began to lay siege to Cornwallis. The British general now had the combined armies to his front and the bay and de Grasse behind him. The Royal Navy, always a source of reinforcements and removal when in extremis, was hundreds of miles away. Cornwallis did the sensible, eighteenth-century thing. He offered to surrender his intact army to Washington and Rochambeau on 17 October – four years to the date after Burgoyne had capitulated at Saratoga.

The news of Cornwallis' surrender led to the collapse of the British war ministry of Lord North and its replacement by the peace party of the Earl of Shelburne. The new government began protracted negotiations with Benjamin Franklin, John Adams and John Jay. At last, on 30 November 1782, the American commissioners signed a peace agreement with England. This was an act of consummate realism that violated the American pledge of 1778 to the French not to withdraw unilaterally from the war, and even Vergennes grudgingly conceded his admiration for the Americans' audacity.

De Grasse was the man who had made victory and independence possible, but he was undone a year after his American triumph. He returned to the West Indies where the climactic encounter in that naval contest came on 12 April 1782: the decisive battle of the Saints. De Grasse faced the British commander, Admiral Sir George Brydges Rodney, who defeated the French fleet, capturing the flagship *Ville de Paris* and de Grasse. This action brought combat in the West Indies to an end, and de Grasse went home in disgrace.[44] But Rodney's victory at sea came too late for the British cause in North America. Peace negotiations had started in Paris that same month.

The Americans had begun their armed struggle with England without a defined military or naval strategy. Both doctrines evolved over the course of the war, sometimes gradually, sometimes suddenly and fitfully. By 1782, the United States had established the foundations of the naval strategy that would guide it for over a century. The crucial elements consisted of commerce-raiding by naval ships as large as frigates as well as by privateers, coastal defense in concert with the army, eagerness for frigate-to-frigate engagements, rejection of line-of-battle ships as the backbone of the navy, avoidance of fleet actions on the high seas, and the projection of naval power – however weak it might be – to distant shores.

In 1890, Alfred Thayer Mahan challenged or radically reshaped each of these formulas, but he was writing for a new age of American industrial might and a revolutionary technology of steel-hulled, steam-driven, armored warships. The fleet actions that he extolled were indeed the historic hallmarks of the great naval powers of Europe, and they became the inspiration of the U.S. Navy of the twentieth century, but they were alien to the men shaping American naval strategy in the War of Independence. It is true that some of them, including George Washington, appreciated the critical value that victorious fleet engagements and command of the sea could offer armies fighting ashore. In September and October 1781, Admiral de Grasse gave Washington the naval component of that winning combination, as a result of which a British general surrendered his army and a British war ministry fell. But de Grasse's superiority in the Chesapeake was necessarily tentative and temporary. Graves and Hood at any moment could have returned with larger fleets and reversed the balance. The French naval superiority at the Virginia Capes and Yorktown therefore conformed much more closely to the models of Sir Julian Corbett than to Mahan's.[45] Corbett argued convincingly that navies could project naval and military force at great distances from their homeland without Mahan's universal command of the seas. It was Corbett's accurate contention that command of the seas was always geographically and temporally limited, never permanent, ubiquitous and worldwide.

To establish a limited Corbettian command of the seas and to achieve victory at Yorktown a European navy had been required, and many American leaders found this dependency deeply troubling. To continue to include numerous ships-of-the-line in post-war American naval planning would require an ally or allies, and allies could drag the fragile young Republic into European wars. Thus it was that one of the premier maritime strategists of the period, President John Adams, went to war against France in 1798–1800 with the purpose of terminating the alliance that had led to victory in 1781 and 1782. The Treaty of Mortefontane closing the Quasi War in 1800 gave him what he sought: bilateral abrogation of the 1778 treaty.[46] Adams' resolution set the American naval standard for the nineteenth century: to sail alone into the future with a reliance on what had been learned from forging strategy and conducting operations during the American War of Independence.

Notes

1 Alfred Thayer Mahan, *The Influence of Sea Power upon History, 1660–1783* (New York: Hill and Wang, 1957). This is one of innumerable editions of a book that has rarely, if ever, been out of print since its publication by Little, Brown and Company in 1890.
2 For an early-twentieth-century rebuttal to Mahan, see Julian S. Corbett, *Some Principles of Maritime Strategy* (Annapolis: Naval Institute Press, 1988), originally published in 1911 by Longmans Green and Co., London. Mahan is sympathetically reconsidered in Jon Tetsuro Sumida, *Inventing Grand Strategy and Teaching Command: The Classic Works of Alfred Thayer Mahan Reconsidered* (Baltimore: Johns Hopkins University Press, 2000).
3 Congressional resolution quoted in Dudley W. Knox, *A History of the United States Navy* (New York: G.P. Putnam's Sons, 1948), p. 7.
4 Congressional resolution quoted in James C. Bradford, "The Navies of the American Revolution, 1775–1783," in Kenneth J. Hagan and Michael T. McMaster, eds., *In Peace and War: Interpretations of American Naval History,* 30th Anniversary Edition (Westport: Greenwood Press, Praeger Security International, 2008), p. 4.
5 They were: *Alfred*, 24, *Columbus*, 18–20, *Andrew Doria*, 14, *Cabot*, 14, *Providence*, 12, *Hornet*, 10, *Wasp*, 8, and *Fly*, 8. Jack Sweetman, ed., *American Naval History: An Illustrated Chronology of the U.S. Navy and Marine Corps, 1775-Present*, 2nd edn. (Annapolis: Naval Institute Press, 1991), p. 1.
6 Kenneth J. Hagan, *This People's Navy: The Making of American Sea Power* (New York: The Free Press, 1991), p. 4. For a history of the Marine Corps, see Allan Reed Millett, *Semper Fidelis: The History of the United States Marine Corps*, rev. and expanded edn. (New York: The Free Press, 1991).
7 Craig L. Symonds, *The Naval Institute Historical Atlas of the U.S. Navy* (Annapolis: Naval Institute Press, 1995), p. 14.

8. Quoted in www.history.navy.mil/faqs/faq59–5.htm, accessed 14 February 2009.
9. Symonds, *Atlas of the Navy*, p. 8. The demise of each ship is explained here.
10. Congressional appointment quoted in Sweetman, *Chronology of the Navy*, p. 2.
11. Congressional orders of 5 January 1776, quoted in Hagan, *People's Navy*, p. 5.
12. Congressional condemnation quoted in ibid., p. 6.
13. Edward L. Beach, *The United States Navy: 200 Years* (New York: Henry Holt and Company, 1986), p. 20.
14. George Washington quoted in Hagan, *People's Navy*, p. 2.
15. Washington quoted in Russell F. Weigley, *The American Way of War: A History of United States Military Strategy and Policy* (Bloomington: Indiana University Press, 1977), p. 12.
16. For Clausewitz' concept of a center of gravity, see Michael Howard and Peter Paret, eds. and trans., *Carl von Clausewitz: On War* (Princeton: Princeton University Press, 1984), Christopher Bassford, *Clausewitz in English: The Reception of Clausewitz in Britain and America, 1815–1945* (New York and Oxford: Oxford University Press, 1994), Hew Strachan, *Carl von Clausewitz's On War* (London: Atlantic, 2007) and Jon Tetsuro Sumida, *Decoding Clausewitz: A New Approach to On War* (Lawrence: University Press of Kansas, 2008).
17. Arnold deserted the Continental Army and joined the British as a brigadier general in 1780, earning iconic status as the quintessential American traitor. For a capsule account, see John Whiteclay Chambers II, ed., *The Oxford Companion to American Military History* (New York: Oxford University Press, 1999), pp. 61–2.
18. Geoffrey Perret, *A Country Made by War: From the Revolution to Vietnam – The Story of America's Rise to Power* (New York: Random House, 1989), p. 39. The author's words.
19. Ibid.
20. Ibid.
21. Symonds, *Atlas of the Navy*, p. 10.
22. Today Penobscot Bay is part of the state of Maine.
23. Symonds, *Atlas of the Navy*, p. 12.
24. Ibid.
25. Whipple quoted in www.whipple.org/abe/commodore.html, accessed 14 February 2009.
26. Symonds, *Atlas of the Navy*, p. 16.
27. See Linda Maloney, "The War of 1812: What Role for Sea Power?" in Hagan and McMaster, eds., *In Peace and War*, pp. 34–46.
28. Morris to Jones, 1 February 1777, quoted in Bradford, "Navies of the American Revolution," p. 9.
29. They were Silas Deane and Arthur Lee.
30. John Paul Jones quoted in Hagan, *People's Navy*, p. 12.
31. In the summer of 1778, the battle fleet of Vice Admiral Charles le Comte d'Estaing tested the British in the Delaware Bay and off New York and Newport, Rhode Island. He spent the fall anchored in Boston harbor. Ibid., pp. 12–13.
32. Symonds, *Atlas of the Navy*, p. 14.
33. *Bonhomme Richard* is conveniently rigged on www.hazegray.org/danfs, accessed 14 February 2009. This is the valuable unofficial online version of the Naval Historical Center's *Dictionary of American Naval Fighting Ships*, 9 vols. (Washington: Government Printing Office, 1959–91).
34. Spain, unlike France, did not recognize the independence of the United States in 1779. Sweetman, *Chronology of the Navy*, p. 9.
35. Franklin quoted in Hagan, *People's Navy*, p. 13.
36. The frigate's description is in Knox, *History of the Navy*, p. 32.
37. Jones is quoted in ibid., p. 35. See also the official website of the Naval Historical Center: www.history.navy.mil, accessed 14 February 2009.

38 The Netherlands signed its first treaty with the United States in 1782. It was one of amity and commerce as contrasted with military alliance. Thomas G. Paterson, J. Garry Clifford, Shane J. Maddock, Deborah Kisatsky and Kenneth J. Hagan, *American Foreign Relations, Volume 1: A History to 1920*, 6th edn. (Boston and New York: Houghton Mifflin Company, 2005), pp. 16–17.
39 Knox, *History of the Navy*, p. 36.
40 Mahan, *Influence of Sea Power*, p. 308.
41 Mahan grudgingly praised Suffren as "a very great man" and evaluated him in terms he usually reserved for praising decisively victorious British admirals. Ibid., p. 416 et passim.
42 George Washington quoted in Mahan, ibid., p. 352.
43 E.B. Potter and Chester W. Nimitz, eds., *Sea Power: A Naval History* (Englewood Cliffs: Prentice-Hall, Inc., 1960), p. 92.
44 Mahan was unsparing in his criticism of de Grasse for failing at the Saints and for his "unsparing and excessive" denunciations of "the conduct of his subordinates on the unlucky 12th of April." *Influence of Sea Power*, p. 449. The victor did not fare much better. In his unrelenting annihilationist stance, Mahan tempers his praise for Rodney with criticism for not aggressively chasing and destroying the entire French fleet. Ibid., pp. 440–9. A concise narrative and judicious evaluation of the battle of the Saints and the two admirals is offered by Potter and Nimitz, eds., *Sea Power*, pp. 97–104.
45 See Corbett, *Some Principles of Maritime Strategy*, passim.
46 See Paterson *et al.*, *American Foreign Relations*, pp. 52–7.

3 British military strategy

Jeremy Black[1]

The discussion of strategy in the American War of Independence faces two main conceptual problems. First, there is the question of the viability of any discussion of the concept of strategy for an age that had at best an uncertain grasp of the very idea of strategy, let alone of what the concept entailed. Second, there is the issue that strategy is usually discussed by military historians in terms of how wars are won. That, however, is to misunderstand strategy or, rather, to operationalize it in terms of military activity when, in fact, the key to strategy is the political purposes that are pursued. In short, strategy is a process of coping with problems and determining goals, and not one of meticulously examining and manipulating the details of the military plans and operations by which these goals are achieved.

British strategy in the American War of Independence has to be understood in this light because the British fought this war very differently than they did the French and Indian or Seven Years' War. In the latter case, the focus had been on conquest and not on pacification. The second goal was very much subservient to the former, although different policies were pursued for the purpose of pacification. These measures included an eighteenth-century equivalent of ethnic cleansing in the expulsion of the Acadians, as well as the very different post-conquest accommodation of the Catholics of Québec.[2]

In the American War of Independence, in contrast, pacification was the strategy, and the question was how best to secure it. The purpose of the war was clear – the return of the Americans to their loyalty – and the method chosen was different to that employed in response to the Jacobite rebellions in Scotland and northern England in 1715–16 and 1745–46, although both cases resembled the American war in that the strategic goal was pacification. In the latter cases, as later in the face of the Irish rebellion in 1798, the remedy had been more clearly military although, in making that argument, it is necessary to note post-war policies for stability through reorganization, such as the introduction of new governmental systems for the Scottish Highlands and Ireland. Obviously, there was no direct corollary with this in the war for America, but one can point to the British efforts to re-establish Royal government, particularly in the southern states, a point to which we will return.

In the case of America, there was not this sequencing by London but, instead, a willingness to consider not only pacification alongside conflict but also new systems as an aspect of this pacification. Indeed, in one sense, pacification began at the outset, with the misconceived and mishandled attempt to seize arms at Lexington and Concord in April 1775. The most prominent instances of pacification were the instructions to the Howe brothers to negotiate as well as fight and, even more clearly, the dispatch in 1778 of the Carlisle Peace Commission, with which the Congress flatly refused to treat. Moreover, the restoration of colonial government in the South was a concrete step indicating, during the war, what the British were seeking to achieve. Alongside that, and more insistently, were the practices of British commanders. Although the Americans were traitors, they were treated with great leniency and suggestions of harsher treatment were generally ignored.

This emphasis on pacification provides an essential continuity to British strategy. An attempt at evaluation faces the classic problem that history occurs forward, 1775 preceding 1776, but is analyzed from posterity with 1775 understood in light of 1776. This approach is unhelpful because the course of the war was affected by two key discontinuities that transformed the parameters. The usual one given is the internationalization of the war with France's entry in 1778, but, prior to that, the declaration of American independence in July 1776 transformed the situation. Alongside that came military unpredictabilities such as the American invasion of Canada in 1775–76, and the British failures at Saratoga in 1777 and Yorktown in 1781. These events were not secondary to the military operationalization of strategy but, instead, helped direct it. The wider political dimension was also affected by events.

This point covers a fundamental aspect of British strategy in the 1770s. Britain was acting as a satisfied power, keen obviously to retain and safeguard its position, but not interested in gaining fresh territory. Representing a satisfied power, British ministers were also wary of getting involved in European power politics. Here the American war fitted into a pattern that had begun with George III's rejection of the Prussian alliance in 1761–62 and had continued with a subsequent refusal to accept Russian requirements for an alliance, as well as with the rejection of French approaches for joint action against the First Partition of Poland of 1772.[3]

Thus, there was to be no recurrence of the situation that existed during the Seven Years' War when Britain fought in alliance with a continental power, a situation that, however unintentional, had proved particularly potent, or had been shaped thus by William Pitt the Elder with his presentation of British policy in terms of conquering Canada in Europe. There would be no alliance with Prussia (nor with anyone else) to distract France and, thus, in military terms, no commitment of the army to the Continent, as had occurred in 1758. Even more, subsidized German troops, such as those deployed in 1757 in an unsuccessful attempt to defend the Electorate of Hanover, would not be used for "German" or European power political purposes. Britain would retain some troops in Europe, Hanoverians for example being sent to serve in the Gibraltar garrison, but most were sent to America where, at peak strength, they comprised nearly 40 percent of the British army. Britain's fundamental strategy thus rested on a cohesion that had military consequences: passivity in Europe combined with the preservation of status in America.[4]

What British strategy appeared to entail in North America, however, varied greatly. The initial British impression was of opposition largely in Massachusetts, and this mistaken perception suggested that a vigorous defense of imperial interests there would save the situation. This view led to British legislation in 1774 specific to this colony, the Coercive Acts, and to a concentration of Britain's North American forces in the Bay Colony. The initial military operationalization of strategy continued after the clashes at Concord and Lexington in April 1775, both because the stress on Massachusetts appeared vindicated and because there were not enough troops for action elsewhere.[5]

This initial effort at coercion failed in Massachusetts and elsewhere. In the former, the military presence was unable to prevent rebellion or to contain it, and eventually, in March 1776, the British had to evacuate Boston when their ships in the harbor were threatened by American cannon. Elsewhere in North America, the lack of troops stemming from the concentration on Boston ensured that British authority was overthrown in the other 12 colonies while the Americans were able to mount an invasion of Canada that achieved initial success, bottling up the British in Quebec.[6]

As a result, the war entered its next stage, one expected neither by most of the Patriots nor by the British government, and that led to a major British effort to regain control that entailed both a formidable military effort and peace-making proposals. Here, again, it is necessary to look at the military options in terms of the political situation. The end of the rebellion/revolution could not be achieved by reconquering the 13 colonies (and driving the Americans from Canada). The task was too great. Instead, it was necessary to secure military results that achieved the political outcome of an end to rebellion, an outcome that was likely to require both a negotiated settlement and acquiescence in the return to loyalty and in subsequently maintaining obedience. This outcome rested on a different politics to that of the conquest of New France (Canada) during the Seven Years' War.

What was unclear was what military results would best secure this political outcome. Was the priority the defeat, indeed destruction, of the Continental Army, as it represented the Revolution, not least its unity; or was it the capture of key American centers? Each goal appeared possible, and there was a mutual dependence between them. The British would not be able to defeat the Americans unless they could land and support troops, and for this capability to be maintained it was necessary to secure port cities. Conversely, these port cities could best be held if American forces were defeated. Doing both of these required troops, both for garrisons and operations in the field. But holding the cities could give further military weight to pacification as such a strategy would produce local Loyalist forces while diminishing the number of Patriots.

The British emphasis possibly should have been destroying the Continental Army, which was definitely a prospect in 1776–77, but, instead, the concentration was on regaining key centers, not least as this was seen as a way of demonstrating the return of royal authority, partially by ensuring that large numbers of Americans again came under the Crown. Indeed, from the period when the Empire struck back in the summer of 1776, the British gained control of most of the key American points, either for much of the war (New York from 1776, Savannah from 1778, Charleston from 1780), or, as it turned out, temporarily (Newport from 1776 to 1779, Philadelphia from 1777 to 1778).[7]

The British though, instead of endeavoring to destroy American military strength, decided to seize territorial objectives; American military strength, it was hoped, would be broken along the way. They proceeded to launch a two-pronged campaign centered on gaining control of the Hudson River, one that accomplished much operationally. But the British commanders forgot the immense value of time.

The advance under Governor General Sir Guy Carleton, launched from Quebec, cleared the Americans from Canada, never to see their return, and pushed into the rivers and lakes of upper New York State. But it was ultimately disappointing. He spent a number of months building vessels to combat the flotilla of Benedict Arnold, failed to take Ticonderoga, even when pressed by his commanders to do so and, in the end, withdrew back to St. Johns. George III judged Carleton "too cold and not so active as might be wished."[8]

The Howe brothers, Admiral Sir Richard and General Sir William, mounted one of the most impressive and complex joint military operations in history against New York City and its environs. The British first landed on Staten Island on 3 July 1776, and eventually brought in over 31,000 troops on hundreds of transports, guarded by 30 frigates and ships-of-the-line, to fight the New York campaign. Naval strength gave General Howe the ability to choose where he should launch amphibious attacks. New York City was impossible to hold with the forces George Washington commanded. British naval power, and Washington's dispersion of his troops, also presented opportunities for the British that more aggressive commanders might have seized. Howe, though he insisted he would seek to destroy Washington's army, failed to do so in the campaign that followed. Howe bore the burden of knowing that defeat would be difficult to reverse and losses hard to replace, while his army had few places to which to withdraw. So, Howe fought a cautious campaign, one that failed to deliver the decisive blow against Washington that he sought.[9] It did produce some success: it returned to British hands the fine port of New York. But the arguably lackadaisical pace of subsequent British action combined with colonial resistance to ensure that the war went on.[10]

General Howe and his subordinates now had the misfortune of dealing with an insurgency, with all its accompanying messiness. They faced the classic problems; and made the classic mistakes. They lacked the men to control and secure the vast areas of New York and New Jersey they had freed from the rebels. The troops Howe did have too often misbehaved, particularly during their march across New Jersey in pursuit of Washington's army. Looting and rape were not uncommon. The German mercenaries proved particularly difficult to control. Howe spread his men in posts over much of western New Jersey and New York, but soon found it necessary to withdraw in the face of insurgent opposition in the form of regular troops and irregulars, demonstrating that he could not keep the Loyalist population safe from the rebels. Too often for the British in the course of this war, those Americans friendly to the Crown became unfriendly, while those unfriendly became more unfriendly still. Worse, the massive effort expended by the British government in support of Howe had gained Britain little beyond the important port of New York City, and two minor posts on the New Jersey shore.[11]

The limited British achievements of 1776 still left important centers, most obviously Boston, that were not under British control. This point indicated the fundamental political problem facing the British and, as is generally true in all military endeavors, whatever they achieved in the field, it would still be necessary to achieve a political settlement, at least in the form of a return to loyalty. The understanding of this issue was an achievement for the British but also posed a problem, while, correspondingly, this understanding was also both an achievement and a problem for the Patriots.

This point helps explain the attention devoted by Patriot leaders throughout the war to politics, as favorable political outcomes were needed to secure the persistence and coherence of the war effort. The British, in turn, could try, by political approaches and military efforts, to alter these political equations within the 13 colonies. Indeed, this had certainly been an element of Howes' 1776 campaign, but the colonials rejected British attempts at negotiation out of hand. Admiral Howe approached Congress, and on 11 September, the sole meeting between officially appointed representatives of the two sides before the final peace negotiations took place. The Declaration of Independence proved to be the stumbling block. Howe declared that it prevented him from negotiating and stated that he could not acknowledge Congress as it was not recognized by the King. The unyielding American delegates stressed the bedrock importance of independence.[12]

At times, the British succeeded in restoring their political authority, as evidenced in the new political prospectus offered in South Carolina following the successful siege of Charleston in 1780, after which British authority was swiftly recognized in tidewater South Carolina. On 5 June 1780, more than 200 of the prominent citizens of Charleston congratulated the British commanders on the restoration of the political connection with the Crown. A loyal address came from Georgetown, South Carolina, the following month, while several of the leading politicians of the state returned to Charleston to accept British rule. This appeared to be a vindication of the British policy of combining military force with a conciliatory policy, offering a new imperial relationship that granted most of the American demands made at the outbreak of the war. It was scarcely surprising that northern politicians, such as Ezekiel Cornell of Rhode Island, came to doubt the determination of their southern counterparts.[13]

The British, though, did not depend solely upon the political approach to resolve their American problem. Howe's initial plans for 1777, sent to the secretary of state for the colonies, Lord George Germain on 30 November 1776, envisaged an autumn attack on Philadelphia and Virginia, followed by a winter campaign in Georgia and South Carolina. The South took at best a minor role in Howe's successive plans, however, while his repeated calls for more troops ensured that there were none to spare for separate operations. Germain was left to hope that it would be possible to engage the Revolutionaries in the South by using Indians.[14]

As Howe believed that it was necessary to defeat the Revolutionaries in a decisive battle, a concentration of British strength was obviously called for. It is easy to understand why British troops were not sent to the South, and yet, in light of the damaging consequences, it is difficult not to feel that more could have been done by troops based in Florida operating alone or in conjunction with a small amphibious force. By leaving crucial decisions to his field commanders, Howe, and Major General John Burgoyne who took command of the army invading from Canada, Lord Germain ensured that the range of British operations was restricted.

Germain had instructed Howe to cooperate with Burgoyne, although he had left both generals considerable latitude in their plans. Alternatively, Germain's instructions can be presented as resulting in a total absence of a clearly defined operational objective. On 18 May 1777, Germain wrote to Howe:

> As you must from your situation and military skill be a competent judge of the propriety of every plan, His Majesty does not hesitate to approve the alterations which you propose; trusting, however, that whatever you may meditate, it will be executed in time for you to cooperate with the army ordered to proceed from Canada, and put itself under your command.[15]

By that stage, Howe's shifting plans made such cooperation implausible. The notion of Howe moving quickly suggests that Germain was out of touch and reveals that he could do little more than hope. The colonial secretary's failure to provide adequate strategic direction was already having its baleful effects.[16] Howe's initial plan, sent to Germain on 30 November 1776 (it reached London on 30 December), was compatible with a march to the Hudson by Burgoyne. He had envisaged a force of 10,000 advancing from New York to Albany, one of 5,000 to defend New York City, another of 10,000 to seize Providence and then march on Boston, one of 2,000, based in Rhode Island, to attack Connecticut, and an army of 8,000 in eastern New Jersey to threaten Philadelphia. Assuming success elsewhere, troops would be shifted to permit an autumn attack on Philadelphia and Virginia, followed by a winter campaign in the South. Howe's plan required 35,000 men, and he called for 15,000 reinforcements, which would have easily given him such a force, as he had 27,000 effectives.[17]

By 20 December 1776, however, Howe had changed his mind. In response to the apparently collapsing American position in the middle colonies, Howe believed capturing Philadelphia offered a better prospect of success than the idea of a march from Rhode Island toward Boston, a proposal that might have resulted in a disaster to match Saratoga. This new plan envisaged no such march.

Instead, 2,000 men were to stay in Rhode Island, 4,000 in New York, 3,000 on the lower Hudson "to cover Jersey on that side, as well as to facilitate in some degree the approach of the army from Canada," while Philadelphia was to be attacked with 10,000 troops.[18]

This plan was a response not only to the more specific opportunities presented by the American retreat, but also to the problem of indicating how an offensive could be conducted if no reinforcements were sent. It did not reach London until 23 February 1777. Five days later, Burgoyne, then in London, sent Germain a memorandum in which he proposed an advance from Canada to Ticonderoga and then on, either to the Hudson, or east through the Green Mountains to the Connecticut River to link up with a force from Rhode Island. In the instructions sent by Germain to Carleton on 26 March, the latter option was ignored, a result of Howe's decision not to base an offensive army on Rhode Island. Instead, an advance to Albany was stipulated, supported by a diversion from Oswego on Lake Ontario down the Mohawk. Major General William Phillips, who served under Burgoyne, was to complain in July 1777:

> I cannot help repining that our march is directed to Hudson's River, the whole country of New England northward and the Connecticut open to us – plans of war made in a Cabinet at several thousand miles distant from the scene of action are not always good.[19]

As Germain had also approved Howe's projected invasion of Pennsylvania, he was aware that Burgoyne could not receive significant support until late in his advance. The fate of delayed operations, such as Major General Sir Henry Clinton's southern expedition of 1776, might have induced caution, as might Howe's unexpected request of 20 January for 20,000 reinforcements, which could not be provided. However, the Pennsylvania plan did not appear to require a lengthy campaign, while, despite the checks inflicted by Washington's midwinter raids at Trenton and Princeton, it was believed that Howe would be able to succeed with only 5,500 fresh troops.

Nevertheless, Howe felt that he could not undertake to support the advance from Canada. On 2 April he wrote to Germain complaining about a lack of reinforcements. Three days later, Howe informed Carleton that:

> having little expectation that I shall be able, from the want of sufficient strength in this army, to detach a corps in the beginning of the campaign to act upon the Hudson's River consistent with the operations already determined upon, the force your Excellency may deem expedient to advance beyond your frontiers after taking Ticonderoga will, I fear, have little assistance from hence to facilitate their approach, and as I shall probably be in Pennsylvania when that corps is ready to advance into this province ... the officer commanding it ... must therefore pursue such measures as may from circumstances be judged most conducive to the advancement of His Majesty's service consistent with your orders.[20]

Howe promised to leave a force to clear the New York Highlands and then possibly to help the northern army, but it was clear that he did not feel bound to assist its operations. On April 20, he wrote to Germain expressing his doubts that he would be able to complete his Pennsylvania campaign in time to help Burgoyne. Howe's decision, communicated in his letter of 2 April which reached London on 8 May, to advance on Philadelphia by sea, rather than across New Jersey, ensured that this would indeed be the case.

The decisions of each of the three principals can be criticized: Lord Germain for failing to reconcile the plans of the two generals; Howe for neglecting the problems of the northern army; Burgoyne for failing to appreciate the strength of the opposition. Major General Clinton argued in July that Howe should cooperate with the operations of Burgoyne's army and move north. But even had Burgoyne fought his way through to Albany, the value of such an advance could be queried. Alexander Hamilton, one of Washington's aides, argued on 5 April 1777:

> as to the notion of forming a junction with the northern army, and cutting off the communication between the Northern and Southern states, I apprehend it will do better in speculation than in practice ... [it] would require a chain of posts and such a number of men at each as would never be practicable or maintainable but to an immense army.[21]

Such criticisms are justified, but it would have been inappropriate for Germain to formulate too rigid a plan, while, however much the operations of two independent armies might assist each other, their fate ultimately depended on their separate campaigns. Advances south from Ticonderoga and north through the Highlands would not have been easy under more favorable circumstances. Howe could defend both his decision to invade Pennsylvania and his chosen approach, via the Chesapeake, instead of the Delaware, or across New Jersey. His goals were unsettled: a decisive battle but also maneuvers to seize major centers, yet he obtained both Philadelphia and two major battles – Brandywine and Germantown.[22] Had Germain wanted to secure Howe's assistance for Burgoyne, he should have sent clearer and firmer orders earlier. Even this, however, would not necessarily have prevented Burgoyne from a Saratoga-type fate; although, had Burgoyne been certain of a major advance coming from New York, he might both have not felt it necessary to send a detachment to Bennington and have held on for a few more days at Saratoga.

Such a discussion is dangerously abstract, not least because it neglects the imponderables of American moves, although these were largely reactive. Any campaign conducted under such circumstances by two independently operating forces faced difficulties, and scholars can be remorseless in their judgments. Had both British armies operated on the axis of the Hudson, then Germain and Howe might have been criticized for neglecting the opportunity to seize Philadelphia, while a successful march south by Burgoyne might have left British positions behind him vulnerable to attack. To have been successful, Burgoyne would have had to defeat Gates decisively. Flexibility in conception when planning a campaign from across the Atlantic seems desirable, and it is possibly more appropriate to criticize the individual commanders, while accepting that had they succeeded – Howe in winning his decisive battle, Burgoyne in reaching Albany – judgments might have been very different.

On the other hand, it could be argued that there was not a British campaign of 1777; rather, there were two totally uncoordinated campaigns. Operating in conjunction with each other, Howe and Burgoyne might have been able to wreck the two American armies, to gain total control of the Hudson River valley, to separate New England from the middle and southern states and to initiate a state-by-state pacification of New England, while the coast was controlled by the Royal Navy.

Operating, however, as two roving columns, and commanded by two lackluster generals, with no overall unity of command and no clearly defined master strategy or guidance from Germain in London, the two armies could not have achieved the potential successes outlined, even had the American forces been defeated. Well-planned and well-coordinated operations do fail, often due to laggardly behavior, but the absence of unity in command was certainly felt in the British planning and execution. Howe and Burgoyne acted with a complete lack of coordination; but, in addition, the situation challenged Eurocentric military thinking, founded as it was on a well-known topography with roads, strategic rivers and towns. In part, this was irrelevant in colonial North America, as was the concept of operating on interior lines. The latter notion was of limited value in America, where in large part the conflict was a war without fronts. New World geography, recruitment and logistics all created a hybrid Euro-American style of war, similar on the surface to European warfare, yet at the same time very different.

The result, though, is what concerns us most. The colonial reaction, and British failures, colluded to produce catastrophic failure. Burgoyne's surrender at Saratoga in October 1777 had the effect of bringing to the forefront something the Crown had thus far banished: additional warfare against one or more Continental European powers. Thus the political element returns in force, reminding us that to treat this conflict, on either side, simply as a military struggle is to underplay the key role of political goals. Indeed, these goals affected not only the moves of armies (a conventional but overly-limited understanding of strategy), but even the nature of the forces deployed by both sides. The British use of German "mercenaries" and, even more, Native Americans and African Americans, provided opportunities for reactive political mobilization on the part of the Patriots, while the American reliance on France correspondingly increased domestic support for war in Britain and diminished sympathy for the Patriots, who could now be presented as hypocrites, willing to ally with a Catholic autocracy that was Britain's historic national enemy, and to side with another Catholic power when Spain joined France in 1779.

These alliances brought the war to a new stage, as there was no inherent clarity about the allocation of British resources between the war with the Bourbons and that with the Americans. Whereas it was relatively easy for the Patriots to abandon the broader American plan of conquering Canada after failure in 1775–76, there was no such agreement over policy in Britain. Partisan politics came into play, not least the politics of justification, with the opposition politicians pressing for a sharp focus on the Bourbons, and the ministry of Lord North unwilling to refocus entirely, partly because it neither wished nor thought it appropriate to abandon hopes of holding onto the American possessions.[23]

Thus, the southern strategy, both military and political, arose after 1778 in large part from the impact of French entry. This entry ended the unusual situation in which Britain was at war solely in North America and therefore able to concentrate attention and resources on it, however ineffectually. Moreover, Britain was essentially pushed into a bifurcated conflict with a struggle for pacification continuing in the 13 colonies (albeit being complicated by the French presence there), while a straightforward military–naval contest began elsewhere. Again, this apparently clear distinction can be qualified by noting that Britain had political options to consider.

The general impression is of progressive moves toward such a bifurcated war, but in practice the political dimension again came first; and was made more complex by the need to consider the goals and moves of various powers, including unpredictable responses to the actions of others. Thus, aside from Britain's relations with the states with which it eventually came to blows, there were also relations with neutral powers, both friendly and unfriendly, to consider. These were linked to the military operationalization of strategy, not least with the possibility that alliances in Europe would yield troops for North America. Furthermore, the European crisis of 1778, which led to the War of the Bavarian Succession of 1778–79 between Prussia and France's ally Austria, created opportunities for Britain and indeed was seen in this light. There has since also been scholarly discussion on the lines that a more interventionist European policy would have distracted France from taking part in the American war with key consequences for British options there.[24]

For a time, those interested in the Americas won the argument. Here, again, politics, or more accurately political interests, played a role. Specifically, South Carolina exiles and their political sympathizers pushed the view that the southern colonies possessed deep wells of political sympathy to the Crown. The suppressed Loyalists only awaited the arrival of the King's troops, whereupon they would rise up and destroy the rebels. Those lobbying for this idea certainly had a point; the South held a great many inhabitants loyal to Great Britain, but their view was in some respects a product of wishful thinking as well, and leads one to draw a comparison between British confidence in deep wells of Loyalist support and the pursuit by many in the administration of Abraham Lincoln at the start of the U.S. Civil War of similar pools of Unionist support in the rebel Confederacy. In the end, the buyers of both proved remorseful.[25]

But the decision to launch this war in the South was made, and the army went. They produced stunning successes: Savannah (1779), Charleston (1780), the Waxhaws (1780) and Camden (1780), breaking formal colonial military power in the region. The political arm of London also intervened here, this time in the form of proclamations that alienated elements of the population. This exacerbated the problem of pacification, one that the British came closer to overcoming than many would like to admit. But, unfortunately for them, in the South the British repeated some of their errors of New Jersey, thereby antagonizing the local population, many of whom supported the Crown. British misconception, combined with poor execution, provided opportunities here upon which the colonials capitalized.[26]

The debate over just where the British should focus their efforts was ultimately settled by the political consequences of General Charles Cornwallis' surrender of his army at Yorktown, Virginia, on 19 October 1781. This capitulation caused Lord North's ministry to fall the following March. It was not succeeded by a similar one, but by one of the opposition under the Marquess of Rockingham, who immediately opened peace negotiations with the American commissioners in London.[27]

As a result, 1782 was a key year of the war. It was a year in which the Patriots had singularly little success, Washington, in particular, getting nowhere with his plan to capture New York. Moreover, this failure was more generally significant as it marked the decline in the Franco-American alliance, a decline caused by both the problems of pursuing very different military priorities and, far more significantly, a war-weariness on the part of the French government that reflected the exhausting demands of wartime European power politics. Moreover, in April 1782 the French fleet in the West Indies was defeated by Admiral Sir George Rodney at the battle of the Saints.[28]

Thus, militarily, the war was going Britain's way. New warships were being launched, public finances were robust, fears of rebellion in Ireland and of disaffection in Britain were largely assuaged, the Bourbons were increasingly unable to attempt another invasion of Britain, Gibraltar had been held, and the British position in both India and Canada was more resilient than had been feared. Yet the politics was now of peace and settlement that were not focused on a return of America to its loyalty. Instead, the priority was the disruption, if not destruction, of the coalition of powers fighting Britain and, hopefully, better relations with an independent United States of America (as it later became). Paradoxically, this strategy was to be successful, which simply underlines the conceptual problems of conceiving of strategy in terms of its military operationalization.[29]

Conclusion and counterfactual considerations

In the American War of Independence, Britain possessed no inherent weakness that made its failure inevitable. Chance and luck, as Clausewitz famously said, often take their part in war, as do the foibles of human nature. Time is also key. Even though the British possessed a strong strategic position in 1782, their best since the French entry in 1778, time, by this point, was no longer on their side. Their options were exhausted.

From the perspective of another time, that of the early twenty-first century, one is driven to ask: had there ever been an alternative to the strategy the British pursued in the war that would revolutionize the future international balance of power? The thesis that post-1763 Britain should have supported Russian demands on Turkey, with which Russia was at war from 1768 to 1774, or, subsequently, Poland, which Russia helped despoil in the partition of 1772, discounts the problems that would have been created by such an alliance. This thesis also exaggerates what the British state could afford to do, and at a time when it was struggling with the burden of unprecedented debt while facing serious political problems in Britain and North America over attempts to raise taxation.

Second, even had Britain allied with Austria, Prussia or Russia after 1763, there is little reason to believe that it would have enjoyed much influence with its ally or allies, or even been consulted by them. This conclusion was suggested by Britain's experience with Austria in 1731–33 and 1748–55, and with Prussia in 1756–63. Moreover, as the three major eastern European powers were at, or close to, war in 1768–74, 1778–89 and 1782–83, the caution of the British ministers was vindicated. Not only were these conflicts in which Britain had only limited interest, but it was also unlikely that these powers would have been able or willing to provide appropriate support to Britain in her confrontations with the Bourbons. Even had they done so, more auxiliaries backing Britain in North America in 1775–83 would have made no more difference than would have a greater number of French troops supporting Emperor Maximilian in Mexico in the 1860s. In each case, there was a powerful domestic opposition in North America able to sustain resistance.

What about the "What if?" of Austrian or Prussian pressure on France, and the possibility of this pressure deterring the latter from helping the Americans from 1778, and thus justifying interventionist British diplomacy? It is pertinent to ask whether such an alliance would not have led, instead, to a highly damaging British commitment to one side or the other in the Austro-Prussian War of the Bavarian Succession (1778–79). The Seven Years' War, in which Britain had allied with Prussia, was scarcely encouraging in this respect. In that earlier war, it initially was far from clear that Britain's involvement in the conflict on the Continent would work out as favorably as it did. In addition, had Britain allied with Austria or Prussia in the War of the Bavarian Succession, then Hanover would presumably have been exposed to attack by its opponent. Hanover was vulnerable, as was repeatedly demonstrated, and had it been overrun, as had happened at the hands of the French in 1757, then its recovery might have jeopardized the military, diplomatic and political options of the British government. In addition, the War of the Bavarian Succession was restricted to two campaigning seasons, but could have been longer, like the Seven Years' War, or speedily resumed, as with the two Austro-Prussian conflicts of the 1740s. Either eventuality would have posed problems for Britain.

Moreover, as another critique of the interventionist counterfactual, and, in this case, specifically the argument that it could have deterred French action and thus ensured British victory, the British had, prior to French entry into the war, already failed to translate victories in North America into an acceptable political verdict. Thus, the "What if no French entry into the war?" is of less moment than might be suggested by a focus on the major French role in the Franco-American defeat of the British at Yorktown in 1781. This point underlines the need to locate speculation about diplomatic options in a context of strategic possibilities.

Goals also need to be borne in mind: it is always a problem if counterfactuals are not adequately grounded in an understanding of contemporary objectives. Britain was a "satisfied" power after 1763, and, as a consequence, it was difficult, if not dangerous, to try to strengthen the status quo by alliances with powers that wished to overturn it. There was also no significant domestic constituency for interventionist diplomacy, and notably none for any particular interventionist course of action. Aside from the practicalities of British power, and the nature of British politics, the Western Question, the fate of western Europe, more particularly the Low Countries, the Rhineland and Italy, had been settled diplomatically in the 1750s by the Austrian alliances with Spain and then France, removing both need and opportunity for British intervention. This shift in power politics was crucial, for the public support for interventionism on the Continent was fragile, if not weak, unless the Bourbons (the rulers of France and Spain) were the target. Indeed, the domestic coalition of interests and ideas upon which public backing for foreign policy rested was heavily reliant on the consistency offered by the resonance of the anti-Bourbon beat. Thus, British military strategy in the American War of Independence cannot be separated from wider currents of political preference and engagement, and they suggest that counterfactuals lose their initial allure upon closer examination.

To Britain, and indeed to all of the powers involved, politics, internal and external, helped to determine the nature of the war. It drove the respective decisions of the various powers to become involved, and exercised an overweening influence on the execution of their respective strategies. The British possessed a clear political goal in regard to the American colonies, but this ultimately meant little because they failed to develop and implement a strategy that allowed them to achieve this political objective.

Notes

1 I am most grateful to Donald Stoker for his helpful comments on an earlier draft.
2 See Fred Anderson, *Crucible of War: The Seven Years' War and the Fate of Empire in British North America, 1754–1766* (New York: Knopf, 2000).
3 Jeremy Black, *A System of Ambition? British Foreign Policy, 1660–1793*, 2nd edn. (Phoenix Mill, Thrupp, Stroud, Gloucestershire: Sutton, 2000), especially pp. 40–5, 234–45.
4 On troops and their dispositions, see Jeremy Black, *War for America: The Fight for Independence* (Phoenix Mill, Thrupp, Stroud, Gloucestershire: Wrens Park, 1991), pp. 27–31.
5 Robert Middlekauff, *The Glorious Cause: The American Revolution, 1763–1789* (Oxford: Oxford University Press, 2005), pp. 269–70; Piers Mackesy, *The War for America, 1775–1783* (Lincoln and London: University of Nebraska Press, 1992), p. 2.
6 John Ferling, *Almost a Miracle: The American Victory in the War of Independence* (Oxford: Oxford University Press, 2007), pp. 80–99, 106.

7 Many British officers certainly wanted to destroy the Continental Army. See Stephen Conway, *The War for American Independence, 1775–1783* (London: Edward Arnold, 1995), pp. 34–5, and Eric Robson, *The American Revolution in its Political and Military Aspects, 1763–1783* (New York: W.W. Norton, 1966), p. 98.
8 Mackesy, *War for America*, pp. 94–6; J.W. Fortescue, ed., *Correspondence of King George the Third: From 1760 to December 1783*, 6 vols. (London: Macmillan & Co., 1927–28), 3:406.
9 Russell Weigley, *The American Way of War: A History of United States Military Strategy and Policy* (Bloomington: Indiana University Press, 1973), p. 3; Ira Gruber, "America's First Battle: Long Island, August 27, 1776," in Charles Heller and William A. Stofft, eds., *America's First Battles* (Lawrence: University of Kansas Press, 1986), pp. 1–32.
10 Ira D. Gruber, *The Howe Brothers & the American Revolution* (Chapel Hill: University of North Carolina Press, 1972), pp. 89–134.
11 David Hackett Fischer, *Washington's Crossing* (Oxford: Oxford University Press, 2004), pp. 160–81, 346–62; Mark V. Kwasny, *Washington's Partisan War, 1775–1783* (Kent and London: Kent State University Press, 1996), pp. 108–9, 112–17.
12 W. Cobbett, ed., *Parliamentary History of England: 1066–1803*, 36 vols. (London: T.C. Hansard, 1806–20), 20:68.
13 J.J. Nadelhaft, *The Disorders of War: The Revolution in South Carolina* (Orono: University of Maine at Orono Press, 1981), pp. 53–4; Charles Derek Ross, ed., *Correspondence of Charles, first Marquis Cornwallis*, 3 vols. (London: J. Murray, 1859), 1:45; Conway, *The War for American Independence*, pp. 216–17, 219–20; Black, *War for America*, p. 189.
14 Germain to John Stuart, 2 Apr. 1777, Public Record Office (hereafter PRO) 30/8/5.
15 PRO, 20/8/5.
16 W.B. Willcox, "Too Many Cooks: British Planning Before Saratoga," *Journal of British Studies* (1962), pp. 56–90.
17 Historical Manuscripts Commission (hereafter HMC) *Stopford-Sackville* 2:49–50.
18 Ibid., 52–3.
19 Ibid., 60–3; Nottingham University Library, Newcastle, Clumber Papers (hereafter NeC) 2, 810.
20 Quoted in G.S. Brown, *The American Secretary: The Colonial Policy of Lord George Germain, 1775–1778* (Ann Arbor: University of Michigan Press, 1963), p. 109.
21 NeC 2369, 2346; Harold C. Syrett and J.E. Cooke, eds., *The Papers of Alexander Hamilton* (New York: Columbia University Press, 1961–87), 1:220.
22 Ira D. Gruber, "British Strategy: The Theory and Practice of Eighteenth-Century Warfare," in Don Higginbotham, ed., *Reconsiderations on the Revolutionary War* (Westport: Greenwood Press, 1978), p. 26.
23 Middlekauff, *The Glorious Cause*, pp. 412–17.
24 Piers Mackesy, "British Strategy in the War of American Independence," *Yale Review* (June 1963): 556; Conway, *The War of American Independence*, pp. 220–2.
25 Paul H. Smith, *Loyalists and Redcoats: A Study in British Revolutionary Policy* (Chapel Hill: University of North Carolina Press, 1964), pp. 77, 82–99; E.D. Townsend, *Anecdotes of the Civil War in the United States* (New York: D. Appleton and Company, 1884), pp. 55–6.
26 William B. Willcox, "Sir Henry Clinton: Paralysis of Command," in George A. Billias, ed., *George Washington's Generals and Opponents: Their Exploits and Leadership*, 2 vols. (New York: Da Capo, 1994), 2:84–7; John Shy, *A People Numerous and Armed* (Ann Arbor: University of Michigan Press, 1990), pp. 198–212; Weigley, *The American Way of War*, pp. 24–39; William B. Willcox, ed., *The American Rebellion: Sir Henry Clinton's Narrative of His Campaigns, 1775–1782* (New Haven: Yale University Press, 1954), pp. 181–2.

27 John Selby, *The Road to Yorktown* (New York: St. Martin's Press, 1976), pp. 179–83; Mackesy, *War for America*, pp. 466–71.
28 Joseph J. Ellis, *His Excellency: George Washington* (New York: Vantage, 2004), p. 137; Samuel Eliot Morison, *The Oxford History of the American People*, vol. 1, *Prehistory to 1789* (New York: Meridian, 1994), pp. 348–51.
29 On the peace, see Richard B. Morris, *The Peacemakers: The Great Powers & American Independence* (New York: Harper and Row, 1965).

4   British naval strategy
War on a global scale

John Reeve[1]

It was naval strategy that made the American War of Independence a global conflict. This so-called "American" war involved the naval forces of Britain, the United States, France, Spain, the Dutch Republic and (indirectly, as the leader of the League of Armed Neutrality) Russia. Warfare at sea was also the connecting link that made the conflict which began with an American rebellion one further round in the Anglo-French struggle which largely defined the "long eighteenth century" from 1689–1815. A better name for the American war would be the Atlantic War of 1775. From the beginning, the principal participants saw it as a global struggle. British concern with the revolt of the colonies, as well as French designs against British power, both derived from contemporary perceptions of North America, including its maritime resources, as the keystone of the British Empire.

The West Indies were, by extension, part of this structure of transatlantic power, which stretched all the way from Canada down to the eastern Caribbean.[2] The key British possessions here were Jamaica and in the Windward and Leeward Islands – the latter groups forming an arc between Puerto Rico and South America. These colonies, as well as being proximate, were economically integral to British North America, depending upon it for the key commodities of timber and food. They were, simultaneously, jewels in the imperial crown, whose exports – notably sugar – made up approximately one-quarter of the value of British imports by the 1770s. The West Indian planters were not, therefore, without political influence in London. The French West Indian colonies were of comparable value and Spain, with its central American empire, had natural interests in the region. The West Indies remained, therefore, a diplomatically and strategically sensitive area and an important theater of military operations, particularly after France and Spain entered the war.

The wider strategic framework of the war was evident even before France became an open participant. By 1778, European waters had become a theater of operations for American privateers, France had initiated covert aid to the rebels via the West Indies, and Britain was attempting to interdict the flow of munitions while not provoking open war with the French. The conflict evolved, and naval strategy was formulated, within a framework of interconnected theaters of operations – all essentially maritime – in Europe, North America, the West Indies and the Indian Ocean.

Our view of the war (and of British naval strategy within it) has been distorted not merely by its retrospective significance for the British and American national stories, but also by the relative invisibility of naval power. As a result, the war has been seen not only as an American parochial episode, but also as a British naval as well as military defeat. The strategic record of the British Royal Navy between 1775 and 1783, however, was one of improvement facilitated by progressive enhancement of its order of battle. This culminated in a major victory in the West Indies, the battle of the Saints in 1782, and in renewed British diplomatic prestige based upon naval power. A further factor contributing to this general historical distortion may be the culture of the Royal Navy, which has never partaken of the British tradition of dealing with defeat by romanticizing it. The Royal Navy is interested in victory, and has never seen the war of 1775–83 as a whole as one of its finest hours.

This war, however, is a remarkable – if complex – case study in naval strategy. It exhibits a host of strategic factors that characterize war at sea. It was, first of all, global, and indicative of the way naval planners draw comprehensive strategic maps. It was also, second, a diplomatic exercise, as naval strategy almost invariably is, and intimately bound up with the British imperial policy and great power politics of the period. Third, the war is a study in sea power as strategy. No conflict has ever made clearer the inherently strategic significance of major warships, nor have outcomes ever been more dependent upon the disposition and use of such ships, both in victory and defeat.

Above all, however, the conflict illustrates the key concepts outlined by Sir Julian Corbett, that great thinker on warfare at sea, a century ago.[3] This war was maritime, rather than strictly naval, in two senses. Its outcome was very much conditioned by the availability of shipping for military transport, as well as by the flow of seaborne trade. Virtually all theaters of the war, moreover, lent themselves to joint maritime campaigns, not just at the operational but at the strategic level. In a sense, the war can be read as a series of episodes in amphibious power projection, some successful, such as the British attack on New York in 1776, some not, such as the Franco-Spanish plan for an invasion of Britain in 1779. In short, the war can be defined as one fought within a maritime strategic environment. The war demonstrates two other cardinal principles of Corbett's theory. As a maritime strategic struggle it revolved, typically, around sea lines of communication, particularly those across the Atlantic. The outcomes of its campaigns were also critically dependent upon local command of the sea – upon one side's ability to use the sea and deny it to the other at particular times and places. The most dramatic example was the inability of the Royal Navy to relieve General Cornwallis at Yorktown in 1781.

Naval strategy in three dimensions

Strategy is about choices conditioned by contexts. It represents the complex interplay of human considerations and decisions with wider circumstantial forces and situations. This interplay is affected in turn by what Carl von Clausewitz conceived of as friction: the fact that in war even the simplest things are difficult to achieve.[4] Just as there was nothing inevitably determined about the naval strategic history of the American War of Independence, nothing escaped the contingent influences of human action or of chaos. We can see these three dimensions reflected in the naval strategic development of the war.

The strategic context

The strategic context of the naval war did not favor Britain. This disadvantage formed a striking contrast with the British experience in the Seven Years' War. In the preceding conflict, William Pitt the Elder's well-coordinated and offensive grand strategy was facilitated by a continental ally, Prussia, and by a major naval victory relatively early in the war, Quiberon Bay in 1759, which effectively gave the Royal Navy command of the sea. The outcome was a victorious treaty in 1763 which saw Britain's arrival as a great overseas territorial power.[5] Such was the extent of the naval victory that the Duke of Bedford, who negotiated the peace, had predicted the creation of a European maritime alliance against Britain.[6] In the ensuing war, this proved to be the case.

The novelty of the war was an enormous strategic challenge for Britain's navy. It was an exception to the general eighteenth-century British pattern of success in global conflict, which combined alliances and naval supremacy to limit or defeat French international ambitions and enhance British power and influence.[7] Britain in this war, by contrast, became the target of a French-led coalition which forced it to defend its global position. Specifically, the American rebellion involved Britain in a trans-oceanic continental war involving formidable logistical difficulties, against a powerful maritime coalition, and without a European continental ally to divide the attention of France. This time it was the French who could challenge British use of the sea while providing financial subsidies and limited land forces to support their continental allies: the traditional British strategy. Contemporaries such as the Earl of Sandwich, Britain's naval minister as First Lord of the Admiralty, understood this reversal of the strategic game. The situation was compounded by late British naval mobilization, despite the urgings of Sandwich himself.[8] The result was that, unusual for the eighteenth century, Britain failed to achieve domination of European waters.[9] This had extensive implications both for the security of the British Isles and for British interests overseas. The central strategic fact of the war was that, with France and Spain united against it, Britain faced a contest for command of the sea. This isolation was further complicated by Dutch involvement, particularly in Europe and in the Indian Ocean.

From the beginning of the American war, the government of Lord North had sought a quick and decisive victory against the rebels. This strategy was linked to budgetary restraints, a function of parliamentary politics and deficient naval preparations. Part of the reason for the latter was diplomacy, and the prevailing view in the Cabinet against provoking France.[10] As a result, there were insufficient small warships, such as frigates and sloops in the American theater, to support military operations, blockade rebel ports and cut off the flow of munitions from Europe.[11] While France had been seriously building up its fleet since 1776, Britain did not start to order up more ships-of-the-line, the major fleet units of navies in the age of sail, until 1777–78.[12] Consequently, by 1780, France and Spain had a combined shipping tonnage approximately 25 percent greater than that of the Royal Navy.[13] Between 1780 and 1782, before Britain's own naval build-up began to bear fruit, there were insufficient British warships of all classes to meet all worldwide strategic commitments, and hence uncomfortable choices to make about global naval deployments. The balance of naval forces in any given theater had implications for that in others. The outcome was the dispersal of forces and a service very seriously overstretched, with no margin for error. The Royal Navy's inability to dominate the Western Approaches to the English Channel, the linchpin of British naval strategy, implied the threats of invasion and of enemy attacks on British trade convoys. As a maritime-commercial power, Britain's official financial structure and war-making capability derived from its ability to trade. Inadequate numbers of warships to blockade French ports or win a fleet action meant, moreover, that overseas theaters of operations could not be quarantined from enemy naval activity.[14] The navy therefore adopted a strategy, uniquely for it in the eighteenth century, of sending detachments overseas in pursuit of enemy forces to try to retain local superiority. This surrendered initiative to the French until the strategy was changed in 1781–82, when an adequate balance of forces in the West Indies enabled Admiral Sir George Rodney to win at the Saints.[15]

As Nicholas Rodger has observed, Britain was generally without the naval strategic initiative for most of the war due to lack of resources. The exceptions were in 1778, after French but before Spanish entry, and in 1782 when the navy finally had the forces to deal with the two Bourbon powers.[16] Without sufficient control of its primary strategic environment – the sea – a maritime power is defeated. It would be easy, therefore, to adopt a deterministic approach, and to argue that the context of the global war made it impossible for Britain to win. Certainly, a disadvantageous strategic framework stacked the odds against the Royal Navy. This was especially true in an age when many encounters between hostile naval forces occurred by chance.[17] But strategic views were adopted and decisions made within the British government which profoundly affected the result of the war.

In the late eighteenth century, British policy was essentially made by the King and Cabinet. King George III was definitely involved in the development of naval strategy. On a general level he had an affinity with the navy, its officers and officials. He also influenced particular strategic decisions, supporting Sandwich, for example, in 1778 in having the decision to deploy ships to America reversed until the destination of Admiral Charles le Comte d'Estaing's Toulon squadron was known.[18] Lord North, the prime minister, and Sandwich were together the central axis of British policy-making during the war.[19] All specific decisions on naval strategy (even about individual ship dispositions) were, however, made by the Cabinet.[20] Within this executive body there were personal and policy tensions, principally between Sandwich and Lord George Germain, secretary of state for the colonies. Sandwich took a global view, arguably underestimating the American rebels as a military force, and sought to concentrate the fleet in European waters. Germain lacked wider concerns and focused on North America with a kind of tunnel vision. Since Germain was an unconstructive bureaucrat, and Sandwich lacked the money and connections needed for real political power, a coordinating authority was necessary, but unforthcoming.[21] North was incapable of assuming overall direction. The result was a lack of clear and decisive strategic policy, competing departmental agendas and oscillating geographical emphases.[22] This was the political manifestation of an overstretched naval power.

Lack of clear direction meant that strategy was formulated in response to events.[23] Between 1775 and 1777, the focus was on the American war, in which the role of the navy was essentially to support the army. Sandwich wanted to concentrate on the potential Franco-Spanish threat, but he had an uphill battle with the Cabinet divided over naval mobilization. He got his way after 1777, once French entry became increasingly likely. Even as the battle fleet was enhanced, however, naval forces were dispersed.[24] Unusually, the Royal Navy won no victory in a fleet action in European waters during the war. Whether one sees this as cause or consequence of strategic difficulty depends on whether one considers the strategy of dispersal or of concentration to be at fault. Sandwich, believing in concentration, wanted most of the ships and the best commanders in home waters or in the West Indies, wishing to reinforce the latter from North America, not Europe.[25] While it is appealing to gravitate toward the counterfactual explanation, and argue that his approach was not properly followed, there is a view which holds that his strategy was not actually defensive enough. Sandwich, according to his biographer, was not sufficiently forceful or articulate in making the case for the role of the Western squadron, in the Western Approaches, as the force most likely to encounter French squadrons and defeat them in detail.[26] As it was, Sandwich had a continual problem in trying to claw back forces from overseas stations and missions, the King himself advocating the high-risk forward strategy of distant imperial defense.

Naval operations and friction

The strategic and operational–tactical levels of naval warfare are intimately connected. This has been so since at least the time of the coming of the modern warship, which is essentially a strike platform with trans-oceanic reach, about the year 1500. Operational issues thus have a great propensity to impact upon strategic situations. The Royal Navy had a remarkable record of victory at the end of the Seven Years' War, and had made considerable professional and technological progress by the 1780s. Its operational effectiveness continued to be limited, however, by the technical, climatic and human factors of the day.

British amphibious operations were aided by a high degree of inter-service cooperation (famously at Quebec in 1759), as well as by increasingly reliable chart-making.[27] It is not, therefore, surprising that there were British amphibious successes during the American war at New York (1776), Philadelphia (1777), Savannah (1778) and Charleston (1780).[28] British convoy protection also improved during the war, aided by Sandwich's policy of having the Channel Fleet cruise late into the summer, which facilitated the safe arrival of convoys from the East and West Indies.[29] Technological developments also enhanced the operational and tactical efficiency of the navy. By 1781, copper sheathing of British warships' bottoms as protection against shipworm and marine growth brought greatly increased speed and an operational fleet approximately one-third larger because there was less need for docking and overhaul.[30] The introduction of the carronade or "smasher," a powerful close-range gun, after 1779 had a psychological as well as tactical effect on the enemy.[31] The progressive introduction of a new firing mechanism, gunlocks, increased the accuracy and rate of British fire at sea. Most importantly, the Royal Navy had an established and ongoing culture of aggression toward the enemy, giving it an invaluable psychological edge over its opponents.[32]

While the sailing warship had an operational independence unmatched until the coming of nuclear propulsion, it was limited in its ability to move and fight by environmental conditions. Bad weather or contrary winds could delay scheduled sailings and prevent engagements. Whole regional weather patterns such as the Caribbean hurricane season, from August to October, or the Indian monsoon, from October to the spring, annually inhibited operations. The mobility of the ship-of-the-line was also predicated upon certain logistical and infrastructural requirements. Shipbuilding materials were basic and the supply of naval stores had to be secured and denied to the enemy. The American rebellion meant that New England timber was no longer available for British masts, and the supply had to be made up from Russia. Britain had the problem of cutting off the flow of Baltic naval stores to France and Spain. Ships-of-the-line had to be refitted, either at home or overseas, after operational service. The only adequate overseas dockyards available to the Royal Navy were at Bombay (Mumbai), India. There were none on the American stations at Newfoundland, North America, Jamaica or the Leeward Islands. With the service overstretched, refitting at home was frequently not an option and ships fell into disrepair.[33] Actual operations could place great strain upon ships and men, which influenced strategic deployments. Blockade of the French Atlantic coast, to cover the fleet at Brest, was a British strategic axiom. Given the difficulties of the close inshore work, "loose blockade" in the Bay of Biscay could be more feasible, with frigates watching closer inshore. The risk was that a French squadron could get away.[34]

Intelligence, always significant in naval warfare, was critical for the British in a conflict in which they were short of capital ships. The unknown destination of the Toulon squadron in 1778 had the whole British political–military command structure on tenterhooks. Britain had excellent intelligence from agents ashore about enemy departures from Europe, but could not intercept opponents or bring them to battle without knowing courses and destinations. Frigates were frequently unavailable or unable to follow and observe. Even with good intelligence, operational responses could be hampered by administrative delays in readying and fitting out ships. They were also subject to poor communications. On average it took nine weeks for a dispatch to reach New York from London.[35] There could thus be no effective central direction of the global war, plans were usually overtaken by events, and even in home waters local commanders needed wide discretionary authority.[36] Local commanders were in turn prisoners of their personal operational picture. They could also be selfish with resources, jealous of their autonomy and querulous.[37] Lack of local flexibility was actually encouraged by the system of fixed overseas stations.[38]

The navy's officer corps could be an unedifying spectacle during the American war, probably as a consequence of professional frustration. Following the indecisive action off Ushant in 1778 – a telling failure to score an early victory over the French – a dispute between the British commander, Admiral Augustus Keppel, and his subordinate, Vice Admiral Sir Hugh Palliser, scandalized the nation and split the navy, especially the Channel Fleet.[39] It is difficult to measure the operational impact of such episodes, but they did not enhance effectiveness. Great and innovative admirals such as George Rodney and Richard Howe served during the war, but the Royal Navy was not yet the force it was to become within 25 years, one with "the habit of victory" and one of the elite military forces of history. In the 1770s and early 1780s, this still lay in the future.

Ways of naval warfare

The naval strategic approaches of all three of the major maritime powers were, paradoxically, ill-suited to the conflict in which they found themselves during the late 1770s. Each discovered that the unfamiliar circumstances posed difficulties, sometimes grave ones. Arguably it was the British who ultimately dealt with this best.

The traditional British maritime or "blue-water" strategy, later articulated by Corbett and propagated by Sir Basil Liddell Hart, was well-suited to imperial aggrandizement. Predicated upon the relative weakness of the eighteenth-century French financial system, it was an attritional strategy, involving a defensive stance in Europe and an offensive one overseas. Tangible British European interests included the security of the Netherlands, Portugal, Hanover and Gibraltar, and access to the Baltic and, to a lesser extent, the Mediterranean.[40] A British strategic philosophy of continental intervention, with deep roots in English history, certainly as far back as the sixteenth century, was expounded during the mid-eighteenth century by those such as Thomas Pelham, first Duke of Newcastle. Its critics were William Pitt the Elder and the "maritime" school. Pitt's raids on the French coast during the Seven Years' War, intended to divert French forces away from the Prussians, had their diplomatic and strategic utility.[41] But given that British interests were inextricably bound up with Europe and its balance of power, a purely maritime approach was not feasible.[42] Both the maritime and continental schools were largely a function of eighteenth-century

British political discourse, and as such tended to be caricatures. In reality, as Paul Kennedy has argued, the two approaches had an organic and long-established inter-dependence.[43] The fundamental problem of the American war for British strategy was that it was *neither* traditionally maritime (there now was a continental war *overseas*, in America), *nor* traditionally continental (there was an absence of allies and of a theater of land operations in Europe).[44]

This hybrid character of the conflict has resulted in one of strategic history's notable legends: that Britain lost the war for America because it lacked a European ally to help dissipate French resources in land warfare at home. This view has had a long life and has not lacked learned advocates.[45] It is not, moreover, without historical foundation. In the early 1760s, the French naval budget was halved to support the war in Germany.[46] Conversely, during the American war, the lack of such a land war was a factor contributing to the increased French effort at sea, which stretched the British naval budget by 50 percent over that for the previous war.[47] One could make a case that an operational consequence was the British strategic defeat at the Chesapeake in October 1781. There is, however, a new scholarly consensus on this complex issue, which locates it within a broader context. The movement has been away from the monocausal emphasis traditionally placed upon the missing continental ally.[48] For one thing, it can be argued that Britain had effectively failed to defeat the American rebellion even before France entered the war.[49] Further, there are a number of variables that cast doubt on the overriding influence of a continental alliance as a factor in British success. These include the relative advantages for Britain and France of a European continental war, the long-term developmental and infrastructural needs of sea power as well as the skilled personnel and stores required, and the viability of government credit structures. One historian has therefore concluded that the relative weakness of France at sea was unconnected to the role of the French army on land.[50]

It is, rather, the whole strategic framework of the American and global war which helps to explain the immense strain it placed upon British war-making capacity. Alongside the enormous expenditure required to combat the Franco-Spanish effort at sea, the financial expense of the war in America was very high. Shipping costs exceeded those in the Seven Years' War. Unlike in the previous conflict, there was no large British colonial military force not paid for by London. France and Spain kept their American military expenses low, thanks to their alliance with the U.S. Continental Army. In short, in comparison with the previous war, Britain made no saving in the cost of land forces (unlike its European opponents), while its naval expenses went through the roof.[51] French policy during the war was linked to a new national emphasis on maritime power after 1750, designed to challenge and contain the British Empire.[52] Britain in fact defended its global position without the aid of a European landward ally. That the absence of such an ally was not singularly decisive in the outcome of the war helps to remove a sense of determinism about the result.

France and Spain also faced strategic adversity. France's leading war minister, the Count de Vergennes, planned a long war of attrition for which his country's financial system was ill-equipped. He appreciated this, ironically, and knew that the British structure of credit was more durable.[53] France was playing for time in a war in which time was not on its side, and would eventually have to choose peace. Neither was Spain financially strong. Both powers, moreover, had built up their navies with a view to redressing the treaty of 1763, but they lacked British operational effectiveness at sea.[54] Further, both Bourbon powers shared a defensive and risk-averse naval strategic approach, ill-suited to an offensive war against a global empire.[55] Britain's aims, by contrast, were ultimately better served by its navy's more aggressive battle-oriented approach, which assisted the regaining of strategic and diplomatic position toward the end of the war. It is true that at home the threat of invasion could tie down large British naval forces, effectively reversing Napoleon's later dictum that British amphibious forces could paralyze 300,000 French troops. But the practical operational problems of mounting an invasion of the British Isles, which included deficiencies of basing, logistics, intelligence and local navigational knowledge, not to mention British naval opposition, meant that such a strategic initiative was unlikely to succeed in anything other than a diversionary fashion.[56]

The failure of British maritime strategy in America, 1775–77

The initial British intention of winning a quick victory over the American rebels ran up against the strategic geography of North America. For a maritime power, it constituted the equivalent of Russia: distant, vast, hostile and without a leading urban center to seize.[57] The Americans, like the Russians, were able to trade space for time.[58] Their evasion of main battle made Washington's army – the Americans' one tangible strategic asset – an elusive target. British strategy, therefore, had to take advantage of its maritime forces to lever amphibious mobility and cut off the flow of munitions to the rebels. Here diplomacy complicated the picture. War in America made peace in Europe – that is, with France – essential for Britain. There was the risk of surprise attack and of a French war of revenge. But only pre-emptive war against France would prevent foreign aid to the Americans so as to reduce the risk of the very European war which would thus be required.[59] This dilemma underlay British strategy. British interests in the American theater did rest, by contrast with the rebels, on a substantial network of armies, fleets and seaborne logistics, all of which came to be targeted by the Americans and their allies.

French policy was the specter haunting British war plans for America. Vergennes was, paradoxically, a conservative statesman who wished to correct what he saw as the European disequilibrium created by British victory in 1763.[60] To him, the American war was an opportunity to bring down British Atlantic maritime power; the danger was of an Anglo-American settlement and attack on the French West Indies. French strategy from 1776 onwards would therefore be naval mobilization, the arming of the rebels, access to French ports for American raiders, and the enlistment of Spanish sea power to outnumber the Royal Navy. Denmark and Holland would also be utilized as neutral suppliers of naval stores to France.[61] Anglo-French relations deteriorated as a consequence, until war came to be seen as inevitable by the middle of 1777.[62]

In 1775, after the battles at Lexington and Concord, British governors and officials in the rebel colonies took refuge on warships. Apart from the besieged troops in Boston, British authority had retreated to the sea.[63] This was in a sense symbolic. America became immediately a theater of joint maritime operations against a hostile shore. But the need for forces in home waters to guard against the French meant that only one-third of the navy – no ships-of-the-line – were on station in America by the end of the year. Five of these 51 warships were needed to protect Nova Scotia, the essential base for a British counterattack. The rest were spread thinly between Boston and Florida.[64] Vice Admiral Samuel Graves was dismissed from his American command at the beginning of 1776, but in truth he lacked the tools to do the job.[65] Warships were not the only vessels required. The British government, in launching a land war in America, did not appreciate the logistics involved. It would have to supply the army from home, across 3,300 miles of ocean, a situation exacerbated in 1778 by the strategy of military dispersal in America. There were 72,000 troops in theater by 1782, with a chronic shortage of shipping for transport throughout the war.[66]

The issue of command of the sea in American waters was of two-fold strategic significance. But the navy was torn between, on the one hand, providing essential mobility, supply and protection for the army and, on the other, enforcing the coastal blockade. Lack of ships-of-the-line – two were present by 1776 – also meant lack of the necessary naval personnel for labor-intensive amphibious work.[67] In the spring of 1776, the navy did successfully evacuate 10,000 troops and Loyalists from Boston to Halifax. Offensive operations that year were intended to recover Canada and crush the American rebellion. Quebec was in fact relieved, and New York was captured in an excellent amphibious operation. But the opportunity to destroy Washington's army by maritime envelopment was lost, and the rebels then shifted to a strategy of avoiding major engagements. New York was an asset as a strategic position and a base, but the Royal Navy had to defend it. By the spring of 1777, Vice Admiral Lord Richard Howe had 72 warships under his command. But the requirement for naval support of the seaborne attack on Philadelphia that year subverted the blockade without gaining any of the strategic advantages of an amphibious movement up the Hudson River. Major General John Burgoyne's surrender at Saratoga in October demonstrated the fate of a British army in America without naval support.[68] The failure of British strategic planning in America that year has been termed appalling and laid at the door of Germain and the generals.[69] Britain retreated to a strategy of attrition for which it lacked the time and resources given the rising prospect of war with France.[70] Thus did a continental defeat overseas help to overturn the naval balance of power in the war.

The initial British decision on the outbreak of the American war had been in favor of continental operations as opposed to a purely maritime campaign against colonial trade. The blockade strategy had not, however, been abandoned. The Prohibitory, or "Capture," Act of December 1775, officially outlawed trade with the rebellious 13 colonies.[71] Despite the navy's difficulties in applying it, strong evidence has been adduced that this did serious damage to the rebel economy.[72] The definition of contraband included weapons, powder, ammunition and "warlike stores" as a military measure to assist British army operations.[73] The rebels initially lacked an arms industry, and for two years their cause depended upon imported munitions.[74] These were procured in Europe and crossed the Atlantic under foreign flags, principally that of France, which aided the rebels by disguising American vessels as French. These goods mostly reached the colonies via neutral West Indian ports: French, Dutch and Danish. At these locations, contraband was trans-shipped to American vessels. The circular and clockwise North Atlantic weather systems, with the established north–south trading patterns of the American hemisphere, meant that operationally the West Indies was the natural area for the Royal Navy to intercept rebel American imports. But there remained for Britain the thorny issue of neutral rights and the diplomatic problem of avoiding war with France, and to a lesser extent Spain. Blockading foreign ports in the West Indies risked international conflict. The British response was therefore a conservative strategy of protests and limited seizures, without real effect.

With the West Indies not a feasible maritime strategic focus for diplomatic reasons, the Royal Navy was left with the task of watching numerous colonial ports along a thousand miles of coastline, as well as supporting the army.[75] A significant rebel advantage in the face of Britain's great military power was the North American seafaring tradition itself. The colonists had a maritime infrastructure, long experience of sea trade and smuggling, and invaluable knowledge of local conditions. All things considered, it is unsurprising that the blockade was highly porous.[76] This illustrates, moreover, the fallacy of assessing maritime strategy in purely numerical terms. The navy seized over 120 American vessels in northern waters during the first year of the war, and destroyed towns in Maine and Virginia. But the blockade failed to stop the flow of arms in any significant way.[77] Thinly dispersed blockading forces could, moreover, be vulnerable to rebel attack at sea. The American Commodore Esek Hopkins, for example, escaped from Delaware Bay in early 1776 with eight vessels under his command. After seizing New Providence in the Bahamas and capturing its munitions, he proceeded to southern New England waters where he engaged the frigate *Glasgow* and captured her tender.

American privateers were a serious threat to British maritime supply lines, as well as to seaborne trade. The fitting out of privateers began as early as May 1775.[78] By the end of the year Britain had authorized the arming of merchant ships and established limited convoying. The Royal Navy escorted vessels carrying war supplies to America, East Indian merchantmen sailing homeward in the Atlantic, and ships departing the West Indies as far as 300 miles out to sea, as well as guarding the Newfoundland fisheries.[79] A serious threat arose with the arrival of American raiders in European waters during 1776. Their intentions were to capture or destroy British shipping, to divert British naval forces from America, and to trigger an Anglo-French war by using French ports and inviting

British blockade.[80] With the lack of small warships, British ships-of-the-line were used to patrol western European waters to little effect.[81] The convoy system was expanded at the request of the merchants. By the end of 1777, virtually every major branch of British maritime trade was being convoyed, and the American navy's 13 new frigates had been defeated or otherwise neutralized, but shipping losses still mounted in home waters and the West Indies. Over 300 merchant vessels were lost to raiders during that year.[82] This American cruiser campaign was a classic attempt at a diversionary maritime war. It did not cause a redeployment of Britain's small warships, the bulk of which were stationed overseas.[83] But the raiders did great damage to trade on both sides of the Atlantic, and brought Britain and France to the brink of war.

British naval forces were dangerously overcommitted by the summer of 1777. Sandwich wrote to Admiral Howe that the seas were crawling with privateers, and that demands for convoying and small warships could not be met.[84] Howe, for his part, told Sandwich that, in the prevailing strategic context, in which support of the army was a priority, the blockade of America would remain a failure. He reported that his fleet was under strain, with its effectiveness being eroded. There was a shortage of seamen, ships were in disrepair, naval logistics were a problem, and crews were stressed by constant service in hostile conditions.[85] The strategic options, moreover, were generally bad. The Admiralty wanted the major New England seaports destroyed so as to deprive the raiders of their bases. But the British commanders in America, Richard Howe and his brother Major General Sir William, favored conventional operations against the Continental Army and American cities; they wanted additional troops and ships-of-the-line. Sandwich was opposed in principle to weakening European waters in the face of the Franco-Spanish threat. Given the local priority attached to supporting the army in America, and given the need to maintain the two-power naval standard against France and Spain in Europe, the strategic failure to deny the seas to American smugglers and raiders was inevitable.[86]

War with France and global naval strategy, 1778

The Franco-American treaties of February 1778 were known of in London four days before France declared them on 13 March.[87] The great strategic gamble of the North government since 1775 that the American war could be localized – that the Americans would not fight in Europe and that France would not intervene – had failed. This has been termed a policy of minimal deterrence, even of appeasement.[88] Its collapse brought on a global conflict in which battle fleets of ships-of-the-line would be the key to strategy.[89] Here Britain was at a grave disadvantage. Sandwich had calculated the previous August that the Royal Navy had 30 vessels in operational condition to face more than 30 French ships in Atlantic ports and 13 at Toulon, as well as at least 11 Spanish ships in Europe. This was far from his principle of superiority over the Bourbon powers in home waters.[90] After having news in December of Burgoyne's surrender at Saratoga, and as France moved toward war during the winter, the British government had realized the need for full naval mobilization, decided upon by the Cabinet on 14 March.[91]

French naval strategy in the war would be diversionary: to occupy the Royal Navy in Europe, drawing Spain into the conflict, while winning in America. The Brest squadron, with the aid of Spain, would operate in the Channel and threaten invasion of the British Isles. The Toulon squadron would have the option of crossing to America. There it might well encounter a British squadron detached from home waters and be cornered. But, by 1778, all of the British army's internal lines of communication in America were by sea. A French naval victory in American waters would isolate British troops and force them into surrender.[92] This strategy would eventually succeed. It is a measure of the British strategic dilemma that Sandwich's credible strategy of concentrating force in home waters would, insofar as it was allowed to be applied, facilitate the French approach.[93]

War with France meant that the Royal Navy could not meet its global strategic commitments.[94] Potentially it had to defend North America, the West Indies, the Mediterranean and India, as well as home waters. Britain would be forced to choose. The Mediterranean was abandoned for the remainder of the war, greatly complicating the task of watching the Toulon squadron.[95] The invidious choice remaining was between home waters and America. It can be argued with the benefit of hindsight that Britain should have given up the rebel colonies at this point, that French entry made victory in America virtually impossible, and that it was political rather than strategic considerations which caused the war there to go on.[96] Perhaps a more plausible argument is that America should have been temporarily relegated as a naval priority, with concentration of the fleet in Europe to defeat France at sea before Spain joined the war.[97] British political divisions at the time created the worst of both worlds. Germain and the King wanted to send ships-of-the-line to America, where at this point there were none. Sandwich wanted consolidation of the Western squadron, given the risk of invasion and the need to seek general command of the sea.[98] The British battle fleet would thus be divided, with politics undermining strategy. In the event, French and British errors would tend to cancel each other out in Europe in 1778.

Sandwich persuaded the Cabinet on 6 April not to reinforce the Mediterranean against the Toulon squadron. This might divide the French fleet but would weaken the Channel in the event the squadron came north. Sandwich would not risk the British Isles for America.[99] The Toulon squadron under Count d'Estaing was in fact dispatched to America on the 13th. This constituted an attempt to strike first in the naval war, but was also a risk: British fleet concentration at home could outnumber the French.[100] British strategy would, however, be reactive.[101] Sandwich, under pressure, agreed to send a squadron to Halifax, but succeeded in prevaricating until the destination of d'Estaing's force was actually known.[102] The squadron, under Vice Admiral John Byron, sailed on 9 June. The Channel Fleet had been placed under the command of Augustus Keppel, an admiral lacking decisiveness and operational experience. He was ordered to cover the French squadrons, engaging them if possible, while guarding against invasion, protecting British trade and enforcing the blockade against contraband to America. The blockade was later extended to French trade, and to neutral vessels carrying military supplies to France: a measure aimed at naval stores from the Baltic.[103] On 27 July, Keppel fought the Brest squadron under Admiral le Comte d'Orvilliers off Ushant, failing to destroy it. The action left the French as a fleet-in-being, whereas the presence of Byron's ships might have been decisive. This was a great lost opportunity to inflict a defeat upon the French before Spain became involved.[104] A political crisis ensued as the parliamentary opposition sought to lever the Keppel–Palliser affair, attacking naval strategy and the conduct of the war but failing to bring down the government.[105] Sandwich and Keppel had been conservative, but their strategy had not failed on its own terms. The Brest squadron had been neutralized without loss of military or trade convoys.[106]

War with France put British strategy in America onto the defensive. Now North America was merely part of a global war of the great powers. Philadelphia was evacuated, and British forces essentially withdrew to their flanks in Nova Scotia and Florida. The navy's major transatlantic presence would be in the West Indies for most of the year, coming north only during the hurricane season.[107] The arrival of French naval forces in America changed the shape of the theater of war, significantly complicating the task of the Royal Navy. The Franco-American alliance had a potential for joint strategy that could act as a pincer movement against the British army. Troops would be vulnerable to attack from the rear, or to siege, if local command of the sea were lost. Howe was forced, therefore, to concentrate his fleet to protect the army and deal with the more-powerful French naval force, Byron's squadron having fallen foul of a gale. Blockade of the coast would be impossible.[108] D'Estaing failed to drive home attacks on New York and Rhode Island during the summer, and then proceeded south to Martinique in the Caribbean. In December he failed in an attack on St. Lucia, recently taken by British forces.[109] Howe resigned his command and left for England in September. North America, now something of a strategic backwater, was left to second-rate British naval commanders for the rest of the war.[110]

The entry of Spain and the League of Armed Neutrality, 1779–80

Anglo-Spanish hostilities effectively began on 16 June 1779.[111] Vergennes had wanted Spain to enter the war to alter the naval balance of power. Against the expected British order of battle for 1779 of 90 ships-of-the-line, Spain added at least 50 to a French force of approximately 66: a dramatic turnaround.[112] French strategy was thus hostage to Spanish war aims: the regaining of Minorca, Gibraltar, West Florida and the coast of Honduras.[113] A major Spanish concern was the security of the annual treasure fleet from America. The plan against Gibraltar, a key issue for Spain, was to besiege it while acquiring British home territory to trade for it. This made Gibraltar one focus of the naval war. It also encouraged the Spanish desire for an invasion of England.[114]

An invasion strategy arose naturally out of Spain's need for a short war; it had limited financial resources and a vulnerable empire.[115] French strategy was not to concentrate on Europe, and Vergennes preferred to attack British trade in home waters, but he had little choice. The allies drew up plans for an occupation of the Isle of Wight and an attack on the fleet base at Portsmouth.[116] The invasion of England was not to be, but one consequence of Spanish priorities would be more difficulty for France in concentrating naval forces overseas.[117] This European strategy did, on the other hand, help to weaken Britain itself overseas, with the Royal Navy guarding against invasion, trying to protect trade, and having to relieve Gibraltar.[118] At the same time, Britain's position in the West Indies was also threatened.[119] War with both Bourbon powers underlined how the American issue was now secondary for Britain, and intensified the need for the global view.[120]

Admiral Sir Charles Hardy had command of the Channel Fleet in 1779. His instructions stressed the security of the British Isles as the major priority.[121] The Franco-Spanish invasion plans underestimated the difficulty of the operation. They depended, above all, on gaining control of the Channel, despite the efforts of the Royal Navy. This was essentially the same problem as faced potential invaders in 1805 and 1940. The combined fleet reached the Western Approaches in mid-August 1779. British strategy was to have it enter the Channel and to fight it there, where the Spanish Armada had been neutralized in 1588. The enemy this time, however, was disinclined to fight. Lacking pilots, provisions, healthy seamen and a safe channel port, it retreated to Brest. The British strategy of deploying a fleet-in-being, aided by poor enemy planning, had been successful.[122]

Meanwhile, Gibraltar was under siege. It would hold out for the duration of the war, but needed relief. The failed invasion of the British Isles enabled a squadron to be sent to the West Indies under Admiral Sir George Rodney, resupplying Gibraltar and Minorca en route. The force sailed on Christmas Day, captured a Spanish convoy, defeated a Spanish squadron in the "Moonlight Battle" off Cape St. Vincent, relieved Gibraltar, supplied Minorca and proceeded to the West Indies. A detached force returning to England captured part of a Spanish convoy.[123] This Mediterranean expedition was the first major British naval victory of the war, and included the destruction of one enemy ship-of-the-line and the capture of eight, as well as the taking of valuable booty and approximately 4,000 prisoners. It was due to adequate force, tactical skill and seamanship, copper bottoms and two fortuitous interceptions.[124]

There was no coordinated British strategic plan for North America in 1779.[125] When d'Estaing's French squadron came north at the end of the summer, there was the added problem of where it might strike. Its arrival caused the British reinforcement of Jamaica against possible invasion to be cancelled.[126] The Royal Navy in America was now facing the combined naval forces of France, Spain and the United States. Yet on land a British strategy of concentration had given way to one of dispersal at the end of 1778. This was vulnerable to enemy achievement of local naval superiority and then landing of troops, such as occurred on the Gulf of Mexico and the Mississippi River.[127] Spanish entry into the war had created enemy positions in Louisiana and Cuba. The sea communications in the Gulf and the Strait of Florida were in fact the main strategic artery of the Spanish empire. This line was threatened by the British gains in Florida under the treaty of 1763. In 1779, therefore, Spain opened a new theater of operations, successfully targeting the British positions in the Gulf, an offensive culminating in the taking of New Providence in the Bahamas in 1782.[128] Jamaica was also threatened by the combined Bourbon positions in the region. Sandwich had his usual priority of home defense, but the King was willing to take risks to save the British West Indies.[129] Here was the background to the appointment of Rodney, a fighting admiral and a political supporter of the government, to command in the Leeward Islands, where the Royal Navy had been fighting under pressure against d'Estaing during 1779.[130]

The primary source of naval stores such as timber, tar, flax, hemp and iron was the Baltic region. Access to Baltic trade was an essential requirement during the war for the European naval powers. The cost of avoiding the British blockade did contribute to French financial strain. But Britain never succeeded in severing the Bourbon powers from these vital commodities.[131] The blockade, moreover, involved the complex legal issues surrounding neutral commercial rights.[132] France promoted these rights in its own strategic interest. The key players here were the Dutch, with a vested interest in neutrality but potentially caught between British naval and French military power. France was pressuring them to take its side by 1779 and wanted to give Dutch merchant shipping warship escort. This promoted the decline of Anglo-Dutch relations, already damaged by the British policy of seizing merchant ships carrying war-like stores, and shots were exchanged in December. Britain declared the Netherlands a hostile neutral in April 1780, with a complete blockade of Dutch shipping to the Bourbon powers.[133] In March, Catherine the Great of Russia, for her own diplomatic reasons, had initiated the League of Armed Neutrality in defense of neutral rights. The Dutch wished to preserve their profits, but if Russia defaulted in the use of protective force, the Royal Navy would destroy Dutch shipping and trade. The Channel Fleet stood between the North Sea and the Bourbon fleets at Brest and Cadiz. Russia, moreover, would make no promise to defend the Dutch overseas empire. By mid-1780, France had outflanked the British naval blockade by land, with Dutch merchants shipping stores to France via inland waterways. Only the use of force by the Royal Navy on the Dutch coast could now hope to cut off supplies. Britain thus had a strategic incentive for war with the Netherlands, which was declared in December 1780. The Dutch joined the League two weeks later. Britain had calculated correctly that Russia would not back the Dutch with force. The League, moreover, had declared the Baltic a neutral area, hence Britain had no need to protect its shipping there.[134]

For the Dutch, war with Britain was an economic and strategic disaster. Dutch naval forces, in theory, were in a position to intercept British Baltic trade and blockade the port of London. But, in 1780, the Netherlands possessed only three-dozen operational warships, including only 16 with 50 or more guns.[135] This meager fleet could not break the British blockade, let alone defend the empire. After a fight with the British at the Dogger Bank in August 1781, the Dutch fleet retreated to the Texel anchorage for the rest of the war.[136] Dutch naval strategy was influenced by a philosophy of port defense in both Europe and the East Indies.[137] Dutch overseas shipping was highly vulnerable to British privateers as well as to the Royal Navy, and 200 vessels were lost during the first month of hostilities. In February 1781, Rodney took the Dutch West Indian island of St. Eustatius, the major commercial center for European aid to the American rebels, which was held for nine months. Other Dutch bases were lost in West Africa, Guyana and the Indian Ocean.[138]

British naval strategy in Europe in 1780 revolved around the familiar themes of home and trade defense, while seeking to prevent the joining of the Bourbon fleets. The Channel Fleet cruised in the Western Approaches and off the Franco-Spanish coast. Old Admiral Lord Hawke recommended the kind of close blockade of Brest that he had implemented during the Seven Years' War. This would not, however, cover Toulon and Cadiz.[139] The British loss of an outward-bound West Indian commercial–military convoy was a disaster, and contributed to the scuttling of an initiative for peace with Spain. The overstretched navy adopted a defensive strategy of diverting homeward trade from the Western Approaches around the British Isles.[140]

The British taking of Charleston in May 1780, with the intention of using it as a naval base, was offset by the developing Bourbon threat in the western hemisphere. French and Spanish convoys left Europe for the Caribbean in February and April respectively, and French reinforcements for Washington's army sailed in May, reaching Newport in July.[141] The British Cabinet decided to reinforce North America, and eight ships-of-the-line were detached from European waters under Rear Admiral Thomas Graves.[142] Rodney, after fighting an indecisive action against the French at Martinique, came north in September. This created a British naval superiority in North American waters. It was wasted, however, due to lack of strategic focus and quarrels between the British commanders.[143]

Defeat in America, 1781

Franco-Spanish priorities largely conditioned the naval strategic agenda during 1781. Spain, although concentrating on the siege of Gibraltar, wanted French assistance in the Americas. France now had a need to defend the Dutch empire, and hence to secure the Cape of Good Hope, the gateway to the Indian Ocean. French squadrons were therefore dispatched in the spring to the West Indies, under Count de Grasse, and to the Cape, under the Chevalier de Suffren, departing Brest as a single force. Plans were developed for a combined Bourbon attack on Jamaica, designed as a possible diplomatic body-blow to force Britain to come to terms.[144] At this point the British Cabinet made a critical decision: to utilize the Channel Fleet in the resupply of Gibraltar. This was achieved, but at a major strategic price. While the fleet took on provisions off Ireland, the French force slipped out of Brest. Rodney, in the West Indies, compounded the situation by having his fleet divided while he pillaged St. Eustatius, allowing de Grasse to reach Martinique in safety.[145] His arrival in the western hemisphere would have far-reaching consequences.

The complex series of strategic–operational decisions and movements – on the part of British, French and American commanders on land and sea – leading to the famous naval encounter at the Chesapeake and the British surrender at Yorktown on 19 October have been elucidated elsewhere.[146] These events were highly fortuitous, but several key influences were at work in one of the more dramatic episodes in strategic history. The three British armies in North America, in the North, the South and Virginia, would each be isolated if Britain lacked command of the sea when and where necessary. There was complacency in London, particularly on the part of Germain, about the potential for Franco-American forces to spring a joint operational trap in such circumstances. Despite British possession of intelligence about enemy plans and movements, including letters from Washington's headquarters indicating the broad allied plan of campaign, there was a lack of collective situational awareness on the part of the British high command. This obliviousness was combined with a general absence of cooperation amongst the British naval and military leaders in North America. Washington, by contrast, showed an ability to combine flexibly and effectively with French naval and military forces, as well as an awareness that the outcome at sea could be crucial.[147] Rodney's decision to leave for England in mid-year took the navy's leading fighting admiral out of the equation. De Grasse, after taking Tobago, had come north, and by 29 August was at the Chesapeake with 26 ships-of-the-line and 3,000 troops to reinforce the Marquis de Lafayette's force against Lord Charles Cornwallis' soldiers. The only salvation for the British army in Virginia was via victory at sea.[148]

Wednesday, 5 September 1781, was the blackest day in the history of the Royal Navy. A fleet engagement off the Chesapeake between de Grasse and a British force under Thomas Graves left the French still in command of the Bay area. They were reinforced six days later by the French Newport squadron carrying the siege train. The combined American and French armies of George Washington and Lieutenant General Comte de Rochambeau arrived by land on the 14th and Cornwallis was doomed. It was the breakthrough for which the French and Americans had worked and one of the greatest demonstrations in history of the strategic value of sea power and of joint and combined warfare. The Chesapeake action led directly to the loss of a second British army in America, but its ultimate significance was political.[149] After Yorktown, the British governing class was no longer willing to fight for the 13 colonies. The Royal Navy's taking of a French military convoy for the West Indies in December could not offset this effect. Sandwich defended the achievements and the conduct of a naval war in which Britain could not be strong everywhere. But Henry Fox, leading the attack in Parliament, argued that the correct strategy of fleet concentration in Europe had been fatally abandoned.[150] In February, the House of Commons voted to abandon offensive war against the Americans, and in March the North government fell. From this point North America ceased to be a significant theater of war, but the global maritime conflict with France continued. Germain defeated Sandwich during the winter of 1781–82 over the issue of naval deployments: by the summer there were more British ships-of-the-line in the West Indies than in Europe: 42 as against 34 out of 96.[151]

War in the Indian Ocean, 1781–83

While Europe and the West Indies would remain the major theaters of war, significant fighting took place in the wider Indian Ocean area. To what extent was the Asian theater an integral part of the global conflict? European interest in India was traditionally commercial rather than territorial. But in the wake of the Seven Years' War, India acquired a diversionary role in French strategy as a place to occupy British naval forces. This, it was considered, would facilitate French superiority in European waters and an attack on the British Isles. As the Atlantic war developed, Dutch involvement made the East Indies a defensive consideration for French strategy. From late 1781, the Indian Ocean became a more offensive French area of operations, with the aim of striking a decisive blow against Britain, such as the taking of Bombay.[152] Despite the relatively small naval forces deployed there, Asia was unquestionably part of the wider war.

The northeast monsoon limited naval operations in the Indian theater to the period from April to September, after which the usual British practice was to withdraw to Bombay and the French likewise to Mauritius in the southwest Indian Ocean. French forces also benefitted from logistical support available in the Dutch East Indies.[153] In the relatively small Indian coastal area, where the opposing naval forces were evenly balanced, the unity of fleets was axiomatic since division could be fatal. India, like Europe and North America, was also a maritime–continental theater of operations. Power at sea meant power on land, and coordination of naval and military forces, although the British lacked it, was essential. Gaining of local command of the sea required possession of a base not dependent upon naval power for security.[154] Such a base was the Dutch port of Trincomalee in northern Ceylon (Sri Lanka), an excellent natural harbor which had been taken by the British but was lost again in 1782. The Cape of Good Hope was a pivotal position on which French use of Mauritius depended. With Dutch entry into the war, it became for Britain an enemy base, from which both British eastern trade and the staging post at St. Helena could be attacked.[155] Suffren, an aggressive fighter and – outside the French mold – a pursuer of decisive fleet action, foiled a British attempt to take the Cape in early 1781, attacking a Royal Navy squadron at Porto Praya in the Cape Verde Islands which are in the Atlantic about 450 miles west of Africa. He arrived in southern India a year later. On land, the French supported the Nabob of Mysore in his war against the British East India Company. At sea, Suffren fought a series of intense and evenly matched battles against the British during 1782–83. Vice Admiral Sir Edward Hughes was aware that the French offensive was aimed ultimately at destroying British trade and settlements, and that the preservation of his squadron was crucial for the survival of the British presence in India.[156] The two equally determined and able sea-fighters broke off their mutual challenge only when news arrived that peace treaties had been signed by Britain, France and Spain early in 1783.

The revival of the British position and the coming of peace, 1782–83

The French strategic aim in 1782 was to keep up the pressure on Britain for one more campaign, so as to force its government to peace. The risk was of a British victory and strategic recovery.[157] By the beginning of the year the Royal Navy had mobilized a fleet equal to the combined force of the Bourbons.[158] Lord Howe was given command of the Channel Fleet by the new Rockingham government, but he was outnumbered with the greatest part of the navy in the West Indies. Yet the British achieved the success of an important convoy interception off Ushant, taking a French ship-of-the-line and 1,000 troops destined for the Indian Ocean. A large Franco-Spanish fleet achieved nothing in the Western Approaches during the summer. Howe resupplied Gibraltar in October, fighting a fleet action off Cape Spartel. The naval war in British home waters was effectively over.[159]

Rodney returned to the Caribbean in February, with Jamaica under threat of a Franco-Spanish invasion. On 12 April, off Dominica, he won a resounding victory at the battle of the Saints, capturing de Grasse, his flagship and four other French ships-of-the-line. Rodney's deputy Samuel Hood later took another two. This contest saved Jamaica, and revived British naval prestige to significant political effect. The perception in London and Paris was that the naval balance of power had been restored to that of the early 1760s: a perception that would greatly influence the peace treaties.[160] Britain reinforced the Royal Navy in the West Indies, guarding its position as the war moved toward a conclusion.[161] To the North, despite a shortage of transport shipping, America was evacuated during 1782–83 after the establishment of peace terms, with tens of thousands of British Loyalists being carried to Canada, Europe and the West Indies.[162]

Britain issued orders for the cessation of hostilities on 13 February 1783. While the terms of the peace essentially reiterated those of 1763, from a naval strategic point of view, Britain's retention of its valuable West Indian sugar islands, of Canada and Gibraltar, and the maintenance of its position in India were the most significant achievements, together with the defense of the British Isles and the protection of trade. This residual global position was underpinned by Britain's maritime infrastructure and fiscal system. The result was the revival of Anglo-American trade and the settlement of Australia, such that the contemporary belief that the loss of America would undermine British power was not borne out. The French attempt to challenge the pre-eminent global naval power on its own ground was finally a failure. While the Royal Navy learned technical lessons from the conflict in such areas as tactics and signaling, the strategic lesson of the importance of the Western Approaches was not lost on a later

British war leader, William Pitt the Younger, prime minister for 20 years between 1783 and 1806.[163] Perhaps above all, a generation of younger British naval officers – Nelson's generation – had experienced the elation of victory and the bitterness of defeat, and further developed the culture of aggression in their determination to exploit opportunities to win.[164]

A case study in global naval strategy

The war at sea is rich in lessons for the student of strategy. The first is to recall the observation of Clausewitz: the supreme requirement of strategy is to understand the nature of a war and prosecute that war in its own terms.[165] In this case the war was fundamentally maritime and global, although not all British strategists at the time perceived it as such. The essential British agenda, therefore, had to be defense of the overall imperial position. In strategy it is the net outcome that counts, and the preservation of the British Empire was, in these terms, a satisfactory result. The war remains, however, a study in what can go wrong with a naval–maritime strategy, as well as in what can go right. The original failure was arguably diplomatic. As Paul M. Kennedy has emphasized, Britain fought this war alone.[166] The context in which there were too many enemies, theaters and commitments resembles the strategic dilemma facing Britain in 1940–41.

The counter-factual question as to how a major British victory in European waters would have altered the course of the American war is, of course, unanswerable.[167] While the "what ifs" of history must ultimately remain speculative, we can say some things with confidence about such a theoretical naval victory and the context in which it would have occurred. In terms of the pattern of Britain's eighteenth-century wars, the lack of such a victory was indeed unusual, and contrasted sharply with the situation during the Seven Years' War. Undoubtedly this contributed to Britain's essential strategic problem during the American war, which was contested command of the sea. Further, such a victory would have increased significantly British strategic and diplomatic leverage in dealing with France and perhaps therefore with the American rebels. Finally, the optimal time to inflict such a blow was after French but before Spanish entry into the war. Given all this, the British naval campaign of 1778 and the action off Ushant were arguably a major lost opportunity to alter the course and possibly the outcome of the war. This of course relates to the issue of how far Sandwich was right, as opposed to Germain, in favoring naval deployments in home waters. While there are learned dissenting voices, historical opinion has tended to back Sandwich, Nicholas Rodger even holding that he was not strategically conservative enough.[168]

The war remains, in the broadest terms, a demonstration of the many dimensions of naval power, showing it to be inherently strategic, indirect, flexible, global, deep, joint, intimately connected with diplomacy and favored by time. It is also dependent upon command, or at least dispute, of its primary strategic environment, the sea. Interestingly, the war saw no overall British command of the sea.[169] Such disputed command, as Corbett points out, is frequently the case.[170] In the context of the war, dispute worked against British offensive strategy in North America, subverting power projection and blockade; in Europe and India, where Britain was on the defensive, it worked in its favor. In the last resort, naval power worked in the war, as it has always worked, as an enabler. Negatively, naval strategic defeat at the Chesapeake led to failure on land and the loss of the colonies. Positively, naval victory at the Saints led to diplomatic leverage and a satisfactory peace.

Notes

1 Financial support for this work was provided by the Royal Australian Navy under the Osborne Fellowship program at the University of New South Wales, Australian Defence Force Academy. The views expressed are those of the author, and in no way constitute official statements of the Australian Government, the Department of Defence or the RAN.
2 N.A.M. Rodger, *The Insatiable Earl: A Life of John Montagu, Earl of Sandwich 1718–1792* (London: HarperCollins, 1993), p. 328.
3 On these issues see, in general, J.S. Corbett, *Some Principles of Maritime Strategy* (London: Longmans, Green and Co., 1911), reprinted, Eric Grove, ed. (London: Brassey's, 1988).
4 Carl von Clausewitz, *On War*, Michael Howard and Peter Paret, eds. and trans. (Princeton: Princeton University Press, 1976), p. 119.
5 N.A.M. Rodger, *The Command of the Ocean: A Naval History of Britain, 1649–1815* (London: Allen Lane, 2004), p. 290.
6 Ibid., p. 287.
7 J.B. Hattendorf, "The Struggle with France, 1689–1815," in J.R. Hill, ed., *The Oxford Illustrated History of the Royal Navy* (Oxford: Oxford University Press, 1995), p. 119.
8 Memorandum for the Cabinet by Sandwich, Sept. 1779, G.R. Barnes and J.H. Owen, eds., *The Private Papers of John, Earl of Sandwich, First Lord of the Admiralty 1771–1782*, 4 vols. (London: Navy Records Society, 1932–38), vol. 3, p. 170.
9 D. Syrett, *The Royal Navy in European Waters During the American Revolutionary War* (Columbia: University of South Carolina Press, 1998), p. x.
10 H.M. Scott, *British Foreign Policy in the Age of the American Revolution* (Oxford: Oxford University Press, 1990), p. 236.
11 D.A. Baugh, "Why Did Britain Lose Command of the Sea During the War for America?" in J. Black and P. Woodfine, eds., *The British Navy and the Use of Naval Power in the Eighteenth Century* (Leicester: Leicester University Press, 1988), p. 155.
12 Ibid., pp. 153–5.
13 J. Black, *The British Seaborne Empire* (New Haven and London: Yale University Press, 2004), p. 136.
14 Rodger, *Insatiable Earl*, p. 273.
15 D. Syrett, "Count-Down to the Saintes: a Strategy of Detachments and the Quest for Naval Superiority in the West Indies," *The Mariner's Mirror* (2001), 87:150–62.
16 Rodger, *Insatiable Earl*, p. 268.
17 Ibid., p. 273.
18 Syrett, *European Waters*, pp. 28–30, 32.
19 Rodger, *Command of the Ocean*, p. 329.
20 Syrett, *European Waters*, p. 13. It is difficult to distinguish between the smaller group of ministers who made routine decisions and the full Cabinet. Scott, *British Foreign Policy*, pp. 18–19.

21 D. Syrett, *The Royal Navy in American Waters 1775–1783* (Aldershot: Scolar Press, 1989), p. 33; Rodger, *Command of the Ocean*, pp. 331–2.
22 Syrett, *European Waters*, p. 152.
23 Ibid., pp. ix–x.
24 Ibid., pp. x, 12–13.
25 Rodger, *Insatiable Earl*, pp. 271, 279, 283–4.
26 Ibid., pp. 271–4.
27 Rodger, *Command of the Ocean*, pp. 274–5, 288 ff.
28 Black, *British Seaborne Empire*, p. 135.
29 Rodger, *Insatiable Earl*, p. 270. French privateering had a limited effect during the American war, with a low level of activity. Without British command of the sea, French convoys were safer, meaning less financial incentive to resort to raiding. Rodger, *Command of the Ocean*, p. 359.
30 Rodger, *Insatiable Earl*, pp. 294–6.
31 Ibid., p. 299.
32 Rodger, *Command of the Ocean*, p. 272.
33 Rodger, *Insatiable Earl*, p. 275.
34 M. Duffy, "The Establishment of the Western Squadron as the Linchpin of British Naval Strategy," in M. Duffy, ed., *Parameters of British Naval Power 1650–1850* (Exeter: University of Exeter Press, 1992), pp. 77–8.
35 Syrett, "Count-Down to the Saintes," p. 152.
36 Rodger, *Insatiable Earl*, p. 273.
37 Black, *British Seaborne Empire*, p. 136.
38 Rodger, *Insatiable Earl*, p. 274.
39 Rodger, *Command of the Ocean*, pp. 3, 37–8.
40 D.A. Baugh, "Great Britain's 'Blue-Water' Policy, 1689–1815," *International History Review* (1988), 10:36–7, 46–7, 56–7.
41 Rodger, *Command of the Ocean*, pp. 269–71. On the maritime and continental schools during the mid-eighteenth century, see R. Pares, "American versus Continental Warfare, 1739–63," *English Historical Review* (1936) 51:429–65.
42 N.A.M. Rodger, "The Continental Commitment in the Eighteenth Century," in L. Freedman, P. Hayes and R. O'Neill, eds., *War, Strategy and International Politics: Essays in Honour of Sir Michael Howard* (Oxford: Clarendon Press, 1992), pp. 51–3.
43 Paul M. Kennedy, *The Rise and Fall of British Naval Mastery* (London: Allen Lane, 1983, repr. Macmillan, 1985), p. 75.
44 D.A. Baugh, "Withdrawing from Europe: Anglo-French Maritime Geopolitics, 1750–1800," *International History Review* (1998) 20:24.
45 See, for example, Syrett, *European Waters*, p. 18.
46 Rodger, *Command of the Ocean*, p. 283.
47 Baugh, "Why Did Britain Lose Command of the Sea?" p. 160.
48 On the historiographical issue, see ibid., pp. 149–51.
49 Black, *British Seaborne Empire*, p. 139.
50 Rodger, "The Continental Commitment in the Eighteenth Century," p. 50.
51 Baugh, "Why Did Britain Lose Command of the Sea?" pp. 159–60.
52 See, in general, Baugh, "Withdrawing from Europe."
53 Baugh, "Why Did Britain Lose Command of the Sea?" p. 161.
54 A. Lambert, *War at Sea in the Age of Sail 1650–1850* (London: Cassell, 2000), p. 128.
55 Rodger, *Command of the Ocean*, p. 273.
56 Rodger, "The Continental Commitment in the Eighteenth Century," pp. 51–2. Napoleon's observation is quoted in Corbett, *Some Principles of Maritime Strategy*, p. 69.
57 The Russian parallel has been suggested by Syrett in *American Waters*, p. 34.
58 Lambert, *War at Sea in the Age of Sail*, p. 130.

59 Scott, *British Foreign Policy*, pp. 207–8, 243.
60 J.R. Dull, *The French Navy and American Independence: A Study of Arms and Diplomacy, 1774–1787* (Princeton: Princeton University Press, 1975), pp. 7–11.
61 Ibid., pp. 9, 31–7; Syrett, *American Waters*, pp. 28–9; Lambert, *War at Sea in the Age of Sail*, p. 131.
62 Scott, *British Foreign Policy*, p. 209.
63 Syrett, *American Waters*, p. 1.
64 The protection of Nova Scotia was necessary in the face of the American military presence in Canada and at sea. Ibid., pp. 11, 29.
65 Ibid., p. 10.
66 D. Syrett, *Shipping and the American War 1775–83: A Study of British Transport Organisation* (London: The Athlone Press, 1970), pp. 243–4.
67 Syrett, *American Waters*, p. 58.
68 Ibid., pp. 23–4, 46 ff., 59, 69–70, 74–5, 85–7, 117.
69 D. Syrett, "The Failure of the British Effort in America, 1777," in Black and Woodfine, eds., *The British Navy and the Use of Naval Power*, pp. 176 ff.
70 Ibid., p. 180; Scott, *British Foreign Policy*, pp. 259–60.
71 D.A. Baugh, "The Politics of British Naval Failure, 1775–1777," *The American Neptune* (1992) 52:221–3.
72 R. Buel, Jr., *In Irons: Britain's Naval Supremacy and the American Revolutionary Economy* (New Haven and London: Yale University Press, 1998).
73 Baugh, "Politics of British Naval Failure," p. 223.
74 Syrett, *American Waters*, p. 60.
75 The preceding analysis is indebted to Nicholas Rodger in *Command of the Ocean*, p. 331. See also Syrett, *American Waters*, pp. 20 ff., 30–1, 89, *European Waters*, pp. 3–5.
76 The blockade, for example, of New England involved 27 warships during March 1777, but was ineffective. A single case study is that of HMS *Orpheus* which in a cruise sighted 90 American vessels but could only intercept 33. Syrett, *American Waters*, pp. 70–1.
77 Ibid., p. 27.
78 Ibid., p. 6.
79 Ibid., pp. 31–2; Syrett, *European Waters*, pp. 5–6.
80 Syrett, *American Waters*, pp. 63–4.
81 Syrett, *European Waters*, pp. 8–9.
82 Ibid., pp. 9–10; Syrett, *American Waters*, pp. 86, 88.
83 Ibid., p. 67. A decision was made in March 1778 to withdraw 20 small vessels from America when war with France was imminent. Syrett, *European Waters*, p. 20.
84 Barnes and Owen, eds., *Sandwich Papers*, 1:294, Sandwich to Howe, 3 Aug. 1777.
85 Syrett, *American Waters*, p. 87.
86 Barnes and Owen, eds., *Sandwich Papers*, 1:235–8, Sandwich to Lord North, 3 Aug. 1777; Syrett, "Failure of the British Effort in America," pp. 174–5.
87 Dull, *The French Navy and American Independence*, pp. 100–1; Syrett, *European Waters*, p. 20.
88 N. Tracy, *Navies, Deterrence and American Independence: Britain and Seapower in the 1760s and 1770s* (Vancouver: University of British Columbia Press, 1988), p. 151; Rodger, *Command of the Ocean*, p. 335.
89 Hattendorf, "The Struggle with France, 1689–1815," p. 103.
90 Barnes and Owen, eds., *Sandwich Papers*, 1:236–7, Sandwich to Lord North[?], 3 Aug. 1777.
91 Baugh, "Politics of British Naval Failure," pp. 239–40; Syrett, *European Waters*, p. 20.
92 Dull, *The French Navy and American Independence*, pp. 107–10; Syrett, *European Waters*, p. 69, *American Waters*, p. 93.

93 As a corollary, Sandwich advocated a fundamental change of strategy in the American theater in favor of military and commercial blockade; he believed that the army had thus far misused the navy for support and should shift to a function of securing bases for warships, together with a joint raiding strategy against rebel ports. He also wanted a separate West Indian naval command to protect the colonies and the Jamaica trade. Barnes and Owen, eds., *Sandwich Papers*, 1:327–35, Sandwich to Lord North, 8 Dec. 1777.
94 Syrett, *European Waters*, p. 165.
95 Ibid.
96 Ibid., pp. 21–2; D. Syrett, "Home Waters or America? The Dilemma of British Naval Strategy in 1778," *Mariner's Mirror* (1991) 77:4, p. 367.
97 Rodger, *Command of the Ocean*, pp. 341–2.
98 Ibid., pp. 335–6.
99 Syrett, *European Waters*, p. 24; Rodger, *Insatiable Earl*, pp. 275–8.
100 Dull, *The French Navy and American Independence*, p. 111; Rodger, *Command of the Ocean*, pp. 341–2.
101 Syrett, *American Waters*, p. 142.
102 Syrett, *European Waters*, pp. 26 ff.; Rodger, *Command of the Ocean*, p. 336.
103 Barnes and Owen, eds., *Sandwich Papers*, 2:369–70, orders to Keppel, Apr. 1778; Syrett, *European Waters*, pp. ix, 23–4, 96–102.
104 Rodger, *Command of the Ocean*, pp. 336–7; J. Black, "Introduction," in Black and Woodfine, *The British Navy and the Use of Naval Power*, p. 16.
105 Syrett, *European Waters*, pp. 51 ff.
106 Ibid., p. 60.
107 Ibid., pp. 94–5; Rodger, *Command of the Ocean*, p. 335; Lambert, *War at Sea in the Age of Sail*, p. 132; Barnes and Owen, eds., *Sandwich Papers*, 1:404–5, summary of instructions to commanders-in-chief in the West Indies, Mar., July 1778.
108 Syrett, *American Waters*, pp. 111–12; Lambert, *War at Sea in the Age of Sail*, p. 132; Rodger, *Command of the Ocean*, pp. 338–9.
109 Ibid.
110 Syrett, *American Waters*, pp. 116, 119.
111 Dull, *The French Navy and American Independence*, p. 150.
112 Ibid., pp. 97–8; Rodger, *Command of the Ocean*, p. 340.
113 Dull, *The French Navy and American Independence*, p. 111; Rodger, *Command of the Ocean*, p. 136.
114 Syrett, *European Waters*, p. 69.
115 J.R. Dull, "Mahan, Sea Power, and the War for American Independence," *International History Review* (1988) 10:1, p. 63.
116 Dull, *The French Navy and American Independence*, pp. 136–43.
117 J. Pritchard, "French Strategy and the American Revolution: A Reappraisal," *Naval War College Review* (1994) 47:4, p. 94.
118 Dull, "Mahan, Sea Power, and the War for American Independence," pp. 63–4.
119 Barnes and Owen, eds., *Sandwich Papers*, 2:179–83, Sandwich to North, 15 Oct. 1778.
120 Ibid., 3:231, Sandwich to Rodney, 25 Sept. 1790; Scott, *British Foreign Policy*, p. 277.
121 Syrett, *European Waters*, p. 68.
122 Ibid., pp. 74–6, 78–81; Lambert, *War at Sea in the Age of Sail*, p. 134.
123 Syrett, *European Waters*, pp. 83–93.
124 Ibid., pp. 93–4.
125 Syrett, *American Waters*, p. 122.
126 Ibid., pp. 129–30.
127 This strategic contradiction has been pointed out by Syrett. Ibid., pp. 118–19.
128 Pensacola was taken, due to lack of British naval support, in May 1781, ibid., pp. 119, 132, 174–5.

129 Barnes and Owen, eds., *Sandwich Papers*, 3:163–71, letter from the king, 13 Sept. 1779, and paper for the Cabinet by Sandwich, Sept. 1779.
130 Syrett, *European Waters*, pp. 81–3. Rodney's appointment was linked to a British strategic decision not to vacate the West Indies during the 1779 hurricane season in an attempt to gain local naval superiority at the beginning of the next campaign. The Leeward Islands, between Venezuela and Puerto Rico, were major strategic and economic assets to the European powers and saw much naval fighting during the war. Syrett, "Count-Down to the Saintes," pp. 150–1.
131 Syrett, *European Waters*, pp. 95–6, 132.
132 These issues are discussed in D. Syrett, *Neutral Rights and the War in the Narrow Seas, 1778–1782* (Fort Leavenworth: U.S. Army Command and General Staff College, 1985).
133 Syrett, *European Waters*, pp. 102 ff.; Dull, *The French Navy and American Independence*, pp. 175–6.
134 Syrett, *European Waters*, pp. 118 ff.; Rodger, *Command of the Ocean*, pp. 347–8.
135 Syrett, *European Waters*, p. 126.
136 Ibid., pp. 130–1.
137 H. Richmond, *The Navy in India 1763–1783* (London: Ernest Benn, 1931), p. 322.
138 Rodger, *Command of the Ocean*, p. 348; Syrett, *European Waters*, pp. 129 ff.; J.I. Israel, *The Dutch Republic: Its Rise, Greatness and Fall 1477–1806* (Oxford: Oxford University Press, 1995), p. 1097.
139 Syrett, *European Waters*, pp. 134–5, 137–8.
140 Ibid., pp. 136–7, 142, 146; Rodger, *Command of the Ocean*, p. 347.
141 Ibid., p. 345; Dull, *The French Navy and American Independence*, pp. 187–92.
142 Syrett, *American Waters*, p. 142.
143 Ibid., pp. 151 ff.
144 Dull, *The French Navy and American Independence*, pp. 216–21, 277–8, 249–53.
145 Syrett, *European Waters*, pp. 139 ff.; Rodger, *Command of the Ocean*, pp. 349–50.
146 See ibid., pp. 351–2; Syrett, *American Waters*, chapters 5 and 6.
147 A.T. Mahan, *The Major Operations of the Navies in the American War of Independence* (Boston: Little, Brown and Co., 1913, repr. New York: Greenwood Press, 1969), p. 4.
148 As Syrett has pointed out. Syrett, *American Waters*, pp. 192–4.
149 Rodger, *Command of the Ocean*, pp. 352–3.
150 This view was also held by Lord Howe. Richmond, *The Navy in India*, pp. 139–40. See also Barnes and Owen, *Sandwich Papers*, 4:281–301, memorandum by Sandwich in defense of his administration, 31 Dec. 1781, pp. 350–5, Sandwich's notes for a parliamentary speech on 6 Mar. 1782; Rodger, *Insatiable Earl*, pp. 301–2; Syrett, *European Waters*, p. 152.
151 Ibid., pp. 152–3.
152 Richmond questions the feasibility of such an offensive plan in the face of local climatic and topographical conditions. Richmond, *The Navy in India*, pp. 18 ff., 318 ff.
153 Rodger, *Command of the Ocean*, pp. 275, 356–7.
154 Richmond, *The Navy in India*, pp. 30–1, 256.
155 Ibid., pp. 25, 126 ff.
156 Ibid., pp. 183 ff., 302, 378–9; Rodger, *Command of the Ocean*, pp. 356–7.
157 Dull, *The French Navy and American Independence*, p. 286.
158 Rodger, *Insatiable Earl*, p. 292.
159 Syrett, *European Waters*, pp. 155, 158–9, 160, 162; Rodger, *Command of the Ocean*, pp. 355–6.
160 Ibid., pp. 353–4; Rodger, *Insatiable Earl*, p. 292; Scott, *British Foreign Policy*, p. 316; Lambert, *War at Sea in the Age of Sail*, pp. 139–40.
161 Dull, *The French Navy and American Independence*, pp. 333–4.
162 Syrett, *American Waters*, pp. 222–6.

163 Rodger, *Command of the Ocean*, pp. 360–1; Syrett, *European Waters*, pp. 167–8.
164 Lambert, *War at Sea in the Age of Sail*, p. 140; Barnes and Owen, eds., *Sandwich Papers*, 3:216, Rodney to Sandwich, 31 May 1780.
165 Clausewitz, *On War*, pp. 88–9.
166 Paul Kennedy, *The Rise and Fall of the Great Powers: Economic Change and Military Conflict from 1500 to 2000* (New York: Random House, 1987), p. 117.
167 This issue is raised by Syrett in *European Waters*, p. xi.
168 Rodger, *Insatiable Earl*, pp. 271–4. See also Richmond, *The Navy in India*, p. 177; Syrett, *European Waters*, pp. 167–8. For different views, see Baugh, "Why did Britain Lose Command of the Sea?" pp. 156–7; P. Mackesy, *The War for America, 1775–1783* (London: Longmans, 1964), pp. 513–16.
169 Rodger, *Command of the Ocean*, p. 359.
170 Corbett, *Some Principles of Maritime Strategy*, p. 338.

5 The King's Friends
Loyalists in British strategy

Ricardo A. Herrera

Variously envisioned as an untapped pool of provincial auxiliaries for the Crown, to a cowed majority awaiting delivery from its Whig oppressors, and everything between, British Loyalists were a chimera, at once Britain's imagined asset and its liability.[1] Because the War for Independence was also a civil war within British America, a "struggle ... often characterised by atrocious cruelty," the significance of the Loyalists loomed large in the minds of British political and military officials. Their place in British strategies for suppressing the American rebellion and winning the war seems to have changed as often as Britain's commanders-in-chief and their hopes and plans for winning the struggle. Indeed, even within the minds of the broad mass of Loyalists, their role was uncertain, their motives diverse, and actions anything but united. Above all, they feared the disorder that would be wrought by revolution and the subsequent overturning of traditional, ordered ways. To a very large degree, therefore, the Loyalists were a screen upon which British strategists projected their hopes and fears.[2]

The best estimate of Loyalist strength is perhaps 15 to 20 percent of the white population, some 2.2 million people, bolstered by an additional 200,000 or so formerly enslaved black Americans, and the various Indian nations, whose own stories of conflicted and often shifting interests, loyalties and civil war paralleled that experienced by British Americans. Although Loyalists were scattered throughout the colonies, their population was concentrated in two broad geographic areas. The first concentration ranged northward through the southern backcountry from around Augusta, Georgia, through the "Regulator" districts of the Carolinas, into Virginia and Pennsylvania, and up through the region edging the Appalachian Mountain chain into Vermont. Most of these backcountry colonists engaged in subsistence farming with limited, even tenuous, ties to local or regional markets. Many were recent immigrants who, because of their recent arrival and settlement (some came as late as the early 1770s), maintained strong ties to the mother country and a corresponding distrust of local Whig oligarchs.[3] The second grouping, found in the more populated coastal regions of the middle colonies of Pennsylvania, New York, New Jersey and Delaware, were generally of older colonial stock, those whose families had lived in the colonies for generations.

In neither case was there economic or social common ground; Loyalists occupied all tiers of colonial society. What they did share was a broad but common fear of disorder. The Revolutionaries threatened to overturn empire, liberty and individual freedom within the security of the imperial order. Loyalists cleaved to the concept of individual liberties within the safeguards of the British constitutional order. Indeed, Loyalists "nourished the idea that the enemy were a mob led by demagogues" bent on self-aggrandizement and the usurpation of power through the overthrow of the traditional order.[4]

In the early stages of the war, British plans and support for the "King's Friends" were, to say the least, wanting. The outbreak of hostilities at Lexington and Concord in April 1775 demonstrated the unpreparedness for war of Lord North's ministry. North called for using every means at hand to crush the rebellion, but he failed to translate his words into action. He assumed that conventional military force would smash the armed resistance and restore order. Moreover, North did not understand the nature of the rebellion and its widespread support. His inability to grasp the popular nature of the struggle and the means necessary for suppressing it highlighted the political and military shifts taking place in the late eighteenth century. The problem was so great that one author even overstates the case:

> none of the great maxims of strategy applied in America. The weighing of ends and means, the magnitude of the object against the cost of achieving it, provided little guidance. For both sides the political objectives of the struggle were absolute.

Britain's inability to comprehend fully the nature of the American War of Independence constrained British strategic foresight in what was a people's war, the struggle for hearts, minds and sentiments spanning a continent. As a result, throughout the war Britain struggled mightily in trying to reconcile political ends through military means.[5]

As early as 1774, General Thomas Gage, commander-in-chief of the British army in America and Royal Governor of Massachusetts, wrote to Lord Dartmouth, secretary of state for the colonies, that while he found the loyal population wanting in energy and direction, he believed that if properly led and supported by British arms it would openly declare for the Crown. Gage's support for and inclusion of Loyalists in his plans for suppressing the Massachusetts rebels, not to mention the steadiness of the Loyalists, was, however, transitory. Left largely to their own devices, an erstwhile corps of 300 New England Loyalists in Freetown, Massachusetts, armed through Gage's offices, was scattered by its rebellious opponents in April 1775.

Gage's fleeting engagement with New England Loyalists notwithstanding, he and his successors, Generals Sir William Howe and Henry Clinton, and many of their fellow officers recognized something of the revolutionary nature of the war, but differed on how best to prosecute it. They divided along the lines of adopting the hard hand of war and a more conciliatory approach. Even within this division distinctions appeared, ranging from a complete pullout from the rebellious colonies to a more indirect approach premised upon British maritime supremacy and denying the rebels outside assistance. These conflicting opinions on the conduct of the war shed light upon the larger issue of Britain's lack of focus and the difficulty it faced in trying to reconcile strategy with the desired state of affairs it hoped to effect in America. In both political and military circles, Britain was at a loss when it came to realistic assessments of Loyalist strength, potential and commitment, and how best it might recruit and employ the King's Friends.[6]

Groping forward, Gage and the ministry looked southward, toward Pennsylvania and Virginia, where yet another scheme to raise the King's Friends foundered when rebel forces captured and imprisoned the newly commissioned leader, Lieutenant Colonel John Connolly. Deeper and more steadfast pockets of Loyalism were found in Nova Scotia, but with the rebellion centered in New England and southward, this was scant consolation. At best, Canadian Loyalists reassured British authorities of their hold on the northern provinces and allowed them to focus on the problem with the 13 colonies.[7]

Shifting its attention even further south, by July 1775 North's ministry was placing great faith in an imagined pool of loyal Americans living in the Carolinas and Georgia. The army, it recognized, was too small to crush the rebellion. Colonial governors' reports fed the ministry's hopes of an inexpensive and effective solution to compensate for the size of the British army, especially after Catherine II had rebuffed British inquiries about hiring Russian troops as auxiliaries. Agreements with German princelings finally secured the much-needed supplementary forces. That accretion notwithstanding, the Loyalist chimera continued pulling at the ministry. Dartmouth's anticipation of North Carolina governor Josiah Martin's efforts to raise his colony's Loyalists resulted in his ordering "ten thousand stand of arms and six light field pieces" for the North Carolinians in September 1775. Martin, a refugee aboard a Royal Navy warship, had written to London about the many thousands of Loyalist signatures on petitions he had received. With adequate support, Martin opined, the King's Friends, including Scottish immigrants, would rise against the rebels and even inspire a western Indian uprising in support of the Crown. Furthermore, Martin believed that the need to keep watch over slaves and disaffected indentured servants would dissipate rebel strength in the low country. Hope, not generally recognized as a principle of war, and the unsubstantiated belief in the size and commitment of Southern Loyalists continued driving the ministry's plans and playing a significant part in planning for Britain's invasion of the southern colonies.[8]

Governor Martin's missives intrigued the ministry, and by October 1775 both North and George III were advocating allocating forces to the South. Major General Howe, who had replaced Gage that month, was opposed to dispersing his limited forces. Once the operation was set in motion, however, it was all but impossible to stop. Rather than fight against it, Howe let it proceed as he planned for other, and, he hoped, more fruitful operations. Lord George Germain, who had replaced Dartmouth as colonial secretary, oversaw the enormous administrative effort behind the southern venture. Germain remained in office until 1782, and thus directed or influenced the formulation, execution and coordination of British strategy in America. His counterpart in planning for the descent on the South was Lieutenant General Sir Henry Clinton. At first they planned to invade

North Carolina with the intention of recruiting, arming and training Loyalist legions to assist regular forces in suppressing the rebellion in North Carolina and Virginia. Once done, regular forces were to withdraw and leave security in the hands of the provincial troops. So confident were Germain and Clinton that they disregarded the rebel threat and potential, preferring to project slighting views on the Revolutionaries' capabilities.[9]

The plan, as originally submitted to Howe, called for an amphibious expedition of five regiments from Ireland under Major General Charles Lord Cornwallis. Convoyed by a 50-gun ship-of-the-line and six frigates under Commodore Sir Peter Parker, the expedition was to rendezvous off North Carolina's Cape Fear River with a smaller element from Boston; together they would land from the river. Once ashore, Governor Martin and his Highlanders were to join with Henry Clinton, the expedition's commanding general. Thereafter, Clinton was left to determine where best he might direct his forces.

As it happened, the plan never came to fruition. Despite the governors of Virginia and North and South Carolina having examined it, they failed to note that the sand bar before the Cape Fear River precluded even the shallower-draft frigates from entering the river's mouth and supporting the landings. In addition, intelligence received by Germain in August 1775 indicated that rebels controlled the littoral zone extending inland as far as one hundred miles, thus confining centers of Loyalism to the Carolina backcountry. Whatever landings there would be would surely be contested, and were there to be an invasion, the landing forces would need naval gunfire support. The news turned worse. In March 1776, Lieutenant General Clinton learned at Cape Fear River that some 1,000 North Carolinian rebels administered a severe drubbing to 1,600 Loyalists at Moore's Creek Bridge in North Carolina. Armed with broadswords and 500 muskets, the Highlanders suffered severely, losing 70 killed or wounded and another 850 captured. On top of these discouraging developments came news that delays in preparing the invasion force in Ireland had pushed the landings so far back that any attempt before the spring or summer of 1776 was out of the question.[10]

Clinton was not dissuaded by these setbacks. Recognizing Britain's limited ability to project power beyond the littoral, Clinton determined to exploit British maritime strength vis-à-vis the Loyalists. The two regions that seemed most promising were the Chesapeake Bay, whose many estuaries and inlets would allow the Royal Navy to exploit its strategic mobility while simultaneously supporting ground forces and denying the region to rebel shipping. Its rich farmlands, easy access to sea lanes and geographic centrality on the eastern seaboard presented the promise of establishing a stable Loyalist region from which to launch expeditions and reassert British power while severing communications between the middle colonies from the southern colonies. The second region centered on the Savannah River, by which expeditionary forces could link up with the garrison at St. Augustine, Florida, and expand zones of British control throughout the backcountry. Both of these options came to naught because of continuing delays with Parker's squadron. Instead, British power descended on one of the least desirable locations in the south, Charleston, South Carolina.[11]

Geography was both the attraction and shortcoming of the city. Its deepwater port and rich hinterlands offered havens for the Royal Navy and for supporting Crown forces; however, Charleston was a poor location from which to expand into the backcountry pockets of Loyalism. It was too distant from the Carolina upcountry to allow easy penetration: the road network, as throughout most of the colonies, was poor, the rivers had limited navigability inland, and its situation on a peninsula bounded by estuarial rivers and malarial swamps made it easily isolated and a potential deathtrap. Clinton, however, saw an opportunity. From recent intelligence he believed that the fortifications on Sullivan's Island, guarding the approaches to Charleston Harbor, were weak and thus presented an opportunity to establish a base at which the King's Friends might concentrate. According to Clinton, his sole intention was the seizure of Sullivan's Island. It was only at the prompting of Commodore Parker and the promise of success that his plans expanded to include capture of the city.[12]

On 28 June 1776, Parker and Clinton launched their furtive attack. From the outset it displayed some of the worst characteristics of eighteenth-century British joint operations – poor planning and faulty reconnaissance compounded even poorer coordination and execution. The fort's sand and palmetto-log walls absorbed all the shot Parker's ships threw at it, as the South Carolinians responded in kind with great accuracy and telling fire. Three badly-damaged ships and nearly 200 casualties later, the expedition set off for New York, leaving Charleston for another day.[13]

Through 1775 and into the summer of 1776, the British army acted as a fire brigade, rushing hither and yon to stamp out the flames of protest and rebellion with little effect. This approach had little to recommend it; Howe's 1776 campaign, however, was meant to remedy this lack of focus. He determined to strike at rebel centers of gravity in order to demonstrate the "futility of further resistance" and destroy their army in open combat. Howe believed that crushing the Continental Army was the surest path to victory and the re-establishment of peaceful relations and colonial subordination. Furthermore, since he believed the rebellion was confined to a handful of locations, that task would not demand too much in the way of men and material. As a result, Sir William minimized the Loyalists' role in the upcoming campaign. They might be entrusted with limited defensive operations, but not in the decisive conventional struggle Howe envisioned.[14]

Despite the subordinate military role envisioned for the Loyalists by Howe, they played a major part in his plans for 1776 and the peace he hoped to conquer. Based on Governor William Tryon's reports, among others, of their strength and sympathies in the middle colonies, Howe focused that year's campaign on the conquest of New York. The city's deep-water harbor and its strategic location at the mouth of the Hudson River–Richelieu River corridor, a traditional north–south invasion route, offered excellent access to northern New England's interior and a base from which to project British power southward. Despite Tryon's claims of several thousand loyal subjects in New York, Howe was more interested in their post-war potential than in their military might. The King's Friends would be essential in the re-establishment of royal government, and in supporting it once re-established.[15]

Howe's easy victories over General George Washington in New York convinced him that peace could be had with only a bit of urging. Peaceful, but very broad and unspecific, overtures from the general and his brother and fellow peace commissioner, Vice Admiral Lord Richard Howe, earned derision from loyal and rebellious Americans alike. Loyal critics took the Howe brothers to task for the vagueness in their calls to "converse" while rebels lambasted them for asking Americans to submit to a humiliating dependence upon a monarch and Parliament that had so plainly treated them with contempt.[16]

By the summer of 1776, it was evident that Loyalists' efforts at mobilizing and organizing themselves into an effective arm of British strategy were haphazard at best, and that a leadership void existed at the juncture of Loyalist eagerness and British need. Geographic dispersion, and superior rebel organization, leadership and communications, militated against the Loyalists establishing a unified or coordinated effort from below. It was not that Gage, Howe, Clinton, North, Dartmouth or Germain failed at some point to recognize that British numbers were not enough to crush the rebellion or that the successful re-establishment of metropolitan authority was predicated upon Loyalist support; British leadership, organization and material support for the Loyalists, as well as strategic vision, clarity and energy, were all in severe want. At even the most basic level, raising provincial regiments or recruits for the regular establishment, British commanders and policy-makers fell short of the mark. Overconfidence, history and interest were the chief culprits.

North's ministry was reluctant to increase the size of the army. Expanding the army was an expensive proposition for what the ministry and army believed would be a short war, and North was reluctant to increase the tax burden on the populace. Ministry and army leadership hewed to the conviction that defeating the Continental Army with regular forces would suffice. Similar to many in the army officer corps, North believed the war would be brief and that rebel forces would be easily swept away. Events, however, told otherwise. Despite a series of easy victories in and around New York in 1776, the Continental Army survived and the rebellion continued. Confronting Washington's army was not enough. Clearly, a strategy that envisioned the contested space as something beyond the battlefield was necessary. It had to include gaining the affections, interests and security of the people in order to allow the sympathetic population to express itself and lend support to the Crown, but also, if necessary, engage in the sort of political intimidation and coercion that could negate or suppress rebel sympathies. Armed force was called for, but the size of the standing army, including German auxiliaries, was far too small to accomplish that mission. Britain needed troops capable of fighting a conventional war, but also a paramilitary arm to secure those areas beyond the reach of conventional forces. Loyalists had the potential to provide both. Enlisting, organizing, arming and supporting greater numbers of loyal Americans was thus a necessary concomitant to British success, but whether and when British strategists would realize it was the rub.

British soldiers, government ministers and Loyalists remembered the difficulties encountered with American provincial soldiers over issues of rank and precedence, pay, discipline, and the terms and limits of enlistments. Provincial troops were not new in imperial conflicts. They had figured mightily in struggles against France and Spain from the late seventeenth century onward. Indeed, British victory in America in the Seven Years' War had come from an intramural effort. The regulars' successes were predicated upon the incorporation of provincial soldiers within the war effort. Examples of this sort notwithstanding, the history of Crown and provincial military cooperation was mixed at best. Some regulars and colonials remembered their service alongside one another fondly. This view, however, was decidedly in the minority. For provincials who had served alongside regulars in the previous war, the prevailing sentiments were decidedly jaundiced, even bitter. The metropolitan view of colonial soldiers was little better. They were a weak and uncertain reed upon which to rely for any but the simplest and least taxing of missions. The officers were unlettered, jumped-up, middling and lower sorts, tradesmen and mechanics whose commissions depended on political favor. They were men with pretensions to gentility and equality with regular officers, but with none of the requisite characteristics.[17]

Historian Paul H. Smith noted that "In addition to imagined abuses and petty personal prejudices, several real objections to enlisting Loyalists into new provincial regiments were raised," particularly their lack of experience and the time it would take to train them. In this, the Loyalists were most like their rebellious brethren. Believing that the war would be short, the ministry and the army neglected serious policy deliberations about raising a provincial corps.[18]

Overconfidence, interest, prejudice and a false sense of economy combined to prevent including Loyalists in a greater military capacity until the end of 1776, when, belatedly, Howe and Germain recognized how widespread the rebellion was and how difficult it was to overwhelm the revolutionary Americans and their armies. Rather than massing his forces in preparation for a decisive contest, Howe now planned to disperse them in New England and the middle colonies. Territory, it seemed, not the destruction of the Continental Army, was his new focus. Requesting 15,000 additional soldiers, General Howe planned to seize and hold Providence, Rhode Island, with a 10,000-man force and, if practicable, to march on Boston. The 2,000-man garrison holding Rhode Island was to harass the Connecticut coast. Another 10,000-soldier expedition was slated for an advance up the Hudson against Albany. Some 5,000 soldiers were to hold New York City, while 8,000 in New Jersey threatened Philadelphia and tied down Washington's army to prevent it from reinforcing Albany. Should circumstances permit, Howe planned to continue his southern offensive into Virginia in the autumn, and if the navy could provide adequate support that winter, he would strike at South Carolina and Georgia.[19]

Proximity and pursuit dictated that Howe pursue Washington into New Jersey. Following his string of successes in New York, Howe's British and Hessian soldiers pursued the Continental Army through the Jerseys. As British forces marched deeper into New Jersey, the colony's Loyalists rose in support of the Crown. Howe believed that a counter-revolution was in the offing. In order to protect the Jersey Loyalists, he parceled his forces throughout the colony in outposts designed to extend his control over the colony while shielding the King's Friends from reprisals. Washington responded to the situation by dispatching a regiment to Monmouth in central New Jersey in November 1776. He ordered Colonel David Forman and his Additional Regiment of the Continental Line to "suppress them." Forman organized the vigilante Association of Retaliation to punish Monmouth County's Loyalists and helped drive that part of New Jersey into a "bitter civil war."[20]

In December 1776 and January 1777, Washington, ever the strategic opportunist, struck back in a series of small but important actions at Trenton and Princeton that changed the strategic equation in New Jersey. British and Hessian outposts were simply too vulnerable to attack by the Continental Army and local militia, so Howe began contracting his lines in January 1777. As Howe's lines shrank, British forces abandoned scores of Loyalists to vengeance-driven militiamen and volunteers. Left to their own devices, "Loyalists began to wonder if imperial loyalty flowed only from the bottom up, not from the top down." So angry, dejected and fearful were some Loyalists that they "changed uniforms of Loyalist green and red for Continental buff and blue."[21]

The enormous expense that would have been entailed by acceding to Howe's request for thousands of additional soldiers had troubled Germain. He feared that public support for the war might wane should taxpayers be asked to shoulder yet more debt and if more men were asked to take the king's shilling. Nearly as pressing was the apprehension that France and Spain would openly enter the war, which would decisively change the nature of the conflict. Howe, after a fashion, came to Germain's rescue, or so it seemed to Germain. Sir William's estimate of the situation in America had changed. Washington's victories in December 1776 and January 1777 at Trenton and Princeton, and the partisan war waged by militia in New Jersey, had led to Britain's virtual abandonment of that colony and its Loyalists. While the Revolutionaries' morale was waxing, all but the most obdurate of Loyalists realized the seriousness of the state of affairs. Howe's new campaign plans focused now on Philadelphia and the purportedly large numbers of Loyalists in Pennsylvania. Henceforth, Howe planned to campaign near centers of Loyalist support and look to expand from these secure bases. To do so, he proposed raising provincial militias that would supplement his core of British regulars and Hessian auxiliaries. Although the provincial regiments would certainly increase the public debt, they would not cost nearly as much as regulars, nor would they tax British manpower at home. On the surface there seemed to be a degree of concurrence; Howe would have the soldiers he needed and the ministry's concern for economy would be addressed. Yet, as Paul H. Smith pointed out, "Howe's plans to use the Loyalists and Germain's expectations were scarcely compatible."[22]

Howe did not intend the provincial soldiery as stand-ins for his regulars. Rather, they were to be used as second-line forces to garrison posts, enforce public order or execute raids so as to free the regulars for more pressing duties.

Whatever units might be raised would also serve as a limited manpower pool from which to flesh out a handful of certain regular regiments. These Loyalist proxies, however, were not replacements for regulars, nor were they proper reinforcements. Nevertheless, Germain clearly had other ideas. His concerns over maintaining public support for the war in the face of increased taxes and the looming Franco-Spanish threat led him to deny Howe's estimate of the situation and instead to argue that the Revolutionaries were weak and their morale depressed. Thus he argued himself into equating Loyalist political or moral support for their military capacity.[23]

Howe's decision to campaign near Loyalist centers of support coupled with "Germain's inability to send proper reinforcements" led to the raising of new provincial corps and to their better integration within the British force structure, including increased staff oversight with a paymaster general, a muster-master general and inspector general, along with their deputies. Heretofore, the regiments raised for service in the "Provincial Line" had been due solely to the efforts of Loyalist leaders. In the summer of 1776, Howe granted Oliver De Lancy of New York and Cortland Skinner of New Jersey authority to raise New York and New Jersey Loyalists respectively, and Robert Rogers of Rogers' Rangers fame permission to raise the Queen's Rangers. That winter Howe authorized Edmund Fanning to raise the King's American Regiment, John Bayard the King's Orange Rangers, Beverly Robinson the Loyal American Regiment and the Royal Guides and Pioneers, and Montforte Browne the Prince of Wales American Regiment. Howe issued warrants to Loyalist leaders in 1777 for even more units. William Allen of Pennsylvania received the authority to raise the Pennsylvania Loyalists and James Chalmers the Maryland Loyalists. While these regiments accounted for less than one-third of the total number of units authorized, they constituted "nearly two-thirds of all Loyalists in arms."

Impressive as Howe's actions looked, they were limited to the administrative realm. For, while Howe had refined the army's oversight of the Loyalists, he and the ministry neglected the reconsideration of policy vis-à-vis the Loyalists. Neither Howe nor Germain had given much consideration over how best to employ them or what particular abilities they might provide the army, or devoted much reflection on their strengths or weaknesses, or their character. It mimicked, disturbingly, the shallow depth of thought and reflection they had given to the nature of the Revolution.[24]

The Loyalist chimera had become a significant feature of British strategic thought in the 1777 season. Lieutenant General John Burgoyne's proposal to divide fire-breathing New England from the more moderate middle colonies by establishing control over the Lake Champlain–Hudson River corridor met little serious reflection from Germain and even less effort on his part to coordinate the movement with Howe. Burgoyne's plan committed precious regulars on an adventure premised upon the belief that Loyalists would make his route secure and that they would provide logistical support for his army. Germain and Burgoyne presumed that the large numbers of Loyalists joining Howe's efforts in Pennsylvania would allow Howe to support Burgoyne. Burgoyne, moreover, naively assumed his journey southward from Montreal would be through friendly territory. He blithely ignored the issue of raising Loyalist regiments, and later professed surprise when he received no support. Thus, in Burgoyne's mind, Loyalists shared a measure of responsibility for his army's demise at Saratoga in October 1777.[25]

Neglect within the broader arena of policy notwithstanding, Loyalists' numbers and British hope and faith in them helped drive the formulation and execution of British strategy. Between 1775 and 1781, Loyalists and Britons raised some 312 companies in 50 or so Loyalist regiments, legions or battalions. Throughout the war, over 15,000 Loyalists served at one time or another in the provincial line; 10,000 alone served between 1780 and 1781, and another 10,000 are estimated to have served in the ranks of Loyalist militias. Impressive as the numbers seem at first glance, they fell far short of British expectations. In the summer of 1776, on Howe's invasion of New York, British logisticians prepared to ship uniforms and equipment for 7,000 Loyalists. Shortly after the victories on Long Island, more equipment was sent, enough to outfit an additional 3,000. Later that year, instead of the projected 10,000 provincials, Howe had but 3,000. The ministry's "overestimation" of the Loyalists' strength and its continuing belief that the Revolution was the handiwork of a small group of radicals contributed mightily to its "chronic inability to formulate realistic policies which would secure their maximum assistance." North believed that once regulars landed, thousands of Loyalists would flock to the colors. It was that simple, or so Howe, North and others believed. Disappointed by the poor showing, the ministry gave scant attention to later pleas to raise regular provincial regiments or to correct abuses and inconsistencies in regulations. Dismayed by the ministry's inattention, dissatisfied with being relegated to militia service and mundane duties like foraging, Loyalists believed their service and patriotism was taken for granted, which was not an altogether incorrect assumption.[26]

The provincial line, like its colonial predecessors, was something of a hybrid, incorporating features of the regular army tempered to colonial circumstances. Local leaders raised their units for rank. Typically, a wealthy Loyalist petitioned the commanding general's permission to raise a regiment. Once permission was granted, the would-be commander nominated his officers, who were required to enlist certain numbers of men in return for a specified rank. Recruits signed on for two years or for the extent of the war. Non-commissioned officers received an enlistment bounty of 200 acres, while privates received 50 acres; all soldiers received pay equivalent to their regular counterparts. Similar to past practices, provincial officers ranked below their regular counterparts. Regular army benefits such as hospital care, gratuities for wounded officers and half pay when furloughed or released from active service did not figure into the provincial equation.

Burgoyne's surrender of 5,000 irreplaceable regulars and France's subsequent open entry into the war in 1778 led to a reappraisal of the place and treatment of Loyalists.[27]

Britain faced a dramatically different strategic situation in 1778 than only a year earlier. Its colonial rebellion had mushroomed into a European war that threatened to expand into an even greater European conflict with Spain and other nations chafing over British treatment of neutral shipping, as well as those looking to exploit what appeared to be British strategic overreach. Under these new circumstances, the ministry withheld regular regiments from overseas duty in order to defend the Home Islands, shifted several from America to provide West Indian garrisons, ordered the dispatch of several thousand regulars for operations against French West Indian islands, and put aside any consideration of new drafts of regulars for duty in America. Considerations of economy were abandoned in order to mobilize the Royal Navy to protect the British Isles from French invasion, extend naval coverage to the Sugar Islands, escort convoys and still maintain some form of blockade on the American coast. The time had come for a reconsideration of Loyalists' place in British strategy.[28]

Beginning in the autumn of 1778, Germain and Clinton, the commander-in-chief since May 1778, nearly simultaneously decided that it was time to accord the provincial line more equitable treatment. Cash bounties were authorized for new recruits, money set aside for hospitalization, gratuities established for wounded officers and, most importantly, provisions made for granting officers regular rank and half pay for life. As dramatic and encouraging as they were, the new policies were a case of "too little, too late." New enlistments fell below the levels attained in 1778 and failed to compensate for discharges, death and desertion. Officering the provincial line proved easy; manning it was an altogether different matter. Friendship and declarations of loyalty did not translate into a willingness to shoulder arms. Apparently, the Loyalists most willing to fight were also those most willing to command but not to serve as common soldiers. At just the moment when Loyalists were most needed to bolster the war effort, British inconsistencies, second-rate treatment and failure to understand and thus properly exploit and reward the Loyalists were having their effects.[29]

French entry into the war expanded the Loyalists' roles as it broadened Britain's strategic concerns and stretched its resources. Germain directed Clinton to launch a 5,000-man attack against the French West Indian island of St. Lucia. Following its capture, the regulars were to be dispersed as garrisons on Britain's Sugar Islands. Another 3,000 were destined for Pensacola and St. Augustine, Florida. The loss of 8,000 soldiers for operations in the Caribbean and garrisoning Florida forced Clinton to abandon Philadelphia in June 1778 and concentrate his forces in New York. Should that post prove untenable, he was enjoined to divide his forces between Rhode Island, Nova Scotia and Upper Canada. The British hold on Rhode Island, moreover, looked increasingly impracticable with the threat posed by the French navy. The outlook was decidedly gloomy, yet British leaders once more turned their attention to the southern colonies.[30]

As in 1775 and 1776, the ministry's faith in the purported strength of Southern Loyalists attracted it to the southern colonies. The June 1776 failure at Charleston had done nothing to allay that interest. Also as in 1775 and 1776, campaigning in the South wasted British strength and resources when the Whig center of gravity, the greatest part of population most committed to the Revolution, the main Continental Army and the Congress was in the North. Furthermore, neither the geography nor the demography of the region played to British strengths, and rebel forces had had the area largely to themselves for three years. War with France, domestic politics and the need to gain the favor of uncommitted Americans drove the decision to shift the seat of war southward. After having committed three years of effort to the struggle, the ministry was loath to give up; a Southern campaign appeared to address its needs. The region's proximity to the West Indies appeared advantageous in light of the focus on St. Lucia and need to protect Britain's Caribbean holdings. It would allow British forces to continue operations, albeit with larger commitments of Loyalists, while demonstrating British strength to uncommitted colonists. Finally, a Southern campaign would help beat back the domestic political opposition of Whigs in England and bolster wavering support by demonstrating the ministry's commitment to a successful conclusion of the war.[31]

Lieutenant General Sir Henry Clinton had believed in prosecuting a southern strategy until early in 1778, but thereafter he developed doubts about it following the expansion of the war and the subsequent reduction of forces available for active operations. However, believing that, if he failed to act, the government's determination to give proper attention to or even to continue the war in America would evaporate, Clinton went ahead with the Southern campaign.[32]

On 27 November 1778, over 3,000 British regulars, Hessian auxiliaries and middle-colony Loyalists, all under the command of Lieutenant Colonel Archibald Campbell, sailed for Savannah, reaching Tybee Island, southeast of the city, on 23 December. Six days later, Savannah fell. A British column out of Florida under Brigadier General Augustine Prevost helped complete the capture of the city's defenses. As was the case with so many British operations, little thought had been given to how best to follow up initial successes and subjugate Georgia. Instead, British forces launched operations that only succeeded in rousing the ire and enmity of the people. Neither Clinton nor Germain developed detailed guidance or plans on how to proceed after capturing Savannah. While loyal Americans took heart from these successes, their enthusiasm and willingness to serve depended on the security provided by British regulars. Bereft of higher guidance, however, Campbell and Prevost failed to destroy their enemies, restore peace or to establish the conditions necessary for a Loyalist rising.[33]

Taking heart from the victories in Georgia, Clinton turned his attention to South Carolina. He and Vice Admiral Marriot Arbuthnot set sail from New York with nearly 8,000 soldiers bound for Charleston on 26 December. Clinton also ordered British forces operating in the Georgia interior to converge on Charleston, which removed support and security from the Georgia Loyalists and left them at the mercy of Whig militias. Landing south of Charleston on 11 February 1780, Clinton's expedition marched inland, cut off the Charleston peninsula and laid siege to the city. With the city besieged and the British commanding the sea, it was only a matter of time before Charleston fell. On 11 May, Major General Benjamin Lincoln surrendered over 5,000 Continentals and militiamen. South Carolina appeared open to reconquest.[34]

The shock and completeness of Benjamin Lincoln's surrender seemed to end the spirit of resistance in South Carolina. Militiamen captured at Charleston were paroled home. So dispirited was the militia beyond Charleston that its leaders too surrendered. They were also paroled and returned home. South Carolinians seemed to have accepted the return of royal government; it appeared that the next step was the restoration of civil administration. The question was how quickly and how best to effect it? Shortly before embarking on the invasion of South Carolina, Clinton and Arbuthnot were jointly appointed peace commissioners. The admiral favored the restoration of royal government as quickly as possible, believing that it would transform South Carolina into a Loyalist haven and set a proper example for the other colonies to follow. In Arbuthnot's eyes, success "depended upon restraining the rapacity of British troops" operating in the backcountry and separating civil authority from its overwhelming reliance on military power. Clinton, however, was not sanguine about the prospect. He believed that military authority would have to remain supreme for an indeterminate time. The Loyalist base was simply not deep enough, or too scattered, or too cowed to assert itself without British bayonets. Furthermore, British policies in South Carolina aggravated the previously disaffected or neutral populations and rekindled the fires of unrest.[35]

Shortly after capturing Charleston, Clinton began forcing South Carolinians to choose sides by declaring their allegiance to the Crown and defending it by enlisting in the Loyalist militia. Later proclamations from Clinton required paroled South Carolinians to submit to oaths of allegiance as a precondition to having their rights restored. Sir Henry finally declared that all paroled men, except those taken at Charleston, were to be released from their paroles and have their rights restored. If, however, they failed to swear allegiance to the Crown they would henceforth be considered in rebellion. Clinton had managed to undermine his own success by forcing the people to take sides. Due to his black and white view of the insurgency and his disdain for the neutrality of the paroled, Clinton restored South Carolina to the revolutionary fold. Convinced of the completeness of his victory in South Carolina, the general turned his attention to an autumn campaign in the Chesapeake. The siren call of the King's Friends beckoned him. On 8 June 1780, Clinton departed for New York, leaving 4,000 soldiers and responsibility for pacifying the southern colonies to Lieutenant General Charles Lord Cornwallis. As far as Clinton was concerned, it was only a matter of the army showing up to bring the Carolina Loyalists forward. Once Cornwallis finished the nearly complete work in South Carolina, he was to sweep northward, establish a base of operations near Hampton, Virginia, and then advance northward to the Hudson River. Clinton belied his strategic ignorance when, in July, he wondered whether Lord Cornwallis might spare excess troops for use under himself.[36]

Cornwallis established a series of fortified posts throughout the Georgia and South Carolina backcountry in order to protect and attract Loyalists. His premise was that a well-disciplined militia stiffened by a handful of regulars would pacify and maintain order in the region. Cornwallis envisioned a two-tiered militia system with older men and those with families serving in their own locales under their own officers. These men would respond to regional threats or insurrections. The active component comprised men under 40 without families. They were to serve six-to-twelve months under officers of their choosing, be free from regular service outside of Georgia and the Carolinas, and receive pay and provisions. Major Patrick Ferguson, a talented and creative officer, was "appointed Inspector of Militia and Major Commandant of the first battalion," and charged with overseeing the recruiting, organizing and training of the militia. Ferguson, however, was poorly suited to the task. More interested in commanding than in his other duties, Ferguson's accomplishments as inspector of militia were uneven. While he organized about 1,500 men into eight battalions around Ninety-Six, South Carolina, he did little in the way of inspecting training or recruitment, or building up the Loyalist militia in such key locations as Camden, Cheraw or Georgetown, South Carolina. Ferguson's mixed attainments were compounded by Cornwallis' inability to find field-grade officers to command the Loyalist militia battalions. Those most qualified were already fighting, had fought or had emigrated.[37]

The war assumed an especially vicious character in the Carolinas, which experienced their own civil war within the larger, imperial civil war. Units like Lieutenant Colonel Banastre Tarleton's Loyalist British Legion pillaged and plundered the Loyalists, Whigs and neutrals without distinction or concern. Forced to choose between the undemanding but weak Revolutionary government and the oppressive and increasingly violent British occupation, most Carolinians chose the former. Neither Clinton nor Cornwallis had the foresight or sensitivity to determine how best to steer between the shoals of revolutionary, neutral and loyal interests, and between leniency and harshness. Instead, British leaders chose to view the conflict in black and white instead of the shades of gray inherent in insurgencies and counterinsurgencies.[38]

North Carolina Loyalists struck while Cornwallis was planning for his move into the colony. The news was not good. At Ramseur's Mill, North Carolina, some 400 mounted, Whig militiamen under Colonel Francis Locke crushed Colonel John Moore's 1,300 indifferently armed and poorly disciplined Loyalists on 20 June. In one battle, North Carolina Loyalism had been extirpated. Other battles followed, and in each case the rebels had taken the initiative. Cornwallis realized that the situation he had inherited from Clinton no longer existed. He believed his only course of action was "immediately launching a bold offensive into North Carolina." It seemed to him that only this aggressiveness could save Georgia and South Carolina and enable him to take the reconquest to the Chesapeake. Leaving scattered posts throughout the Georgia and South Carolina backcountry, Cornwallis advanced northward. At Camden, South Carolina, he destroyed the Continental Army under the command of Major General Horatio Gates, the hero of Saratoga. It looked to Cornwallis as though he had begun to reverse British fortunes. It did not, however, last long. Within a fortnight of his victory, Cornwallis had already begun fearing that the Loyalist militia was unable to sustain itself, much less approach British feats of arms. In desperation, he ordered the executions of men who enlisted in Loyalist militias only to desert to the enemy.[39]

Cornwallis marched into North Carolina in order to cut off South Carolinian rebels from their sources of supply. He did not believe that his Loyalists would be able to pacify South Carolina if the rebels were well supplied. North Carolina, however, turned out to be a hornets' nest. The glowing reports from Loyalist leaders were exaggerations that fed a British appetite hungry for good or at least promising news. Rather than retire to South Carolina to pacify the province, Cornwallis focused on conducting combat operations in North Carolina. He was convinced that without victory in North Carolina there would be no peace in the South.[40]

Advancing northward, British forces occupied Charlotte, North Carolina, on 25 September 1780. The British advance left a vacuum in South Carolina that Loyalist garrisons manning backcountry posts were unable to fill. This demonstrated a fatal flaw in Britain's southern strategy: the Loyalists could not play the role the British plan dictated. Revolutionary militias attacked their lines of communication and all but reclaimed the countryside. Moreover, partisans had begun harassing Cornwallis' army and its lines of communication. Charlotte, in the meantime, had proven a poor prize. It held no supplies and it was a hotbed of rebellion. Unable to advance or forage, Cornwallis awaited resupply from stores at Camden. As he waited, Major Ferguson and his Loyalist militiamen advanced northward along the western border of the Carolinas. He had convinced Cornwallis of his men's dependability and his own command of the situation. Operating beyond the zone of British influence, Ferguson and his 1,000 Loyalists made a tempting target for Revolutionary militiamen from over the Appalachian Mountains in present-day Tennessee and Kentucky. On 7 October 1780, an equally sized force attacked Ferguson, ensconced atop Kings Mountain in South Carolina, and destroyed the young Scot and his provincials. The loss of so many men at Kings Mountain, the risings in the backcountry, and Cornwallis' inability to project and restore British power beyond the range of his muskets forced him to retreat to Winnsboro, South Carolina. Before he could think of continuing with the offensive, Cornwallis had first to put South Carolina into order.[41]

By the time Cornwallis began his march anew on 7 January 1781, the situation in South Carolina had taken a turn for the worse. Major General Nathanael Greene had replaced Horatio Gates as commander of the Continentals' Southern Department. With him was a skilled backwoodsman and gifted commander, Brigadier General Daniel Morgan. Cornwallis divided his army, larger since having received reinforcements under Major General Alexander Leslie, in order to pursue and destroy Morgan's "Flying Army," while shadowing the main rebel force under Greene. Lieutenant Colonel Tarleton, Cornwallis' most skilled leader of provincials, drove his Legion after Morgan. Morgan brought him to battle on ground of his own choosing – Cowpens, South Carolina, on 17 January 1781, where he defeated Tarleton and killed or captured nearly 1,000 British Loyalist and regular troops. The victory was a much-needed tonic for the revolutionary cause. It also forced Cornwallis to pursue his enemy in order to reverse the humiliation. Greene drew Cornwallis on toward Virginia in a race for the Dan River, dividing North Carolina from Virginia.[42]

Cornwallis doggedly pursued Greene, even burning his own baggage train in order to increase his army's rate of advance. Greene marched northward; his Continentals and the militia denuded the route of march and intimidated would-be Loyalists into quiescence. As Cornwallis pursued, he left a strategic vacuum that the Loyalists could not fill. Rebel militia rose in the absence of British regulars and enforced the Whig political order. Greene allowed Cornwallis to catch him at Guilford Courthouse, North Carolina, on 15 March. Although Cornwallis prevailed, it was a victory he could ill afford. Greene was able to retreat, maintain the discipline of his army, and return to South Carolina where he waged a skillful and unremitting war against the British occupation. Cornwallis instead marched his army to Wilmington on the North Carolina coast. As he marched, Cornwallis was surrendering North Carolina to his enemy.[43]

Following a two-week stay in Wilmington, Cornwallis informed Clinton that he intended marching to Virginia. In a letter to Germain, he summarized the mortal failure of Britain's southern strategy:

> our experience has shewn that their [Loyalists] numbers are not so great as had been represented and that their friendship was only passive; For we have received little assistance from them since our arrival ... and altho' I gave the strongest and most publick assurances that ... I should return to the upper Country, not above two hundred have been prevailed upon to follow us either as Provincials or Militia.

According to Cornwallis, one of the principal reasons for the "Winter's Campaign" was the "hopes that our friends in North Carolina ... would make good their promises of assembling and taking an Active part with us, in endeavoring to reestablish His Majesty's Government."[44]

In the end, Cornwallis gave up on the Southern campaign and on the Loyalists upon whom so much was expected. Disingenuously, he placed blame for his losses upon the King's Friends. He intimated that they were to have constituted an active part of the army suitable for extended, offensive field operations when, in fact, they were to have been a defensive force pacifying the country and manning strategic posts.[45]

British military and political leadership had never fully understood the nature of the American Revolution. Because they insisted that it was the work of a handful of dedicated radicals, they failed to see the deeper roots and broader appeal of the revolutionary cause. They also neglected serious consideration of Loyalists' strengths, weaknesses and basic motivations. British leaders had assumed until 1778 that ending the rebellion was a purely military affair and one that need not involve provincial forces. From the outset, the Loyalists were often ignored or treated dismissively. Despite slighting treatment, Loyalists volunteered and ably served the Crown. It was not until France entered the war in

1778 that the ministry and the army finally paid serious attention to recruiting, training and retaining a provincial line on par with the regular establishment. As British resources became increasingly strained, the Loyalists' place in British strategy grew; the greater the stress on British resources, the more hope that was placed on the Loyalists. Far too late in the war, Britain turned to the Loyalists, and when Britain did turn to them it expected too much of them.[46]

Notes

1 For the purposes of this chapter, Whig is used synonymously with Patriot.
2 Stephen Conway, "Britain and the Revolutionary Crisis, 1763–1791," in P.J. Marshall, ed., *The Oxford History of the British Empire: The Eighteenth Century* (New York: Oxford University Press, 1998), vol. 2, pp. 339–40; Paul H. Smith, *Loyalists and Redcoats: A Study in British Revolutionary Policy* (Chapel Hill: University of North Carolina Press for the Institute of Early American History and Culture, 1964), p. ix; John Derry, "Government Policy and the American Crisis, 1760–1776," in H.T. Dickinson, ed., *Britain and the American Revolution* (London: Longman, 1998), p. 59; William H. Nelson, *The American Tory* (London: Oxford University Press, 1961; repr., Boston: Northeastern University Press, 1992), p. 1; Piers Mackesy, *The War for America, 1775–1783* (Cambridge: Harvard University Press, 1964; repr., Lincoln: University of Nebraska Press, 1993), p. 4.
3 See Robert V. Wells, "Population and Family in Early America," in Jack P. Greene and J.R. Pole, eds., *The Blackwell Encyclopedia of the American Revolution* (Cambridge: Blackwell, 1991), pp. 40–3; Nelson, *The American Tory*, pp. 87–9; Colin G. Calloway, *The American Revolution in Indian Country: Crisis and Diversity in Native American Communities* (Cambridge: Cambridge University Press, 1995), pp. 29–42; Harry M. Ward, *The War for Independence and the Transformation of American Society* (London: UCL Press, 1999), pp. 193–209; Ann Condon, "Marching to a Different Drummer: The Political Philosophy of the American Loyalists," in Esmond Wright, ed., *Red, White and True Blue: The Loyalists in the Revolution* (New York: AMS Press, 1976), pp. 2–5; James E. Bradley, "The British Public and the American Revolution: Ideology, Interest and Opinion," in H.T. Dickinson, ed., *Britain and the American Revolution* (London: Longman, 1998), p. 139; N.E.H. Hull, Peter C. Hoffer and Steven L. Allen, "Choosing Sides: A Quantitative Study of the Personality Determinants of Loyalist and Revolutionary Political Affiliation in New York," *The Journal of American History*, 65, no. 2 (Sept. 1978), pp. 344–66; Ruth M. Keesey, "Loyalism in Bergen County, New Jersey," *The William and Mary Quarterly*, 3rd ser., 18, no. 4 (Oct. 1961), pp. 558–76; see also Albert H. Tillson, Jr., "The Localist Roots of Backcountry Loyalism: An Examination of Popular Political Culture in Virginia's New River Valley," *The Journal of Southern History*, 54, no. 3 (Aug. 1988), pp. 387–404 for an examination of Loyalism and localism.
4 Ibid.; Mackesy, *War for America*, p. 31; Smith, *Loyalists and Redcoats*, p. 10; Ward, *War for Independence*, pp. 35–8; Bruce G. Merritt, "Loyalism and Social Conflict in Revolutionary Deerfield, Massachusetts," *The Journal of American History*, 57, no. 2 (Sept. 1970), pp. 277–89; Keesey, "Loyalism in Bergen County," pp. 558–76; see also Keith Mason, "Localism, Evangelicalism, and Loyalism: The Sources of Discontent in the Revolutionary Chesapeake," *The Journal of Southern History*, 56, no. 1 (Feb. 1990), pp. 23–54.
5 Ian Christie, "The Imperial Dimension: British Ministerial Perspectives During the American Revolutionary Crisis, 1763–1776," in Esmond Wright, ed., *Red, White and True Blue: The Loyalists in the Revolution* (New York: AMS Press, 1976), pp. 154–8; H.T. Dickinson, introduction to H.T. Dickinson, ed., *Britain and the American*

Revolution (London: Longman, 1998), pp. 13–17; Stephen Conway, "British Governments and the Conduct of the War," in ibid., p. 159; Smith, *Loyalists and Redcoats*, p. 10; Mackesy, *War for America*, pp. 32–3; Paul David Nelson, "British Conduct of the American Revolutionary War: A Review of Interpretations," *The Journal of American History*, 65, no. 3 (Dec. 1978), pp. 623–53; Eric Robson, "The Expedition to the Southern Colonies, 1775–1776," *The English Historical Review*, 66, no. 261 (Oct. 1951), p. 535. See also Matthew H. Spring, *With Zeal and With Bayonets Only: The British Army on Campaign in North America, 1775–1783* (Norman: University of Oklahoma Press, 2008) for a recent tactical and operational analysis on the close connection between military success and political victory.

6 Smith, *Loyalists and Redcoats*, pp. 12–18; Stephen Conway, "To Subdue America: British Army Officers and the Conduct of the Revolutionary War," *The William and Mary Quarterly*, 3rd ser., 43, no. 3 (July 1986), p. 382; Ira D. Gruber, "Lord Howe and Lord George Germain, British Politics and the Winning of American Independence," *The William and Mary Quarterly*, 3rd ser., 22, no. 2 (Apr. 1965), pp. 225–43.

7 Smith, *Loyalists and Redcoats*, pp. 12–18; Conway, "To Subdue America," p. 382; Gruber, "Lord Howe and Lord George Germain," pp. 225–43.

8 Smith, *Loyalists and Redcoats*, pp. 18–23; Mackesy, *War for America*, p. 43; Conway, "British Governments," pp. 158–9; Robson, "Expedition to the Southern Colonies," p. 538.

9 Smith, *Loyalists and Redcoats*, pp. 21–4; Mackesy, *War for America*, pp. 43–4, 62–4; Roger Kaplan, "The Hidden War: British Intelligence Operations During the American Revolution," *The William and Mary Quarterly*, 3rd ser., 47, no. 1 (Jan. 1990), pp. 118–19.

10 Smith, *Loyalists and Redcoats*, pp. 24–5; Mackesy, *War for America*, pp. 43–5, 56, 61–3; Don Higginbotham, *The War of American Independence: Military Attitudes, Policies, and Practice, 1763–1789* (New York: Macmillan, 1971), pp. 136–7; David K. Wilson, *The Southern Strategy: Britain's Conquest of South Carolina and Georgia, 1775–1780* (Columbia: University of South Carolina Press, 2005), pp. 19–35; Michael A. Capps and Steven A. Davis, *Moores Creek National Battlefield: An Administrative History*, National Park Service, Department of the Interior, June 1999, www.nps.gov/history/history/online_books/mocr/adhi_1.htm (accessed 22 Jan. 2007); John Ferling, *Almost a Miracle: The American Victory in the War of Independence* (Oxford: Oxford University Press, 2007), pp. 126–7.

11 Smith, *Loyalists and Redcoats*, pp. 25–6; Wilson, *Southern Strategy*, pp. 36–40.

12 Mackesy, *War for America*, p. 86; Robson, "Expedition to the Southern Colonies," p. 554; Smith, *Loyalists and Redcoats*, pp. 28–9; Wilson, *Southern Strategy*, pp. 36–40; Ferling, *Almost a Miracle*, pp. 128–9.

13 Wilson, *Southern Strategy*, pp. 38, 45, 51–53; Smith, *Loyalists and Redcoats*, p. 29.

14 Smith, *Loyalists and Redcoats*, pp. 36–40.

15 Ira D. Gruber, *The Howe Brothers and the American Revolution* (Chapel Hill: University of North Carolina Press for the Institute of Early American History and Culture, 1972), pp. 83–4; Ferling, *Almost a Miracle*, pp. 410–41.

16 Gruber, *Howe Brothers*, pp. 124–6.

17 Smith, *Loyalists and Redcoats*, pp. 32–33; Higginbotham, *War of American Independence*, pp. 137–9; John W. Shy, *Toward Lexington: The Role of the British Army in the Coming of the American Revolution* (Princeton: Princeton University Press, 1965), pp. vii–viii; Stephen Brumwell, *Redcoats: The British Soldier and War in the Americas, 1755–1763* (Cambridge: Cambridge University Press, 2001), p. 76; see also Fred Anderson, *A People's Army: Massachusetts Soldiers and Society in the Seven Years' War* (Chapel Hill: University of North Carolina Press for the Institute of Early American History and Culture, 1984); Fred Anderson, *Crucible of War: The Seven Years' War and the Fate of Empire in British North America, 1754–1766*

(New York: Knopf, 2000); and James Titus, *The Old Dominion at War: Society, Politics and Warfare in Late Colonial Virginia* (Columbia: University of South Carolina Press, 1991).
18 Ward, *War for Independence*, pp. 40–1; Smith, *Loyalists and Redcoats*, pp. 34–6.
19 Gruber, *Howe Brothers*, pp. 174–5, 199–200; Smith, *Loyalists and Redcoats*, pp. 44–5.
20 David Hackett Fischer, *Washington's Crossing* (New York: Oxford University Press, 2004), pp. 171–2; Francis B. Heitman, *Historical Register of Officers of the Continental Army during the War of the Revolution, April, 1775 to December, 1783*, rev. & enl. (Washington, DC: Rare Book Shop, 1914), p. 24.
21 Fischer, *Washington's Crossing*, pp. 346–50.
22 Gruber, *Howe Brothers*, pp. 165, 174–5; Smith, *Loyalists and Redcoats*, pp. 45–6.
23 Smith, *Loyalists and Redcoats*, pp. 46–7.
24 Ibid., pp. 48–50, 59; Ferling, *Almost a Miracle*, pp. 415–17.
25 Smith, *Loyalists and Redcoats*, pp. 50–6; Mackesy, *War for America*, pp. 134–5.
26 Smith, *Loyalists and Redcoats*, pp. 60–2; Ward, *War for Independence*, pp. 40–3.
27 Smith, *Loyalists and Redcoats*, pp. 63–4.
28 David M. Griffiths, "An American Contribution to the Armed Neutrality of 1780," *Russian Review*, 30, no. 2 (Apr. 1971), pp. 164–72; Smith, *Loyalists and Redcoats*, p. 72; see also David Syrett, *The Royal Navy in European Waters During the American Revolutionary War* (Columbia: University of South Carolina Press, 1998); Andrew Jackson O'Shaugnessy, *An Empire Divided: The American Revolution and the British Caribbean* (Philadelphia: University of Pennsylvania Press, 2000).
29 Smith, *Loyalists and Redcoats*, pp. 73–8.
30 Ibid., pp. 85–6.
31 Ibid., pp. 86–8; Higginbotham, *War of American Independence*, pp. 353–4; Wilson, *Southern Strategy*, pp. 2–4.
32 Smith, *Loyalists and Redcoats*, pp. 90–4; Ferling, *Almost a Miracle*, pp. 409–11; Robert K. Middlekauff, *The Glorious Cause: The American Revolution, 1763–1789*, rev. and exp. (New York: Oxford University Press, 2005), pp. 440–1.
33 Smith, *Loyalists and Redcoats*, pp. 100–2; Higginbotham, *War of American Independence*, pp. 354–5; Conway, "British Governments and the Conduct of the War," pp. 164–6.
34 Smith, *Loyalists and Redcoats*, pp. 126–7; Higginbotham, *War of American Independence*, pp. 356–7.
35 Smith, *Loyalists and Redcoats*, pp. 128–30; Mackesy, *War for America*, pp. 341–2; K.G. Davies, "The Restoration of Civil Government by the British in the War of Independence," in Esmond Wright, ed., *Red, White and True Blue: The Loyalists in the Revolution* (New York: AMS Press, 1976), pp. 111–33.
36 Smith, *Loyalists and Redcoats*, pp. 130–5.
37 Ibid., pp. 136–40; Mackesy, *War for America*, pp. 342–4.
38 Smith, *Loyalists and Redcoats*, pp. 140–2; Higginbotham, *War of American Independence*, pp. 36–61; Mackesy, *War for America*, pp. 344–5; see also John Shy, *A People Numerous and Armed: Reflections on the Military Struggle for American Independence* (New York: Oxford University Press, 1976); Wayne E. Lee, *Crowds and Soldiers in Revolutionary North Carolina: The Culture of Violence in Riot and War* (Gainesville: University Press of Florida, 2001).
39 Smith, *Loyalists and Redcoats*, pp. 142–6.
40 Ibid., pp. 155–6.
41 Ibid., pp. 147–9; Ferling, *Almost a Miracle*, pp. 459–62.
42 Smith, *Loyalists and Redcoats*, pp. 149–51; Higginbotham, *War of American Independence*, pp. 367–8.
43 Smith, *Loyalists and Redcoats*, pp. 151–3.

44 Cornwallis to Germain, 18 Apr. 1781, in Benjamin Franklin Stevens, *The Campaign in Virginia: An Exact Reprint of Six Rare Pamphlets on the Clinton–Cornwallis Controversy....* (London: B.F. Stevens, 1888), vol. 1, p. 362, quoted in Smith, *Loyalists and Redcoats*, p. 155.
45 Smith, *Loyalists and Redcoats*, pp. 155–6.
46 Ibid., pp. 168–74.

6 Ambivalent allies
Strategy and the Native Americans

Karim M. Tiro[1]

Introduction

Lieutenant General John Burgoyne, explaining what he termed the "perplexities" of "the alliance" of German, Canadian, British, Loyalist and Indian troops he led, singled out the Natives Americans as "liable to suspicion of treachery." He was not alone in this feeling. Although Indian allies were sometimes praised by those whom they served, they were also often described as cowardly, brutal, undisciplined and capricious. Comments of this nature, uttered by persons who should have been sympathetic to the Indians, testify to Europeans' failure to understand Indian ways of war or the motives that lay behind Native American participation in the war. Unfortunately, in considering Indian participation in the American War of Independence, historians have generally followed these assessments – or, worse still, the propagandistic debates surrounding the employment of Native American allies and the sensationalized reports of their actions. Indians have thus been afforded insufficient historical consideration or appreciation. This chapter surveys the Indians' patterns of involvement in the war. Although varied, Native American actions were sufficiently consistent to allow us to make some generalizations about their objectives and strategies.[2]

In the American Revolution, Native American nations shared the primary objectives of retaining their autonomy and their land. Because the War of Independence on the frontier was itself a war of territorial expansion, it became for the Indians an "anticolonial war of liberation," a "War of Independence," in the words of historian Colin Calloway.[3] Considerations of trade and supply were decidedly secondary, although Native Americans could hardly ignore their need for ammunition, guns, tools, textiles and other items they did not manufacture themselves. However, outright mercenary considerations proved crucial primarily where Britain or the North American colonists had real difficulty meeting even minimal demands. Although all Indian communities encouraged both the British and Americans (or Spanish) to bid high and often for their help, goods determined loyalty only where the territorial threat posed by settlers had yet to materialize and where combat was more limited, such as the western Great Lakes region and the Mississippi Valley.[4]

As a strategy to protect their lands and secure supplies, Native Americans entered into limited alliances with either the British or the Americans. In general,

Indians in the American Revolution did not act autonomously, but neither did they follow orders they deemed contrary to their interests. Native Americans dispensed assistance of various kinds in careful doses according to their particular situation. With regard to the Iroquois during the colonial period, historian Jon Parmenter has argued that the Indians' participation as allies in colonial wars should not be understood as evidence of their subordination, but rather as one of their many creative adaptations to the colonial environment. Alliance yielded supplies, intelligence, an outlet for warriors' military ambitions, leverage to affect the war's prosecution, a burnished reputation for military prowess and captives for ritual use or population augmentation. Indians approached the American Revolution sensing its possibilities in these terms, and their participation reflected these aims, which reinforced their larger goal of independence.[5]

Linguistically and culturally diverse, and proudly autonomous, Native Americans had little reason to unify in support of the Crown or the rebels. Neither Britain nor the United States demonstrated the ability to win the war at any point during its prosecution, and the Indians did not have the collective power to determine the outcome. Thus, the glib observation that tribal divisions among the Indians worked to their detriment is inaccurate here. Each tribe naturally stood in a slightly different position vis-à-vis the British and the Patriots in terms of strength and security. For most, it was clear that the British offered a measure of protection against the openly expansionist colonists, as well as superior access to goods. This predisposition toward Britain was, however, tempered by experience. As allies, protectors and trade partners of indigenous peoples, the British never inspired as much confidence as the French had in earlier days. Southern Indians in particular noted Britain's role in promoting the long-running conflict between the Creeks and Choctaws. On the other hand, the colonists' sheer numbers made Native Americans fear invasion of their territory. Thus, allegiances fluctuated according to events, and tribes in greater proximity to Patriot settlements were more likely to provide the rebels with intelligence or active assistance.

Adding to the complexity of the situation was the fact that decision-making took place at the village level. There, peace and war chiefs competed vigorously to recruit support from among their friends and kinfolk. Internal village political divisions had been exacerbated over the course of the colonial period by warfare, disease, migration and missionary activity. Decentralization and factionalism did not necessarily disable strategic planning. Shared values, kinship connections and structural considerations dictated that many villages ultimately identified similar interests and pursued similar policies. By the Revolutionary era, political divisiveness had abated somewhat as Native Americans sorted themselves into different villages where politics might proceed less acrimoniously. Villages of like-mind and similarly situated peoples formed loose confederations. Even still, they did not necessarily reach the same decisions all the time, let alone simultaneously. As a result, important fissures opened and closed regularly among the constituent villages and factions of tribes like the Shawnees and confederacies like the Creek, Cherokee and Iroquois. On the one hand, the resolute localism of

Native Americans' politics cannot be ignored; nor, on the other, should particularism obscure the underlying coherence of their actions.[6]

During the Revolution, Indians rarely consented to attack Indian targets, especially when loss of Native American lives would likely ensue. This restraint illuminates ethnic confederate identities such as Choctaw or Iroquois, and even a broader emerging Indian identity.[7] Native Americans correctly understood the Revolution as a Euro-American war in which territorial expansion was the key objective of the tens of thousands of backcountry Patriots who fought hard but were virtually untouched by British taxation and expressed limited interest in republican ideology. According to legal scholar John Wunder, Native Americans heard in the Declaration of Independence, with its histrionic condemnation of Indians, "a cruel myth and a dire geopolitical statement of purpose."[8] For Indians, the Revolution was a distinct phase in a larger struggle for control of the trans-Appalachian West that lasted from the outbreak of the Seven Years' War until the death of the great Shawnee chief Tecumseh in the battle of the Thames in October 1813.

Militarily, the impact of Indians on the American Revolution was out of proportion with the relatively small number of participants. As Patriot trader-agent George Galphin observed, "Thirty or forty straggling Indians made the Greatest part of Georgia run."[9] Most Native American men had a thorough knowledge of regional topography and had cultivated hunting and fighting skills from an early age. Thus, Indians were sought by both sides as scouts, spies and trackers. They distinguished themselves in irregular combat operations as well. Confident in their own capabilities, they did not defer to white commanders, and exercised their operational independence with regard to target selection and timing. As befitted small-scale societies – and particularly ones still being wracked by imported diseases – attackers could accept few casualties. Especially with smallpox afoot, they were not inclined to linger among the soldiery in anticipation of further engagements. Their contributions reflected what historian Wayne Lee has identified as the "cutting off" style of warfare, in which a select segment of the enemy was targeted for killing while the attackers minimized their vulnerability to retaliation. Tactically, ambush and surprise were thus crucial elements of what had already been described pejoratively as "the skulking way of war." Seeking maximum impact consistent with the preservation of their own lives, Native Americans selected dispersed targets, and sometimes unarmed ones. Indian raiders allied with the British thus kept the entire backcountry in a state of alarm during much of the war, complicating recruitment by Patriots and stalling or even reversing colonial settlement in some areas.[10]

By entering into limited alliances with one or the other of the war's antagonists, the Indians were not able to permanently halt or push back the bounds of Euro-American settlement, or to prevent damaging – and sometimes devastating – raids on their own villages. However, many Indian nations were able to gain some temporary material and political considerations, as well as intelligence, captives and coups. Most survived the Revolution with their military capabilities largely intact. This enabled them to thwart the attempt of the United States to consolidate its claims to much of the territory relinquished by Britain at the Treaty of Paris in 1783. Native American military resistance forced political concessions on the new nation and delayed trans-Appalachian U.S. expansion for more than a decade, until the battle of Fallen Timbers and the Treaty of Greenville in 1794–95.

Decay of the colonial order

The American War of Independence presented the Indian tribes of eastern North America with a choice between two unattractive contenders to power. The events of the last ten to fifteen years had clearly demonstrated both the colonists' expansionist desires and the limited nature of British goodwill. After the Seven Years' War, many Native Americans lamented the departure of France, whose empire had been dependent economically upon Indians' furs, dependent strategically upon Indians' martial skills and interested ideologically in the conversion of the Indians' souls. They did not appreciate all French overtures equally, but on the whole the French were relatively circumspect in their intrusiveness. The British, by contrast, were more interested in the Indians' land and were not reliant upon them for defense. Thus, the Native Americans' demands could be more easily refused. And that is precisely what the departure of France enabled Britain to do, or so it seemed to the commander-in-chief in America, installed in 1761, Sir Jeffery Amherst. Amherst broke with French precedent by abruptly curtailing the supply of ammunition to the interior tribes – thereby harming Indian hunters – and occupying forts in the interior – thereby threatening Indian communities strategically. These and other unilateral actions contributed to the outbreak of Pontiac's War (1763–66) across the Upper Ohio Valley and Great Lakes regions.[11] Britain recalled Amherst and reopened the flow of goods, but they remained culturally tone-deaf and miserly compared to the French. The Indians understood that British openhandedness was mostly a function of their own power to create costly disruptions.

Colonial settlers had welcomed the French defeat, and they celebrated by striking out for trans-Appalachian lands. The British attempt to prohibit this expansion even temporarily, most notably through the Proclamation of 1763, failed miserably. Indeed, not only did the Proclamation Line fail to stop trespasses, the mere attempt alienated settlers and speculators, and contributed to the crisis of imperial authority.[12] As a result of this failure, the formal boundaries of Indian country were consistently revised westward during the 1760s. In various treaties, Native Americans accepted payment for lands that they were unable or simply unwilling to defend against colonists, and some of which had already been settled illegally. At the Treaty of Fort Stanwix in 1768, the British Superintendent of Indian Affairs for the Northern Department, Sir William Johnson, negotiated a new boundary in which the Six Nations, or Iroquois Confederacy, preserved much of their territory in present-day central and western New York, in large part by ceding claims to extensive territories south of the Susquehanna and Ohio Rivers – territories that were occupied by other tribes. The Ohio River boundary between the colonies and Indian country would be disputed for more than two decades to come, turning Kentucky into a crucible of conflict. That same year, at Hard Labor, South Carolina, Johnson's Southern Department counterpart, John Stuart, negotiated a new boundary with other tribes. This line was less draconian in its effects on Indian peoples, but it did not hold. Needful of goods and pressured by settlers swarming across the boundary, Indians continued to part with more lands. In the 1770 Treaty of Lochabar, the Cherokee ceded lands in Virginia, West Virginia, Tennessee and Kentucky. Georgia made inroads into Creek and Cherokee country with its "New Purchase" in 1773. Indeed, the 14,000 Creeks, whose Lower Towns were feeling the press of settler colonialism most directly, called Georgians *Ecunnaunuxulgee*, which translated as "People greedily grasping after the lands of the red people." In the 1775 Treaty of Sycamore Shoals, Cherokee headmen signed away 27,000 square miles in Kentucky, Virginia and Tennessee to private speculators.[13] By 1774, the number of colonists beyond the Appalachians approached 50,000. Although the Indians still outnumbered them there, the colonial population had swelled beyond two million, whereas the total indigenous population east of the Mississippi was probably one-eighth that.

The aggressive spread of colonial settlement made it easier for Native Americans to develop a modicum of unity across the lines of tribal identity. The epicenter of pan-Indian organizing was the Upper Ohio Valley, among the roughly 5,800 Shawnees and Delawares. Not coincidentally, these nations had been at the center of Pontiac's War and had been the tribes most ill-served by the Treaty of Fort Stanwix. Their emissaries received a sympathetic hearing among southern tribes, who shared their concern over the fate of their common Kentucky hunting grounds. At a summer 1770 Indian gathering on the Scioto River in the Ohio country, delegates from northern and southern nations alike declared peace with one another. Diplomatically, this was quite a coup. However, the gesture of solidarity fell well short of making them capable of effective, coordinated military or political action in the war to come.[14]

Lord Dunmore's War in western Virginia in 1774 was the most dramatic example of frontier tension – and of the limits of intertribal unity. Virginians massacred Indians, provoking a brief, bitter conflict. The Shawnees asked for, but did not receive, the military support of their Delaware, Miami or Seneca neighbors, who were persuaded by the British and Iroquois that their interests lay in remaining neutral, not widening the conflict.[15] The Shawnees were nominally defeated in October at Point Pleasant and forced to cede their claims to Kentucky, thereby fulfilling the Virginians' aims. Many Shawnees understandably welcomed the American War of Independence as an opportunity to renew the border war, especially since its outbreak pre-empted the planned negotiations for a permanent peace settlement.[16] Most Indian nations, however, mirrored the earlier caution of the Shawnees' neighbors. They articulated a desire to remain neutral in a conflict where they saw much to lose and little to gain.

Fragile neutrality, 1775–76

Rival European empires had long vied for Indian support, as did individual English colonies, and the Native Americans had made the most of the opportunities presented by playing colonial competitors off one another. Premature commitment was never desirable, and by the time of the American War of Independence, the Indians were warier than usual since the very nature of the rift between colonists and mother country appeared somewhat opaque. The earlier colonial wars had pitted European empires against one another, but never divided one against itself. A British official lobbying a Chickasaw chief complained "I had ... the greatest difficulty to make him comprehend that [the Patriots] had forfeited their right to the protection of the Great King and the British nation by their apostasy and rebellion." The Oneida council observed that "the present situation of you two brothers is new and strange to us." The Indians nevertheless took this as an opportunity to air grievances in the hopes that the looming conflict might conduce to their resolution. Not surprisingly, some of the complaints involved land deals.[17] Another disincentive to hasty alignment was the flow of gifts into Indian country that rose commensurately with the tensions between Britain and its colonies. As both the rebels and the imperial government curried favor with the Indians, the tribes that benefitted from such blandishments were induced to prolong the courtship. American commissioner Tench Tilghman complained that "it was plain ... that the Indians understand their game, which is to play into both hands." British agent David Taitt likewise observed that the Creeks by and large "wish[ed] to enjoy the advantages of a neutrality by being paid from both parties."[18]

Adopting a posture of neutrality also papered over internal divisions that existed within most tribes. Younger warriors were relatively eager to seize opportunities to go to war to demonstrate their prowess and establish their masculine identities. Moreover, since the warriors were the ones who used hunting grounds, and since game populations declined as colonial settlement approached, they had a more expansive definition of territory worthy of defense. By contrast, older, peacetime chiefs generally counseled patience. Since these chiefs maintained their status through the redistribution of goods obtained through diplomatic channels and at treaty gatherings, they inclined toward peace and lots of meetings. The goods were particularly important because the peace chiefs lacked the authority to coerce the warriors to abide by their judgments. However, the peace chiefs could usually count on the support of the women, who also wielded significant influence over whether or not the nation went to war. Women's relative reluctance to support war was rooted in several roles they played. As full-time residents of villages and practitioners of a land-intensive horticulture, women's activities were less sensitive to settler encroachment. Since most Eastern Woodlands societies were matrilineal, women embodied the clans and were responsible for maintaining the clan's numbers and residences. Since withdrawal was the customary late-eighteenth-century Native American strategy in the face of an enemy assault, women's consent to a policy of war was tantamount to granting permission for their villages and fields to be destroyed. The peace chiefs hoped that, with a little more time and talk, a course of action around which a village consensus could be created might become apparent.[19]

Both the British and the Americans were initially supportive of Indian neutrality. The British limited their recruitment to avoid the negative publicity that enlisting Indians would generate both at home and among the colonists, as well as to buy time until they could be more effectively organized.[20] For their part, the Patriots tried to keep Native Americans on the sidelines because they knew that they faced an insurmountable disadvantage in recruiting them. From the coastal rebel perspective, the task of fighting Great Britain was tall enough; the prospect of fighting Indians on another front appealed to only the most land-hungry colonists. And yet appeal it did. Addressing the Georgia Assembly, General Robert Howe declared himself

> convinced, that some of the back Inhabitants of your State, from the Inveteracy they bore the Indians, from some motives of Interest I could not discern, or some strange Infatuation not to be accounted for, would ... contribute to, or indeed create an Indian War.

The Continental Congress sounded a similar caution, pointing out that such a conflict would "entail great injury and expense to the United States."[21]

The Cherokee War of 1776 was the major exception to Indian neutrality in the first phase of the War of Independence and to the general disinclination to act independently. It pitted a Cherokee faction led by war chief Dragging Canoe against Virginia, the Carolinas and Georgia. Although the British and most of the roughly 9,000 Cherokees in the region had counseled against it, about 600 Cherokee warriors were moved to action by a visiting delegation composed of Mohawks, Mingos, Shawnees, Nanticokes, Delawares and Ottawas. Antagonized by illegal colonial settlements on their land, a Shawnee emissary convinced many that it was "Better to die like men than to diminish away by inches."[22] The revolutionary ferment provided an apparent opportunity to strike at the frontier, and the warriors undertook an extensive raiding campaign against border settlements between Virginia and Georgia during June and July 1776.[23] A response was not long in coming. In August, 600 South Carolina militiamen and a battalion of Continentals destroyed the Cherokee Lower Towns. In September, South Carolina and North Carolina forces destroyed the Middle Towns. Many of the Overhill (Tennessee) Towns were spared by Virginia, but only after they agreed to provide land, hostages and future assistance. The actions of Dragging Canoe and his followers had brought considerable destruction upon the more peaceable majority, prompting the former to remove themselves to their own towns in Tennessee, where they became known as the Chickamaugas.[24] Dragging Canoe's actions proved particularly counterproductive because they thrust those frontier folk who were politically loyal to the Crown into the fold of the Patriot militia that had come to their aid, thus strengthening the rebel cause.[25]

Southern caution, northern destruction, 1777–78

By 1777, Indian activity increased where the conflict intensified. The exigencies of war had caused both the British and the Patriots to recruit Indian allies more vigorously. In the South, British overtures received a tepid response. The example made of the Cherokees had been heeded by other Native American peoples of the region.[26] John Stuart received promises of support from Creek, Chickasaw and Choctaw towns, but their lackluster performance in 1777 and 1778 suggested that these promises were more calculated to appease the British and shake loose supplies than actually promote a Crown victory. Seminoles and Lower Creeks assisted the Florida Rangers in driving off Patriots' cattle to help provision St. Augustine, but they took many head for themselves. Chickasaws and Choctaws patrolled the Mississippi and Tennessee Rivers, but only half-heartedly. Creek warriors assisted the British in the defense of St. Augustine, a principal channel of trade, and attacked settlers who came onto their lands, but their numbers were reduced to a handful for more offensive actions. In sum, Southern Indians could be recruited readily only for defensive actions. In the wake of the Cherokee War, they would not act independently, and were tentative in their cooperation with Britain. Until the British demonstrated their ability to win, the Indians of the South remained shy.[27]

To the north, by contrast, Indians made themselves more extensively useful to both sides, particularly as combat auxiliaries to the British. Mingos, Wyandots and Shawnees – including those who induced the Cherokees to undertake their ill-conceived hostilities – assisted the British at Detroit by raiding settlements in western Pennsylvania and Virginia.[28] In the northeast, the Mohawks, one of the Six Nations Iroquois, stood at the head of Indians allied with Great Britain. Their decision to support Britain arose in part from their close relations to the recently deceased Sir William Johnson, who had married into that tribe. Some Mohawks saw the war as the last chance to recoup lands lost to Euro-American colonists. Many Senecas and Cayugas thought assisting the British an easy way to deal a blow to settlers and appease the likely victor while picking up valuable trade goods.

In the North, the battle of Oriskany fought in August 1777 was the most significant confrontation in which Indians participated in large numbers. Some 400 Iroquois warriors, led by Seneca chief warriors Cornplanter and Old Smoke, and assisted by Sir John Johnson's Royal Greens, ambushed a column of militiamen accompanied by Oneida Indians. Between 200 and 400 rebels and Indians were killed, as well as a smaller but unknown number of Loyalists and Indians.[29] The Senecas' loss of 36 warriors out of a population of roughly 4,000 transformed their participation in the American Revolution into a traditional "mourning war." A mourning war was undertaken after losses to replenish clan power by appropriating the power of enemies. The preferred mode of accomplishing this was by taking live captives and adopting or ritually executing them, although scalps would sometimes suffice. This imperative, which was a primary purpose of war in Iroquois culture until the late seventeenth century, now dovetailed nicely with British military needs.[30]

British–Iroquois raids on Pennsylvania frontier settlements multiplied in the spring of 1778, and in June the ferocious assault on Pennsylvania's Wyoming Valley led by Major John Butler and Old Smoke signaled an increase in their scale as well. Some 400 Indians, principally Senecas, and 100 rangers forced two small forts to capitulate before moving on to the largest fort in the area. Local militiamen insisted upon a confrontation, and were ambushed en route. Approximately 300 died, most while attempting to retreat. Some prisoners were executed in ritual fashion. One British officer reported that he had to plead with the Indians to spare prisoners' lives because "the Indians were so exasperated with their loss last year near Fort Stanwix." A Patriot interpreter reported that some were nevertheless "tommahawk'd ... particularly five who were given to make up the loss of the Ax Carrier, a Seneca Warrior killed last summer near Oriske." The mourning war continued in November, at Cherry Valley in New York, where 33 civilians were killed.[31]

The Patriots were not without Native American assistance in the North, but it was less substantial. Indeed, even though Thomas Gage ballyhooed American recruitment of Indian allies as evidence of Patriot perfidy, he judged those who answered the call as "not of great worth" militarily. They were, he said, "what the French would call *domiciliés*," in other words, Indians who resided among colonists, as opposed to "distant Indians."[32] The Stockbridges, Pequots, Wampanoags and other Indians already surrounded by colonial settlement in New York and New England had stepped forward to prove their bona fides to their Patriot neighbors. For these Native Americans, ingratiating themselves during the present conflict would earn them greater autonomy and respect in the future, or so they hoped. Their greater degree of acculturation was reflected in their generally more conventional service. However, they also supplied emissaries whose linguistic skills and cultural knowledge were put to use helping the Patriots manage their relations with other tribes. In the South, the Catawbas had also fallen within the colonial compass, and they supplied 20 scouts for the South Carolinians against the Cherokees, who conveniently happened to be their traditional foes. When the war later grew more intense in the South, Catawba warriors were present at many significant engagements, including Hanging Rock (August 1780) and Guilford Courthouse (March 1781).[33]

Ultimately, the Indian nation that stepped forward to provide the Patriots with their most effective auxiliaries did indeed prove to be one more "distant," the Oneidas of present-day central New York.[34] Like the Mohawks, the Oneidas were members of the Iroquois Six Nations Confederacy. Unlike the Mohawks, however, the Oneidas still retained most of their land base in 1777, and they wished to keep it. Living just outside the zone of colonial settlement, and occupying a strategic portage, they were keenly aware of their vulnerability to Patriot invasion. Oneida warriors therefore mustered with the militia of adjacent Tryon County from an early date, and they supplied their rebel neighbors with scouts, spies and diplomats as well. When their fellow Iroquois marched into their territory in support of British Colonel Barry St. Leger, the Oneidas met them in fierce combat at Oriskany. The killing of Iroquois warriors by other Iroquois has led some historians to view the battle of Oriskany in August 1777 as the start of an "Iroquois civil war."[35] However, although pro-American and pro-British Indians did sack one another's villages in Oriskany's wake, this was the last time during the war that the Iroquois on either side permitted such a deadly confrontation to take place. Britain's Indian allies "ran off through the wood" before they would have met the Oneidas fighting at Saratoga in October.[36] For their part, the Oneidas shifted their combat activities for 1778 southward, to eastern Pennsylvania. There, after the battle of Barren Hill in May 1778, Marquis de Tousard praised "their hability [sic] in firing." By way of recognition for the services they had rendered, the Oneidas were granted 11 officers' commissions at the ranks of captain and lieutenant.[37]

Although the Oneidas wished and worked hard for a Patriot victory, they never judged their goals to be isomorphic with those of the United States. When goals diverged, the Oneidas acted in their own interest. In small-scale encounters, this meant occasionally ignoring the tracks of, or meeting clandestinely with, pro-British Indians, as well as "accidentally" allowing Indian captives to escape. The Native Americans appreciated the value of cultivating sympathy and contacts on the opposing side of the conflict. Exchanges of intelligence were crucial to independent decision-making. The Oneidas expended some of the capital they had accrued with Patriot officers to secure the release or better treatment of hostile Indian prisoners, as well as more lenient policies toward hostile Indian nations. Such courtesies were reciprocated.[38]

On a larger scale, Oneidas exercised strategic autonomy by withholding support from the Continental Army's largest undertaking in 1779, Major General John Sullivan's campaign against the western Iroquois nations. General Washington ordered the campaign to quiet the northern tribes – as well as the anxious pleadings of the congressional representatives of the ravaged frontier. Sullivan marched four brigades through central and western New York destroying villages and fields. The Senecas, Cayugas and Mohawks declined to engage them, thereby avoiding needless casualties. Sullivan upbraided his Oneida allies for sending him only a handful of men and a guide who was unfamiliar with the area, or at least pretended to be. But Sullivan's complaint changed nothing. The Oneidas' long-term interests would surely have been harmed had the campaign succeeded in severely weakening the Six Nations.[39]

Mobilizing against the United States, 1779–82

The Sullivan campaign was only the largest of many events in the middle of the war that dimmed most Native Americans' already gloomy assessment of the prospects for future peaceful co-existence with the United States. Although Sullivan accomplished his goals without substantial resistance, the campaign only hardened Iroquois antagonism toward the U.S. In formulating his strategy against the western Iroquois, George Washington had failed to appreciate that the Seneca and Cayuga were not the Cherokee. Britain enjoyed broader support among the Six Nations' population, and British Fort Niagara was close enough to shelter them in their hour of need. Thus, the Iroquois responded as they had to large-scale French invasions in 1666 and 1687. They withdrew, accepting their material losses and biding their time until they could launch retaliatory raids on their own terms. Historian Joseph Fischer has dubbed Sullivan's campaign "a well-executed failure" because the Continental Army's operational success did not prevent British–Iroquois raids from resuming the following spring with greater intensity than ever. Indeed, in May 1780 Fort Niagara's commanding officer, British Lieutenant Colonel Mason Bolton, wrote Quebec's governor and commander-in-chief, Frederick Haldimand, that "we would not have had one third of the Six Nations in our interests at this time" had Sullivan exercised "more prudence & less severity."[40] In November, Colonel Guy Johnson reported that Loyalist and Indian raiders on the northern frontier captured 14 rebel officers and 316 men while destroying more than 700 structures, including small forts and mills.[41] The frontier of American settlement was rolled back as far east as Schenectady, a mere 16 miles from the Hudson River.

In the Ohio Valley, Native American opinion had followed a similar trajectory. There, it was not so much the result of the failure of Washington's 1779 strategy as it was of independent, and often contradictory, efforts by backcountry officers with sensibilities and objectives of their own. Just as the Chickamauga warrior faction had defied the tribal leadership to pursue particular interests and provoke conflict, so did backcountry militiamen whose antipathy toward Indians and desire for land far exceeded Washington's. The Delaware experience exemplifies this pattern, while illuminating that group's exceptionally dogged pursuit of neutrality. Under the leadership of war captain White Eyes, a portion of the Delaware had succeeded in remaining uncommitted through 1778 despite threats and demands from both sides. Their neutrality even withstood deadly provocations from the Americans, such as the 1778 "Squaw campaign," so-called because most of its casualties and prisoners were Native American women.[42] While warriors from other divisions of the Delaware had joined militant Shawnees to assist British operations out of Detroit, White Eyes' strategic calculation remained the same, and he sought land guarantees from the United States in exchange for the abstention of most his Delawares from the conflict. As gestures of goodwill, White Eyes also offered the Americans valuable intelligence, guides and diplomats who might be able to head off trouble with Britain's Indian allies. In the event the peacemakers failed, White Eyes also offered the Americans posts in Delaware country, posts where Delawares themselves might take refuge. Apparently preservation of these Delawares' relatively helpful, non-aggressive stance was so important to the United States that Patriot agents agreed in the 1778 Treaty of Fort Pitt "to form a state whereof the Delaware nation shall be the head, and have a representation in Congress."[43] This appreciative sentiment was not, however, shared by backcountry militiamen. Although White Eyes represented one of the United States' few valuable strategic allies in Indian country, they murdered him toward the end of that year. With White Eyes gone, and the Americans unable to sustain an adequate level of supply for these Delawares, their neutrality weakened. By the end of 1781, most neutral Delawares were supporting Great Britain.[44]

From 1780 onwards, British–Indian raiding picked up, particularly in northern Kentucky. The British sought to protect Detroit, and the Indians wanted to defend the Ohio River boundary. However, in joint operations, where British and Native American aims diverged, the latter won out. When Captain Henry Bird wished to attack the United States forts at and around the Falls of the Ohio (Louisville) in 1780, the leaders of the 700 Indians under his command vetoed the idea, "giving for their reason that it could not be prudent to leave their villages naked & defenceless." It was a complaint heard frequently by those seeking to raise both Indian warriors and colonial fighters. Bird compromised with the Indians and struck two other forts farther east. Once again, however, the warriors departed from his commands. Contrary to Bird's wishes, immediately upon the surrender of both forts, Indians rushed in and seized captives and killed livestock. From the Native American perspective, taking captives in war fulfilled an important social imperative, and livestock was a key symbol of obnoxious European settlement. Then, upon hearing a retaliatory force was en route, the Indians quickly fled.[45]

In the South, Indians grew more hopeful that co-existence with the Americans would not be necessary, and increased their efforts toward that end, albeit somewhat less vigorously than their northern counterparts. Creeks, Choctaws, Chickasaws and Chickamauga Cherokees stepped up their contributions, especially following Britain's December 1778 capture of Savannah. Dragging Canoe's Chickamauga Cherokees resumed hostilities against the Americans. Although this time they enjoyed unambiguous British support, the result was further defeat. Nevertheless, the Chickamaugas continued raiding frontier Patriot settlements through 1781, buoyed in part by British promises and anger over the indiscriminate character of the Patriots' retaliation.[46] Over the spring and summer of 1779, 300 Creek warriors raided South Carolina settlements and searched swamps for deserters. In 1780, the assistance of 1,235 Creek warriors, 236 Choctaws and 31 Chickasaws helped the British deter a Spanish invasion of Pensacola, as the Spanish were more concerned with the Indians in the vicinity of the fort than the British soldiers within it. To ensure its capitulation, the Spanish had to return the following year with overwhelming force. The Creeks also assisted the British in repelling the 1780 Patriot attack on Augusta, and proceeded to wreak havoc on the countryside in pursuit of the retreating attackers. Although Augusta fell to the Patriots in the spring of 1781, Creek warriors actively assisted the British into the following year, even stealing into General Anthony Wayne's camp and attacking in the dead of night. The Chickasaws' most emphatic actions came as a direct response to American provocation in the form of the construction of Fort Jefferson on Chickasaw territory. The Chickasaws harassed the fort until the Patriots chose to abandon it.[47]

With their own objectives in mind, Southern Indians also operated with more autonomy than their commanding officers could accept. For example, when Creeks "saw the King's Army Seize upon all the Negroes they could get," the Indians "did the same and intend[ed] to carry them to the Nation," where the blacks would have remained chattel or been adopted or sold. And after a Creek encampment was attacked by surprise, they disappeared. When a party of Cherokees sensed themselves dangerously outnumbered in an impending encounter in 1779, they did the only thing they thought reasonable under the circumstances: they deserted. An exasperated Brigadier General Augustine Prevost complained his Native American warriors were not just few in number but also "so very cautious that no real service can be had of them."[48] The Indians did not obey British officers, who were perennially frustrated by the fact that the paradoxical practice of Indian warfare remained to gain people, not lose them.

In the trans-Appalachian region, the American Revolution was a border war – and a race war.[49] That the war intensified there after the battle of Yorktown in October 1781 suggests its distinct and semi-autonomous character. Although George Rogers Clark had burned Shawnee towns north of the Ohio in 1780, it had so little effect that he felt compelled to repeat the exercise in response to the Indian raiding of the so-called "Bloody Year" of 1782. In March 1782, Pennsylvania militiamen at Gnaddenhutten methodically killed more than 90 Delawares – mostly women and children, all pacifist Moravian converts – and Ohio Indian hostility spiraled.[50] Indians escalated their attacks in its wake. In early June, Shawnees, Delawares, Mingos and Wyandots defending Sandusky, a Delaware town north of the Ohio, defeated 400 frontier militiamen. The latter were ambushed as they retreated in small groups. Missionary David Zeisberger noted that, of the prisoners they took, if "any ... had part in that affair [i.e., Gnadenhutten], he is forthwith bound, tortured, and burnt."[51] At this point, most of the Ohio Indians probably considered their immediate goals to have been fulfilled: they had successfully defended Sandusky and chastised the Pennsylvania militia in the process. With that, most returned home when they were satisfied no invasion force would be coming from Kentucky. However, Captain William Caldwell and a small party of rangers, including several British agents, accompanied 300 Wyandots and "Lake Indians" into Kentucky, where they besieged Bryan's Station and then decisively defeated Kentucky militiamen at Blue Licks in August. Clearly, the Indians of the Old Northwest held the initiative in 1782. They had not stopped the settlement of Kentucky, nor were they able to prevent militiamen from raiding Indian towns north of the Ohio River. The Indians had, however, demonstrated their power and greatly raised the costs of settling Kentucky and approaching the Ohio River.[52]

"Conquest": 1783–94

Great Britain had received valuable military assistance from Indians during the war, but once again demonstrated its fundamental disregard for them by ignoring their interests at the treaty table in Paris. British negotiators ceded to the Americans the Crown's sovereign claims south of Canada and east of the Mississippi without condition. There was no acknowledgment that Indians retained aboriginal title to territories they never ceded to Britain, or any stipulation that colonial treaties would be honored. This contrasted with the French surrender in 1760, which shielded Native American allies from dispossession and retribution.

Tidings of this betrayal came as a shock to many Indians allied with the Crown, as well as to the British officials in America, who were reduced to dissembling in the hopes that the news would turn out to be false. Indians expressed their incredulity that the "King could pretend to cede to America what was not his own to give," especially in light of their generally successful operations.[53] In stating that "the peacemakers and our Enemies have talked away our Lands at a Rum Drinking," the Cherokee Little Turkey suggested that perhaps the British negotiators had fallen victim to the vicious arts by which Indian treaties were too often concluded.[54] Although the British agents sought to reassure Native Americans that the boundaries of colonial treaties would remain effective, they suspected that the United States would self-servingly interpret the concessions in the Treaty of Paris (1783) in the broadest terms possible. Indeed, despite Native American military domination of the northern frontier at war's end, the United States proceeded to insist that Britain's Indian allies had been conquered merely by association with the Crown, and that their aboriginal land title was therefore null and void.[55]

At the 1784 Treaty of Fort Stanwix, the United States demanded of the hostile Six Nations not only millions of acres of land, but hostages as well. Such demands ran directly counter to the assertion of a Mohawk chief that "We are free, and independent." According to one observer, the Americans' grandiose claims of conquest and their immediate demands "made the Indians stare."[56] Lieutenant Colonel Josiah Harmar, at the Fort McIntosh Treaty of 1785, observed that the United States representatives calculatingly replied "in a high tone" when the Wyandots, Ojibwe, Delawares and Ottawas declared "that they still looked upon the lands which the United States held by the treaty with Great Britain as their own." The Americans bluntly stated:

> that, as they had adhered during the war to the king of Great Britain, they were considered by us as a conquered people and had therefore nothing to expect from the United States, but must depend altogether upon their lenity and generosity.[57]

Although they lacked the authority to do so, the chiefs present acceded to American demands of land for peace. The process was repeated with the Shawnees at Fort Finney in 1786 and the Choctaws, among others, at Hopewell in 1785 and 1786.[58]

Individual states exacted cessions as well. For example, in 1783, Georgia compelled the Cherokees to cede 1,650 square miles of land. Cherokee leaders expressed how they were also "Distrest by the No. Carolina People.... They have got all our Land from us. We have hardly as much as can stand on, and they seem to want that little worse than the Rest."[59] In 1785, they ceded more than 6,000 square miles in western North Carolina and Tennessee to the United States. New York even dispossessed the Oneidas, who had served the Patriots so effectively, of the great preponderance of their lands within five years of the war's conclusion. Neither the Mashpees nor the Stockbridges fared much better at the hands of the states in whose limits they had claims, although the Catawbas were more successful at using their service to secure some rights.[60] Ultimately, although the British and Patriots complained that the Indians did not meet their expectations as allies, it was the Indians who truly felt the force of the limits of that relationship.

Epilogue: war in the West, 1786–95

Nevertheless, events that transpired in the decade that followed the American War of Independence suggest that, although the Indians' wartime strategies had failed to protect their villages, fields and hunting territories, they had not been without important effect. The Native Americans retained their capacity to prevent U.S. consummation of its pretended conquest. As the British army withdrew, Indians in the trans-Appalachian region saw their strategic options narrowed but also clarified. Through the post-war federal treaties, the United States had broadcast its contempt for Indians and made the immediacy of its expansionist agenda unambiguously, indeed, terrifyingly, clear. As a result, political unity among the Indian nations increased. A well-organized Indian resistance to the settlement of the Ohio country, the "United Indian Nations," emerged to challenge the post-war federal treaties and claim collective ownership of the land. And, although northern Indians could no longer fight alongside the British, they could still draw British support and supplies from as-yet-unevacuated British posts from Lake Champlain to Michilimackinac. In the South, Native Americans drew similar lessons, and found that Spanish officials in New Orleans actively supported Indian resistance to American expansion.

Although diplomacy kept a lid – barely – on violence between settlers and Indians in the South, the Cumberland Valley caught fire once again, thanks to the redoubtable Chickamaugas. Farther north, military exchanges between Indians and Kentuckians in the Ohio Valley by 1788 had again reached wartime levels. In the Ohio country, Native Americans inflicted heavy losses on the United States when General Josiah Harmar marched 1,500 men against the Shawnee and Miami in October 1790. He lost about 200 of them when Indians, probably led by Miami chief Little Turtle, whose losses were half that, ambushed militiamen who had been carelessly separated from the main body of troops. As historian Michael Warner observed, "the Ohio Indians proved in 1791 that they possessed enough strength to annihilate an army larger than Harmar's."[61] The lesson was demonstrated a year later, when Little Turtle encircled the encampment of General Arthur St. Clair. While the Indians suffered 21 killed and 40 wounded, the U.S. suffered 647 killed and nearly 300 more wounded. Historians have pointed out that St. Clair lost more men than were killed at the bloody Revolutionary War battles of Camden and Long Island combined.[62]

Having failed to capitalize on the shock the Indians felt at British abandonment, and well understanding the serious costs of Native American hostility, the administration of President George Washington modified U.S. Indian policy. It abandoned the fanciful conquest theory and again recognized the Indians' right of occupancy and sovereignty in two treaties signed at Fort Harmar in 1789, one with the Wyandots and the other with the Six Nations.[63] In order to prevent more trouble, the federal government in 1790 passed the Trade and Intercourse Act which sought to curtail the illegal and abusive trade and treaty practices of private individuals and states. The federal government also entered into treaties with Native American nations that permitted the latter to retain comparatively more land – even returning some – as in the 1790 Treaty of New York with the Creeks and the 1794 Treaty of Canandaigua with the Six Nations. The United States also pursued non-military strategies to encourage Indians to cede land. These included missionary work, technical assistance in building mills and European-style farms, and trade. Although these strategies were implemented only fitfully in the early republic and then weakened during the Jacksonian Era from about 1820 to 1845, over the long term they helped Indians consolidate themselves socially and politically within American society.[64]

Because the Indians had not been conquered militarily in the American Revolution, the Washington administration was also compelled to create the Legion of the United States under General Anthony Wayne. Not only was the force three times the size of the previous expeditions, its men were more integrated operationally and systematically trained in *petite guerre* operations like ambush and scouting.[65] Unlike its predecessors, the Legion did not collapse when attacked by a force of 1,500 Ottawas, Shawnees, Wyandots, Miamis, Delawares and others at Fallen Timbers in 1794. The warriors suffered about 40 killed and fled. But it was the British who delivered the coup de grace to the Indians. Although nearby Fort Miamis was in British hands, no support for the Indian warriors came forth. Britain's willingness to sustain conflict with the U.S. through Native American proxies was sapped by the challenge presented by Napoleon. The Legion underscored its presence by proceeding to destroy Indian settlements in the area with impunity. Spain, in even more serious disarray at home as a result of Napoleonic depredations, also withdrew its support for Native American resistance in the South.

The confederated Indians found themselves in a situation more akin to that of the Cherokees in 1776 than the Senecas or Cayugas in 1779. They accordingly sued for peace and ceded most of the Ohio country at the 1795 Treaty of Greenville. Their agreement to cease hostilities acknowledged that the successful military defense of their lands and rights presupposed two conditions. The first was the assistance of a European ally to supply arms and ammunition. The American War of Independence had increased the potential for such alliances, with their attendant rewards and dangers, and the Native Americans made what they could of them. In the decade that followed the Treaty of Paris, Britain and Spain continued to offer assistance, but only in a much more limited way. The second condition was a foe that was averse to casualties and had a limited mental or economic capacity for conflict. There had to be some fathomable limit to the risk that settlers and their state were willing to accept for Indian lands. But the new American nation was not that kind of beast. By 1795, the withdrawal of their European allies led most Eastern Indians to recognize that there would be no military solution to what was essentially a demographic phenomenon.[66]

Notes

1. The author wishes to thank Carl Benn and Wayne Lee for their comments on an earlier draft of this chapter.
2. John Burgoyne, *A State of the Expedition From Canada, As Laid Before the House of Commons* (London: J. Almon, 1780), p. 101; S.F. Wise, "The American Revolution and Indian History," in John S. Moir ed., *Character and Circumstance: Essays in Honour of Donald Grant Creighton* (Toronto: Macmillan of Canada, 1970), pp. 182–200. Recent surveys of Native American participation in the Revolution breaking with this tradition include Colin G. Calloway, *The American Revolution in Indian Country: Crisis and Diversity in Native American Communities* (New York: Cambridge University Press, 1995); Armstrong Starkey, *European and Native American Warfare 1675–1815* (Norman: University of Oklahoma Press, 1998), pp. 111–36; John Grenier, *The First Way of War: American War Making on the Frontier, 1607–1814* (New York: Cambridge University Press, 2005), pp. 146–69; Gregory Evans Dowd, *A Spirited Resistance: The North American Indian Struggle for Unity, 1745–1815* (Baltimore: The Johns Hopkins University Press, 1992). Key regional studies are James O'Donnell, *Southern Indians in the American Revolution* (Knoxville: University of Tennessee Press, 1973); Barbara Graymont, *The Iroquois Indians in the American Revolution* (Syracuse: Syracuse University Press, 1972); Robert S. Allen, *His Majesty's Indian Allies: British Indian Policy in the Defence of Canada, 1774–1815* (Toronto: Dundurn, 1992).
3. Calloway, *American Revolution*, p. xiii; Grenier, *First Way of War*, p. 162.
4. Greg O'Brien, "The Choctaw Defense of Pensacola in the American Revolution," in Greg O'Brien, ed., *Pre-Removal Choctaw History: Exploring New Paths* (Norman: University of Oklahoma Press, 2008), pp. 128–9; Susan Sleeper-Smith, "'Ignorant bigots and busy rebels': The American Revolution in the Western Great Lakes," in David Curtis Skaggs and Larry L. Nelson, eds., *The Sixty Years' War for the Great Lakes, 1754–1814* (East Lansing: Michigan State University Press, 2001), pp. 145–66; Richard White, *The Middle Ground: Indians, Empires and Republics in the Great Lakes Region, 1650–1815* (New York: Cambridge University Press, 1991), pp. 366–412.
5. Jon W. Parmenter, "After the 'Mourning Wars:' The Iroquois as Allies in Colonial American Campaigns, 1675–1760," *William and Mary Quarterly*, 3rd ser., 64 (2007), passim; Karim M. Tiro, "The Dilemmas of Alliance: The Oneida Indian Nation in the American Revolution," in John Resch and Walter Sargent, eds., *War & Society in the American Revolution: Mobilization and Home Fronts* (DeKalb: Northern Illinois University Press, 2007), pp. 215–34; Sharon Sauder Muhlfeld, "Preserving Independence: Native American Responses to the Revolution in the Ohio Valley," in David Naumec, ed., *Proceedings of the Northeastern Native Peoples & the American Revolutionary Era: 1760–1810 Symposium* (Mashantucket: Mashantucket Pequot Museum & Research Center, 2008), pp. 49–55; Daniel Usner, *Indians, Settlers, and Slaves in a Frontier Exchange Economy: The Lower Mississippi Before 1783* (Chapel Hill: University of North Carolina Press, 1992), pp. 85, 101–2; James R. Atkinson, *Splendid Land, Splendid People: The Chickasaw Indians to Removal* (Tuscaloosa: University of Alabama Press, 2004), pp. 101–2.
6. Daniel K. Richter, "Native Peoples of North America and the Eighteenth-Century British Empire," in P.J. Marshall, ed., *The Oxford History of the British Empire*, vol. 3: *The Eighteenth Century* (New York: Oxford University Press, 1998), pp. 349–63; J. Leitch Wright, *Creeks & Seminoles: The Destruction and Regeneration of the Muscogulge People* (Lincoln: University of Nebraska Press, 1986), pp. 113–14; O'Brien, "Defense of Pensacola," p. 126.
7. Karim M. Tiro, "A 'Civil' War? Rethinking Iroquois Participation in the American Revolution," *Explorations in Early American Culture*, 4 (2000), pp. 148–65; Par-

menter, "After the 'Mourning Wars,'" pp. 40, 44; Timothy J. Shannon, "War, Diplomacy, and Culture: The Iroquois Experience in the Seven Years' War," in Warren R. Hofstra, ed., *Cultures in Conflict: The Seven Years' War in North America* (Lanham: Rowman & Littlefield, 2007), p. 88; O'Brien, "Defense of Pensacola," p. 127.

8 Malcolm J. Rohrbaugh, *The Trans-Appalachian Frontier* (New York: Oxford University Press, 1978), p. 16; Eric Hinderaker, *Elusive Empires: Constructing Colonialism in the Ohio Valley, 1673–1800* (New York: Cambridge University Press, 1997), p. 187; John R. Wunder, "'Merciless Indian Savages' and the Declaration of Independence: Native Americans Translate the *Ecunnaunuxulgee* Document," *American Indian Law Review*, 25 (spring 2001), p. 66.

9 Quoted in Kathryn E. Holland Braund, *Deerskins and Duffels: The Creek Indian Trade with Anglo-America 1685–1815* (Lincoln: University of Nebraska Press, 1993), p. 167.

10 Elizabeth Fenn, *Pox Americana: The Great Smallpox Epidemic of 1775–1782* (New York: Hill & Wang, 2001); Wayne E. Lee, "Fortify, Fight, or Flee: Tuscarora and Cherokee Defensive Warfare and Military Culture Adaptation," *The Journal of Military History*, 68 (July 2004), pp. 718–19; Patrick M. Malone, *The Skulking Way of War: Technology and Tactics Among the New England Indians* (Baltimore: The Johns Hopkins University Press, 1993); O'Donnell, *Southern Indians*, p. 109; R. Douglas Hurt, *The Ohio Frontier: Crucible of the Old Northwest 1720–1830* (Bloomington: Indiana University Press, 1996), p. 86; O'Brien, "Defense of Pensacola," p. 124.

11 Richard Middleton, *Pontiac's War: Its Causes, Course, and Consequences* (New York: Routledge, 2007), pp. 17–32.

12 Woody Holton, *Forced Founders: Indians, Debtors, Slaves, and the Making of the American Revolution in Virginia* (Chapel Hill: University of North Carolina Press, 1999), pp. 6–7; David Dixon, *Never Come to Peace Again: Pontiac's Uprising and the Fate of the British Empire in North America* (Norman: University of Oklahoma Press, 2005), pp. 245–7, 273–5.

13 Michael D. Green, *The Politics of Indian Removal: Creek Government and Society in Crisis* (Lincoln: University of Nebraska Press, 1982), p. 26.

14 Holton, *Forced Founders*, pp. 14–26; Dowd, *Spirited Resistance*, pp. 43–4; Michael D. Green, "The Creek Confederacy in the American Revolution: Cautious Participants," in William S. Coker and Robert R. Rea, eds., *Anglo-Spanish Confrontation on the Gulf Coast During the Revolution* (Pensacola: Gulf Coast History and Humanities Conference, 1982), pp. 61–2.

15 Michael N. McConnell, *A Country Between: The Upper Ohio Valley and its Peoples, 1724–1774* (Lincoln: University of Nebraska Press, 1992), pp. 270–9; John K. Mahon, "Anglo-American Methods of Indian Warfare, 1676–1794," *Mississippi Valley Historical Review*, 45 (1958), p. 272.

16 Hinderaker, *Elusive Empires*, p. 194.

17 Atkinson, *Splendid Land, Splendid People*, pp. 100, 104 (quote); Joseph P. Glatthaar and James Kirby Martin, *Forgotten Allies: The Oneida Indians and the American Revolution* (New York: Hill & Wang, 2006), pp. 88 (quote), 93–4, 121–2; William N. Fenton, *The Great Law and the Longhouse: A Political History of the Iroquois Confederacy* (Norman: University of Oklahoma Press, 1998), pp. 582–98.

18 Tench Tilghman, *Memoir of Lieut. Col. Tench Tilghman* (New York: New York Times/Arno, 1971 [1876]), p. 88; Taitt quoted in Calloway, *American Revolution*, p. 45.

19 Greg O'Brien, *The Choctaws in a Revolutionary Age, 1750–1830* (Lincoln: University of Nebraska Press, 2002), pp. 27–49; O'Brien, "Defense of Pensacola," p. 142; O'Brien, "The Conqueror Meets the Unconquered: Negotiating Cultural Boundaries on the Post-Revolutionary Southern Frontier," in *Pre-Removal Choctaw History*, p. 151; Nathaniel Sheidley, "Hunting and the Politics of Masculinity in Cherokee Treaty-Making, 1763–75," in *Empire and Others: British Encounters with Indigenous*

Peoples, 1600–1850 (Philadelphia: University of Pennsylvania Press, 1999), pp. 167–77; Theda Perdue, *Cherokee Women: Gender and Culture Change, 1700–1835* (Lincoln: University of Nebraska Press, 1998); Lee, "Fortify, Fight, or Flee," pp. 757–68.

20 O'Donnell, *Southern Indians*, pp. 13–14; Andrew McFarland Davis, "The Employment of Indian Auxiliaries in the American War," *English Historical Review*, 2 (1887), pp. 709–28.

21 Robert Howe to the Speaker of the Georgia Assembly, 4 Sept. 1777, *Papers of the Continental Congress*, reel 87, i73:7; *Journals of the Continental Congress*, 9:823–4; Kenneth Coleman, *The American Revolution in Georgia 1763–1789* (Athens: University of Georgia Press, 1958), pp. 72, 113–14. Spelling modernized by editor.

22 Calloway, *American Revolution*, pp. 194–7 (quote, p. 195); Dowd, *Spirited Resistance*, pp. 47–9 (quote, p. 47).

23 O'Donnell, *Southern Indians*, pp. 40–3.

24 Ibid., pp. 40–9; M. Thomas Hatley, *The Dividing Paths: Cherokees and South Carolinians Through the Era of Revolution* (New York: Oxford University Press, 1993), pp. 217–28; Parmenter, "Dragging Canoe (Tsi'yu-gûnsi'ni): Chickamauga Cherokee Patriot," in Nancy L. Rhoden and Ian K. Steele, eds., *The Human Tradition in the American Revolution* (Wilmington: SR Books, 2000), pp. 118–26.

25 Jim Piecuch, "Incompatible Allies: Loyalists, Slaves, and Indians in Revolutionary South Carolina," in Resch and Sargent, eds., *War & Society*, pp. 197–9, 210; Rachel N. Klein, *Unification of a Slave State: The Rise of the Planter Class in the South Carolina Backcountry, 1760–1808* (Chapel Hill: University of North Carolina Press, 1990), pp. 91–5.

26 Helen Hornbeck Tanner, "Pipesmoke and Muskets: Florida Indian Intrigues of the Revolutionary Era," in Samuel Proctor, ed., *Eighteenth-Century Florida and Its Borderlands* (Gainesville: University Presses of Florida, 1975), pp. 22; O'Donnell, *Southern Indians*, p. 52; Green, "Creek Confederacy," p. 65.

27 Calloway, *American Revolution*, pp. 222–4; J. Russell Snapp looks closely at the British supply of the Indians, and ultimately perceives Indians' "strong and tenacious support" of Great Britain, *John Stuart and the Struggle for Empire on the Southern Frontier* (Baton Rouge: Louisiana State University Press, 1996), esp. pp. 197–203; Tanner, "Pipesmoke," pp. 22–3; Atkinson, *Splendid Land*, pp. 103–4; Green, "Creek Confederacy," pp. 65–6; O'Donnell, *Southern Indians*, p. 72; David H. Corkran, *The Creek Frontier, 1540–1783* (Norman: University of Oklahoma Press, 1967), pp. 288–308.

28 Calloway, *American Revolution*, p. 167.

29 Glatthaar and Martin, *Forgotten Allies*, pp. 163–9; Thomas S. Abler, *Chainbreaker: The American Revolutionary Memoirs of Governor Blacksnake* (Lincoln: University of Nebraska Press, 2005), pp. 83–91.

30 On mourning war, see Daniel K. Richter, "War and Culture: The Iroquois Experience," *William and Mary Quarterly*, 3rd ser., 40 (1983), pp. 528–59; Thomas S. Abler, "Scalping, Torture, Cannibalism and Rape: An Ethnocultural Analysis of Conflicting Values in War," *Anthropologica*, 34 (1992), p. 7.

31 James Dean to Philip Schuyler, 19 July 1778, reel 7, Schuyler Family Papers, New York Public Library, Astor, Lenox and Tilden Foundations; James Folts, "The 'Wyoming Massacre' Revisited," paper presented at the 2007 Conference on Iroquois Research, Rensselaerville; Joseph Fischer, *A Well-Executed Failure: The Sullivan Campaign Against the Iroquois, July–September 1779* (Columbia: University of South Carolina Press, 1997), pp. 27–31; Graymont, *Iroquois*, pp. 165–91.

32 Quoted in Patrick Frazier, *The Mohicans of Stockbridge* (Lincoln: University of Nebraska Press, 1992) p. 206.

33 James H. Merrell, *The Indians' New World: Catawbas and Their Neighbors From European Contact Through the Era of Removal* (Chapel Hill: University of North

Carolina Press, 1989), pp. 215–17; Calloway, *American Revolution*, pp. 92–4; Frazier, *Mohicans of Stockbridge*, pp. 194, 203–4; Jack Campisi, *The Mashpee Indians: Tribe on Trial* (Syracuse: Syracuse University Press, 1991), pp. 87–8; D. Naumec, "Connecticut's Native Troops, 1775–1783: Militia, Connecticut Line, and Continental Service," in D. Naumec, ed., *Northeastern Native Peoples*, pp. 56–80.
34 Glatthaar and Martin, *Forgotten Allies*; Tiro, "Dilemmas of Alliance," pp. 215–34.
35 Graymont, *Iroquois*, pp. 142–43; Calloway, *American Revolution*, pp. 33–4; Glatthaar and Martin defend the notion of the Iroquois civil war in *Forgotten Allies*, p. 360, note 21.
36 Quoted in Graymont, *Iroquois*, p. 155.
37 Tousard to unidentified correspondent, 23 May 1778, M247, reel 95, i. 78:157–60, *Papers of the Continental Congress*; Glatthaar and Martin, *Forgotten Allies*, p. 235.
38 Isabel Thompson Kelsay, *Joseph Brant 1743–1807: Man of Two Worlds* (Syracuse: Syracuse University Press, 1984), pp. 226–7; Tiro, "Dilemmas of Alliance," pp. 222–3; Calloway, *American Revolution*, p. 96; Graymont, *Iroquois*, pp. 178, 234; Parmenter, "After the 'Mourning Wars'," pp. 39–76.
39 Fischer, *Well-Executed Failure*, pp. 33, 36; Tiro, "A 'Civil' War?" pp. 157–62.
40 Fischer, *Well-Executed Failure*, pp. 191–7; quoted in White, *Middle Ground*, p. 406. Glenn F. Williams takes a contrary position in "NOT MERELY OVERRUN BUT DESTROY: George Washington's 1779 Campaign Against the Iroquois," in Naumec, ed., *Northeastern Native Peoples*, pp. 126–38.
41 Allen, *His Majesty's Indian Allies*, pp. 54–5.
42 White, *Middle Ground*, esp. pp. 366–412. The murder of the Shawnee neutralist Cornstalk is a parallel example; Dowd, *Spirited Resistance*, pp. 75–7.
43 Francis Paul Prucha, *American Indian Treaties: The History of a Political Anomaly* (Berkeley: University of California Press, 1994), p. 33.
44 Dowd, *Spirited Resistance*, pp. 65–78.
45 White, *Middle Ground*, p. 407; Starkey, *European and Native American Warfare*, p. 129; *Michigan Pioneer Historical Records Collections*, 10:416–17, 19:538–43; Virginia DeJohn Anderson, *Creatures of Empire: How Domestic Animals Transformed Early America* (New York: Oxford University Press, 2004), pp. 175–90, 228–30.
46 O'Donnell, *Southern Indians*, pp. 83–5, 103, 107; Cashin, "But Brothers," p. 268; Hatley, *Dividing Paths*, pp. 226–7; Snapp, *John Stuart*, p. 204.
47 Atkinson, *Splendid Land, Splendid People*, p. 108; O'Donnell, *Southern Indians*, pp. 81–2, 98–9, 113; O'Brien, "Defense of Pensacola," pp. 123–47; Tanner, "Pipesmoke," p. 27; Cashin, "But Brothers," pp. 266–72; Henry Lee, *Memoirs of the War in the Southern Department of the United States*, Robert E. Lee, ed. (New York: University Publishing Company, 1869), pp. 556–61; Calloway, *American Revolution*, p. 227; Atkinson, *Splendid Land*, p. 108; Corkran, *Creek Frontier*, pp. 317–22.
48 O'Donnell, *Southern Indians*, pp. 81–2, 85; Claudio Saunt, *A New Order of Things: Property, Power, and the Transformation of the Creek Indians, 1733–1816* (New York: Cambridge University Press, 1999), pp. 54–60, 111; Tanner, "Pipesmoke," pp. 22–3; quoted in David K. Wilson, *The Southern Strategy: Britain's Conquest of South Carolina and Georgia, 1775–1780* (Columbia: University of South Carolina Press, 2005), p. 117.
49 Grenier, *First Way of War*, p. 162.
50 White, *Middle Ground*, pp. 389–90; Dowd, *Spirited Resistance*, pp. 85–8; Milo M. Quaife, "The Ohio Campaigns of 1782," *Mississippi Valley Historical Review*, 18 (1931), pp. 517, 521.
51 Dowd, *Spirited Resistance*, pp. 87–8 (quote, p. 88); Mahon, "Anglo-American," p. 273.
52 Quaife, "Ohio Campaigns," pp. 522–4; Starkey, *European and Native American Warfare*, p. 129; John Mack Faragher, *Daniel Boone: The Life and Legend of an American Pioneer* (New York: Henry Holt, 1992), pp. 188, 217–24.

53 Denys Delâge and Jean-Pierre Sawaya, *Les Traités des sept-feux avec les Britanniques: Droits et pièges d'un héritage colonial au Québec* (Sillery: Septentrion, 2001), pp. 63–9; Allen, *His Majesty's Indian Allies*, p. 55.
54 Quoted in Colin G. Calloway, *Crown and Calumet: British–Indian Relations, 1783–1815* (Norman: University of Oklahoma Press, 1987), p. 12.
55 Stuart Banner, *How the Indians Lost Their Land: Law and Power on the Frontier* (Cambridge: Harvard University Press, 2005), pp. 121–9.
56 Prucha, *American Indian Treaties*, pp. 43–8 (quote, "independent," p. 46); quote "stare" in Anthony F.C. Wallace, *The Death and Rebirth of the Seneca* (New York: Vintage, 1970), p. 198.
57 Josiah Harmar to John Dickinson, in Consul Willshire Butterfield, ed., *Journal of Capt. Jonathan Heart* (Albany: Joel Munsell's Sons, 1885), p. 53.
58 Allen, *His Majesty's Indian Allies*, pp. 62–5; Greg O'Brien, "The Conqueror Meets the Unconquered: Negotiating Cultural Boundaries on the Post-Revolutionary Southern Frontier," in *Pre-Removal Choctaw History*, pp. 148–82.
59 Calloway, *American Revolution*, p. 284.
60 Graymont, "New York State Indian Policy After the Revolution," *New York History*, 78 (1997), pp. 374–410; Frazier, *Mohicans of Stockbridge*, pp. 234–45; Campisi, *Mashpee Indians*, p. 88; Merrell, *Indians' New World*, pp. 216–23.
61 Michael S. Warner, "General Josiah Harmar's Campaign Reconsidered: How the Americans Lost the Battle of Kekionga," *Indiana Magazine of History*, 83 (1987), pp. 43–64.
62 Leroy V. Eid, "American Indian Military Leadership: St. Clair's 1791 Defeat," *Journal of Military History*, 57 (1993), p. 71.
63 Banner, *How the Indians Lost Their Land*, pp. 133, 139.
64 Francis Paul Prucha, *American Indian Policy in the Formative Years: The Indian Trade and Intercourse Acts, 1790–1834* (Lincoln: University of Nebraska Press, 1970); Merrell, "Declarations of Independence," in Jack P. Greene, ed., *The American Revolution: Its Character and Limits* (New York: New York University Press, 1984), pp. 197–208; Reginald Horsman, *Expansion and American Indian Policy, 1783–1812* (Norman: University of Oklahoma Press, 1992 [1967]), p. 72.
65 Andrew J. Birtle, "The Origins of the Legion of the United States," *Journal of Military History*, 67 (2003), pp. 1255–7; Grenier, *First Way of War*, pp. 199–200.
66 Grenier, *First Way of War*, pp. 201–3; Russell Weigley, *The American Way of War: A History of United States Military Strategy and Policy* (New York: Macmillan, 1973), p. 44; Lawrence H. Keeley, *War Before Civilization* (New York: Oxford University Press, 1996), pp. 71–81.

7 French strategy and the American Revolution
A reappraisal

James Pritchard[1]

The question of French involvement in the American War of Independence frequently becomes entangled in much larger issues that often obscure the reasons France became involved in the first place and what the consequences were for subsequent French history. Overly simple assumptions are commonly asserted about eighteenth-century French foreign policy and Franco-British animosity, on the one hand, and excessively large, often indemonstrable, historical claims are frequently made on the other. Both are too easily accepted by scholars and students, with the result, among other things, that the question of French naval strategy during the war is poorly handled, treated only obliquely as an adjunct to British strategy, and frequently so misunderstood that only a caricature remains.

Historians often view France's chief strategical problem as defined by the nation's role as "a classical hybrid power," torn between its Continental aims and its overseas ambitions.[2] By accepting the permanent existence and reality of this geopolitical model, they are drawn to conclude that even during the American War of Independence – when for once, in Paul Kennedy's phrases, the French "resisted the temptation to attack Hanover or to bully the Dutch," "fought *only* overseas" and "concentrated their resources upon a naval and colonial war" – they failed to conquer, and managed only to humiliate, their British foe.[3] In these analyses, French war aims are never identified, except to say that somehow France failed to achieve defeat of the enemy, as opposed to conquest. Whatever the aims were, however, France in some way was unable to achieve them, accepting the discomfiture of the enemy as a sort of half-measure.[4] This is a summary of fairly common views concerning the role of France during the American War of Independence.

A second issue involves conclusions generally held about the connection between France's involvement in the American war and, a few years later, the French Revolution: first, that France was chiefly responsible for the independence of the United States of America; and second, that the war's burdens led directly to the collapse of the monarchy and the advent of the Revolution.[5] The latter can be found even in distinguished and specialized works. The diplomatic historian Jonathan Dull, for example, claims to show how the war "raised dangers from within the monarchy far greater than those which threatened it from without," but nowhere, however, does he demonstrate that the war brought about the monarchy's downfall or even that it led to any internal destabilization of the regime.[6]

In view of the ubiquity of such a flawed geopolitical model, and also having in mind the propensity of many (especially political economists) to ignore the roles in history of the particular and the idiosyncratic, and to play down the factors of character and circumstance, we should guard against misleading generalizations and reductionism. In the case of France's involvement in the War of Independence, although France did not in fact threaten the Electorate of Hanover, whose ruler was also the King of England, or any other part of Germany and, far from bullying the Dutch, struggled hard (for very good reasons) to ensure their neutrality, it did not fight only overseas. Further, though this was in fact a naval war and the French were able to apply their resources accordingly, it was never solely a colonial war (as Kennedy would have it), and they were not free to concentrate their naval forces in the American theater. Indeed, it was precisely because France had to retain so much of its naval strength in Europe that its strategy frequently appeared hesitant and ambiguous. Finally, France did not just "settle for" the humiliation of Great Britain in lieu of better goals; in fact, its leaders never intended anything else. Indeed, they explicitly rejected any other plan.

The study of French naval strategy may well be an excellent introduction to certain larger issues, for it reveals that although French naval strategy may have appeared uncertain, ambiguous and hesitant, that imprecision is due in part to the character and conduct of senior French naval commanders. One sees, however, that it was also a reflection of the internal weakness of the French political economy and the challenges and difficulties facing French political leaders as those men took the momentous decisions that led France to intervene in the rebellion of the British American colonies and join the latter's struggle for independence. In the end, at Yorktown in October 1781, the French navy forced the surrender of the only large British field army remaining on American soil. Whether this achievement should be seen as the major cause of the independence of the United States, let alone as having anything to do with the French Revolution, is debatable. To study French naval strategy, then, is to deal rather with the events and campaigns of the war.

French strategy in the American war was a product of men whose character and perceptions of the world must be considered in order to understand their strategies, ambiguities and hesitations. Several recent studies of their careers also provide a more complete understanding than heretofore of French foreign and domestic policies that influenced strategy. Chief among the persona is Louis XVI himself, whose recent biographers have seen in him less the dullard of their predecessors than a ruler who was thoughtful, informed and devoted, if neither strong-willed nor determined.[7] Three of his ministers have also been subjects of new revisionist studies which are especially pertinent. The first is Jacques Necker, whose place or position in French history has been completely altered during the past 30 years. Louis XVI made him director general of finances in 1776, after the only real opponent of the war, Anne-Robert-Jacques Turgot, resigned from the Royal Council. A Protestant, commoner and foreigner, Necker was responsible for a conscious policy decision to finance the war through borrowing rather than raising taxes. Historian Robert Harris has shown convincingly that Necker's conduct throughout the war was a model of fiscal restraint, financial responsibility and prudent management.[8]

The second minister is Gabriel de Sartine, former lieutenant general of the Paris police, who served as Louis XVI's first secretary of state for the navy from 1774 until 1780. He was primarily responsible for resuming the reform and rebuilding of the navy and stockpiling matériel in the dockyards in anticipation of the coming war with Great Britain, a policy that had been suspended since the dismissal of Duc de Choiseul in 1770.[9] Sartine also succeeded in obtaining the largest French annual naval appropriations of the eighteenth century in order to accomplish his task, but he went too far when, in 1780, he allowed the treasurer general of the navy to issue unauthorized anticipations, short-term notes issued by financiers on future revenues. These notes, in the amount of 21 million livres, forced up the interest rate on French government borrowings by half a percentage point, thereby upsetting Necker's calculations. In October of that year, the director general of finances engineered the downfall of Sartine and his replacement with an ally, Charles de la Croix, Marquis de Castries, a lieutenant general of the army.[10]

Castries was an excellent choice at the time, probably superior to Sartine, whose ambiguous instructions to naval commanders revealed the uncertainty of his aims.[11] A soldier and veteran of the mid-century wars, Castries was also a reformer; he introduced much-needed vigor and a personal interest in the naval campaign that had been lacking. He was chiefly responsible for the aggressive strategy of 1781 and for the selection of new commanders, especially Admiral de Grasse, for the fleets being readied that year.

Necker's success in replacing Sartine was matched two months later, in December 1780, when he maneuvered to replace the Comte de Montbarey, the war minister, with the Marquis de Ségur, like Castries an army lieutenant general, a veteran of the mid-century wars and an ally. But this demonstration of Necker's growing influence, combined with his peace feelers to Great Britain, threatened the two most important men in the government, the elderly Comte de Maurepas, the King's chief advisor, and the Comte de Vergennes, secretary of state for foreign affairs and the chief architect of French war strategy.[12] When, in February 1781, Necker published his famous *Comte rendu au roi*, which explained his financial policies to the French public, he roused the ire of both men, and his days were numbered. He was dismissed from office three months later, and his reforms and prudent management rapidly began to unravel.

In brief, then, French naval strategy was neither economically determined, nor the product of geopolitical forces. It was designed by men. Just as historian Piers Mackesy showed on the British side, that strategy itself must be restored to its place alongside diplomacy and military operations as a legitimate part of the history of the American War of Independence, so too must the perceptions and prejudices of the French political actors be given importance in accounting for the origins, features and modifications of war strategy in general and naval strategy in particular.[13] Of no one was this truer than Charles Gravier, Comte de Vergennes, the third of Louis' subordinates to receive recent attention. Louis XVI appointed Vergennes minister and secretary of state for foreign affairs in 1774 and relied on him until his death in 1787.[14]

Two conceptions of international politics dominated Vergennes' thinking, and it was both his strength and his weakness that they guided his foreign policy and his war strategy. First was an ambition to restore France to its traditional – in French eyes, rightful – place as arbiter of relations between the powers in the European competitive state system. Second was his understanding that France's reduced position in the 1770s was chiefly the result of the outcome of the great and multifarious mid-century struggles known collectively as the War of the Austrian Succession (1740–48) and the Seven Years' War (1756–63). These conflicts, by bringing France and Great Britain into direct confrontation overseas, had undermined the traditional primacy of Continental issues in the interstate system. The existence of a new and largely independent competitive arena overseas marked international affairs in the years leading up to the American War of Independence and would continue to do so during, and after, that conflict. France, unable to break free from membership in the Eastern European, anti-Prussian alliance, had few attractive Continental options for improving directly its position in that theater, Therefore – though already trapped in other overseas commitments and although doing so further constrained its role in European affairs – France directed its foreign policy overseas against Great Britain.

The purpose of this anti-British policy, then, was to end British preponderance and restore the "natural" balance of power in order to pursue more fully French interests on the continent. At no time was the Comte de Vergennes interested in destroying Great Britain. He was far too experienced to imagine that the other great powers would permit such a thing, even had it been possible. His own words, written to the French ambassador to Spain, make this perfectly clear:

> We must work resolutely to weaken this enemy of ours, but we must not display intentions which would only do us harm because the jealousy they would arouse against the House of Bourbon [i.e., the French Crown] would give England friends and allies.[15]

The challenge to French strategy by the late 1770s was far greater than is sometimes imagined by those who see merely the need to resist the temptation to attack Hanover or the United Provinces (modern Holland) in order to concentrate resources on an overseas naval war. What needs to be made clear is that French naval strategy – and this key fact accounts for much of the real and apparent hesitation with which it was executed – could not be made by France alone. Vergennes was deeply aware in 1778 that, despite four years of naval rearmament, France remained too weak to proceed by itself. France required all the assistance that Spain, its Bourbon ally, could provide. Unfortunately, no one knew that better than the Spanish foreign minister, who had not the slightest interest in supporting American insurgents, acknowledging the independence of the United States or serving as powder monkey to the French navy. Throughout the American War of Independence, Spain had its own agenda, one that included controlling and directing French strategy when and wherever possible.

Also, a strategy of striking at Great Britain overseas had serious limitations arising from the nature of the opponent.[16] Vergennes' view of the need to weaken Great Britain and his awareness of the need for the most subtle, complex diplomacy to restore French influence in Europe combined with his mercantilist outlook.[17] He assumed that British wealth and power were built on its flourishing distant overseas trade, which contributed to the nation's economic growth, encouraged the development of naval power, provided valuable revenues to the state and connected Britain to its colonies, where plentiful supplies of cheap raw materials were exchanged for valuable metropolitan manufactures. While this recipe for power was true (and has attracted navalists, including Alfred Thayer Mahan and Sir Julian Corbett, for two centuries and more), it was not the whole truth. The fundamental source of British wealth remained its expanding and diversified agriculture, increasing industrial production and its rapidly growing domestic transportation network, which contributed to additional consumption. Also very important, as Napoleon's Continental blockade later showed, was trade with other European nations.

In fact, a critique along these lines had been offered by Turgot, Necker's predecessor in finances and an opponent on principle of colonies and monopolies. Turgot's arguments, which were in favor of peace and continued until his dismissal in 1776, had been more perceptive than those of others. In the first place, he believed American independence would occur whether France intervened or not; second, he had argued that an independent America would contribute rather more than less to British trade.[18] Nevertheless, it was Vergennes' perceptions and not Turgot's that prevailed, and they account for the French naval strategy of sending major thrusts to America and the West Indies. For France's foreign minister, the independence of the American colonies was the specific overseas, or peripheral, lever that would help him achieve his greater goal, in two stages: restoring the colonial balance of power and thereby also restoring French influence in the central arena, the European competitive state system.

A key to understanding why Vergennes embarked upon so problematic a strategy was his own failure to comprehend the financial weakness of France that made naval and military reform very slow processes. A career diplomat who had spent all but two of the last 35 years prior to his ministerial appointment outside France, he was a man with no family or social connections at court (except for the king's aunt, to whom he owed his appointment). He had little awareness of the domestic political situation and no appreciation of the forces that had led in 1770 to the show of monarchical power and reforms that preceded his own appointment. Unlike Turgot, he had no grasp at all of the socioeconomic conditions in the nation, nor did he have any interest in them; Vergennes saw domestic politics only in the context of international *raison d'état*. In his eyes, war with Great Britain was unavoidable, because the latter's situation was so unnatural that peace could not last. The great strategic problem, then, was to control when, where and under what conditions France would fight that war.

Vergennes' geopolitical views had other shortcomings as well that make the flaws in his strategy clear. First, his aim to fight Great Britain, in however limited a way, was based on his conviction that France's lost prestige and reduced position in Europe was entirely due to that nation's rise. In response, he sought for France the role of arbiter. He did not grasp that none of the five great powers could now control the conditions governing the relative strengths of the others. Second, the ideological paradox of an absolute monarchy aiding a republican uprising bothered Vergennes not a whit. For him the problem was not the independence of the United States but how France could benefit from intervening in Britain's growing troubles in America.

On the other hand, Vergennes was to achieve in this war a marriage of diplomacy and military strategy of a very high order, whereas even students of purely military strategy will grant – and Napoleon's career is the paramount demonstration – that strategy without diplomacy can have no long-term effect. His astuteness lay in five things, the first of which was his timing of the French intervention in America. Beginning by authorizing secret financial and material assistance to the insurgents in May 1776, he gave diplomatic recognition to the United States at the end of 1777. A formal alliance committing France to achieving American independence followed shortly; finally, an expeditionary force was sent "when it became necessary" two years later.[19] The second was the subtle and difficult diplomacy used to develop the anti-British coalition.

Vergennes' qualities of timing and astuteness toward the Americans were evident in their coordination in a Continental initiative by which he coaxed Spain into war (1779), fostered the League of Armed Neutrality (1780), prevented a new German war breaking out in Central Europe and blocked the dismemberment of the Ottoman empire.[20]

Third, Vergennes never forgot that however questionable Spanish resources might be, they were indispensable; France had insufficient strength to attack Great Britain alone. Fourth, Vergennes knew when it was time to make peace, and the Treaty of Versailles (or of Paris, 1783) is his monument. Finally, it also needs to be remembered that Vergennes developed an original set of relations with the United States of America, foiling those Americans who sought a compromise peace with Great Britain while checking those in France and Spain who sought to negotiate with Great Britain, leaving American independence unachieved and France alone opposing Great Britain.

During 1778 and 1779, then, French naval strategy was ambivalent in essence and hesitant in execution for a variety of reasons, but its chief outlines are clear enough. Although a 12-year-old plan to concentrate France's entire effort during the coming war on an invasion of England had been updated as recently as 1777, the French naval ministry had quite different ideas. There is no evidence that Vergennes was attracted before the spring of 1779 to any invasion plan or even an attack on the British navy's chief base at Portsmouth.[21] Invasion required France to draw as many ships as possible away from the British Home Squadron, by feints or minor thrusts against British colonies and attacks on British overseas trade, and then to strike across the Channel. The actual French naval plan was precisely the opposite: to keep the attention of the British home forces riveted on Brest and launch the primary attacks overseas in America, the West Indies and the Orient.[22]

The drafter of this plan remains virtually unknown: Charles-Pierre de Claret, Chevalier (later Comte) de Fleurieu, a former student of scientific navigation, who occupied the position of director general of ports and arsenals and served as chief administrative assistant of Sartine, the naval minister. Though Piers Mackesy refers to "the French Admiralty's planning staff," there was no such body.[23] Fleurieu was the sole French naval officer of the day who might be called a general staff officer, and it was he who drew up for the minister's signature instructions for naval commanders during the war.[24]

Therein lay one of the major weaknesses of the French navy: the absence of a collective body of seagoing officers to advise the minister concerning policy on the conduct of operations. The results of this institutional shortcoming were that a great deal was left to improvisation; naval doctrine remained undeveloped; and despite recent reform efforts, administrators continued to wield too much power over operations. The absence of any institutional vehicle for the expression of professional opinion such as the Board of Admiralty in Great Britain's Royal Navy also exacerbated the savage factionalism that wracked the navy throughout the eighteenth century and was unchecked during the American war.[25] Even the foremost French admirals of the war, d'Estaing and de Grasse, were both to suffer the effects of insubordination and the ill-will, even hatred, of some of their captains.[26] Perhaps only in the French navy, where a corps of haughty, conservative nobles virtually ignored the hierarchy of rank in favor of that of birth, would a junior captain refer to Vice Admiral d'Estaing, senior officer afloat, as "chicken-hearted and witless" (*un poltron et un homme sans talents*).[27]

The 1778 campaign mirrored Vergennes' strategy exactly, and by and large it was remarkably successful. Far from being examples of muddle-headedness and "oafish tactics," as has recently been claimed, the conduct of 68-year-old Admiral Louis-Guillouet, Comte d'Orvilliers, off the west coast of France and that of the much younger, but senior Admiral Jean-Baptiste-Charles-Henri-Hector, Comte d'Estaing, deserve closer examination.[28] Vice Admiral d'Estaing left Toulon in April on a multiple mission: to attack the English in Delaware and New York or anywhere he thought practicable; to support American land operations (but only north of the United States, in Nova Scotia or Newfoundland); and, after the hurricane season had passed, to proceed to Martinique in the West Indies to take British possessions in the Windward Islands and protect French islands and their shipping before leaving for France.[29]

In the Channel, French strategy was to divert British attention from d'Estaing's major thrust to America and, just as important, provoke a British attack. In order to prevent Britain from exercising the terms of its defensive alliance with Holland and thus bring the Dutch into the war, and also to avoid disturbing the extremely delicate state of Franco-Austrian relations, Vergennes needed to be able to point to British aggression. This is perhaps a good illustration of the limits of strategy designed by a diplomat; but it was no accident that France dated the outbreak of war with Great Britain at the attack of HMS *Arethusa*, frigate, on *La Belle Poule*, 26-guns, on 17 June 1778.[30] Throughout the next five years of war, France maintained the fiction of British aggression, though not one power in Europe accepted the elaborate fraud.

When Admiral d'Orvilliers sailed from Brest in command of 32 ships-of-the-line, his original instructions urging aggressive tactics were cancelled, and new ones from Sartine ordered him to avoid all risks. His chief tasks were to draw British attention to the Channel and hold it there, disguise the significance of d'Estaing's departure from Toulon, and prevent any morale-destroying British landings on the French coast.[31] Putting the best face on the events of the indecisive engagement that resulted, known to history as the Battle of Ouessant, or Ushant to the English, scholar Etienne Taillemite recently concluded that, although serious tactical weaknesses remained in matters of command, conception of operations and handling of large forces, the engagement had an important effect on morale by demonstrating to the French navy that it could engage the largest navy in Europe with some success.[32] The main point, however, is that the French commander had acted as he had been instructed and trailed his coat.

The seemingly strange behavior of d'Orvilliers at Ouessant does shed light on a larger issue bearing upon French naval performance during the eighteenth century, that quite contrary views of the purpose and aim of naval battles prevailed in France and in Great Britain. Whose views were the more valid is a separate issue; but it is clear from examples that can be drawn from the previous 50 years or more, that the general French aims of war at sea were to attack seaborne trade, launch land assaults against enemy colonial possessions, reinforce French interests overseas and escort French trade. As early as the 1730s, senior French officers denied that any good could come from fleet actions, and a similar attitude prevailed throughout the American war.[33]

The hesitancy in the handling of the French fleets also owed much to their commanders' inexperience. Sartine's own uncertainty as secretary of state for the navy probably communicated itself as well. The latter may have stemmed from the enormous effort it had cost during the previous four years to rebuild the navy, and also from the contradictory policies advocated by colonial planters on the one hand and metropolitan merchants, who feared the threats war posed to their investments at sea, on the other. As a miserly French merchant might have been, Sartine was anxious to preserve the great horde of wealth that the navy represented. He may have feared to risk it without a guarantee of success.[34] His hesitation, and also his surprising orders to open the French West Indies to American and neutral shipping in response to the refusal well before war broke out of metropolitan merchants to fit out new trading ventures, lend support for this view.

Admiral d'Estaing, once a lieutenant general of the army, had been "parachuted" into the navy 16 years before the American war and had never been in a naval battle, and neither he nor d'Orvilliers had ever before maneuvered large squadrons of ships. His conduct in America has often been criticized on the basis of his refusal in July 1778 to engage Vice Admiral Lord Richard Howe near Sandy Hook at the entry to New York harbor, and for failing to strike some positive blow to assist his American allies.[35] Recently, however, it has been appreciated that in pursuing, as instructed, his vaguely defined mission, d'Estaing on that occasion imposed upon the British a major change of strategy, one that greatly favored the American insurgents. Despite his maladroitness and failure a second time to engage the British, off Newport in August, and though a major storm subsequently damaged both fleets, forcing the British into New York and the French into Boston, the mere presence of d'Estaing's squadron, with or without local superiority, forced the British to alter their own strategy of suppressing the insurgents and to abandon their blockade of the American coast.

By September, the British navy had been reduced to defending three urban centers – New York, Newport and Halifax – thus opening the entire coast as far south as Florida to insurgent trade and privateering.[36] French strategy had delivered a major blow to the British war effort. The news of d'Estaing's imminent arrival in the spring of 1778 had forced the evacuation of Philadelphia. By its presence alone, the French navy had reduced British counterinsurgency to a secondary priority. No clearer demonstration could be had than what followed.

When the French fleet finally sailed from Boston for the West Indies in November 1778, the British navy followed, taking 5,000 troops and sending 3,000 more to Florida the same month.[37] In short, the French had deprived the British navy of the strategic initiative and reduced it to reacting defensively. The French began the next season's campaign enjoying strategic freedom, controlling the pace of the maritime agenda. The question remains as to how well they used it.

In the event, in 1779 the need to rely on Spanish support forced France to turn from its overseas, or peripheral, strategy back to a European, or central, one. Although Sartine and Vergennes had believed that France enjoyed effective naval parity with Britain for a few months in the spring of 1778, they had not expected French strength alone to bring results. From the beginning, they knew that Spanish naval assistance was a prerequisite to success, and French diplomacy in the latter half of 1778 focused on Spain as never before. By early 1779, Spain's reluctance to enter the war had driven Vergennes to desperate eagerness to agree to any and all Spanish demands, including an invasion of Great Britain, in order to get an alliance. Fortunately, a combination of British ineptitude and arrogance pushed Spain toward France and, on 12 April, the two nations signed an offensive alliance in the Convention of Aranjuez. Whether the Convention amounted to a great accomplishment of French diplomacy in that war, however, remains problematic; it allowed Spanish strategy to focus at will either at home or overseas, on Gibraltar and Minorca, or Jamaica and Florida, even Honduras and Newfoundland if one wanted to stretch the point.[38] Spain had much more to lose overseas than France, and lacked the resources for a long conflict. It was

Spain's desire for a short and decisive war rather than a long-drawn-out one that was the basis of the Franco-Spanish plan ultimately settled upon for 1779 – to invade Great Britain.[39]

The history of the "grand design," as the invasion became known, and of its deterioration into a naval and military disaster of tragic proportions, with the thousands of lives lost, has been well told elsewhere.[40] However, the plan was the preference of neither French foreign policy nor naval strategy but a reflection of military and economic weakness; it was the price for support elsewhere demanded by Spain, which had not the slightest interest in the re-establishment of French prestige in Europe. Aside from the enormous loss of human and material resources resulting from the failure of the invasion, Spanish aims produced two major detrimental effects. First, they ensured that France would have to fight a much longer war than originally planned, and that the strain on the government's already weak financial structure would accordingly increase. Second, Spanish demands made it much more difficult from 1779 on for the French to concentrate sufficient resources overseas to achieve local superiority. Indeed, far from being a great accomplishment of French diplomacy, the Franco-Spanish alliance rendered French strategy after the failure in the Channel more ambiguous and hesitant than before. Support that had once been a prerequisite for victory had quickly become to some degree an impediment.

The 1779 campaign in America supports such an interpretation. On 30 December 1778, British naval reinforcements and troops from New York captured St. Lucia, to windward of Martinique, and provoked a counterattack by the slow-sailing d'Estaing, who had arrived in the Antilles behind the British. Following an exchange of fire with the inferior British fleet, d'Estaing personally led his troops ashore, was repulsed by the new occupiers and retreated to Martinique.[41] British possession of St. Lucia was of decisive tactical importance for the duration of the war. For a third time, with superior numbers, d'Estaing had abandoned the scene of battle. At Martinique, d'Estaing quarreled with the vigorous governor general, the Marquis de Bouillé, who three months earlier had captured, with local forces, the island of Dominica, lying between Martinique and Guadeloupe. Bouillé was justifiably angry at the threat posed to Martinique by the new British conquest.

During the winter and spring of 1779, the French lost tactical superiority in the West Indies as British ships arrived in substantial numbers; but French reinforcements, because of the great demand for ships in Europe, only trickled in. Commodore (later Admiral) de Grasse arrived with five ships-of-the-line in February, and two more escorting a convoy came in April. In June, with the aid of some of d'Estaing's ships, Bouillé captured the island of Saint Vincent, but more significant – even though it had been accomplished only by cancelling the departure of a squadron destined for India – was Commodore Toussaint-Guillaume de La Motte-Picquet's arrival soon after with five more ships, which gave d'Estaing local superiority.[42]

D'Estaing acted immediately, sailing to attack Barbados. Contrary winds forced him to a new destination, Grenada, and on 2 July he landed with his troops and took the island along with 30 richly laden merchantmen. Four days later, d'Estaing successfully defended his conquest against an inferior British fleet. He did not then annihilate that force, and naturally he has been criticized for this; yet, he had carried out his mission. In fact, considering that the original 12 ships of his fleet had been away from France for 15 months, his reluctance may well be deemed prudence.[43] In all of 1779, only 12 more ships-of-the-line were sent to the Caribbean, and none to America. Thus, after d'Estaing received orders to bring his heavily fouled ships home in advance of the hurricane season, he left only 12 of-the-line in the West Indies.

During the winter of 1778–79, urgent appeals from the Americans for aid against the British who had overrun Georgia and captured Savannah reached d'Estaing at Martinique. He could do nothing at the time, for good reasons: his numbers were then inferior, and he could not leave Martinique except for the fortnight it took to attempt to retake St. Lucia. Also, the preservation of French possessions took priority over retaking Georgia, which he thought impossible in any case. Finally, he planned to attack farther north, at Halifax or in Newfoundland.[44] Nevertheless, later in August, on his way out of the Antilles, the much maligned admiral responded generously. Ignoring his most recent orders, d'Estaing sailed with all his ships for Savannah on a mission more in accord with his original instructions, which had been to strike a blow in aid of his American allies. Perhaps his earlier failure to do so now rankled, but that is unknown. As he had at St. Lucia and Grenada, d'Estaing put his troops ashore and led them himself in a ground assault on the British entrenchments. The French attack failed, and the admiral was wounded.[45] Getting the troops back on board the ships de Grasse had brought in February so that they could return to the West Indies, he collected his original squadron and sailed for France. Storms scattered his ships, and they reached France only a few at a time.

Such a miserable end has obscured for historians the strategic accomplishments of the 1779 campaign, its extraordinary duration and the fact that d'Estaing had not lost one ship to the enemy. Nevertheless, d'Estaing had shown himself to be, to say the least, a strange naval leader. His chief military activity had been leading troops in land assaults. His naval actions were utterly undistinguished; he seemed never to have grasped the nature of sea power at all. "Much more noise than work is only too often the net product of naval engagements," he reported to Vergennes.[46] No better evidence could be had of the traditional French view of naval strategy.

On the other hand, such an attitude was no indication at all of the admiral's personal courage. "If only Monsieur d'Estaing was as able a naval officer as he is brave as a man," wrote one of his captains.[47] The author was Pierre André de Suffren, who during this campaign may have learned the lessons that were to be reflected in his aggressive conduct in the Indian Ocean only a year later. One final irony remains: that d'Estaing's last appearance in America in fact accomplished what his earlier efforts had failed to do. On learning that the French admiral had appeared at Savannah, Sir Henry Clinton decided he could no longer hold both Rhode Island and New York, and evacuated the former. The following summer, a French expeditionary force under the command of the Comte de Rochambeau would occupy Narragansett Bay and Newport without firing a shot.

French naval tactics of 1779 have often drawn much criticism, but the success of that year's strategy should not be overlooked. In 1780, however, French strategy became weaker and less focused. Dissension and military ineffectiveness among the Americans discouraged Vergennes, as did the continued vigorous response of the British. Spanish emphasis on besieging Gibraltar and refusal to cooperate in joint operations in the Caribbean also contributed to hesitancy and uncertainty.[48] The French navy returned to its American strategy, but with even more serious impediments to its coherence than before. In January, the British navy's successful relief of Gibraltar and destruction of the blockading force there delivered such a severe blow to morale that the Spanish government began to consider separate negotiations with Britain out of fear for the security of its overseas possessions.[49] Anticipating a threat there, Spain announced plans to send 10–12 of-the-line and 10,000 men to the West Indies as early as May.[50] French naval strategy now acquired a new obligation, to prevent a defection or defeat of the Spanish, who well remembered the loss of Havana and Florida less than 20 years before. In keeping with their larger aims, the French saw as their first priority not aiding the Americans but ensuring the safety of their own and Spanish possessions in and around the Caribbean.

Sartine, the naval minister, planned to place a combined fleet off the Azores to intercept commerce and hold the attention of the enemy's home fleet, but to send his main thrust once more to America. The need to contribute ten ships-of-the-line to the mid-Atlantic Franco-Spanish force, however, strained French resources to the limit and made local superiority in the West Indies nearly impossible to achieve. A total of 16 ships-of-the-line, nine lighter warships and 83 merchantmen and transports carrying 4,400 troops were sent to the West Indies under the command of the elderly Admiral de Guichen, whose instructions were exclusively defensive: to protect his convoy and colonial commerce, ensure free communication for French shipping and guard the French islands from all attack. As in the past, Sartine ordered him *"ne rien entreprendre qu'avec la certitude du succès"* – not to risk his fleet without the certainty of success.[51]

Luc-Urbain du Bouexic, Comte de Guichen was (unlike d'Estaing) a typical French naval officer of the ancien régime. His origins in provincial Breton, long service, lack of sea experience, slowness of promotion and traditional tactics all combined to earn him disdain and reproach for excessive caution and lack of initiative.[52] Guichen's orders in 1780 were "to keep the sea, so far as the force maintained by England in the Windward Islands would permit without too far compromising the fleet entrusted to him."[53] Mahan remarks that the French admiral had no alternative but to shrink from a decisive engagement; more to the point is the fact that Guichen operated under defensive instructions that reflected not only the traditional mission-oriented strategy of the French navy – epitomized by d'Estaing's comment about naval engagements – but also the transformation of the Spanish from an asset to a liability, one that could not be ignored.

After reaching the Antilles and attaching the ships under Commodore de Grasse's command, Guichen had 22 ships-of-the-line and enjoyed a slight superiority in numbers over British Admiral Sir George Rodney, who arrived shortly after him. But virtually nothing would be accomplished, due to the French admiral's instructions, which reinforced his habitual prudence. Under the urging of governor-general of the Windward Islands, the Marquis de Bouillé, Guichen planned to attack St. Lucia. The battle that ensued off Martinique on 17 April occasioned much vilification from the British admiral against his own captains, and has been the subject of debate ever since; the chief results, however, were that the future victor at the battle of the Saints failed to put a crimp in the well-handled French forces, whereas the cautious French tactician withheld his attack from St. Lucia.[54] Guichen and Rodney met twice again a month later, but after two weeks of maneuvering to allow each to fight on his own terms, they broke off and returned to Martinique and Barbados, respectively. Rodney had successfully thwarted the planned French attack on St. Lucia.[55]

All accounts of French strategy here ignore the Marquis de Bouillé, which is a serious mistake. For, although the naval strategy called for the capture of British islands, in fact those that fell into French hands did so chiefly due to the vigorous conduct of the governor who spent most of the war – when he was not himself capturing islands – railing against the excessive caution of naval commanders.[56] Toward the end of the war, Bouillé wrote of the French squadron: "Since the war [began], on the offensive as on the defensive, it has been much more prejudicial than useful to the king's service in the colonies where, in general, the navy has done only silly things."[57] Bouillé described one of Guichen's divisional commanders, Commodore de Sade (cousin of the notorious novelist and playwright), as a "seventy-year-old man, half-witted and ignorant, but brave."[58]

Bouillé was a trifle hard on the navy. Guichen and Rodney met three times during 1780, and in each case the British admiral accomplished little. For the French, however, this campaign marked a turning point in the war, in that the Spaniards would not have accepted another setback.[59] Guichen's eventual success was owed not to his tactical maneuvering against Rodney but to the arrival off Martinique in June 1780 of the promised Spanish fleet, with 12 ships-of-the-line, 146 merchantmen and transports and 11,000 troops. The French admiral now slipped out of Fort Royal (Fort-de-France) with 15 sail and joined the Spaniards; but the latter, who had many sick on board, had no thought of combined operations and insisted instead on being escorted northward. Early in July, the allied fleet departed the Windward Islands and separated at the eastern end of Cuba, the Spaniards to make for Havana and the French for Cap François (Cap Haitien) on the northern coast of Hispaniola. There Guichen found entreaties from the Marquis de Lafayette and the French minister to the United States to bring his forces to the American mainland, but the ever-cautious admiral refused to disobey his orders which made no mention of North American waters. Convoying a homeward-bound fleet of nearly 100 heavily laden merchantmen that he had escorted from Martinique to St. Domingue (Haiti), in mid-August he sailed for Cadiz to avoid the onset of the hurricane season.

By July 1780, however, another French force arrived in the western Atlantic, this time at Narragansett Bay, Rhode Island. It was commanded by Commodore Chevalier d'Arsac de Ternay, and it carried a French expeditionary force under the Comte de Rochambeau. Where the outcome in the West Indies had been unclear, the French strategy in America met with success. That these seven ships-of-the-line and 32 transports with 5,500 troops had arrived safely indicated that, even on the defensive and in an uncertain situation, the peripheral strategy remained effective. Certainly Rodney's appearance in mid-September at Sandy Hook with 14 ships confirms that the British thought it was.[60] Although the British now had three times the number of French ships in America, their commanders chose to quarrel among themselves. This shows that the French were not the only ones whose personal animosities affected outcome, which suggests that too much weight should not be given to the factional divisions among French officers.

At Narragansett Bay, Ternay was astride the communications between New York and Halifax and, for that matter, in position to strike anywhere along the coast to the south. As autumn wore on and the danger of hurricanes subsided, he also presented a growing threat to the West Indies. The strategy was clearly intended to force the British navy to react, leaving the French in control of the pace of the war. Ternay had to be watched, and during the last six months of 1780 the Royal Navy did little else. In November, Rodney returned, like Guichen before him, to Europe; but a superior British field force remained at New York keeping an eye on the French at Newport, this at a time when British forces in the southern colonies were becoming ever more deeply mired in a murderous war of terror and counterinsurgency. Nevertheless, the French did not develop their strategic initiative in America; that failure proved deeply disappointing and combined with altered circumstances in Europe to increase the need to seek a resolution.

In France, political events that autumn also led to important changes. Some in the Royal Council favored initiating peace, but others, accepting that any hope for a short war was already a thing of the past, advocated expanding the conflict. Although earlier in the year the combined Franco-Spanish fleet, which had spent the campaign season in Cadiz and off the western approaches to Europe, had made the largest capture of a British convoy in the eighteenth century, French policy-makers had become deeply dissatisfied with its non-tactical role. Also, the secretary of state for the navy was becoming difficult; Sartine's request for the enormous sum of 173 million livres for the 1781 campaign suggested that he had become uncontrollable. This perception, combined with serious flaws in his program of naval rearmament and his choice of commanders, left him politically vulnerable. The Spanish alliance, too, continued to be a problem; in September 1780, the Spanish foreign minister had proposed a combined attack on Jamaica, which would force the French to abandon their current strategy in favor of a Spanish aim of reconquest.[61] Finally, the growing war of attrition had become unbearably costly. Even Vergennes agreed that the coming campaign must be the last: "The means to support it are daily becoming exhausted," he wrote in February 1781.[62]

The Marquis de Castries, secretary of state of the navy after October 1780, demanded an escalation of the war, but he was totally opposed to Spanish demands for a combined attack on Jamaica and to those in the Royal Council who dared even consider it. He was also adamantly opposed to the current chiefs, d'Estaing and Guichen. In one of his first moves, Castries ordered home all the French naval units at Cadiz, including Guichen's ships recently arrived from the West Indies. For Castries, the American war must be expanded and a fresh commander-in-chief given a new freedom to determine strategy in the field. Louis XVI had promised command of the West India squadron to the older, more senior Admiral Charles-Auguste de La Touche-Tréville, but Castries successfully imposed his will in Council, and the King named the 58-year-old Comte de Grasse.[63] The naval minister travelled to Brest in March 1781 to inspect the new rear admiral's fleet. Castries also wrote to Ternay, instructing him "to be more enterprising and not to sentence himself to a punctilious residency in Newport harbor."[64]

With no military reinforcements available for Rochambeau at Newport, in part because of the deteriorating situation in Europe, Castries directed de Grasse to act according to his new strategy of aggression and expansion, operating in coordination with the land commanders in America to strike a strong blow during the coming fourth campaign of the war. Commodore Barras de Saint-Laurent, who went out in the spring to take command of the Newport force, was ordered to send to the West Indies American pilots familiar with the Chesapeake. A week after leaving Brest with his enormous convoy, de Grasse dispatched a frigate to Newport with proposals addressed to Rochambeau and General George Washington to coordinate action later in 1781. At that point he parted company with Captain the Chevalier de Suffren, who was to expand Castries' peripheral strategy to the South Atlantic and India.[65]

Before de Grasse sailed for the West Indies, however, the French strategic situation had worsened. The British declared war against the United Provinces, which led to the seizure of St. Eustatius and other Dutch Islands in the West Indies. France had always sought to preserve Dutch neutrality, knowing full well that the Dutch colonies and Amsterdam's commitment to neutral rights and trade were of far greater strategic advantage to both France and the United States than any alliance.[66]

During the next four months after de Grasse appeared at Martinique in April 1781, little occurred beyond the French capture of Tobago. The campaign appeared to be heading toward a repeat of the previous year's passive strategy, preserving the fleet rather than striking a blow. In August, the onset of the hurricane season led de Grasse to seek more northerly seas. Reaching St. Domingue after leaving the Windward Islands, however, de Grasse found replies from the American military commanders to his earlier letters and also their pleas for immediate assistance. De Grasse obtained 3,300 troops from the governor of St. Domingue and, in response to Rochambeau's news that French troops had not been paid for two months, he sent a frigate to Havana where, on his personal promise to pay, five million livres were raised from Spanish merchants in a single day.[67] French merchants had previously refused to provide the necessary funds. Less than two weeks later, on 30 August, Admiral de Grasse entered Chesapeake Bay, and the prelude to one of the most significant naval battles in history was over.

The subject of French naval strategy does not require any examination of the battle of the Virginia Capes of 5 September 1781 that led directly to General Cornwallis' surrender on 19 October, or of the conduct there of Admiral de Grasse. If his military capacity was not conspicuous, his energetic response to the news awaiting him at St. Domingue contributed to the speed and concentration that left the enemy outnumbered off Yorktown and conditioned the successful outcome of French strategy. It is true, however, that the European half of French strategy in 1781 severely modified the American half – but also reinforced its success. That is, although the Marquis de Castries favored expanding the war overseas, Spanish demands and Vergennes' larger concerns forced modification of a strategy so obviously in the French interest.

Meanwhile, growing pressure among the allies for peace challenged the strategy in yet another way. France had not gone to war to destroy Great Britain or its international influence, or to further Spanish interests, but to regain its position in Europe, which it hoped to achieve by redressing the colonial balance of power. By the end of 1781, both had been largely accomplished, the latter owing in part to the successful achievement of the half of French strategy concerned with the center, that is Europe.

During the summer of 1781, allied naval forces achieved success in European waters. In the North Sea, the Dutch usefully kept a British squadron occupied and contributed to stretching British naval resources to their limits.[68] More dramatically, a combined Franco-Spanish assault carried the island of Minorca. The expeditionary force was larger than anything in American waters; in July the French naval component, 18 ships-of-the-line from Brest under the command of the Comte de Guichen, placed itself under the overall command of Admiral Don Luis de Córdoba, whose combined fleet of 30 sail and 100 transports safely landed 14,000 men on the island. Thereafter, the ships of the combined fleet spent most of the summer of 1781 cruising on the Soundings, westward of the English Channel and far from Minorca. Its aim was primarily to prevent the British from operating in the Mediterranean, but also to intercept British convoys and, in view of its numerical superiority, to provoke a general action.

It was in fact a fateful year in both theaters, and early that autumn, despite Spanish aims that concentrated resources against the British in Europe, French fortunes overseas also seemed to be at a crest. In October 1781, the British surrendered their last remaining field army in the American colonies at Yorktown, but by then the British had lost more than that to the allied enemies. Spanish colonial forces from Cuba and Louisiana, culminating in May in a two-year effort, had seized (with the assistance of French ships and troops) Pensacola on the coast of the Gulf of Mexico.[69] Also, during the autumn, the ever-active Marquis de Bouillé recaptured St. Eustatius.

Already, however, reverses were occurring. In early September the Spanish contingent of the combined fleet returned to Cadiz, forcing the now inferior French fleet to fall back into Brest. The whole Spanish alliance was thrown into jeopardy. The French reaction, at the insistence of Castries, was to plan a return in 1782 to the peripheral strategy; the focus would be on the West Indies and India, and even the cancelled attack on Hudson Bay was to go forward. In rapid preparation, reinforcements for these overseas campaigns were readied in the autumn and dispatched from France in December. Now occurred a second series of setbacks: over 80 percent of those reinforcements intended for de Grasse in the West Indies were captured, and in early 1782 a second convoy, bound for Suffren in India, was also lost.[70]

The consequences of these losses were severe. They redoubled the financial strain on the government brought on by Necker's removal from office; and the defeat of de Grasse at the battle of the Saints in April 1782 (of which more presently) was in some part due to the missing guns, munitions, spars and naval stores. Just how much his defeat can be blamed on this cause is unclear, but a strong argument can be made in the case of Commodore de Suffren in India. His campaign was to be continually checked and inhibited by lack of manpower and matériel, as well as by disobedient subordinates.

Despite these disasters, French strategy for 1782 remained to attack on the periphery, but now its aim became three-fold: to force Great Britain to the peace table, keep Spain in the war and prevent the Americans from leaving it. The French navy, however, was strained to its limits; no growing "military–industrial complex" existed at home to replace its losses. Manpower, matériel and financial resources were exhausted.[71] And if Vergennes, Castries and the Spanish foreign minister controlled strategy at the center, in 1782, de Grasse had chief direction of the campaign in the West Indies, and he failed.

On returning to Martinique after the battle of Chesapeake Bay, de Grasse and the Marquis de Bouillé decided upon a campaign to conquer all of the British possessions in the Windward Islands. In January came the French attack on St. Kitts (St. Christophe); Admiral Samuel Hood's attempt to raise the siege was beaten off and the island's fortress surrendered on 12 February.[72] At the end of March, de Grasse received some reinforcements, three ships-of-the-line, but they carried new instructions that French forces were to effect a juncture with a Spanish force of warships and transports en route to the Antilles and attack Jamaica. Castries left it to de Grasse to choose the time of the landings. In the event, Admiral Rodney's arrival at Barbados in February gave the British numerical superiority, and defensive advantage in the British Windward Islands.

According to John Creswell, more has been printed about the engagement that followed, known as the battle of the Saints, and fought off the Island of Dominica on 12 April 1782, than any other British naval battle except Trafalgar.[73] In short, it was a disaster for the French, who suffered the capture of the admiral commanding and three captains, and also the deaths of eight captains. In the aftermath, command of the French forces passed to the Marquis de Vaudreuil. He gathered the surviving vessels around the convoy carrying troops of the expeditionary force that had been the original reason for sailing, and made off for Cap François, which he reached on 25 April. Vaudreuil had but 16 vessels and, following a council of war between French and Spanish officers and officials, he organized two convoys of homeward-bound merchantmen escorted by eight ships-of-the-line. He kept with him only those ships that were copper-bottomed and, with less bottom fouling, were therefore faster. Although the planned rendezvous with 15 Spanish vessels now occurred, giving the allies numerical superiority, the entire offensive strategy had been shattered. Dissension and recrimination greatly increased among the French officers in the wake of the battle, and the planned attack on Jamaica was called off.[74] The French pursuit of an offensive strategy in the Western Hemisphere ended; the fleets in the West Indies remained on the defensive until the end of the war.

Franco-Spanish strategy at the center now focused on Gibraltar; but with the failure of yet another assault on 13 September, the naval war effectively came to an end. A month later, the British successfully relieved the fortress once again.[75] The ensuing engagement decided nothing; the signing of the preliminaries of peace on 20 January 1783 was exactly three months away.

France's involvement in the American war neither caused American independence, though it made a major contribution, nor did it make the French Revolution inevitable. The war certainly weakened France's financial system, as had previous crises, but this time the government proved unable to gain control of its debt – not because the task was impossible but because political opposition prohibited the employment of usual solutions. Men, not fate or historical forces, led France toward the Revolution.[76] This chapter has sought to demonstrate that French intervention in American affairs and the effect of purely military factors on French objectives in the American war were never as important as the influence exerted on the intervention itself by domestic politics, the Spanish alliance, and the exigencies of the colonial situation.

French intervention in the American War of Independence did allow France to resume, however briefly, the position in the competitive states system that it had lost 20 years earlier. From the Comte de Vergennes' point of view, intervention succeeded magnificently. The decision to aid the American insurgents, the choice to fight the war against Great Britain overseas while struggling against Spanish efforts to co-opt France in its own interests and the dispatch of the several French expeditionary corps were all primarily due to him. The 1783 Treaty of Versailles not only acknowledged the independence of the United States but re-established the prestige of France, by restraining the appetites of Prussia and the Hapsburg house of Austria, playing off the Ottoman empire against the steadily mounting pressure of Russia and also the United Provinces against the Hapsburgs, and by reinforcing the Spanish alliance to counterbalance British power.

This was no mean feat, considering that Vergennes, unable to rely on French resources alone, had been forced to depend upon strength outside French control. Notwithstanding, and although the French seized a high degree of strategic initiative at the beginning of the war, in general their naval operations were inhibited. They never succeeded in shaking off the moral advantage possessed by the enemy, with his experience, skill and arrogance. Nor did they shake off their own traditional strategic and tactical doctrines which rejected fleet actions to destroy enemy sea forces – though it remains debatable whether the latter deserved the outright condemnation it has received from later navalists. French naval strategy also failed to rise above the ambitions and collective interests, insubordination and inexperience of the officer corps. While this aspect needs to be taken into account, it seems scarcely surprising; strategy is, after all, socially as well as politically constructed. Personal factors neither prevented, nor caused, final French success. In fact, French naval strategy during the American War of Independence was more than a matter of keeping peace in Europe and sending major naval forces to America. Its success was due to something else entirely.

During the American war, French naval strategy took the form of an interlocking relationship between the center and periphery, between the European and American theaters. French naval planners initially called for major thrusts to America, chiefly to the West Indies. Having to assign naval resources to the center seemed to them a constraint, the price paid for the Spanish support that filled the vacuum of French naval weakness. Historians without exception have accepted this notion, finding that France achieved success in proportion to the degree to which it freed itself from European entanglements. But it can be argued that this "price," the invasion of England and later the conquests of Gibraltar and Minorca, may not have been detrimental to French naval strategy after all. Rather than weighing against the effectiveness of naval forces deployed to the periphery, that large French forces remained in Europe in support of the Spanish aims was the key to the former's effectiveness. Had the Spanish insisted instead on protection of their own colonial possessions or conquest of British possessions in the Caribbean, e.g. Jamaica, as their primary demand, it is unlikely that French naval resources would have been so available to support the Americans. At the same time, the Spanish aims, pursued with French support, considerably increased British uncertainty throughout the war, forcing the latter to retain forces in home waters beyond what the French alone would have tied up. France had not disengaged itself from Europe in order to concentrate resources in America, but rather owed its final success in America to its continued involvement in Europe. It locked the central and peripheral strategies into one.

Notes

1 This chapter was first published in *Naval War College Review* (Fall 1994), vol. 47, pp. 83–108.
2 See, for example, Paul Kennedy, *The Rise and Fall of the Great Powers: Economic Change and Military Conflict from 1500 to 2000* (London: Unwin Hyman, 1988), pp. 88–90, 169.
3 Ibid., pp. 117–18, my italics.
4 Ibid., p. 89.
5 For the first claim, e.g., William J. Eccles, *France in America*, rev. edn. (Toronto: Fitzhenry & Whiteside, 1990), p. 251.

6 Jonathan Dull, *The French Navy and American Independence: A Study of Arms and Diplomacy, 1774–1787* (Princeton: Princeton University Press, 1975), pp. 11 and 343–4.
7 J.F. Bosher, *The French Revolution* (New York: W.W. Norton, 1988), p. 67; also Simon Schama, *Citizens: A Chronicle of the French Revolution* (New York: Alfred A. Knopf, 1989), pp. 51–9.
8 Robert D. Harris, *Necker: Reform Statesman of the Ancien Régime* (Berkeley: University of California Press, 1979) is the most complete study; but see also J.F. Bosher, *French Finances, 1770–1795: From Business to Bureaucracy* (Cambridge: Cambridge University Press, 1970), chapter 8, pp. 142–65.
9 For a somewhat uncritical view in praise of Sartine, see Dull, *The French Navy*, pp. 14–15, 23–5 and 58–60. See Jacques Michel, *Du Paris de Louis XV à la marine de Louis XVI, l'oeuvre de Monsieur de Sartine*, 2 vols. (Paris: Edition de l'Erudit, 1984) for a more complete study.
10 Dull, *The French Navy*, pp. 199–202 admits Necker's influence, but attributes Sartine's dismissal to the secretary of state for foreign affairs, Vergennes, who sacrificed him to the demands of Franco-Spanish diplomacy. Harris, *Necker*, pp. 208–9, is more convincing that the reasons were financial.
11 On Castries, see René de La Croix, Duc de Castries, *Le Maréchal de Castries (1727–1800)* (Paris: Flammarion, 1956).
12 One of the most enigmatic and controversial figures of eighteenth-century French governments, Maurepas has never been the subject of a scholarly biography; a good place to gain some insight into his pervasive influence in government and at court during the reign of Louis XVI, however, is Jehan de Witte, ed., *Journal de l'Abbé de Véri*, 2 vols. (Paris: Plon, 1933).
13 Piers Mackesy, *The War for America, 1775–1783* (London: Longmans, 1964).
14 In addition to Dull's sketch of Vergennes in *The French Navy*, pp. 6–8, 294–5 and 334–5, see Orville T. Murphy, *Charles Gravier, Comte de Vergennes: French Diplomacy in the Age of Revolution, 1719–1787* (Albany: State University of New York Press, 1982) for the most complete study; and also J.F. Labourdette, *Vergennes, Ministre principal de Louis XVI* (Paris: Editions Desjonquières, 1990) whose study complements Murphy's by focusing on the politics of the French court and Royal Council.
15 Archives des Affaires Etrangères, Espagne, tome 590, folio 141. Vergennes to Comte de Montmorin, 31 July 1778, quoted in A.T. Patterson, *The Other Armada: The Franco-Spanish Attempt to Invade Britain in 1779* (Manchester: Manchester University Press, 1960), p. 37; also Dull, *The French Navy*, p. 165 for a similar expression to the same correspondent 14 months later.
16 For a broad overview and comparison of French and British economies during the half-century before the American war, see François Crouzet, "England and France in the Eighteenth Century: A Comparative Analysis of Two Economic Growths," reprinted in his *Britain Ascendant: Comparative Studies in Franco-British Economic History* (Cambridge: Cambridge University Press, 1990), pp. 12–43 (French original in *Annales E.S.C.*, v. 2 [1966], 254–91); see also Ralph Davis, *The Rise of the Atlantic Economies* (London: Methuen, 1973), chapters 17 and 18, pp. 288–316, for a critical variation on the same theme.
17 Murphy, *Vergennes*, p. 256; and Dull, *The French Navy*, pp. 138–9.
18 Schama, *Citizens*, pp. 79–87; also Dull, *The French Navy*, pp. 46–7.
19 Harris, *Necker*, p. 119.
20 Murphy, *Vergennes*, chapters 21–5, pp. 261–330.
21 See E.H. Jenkins, *A History of the French Navy* (London: Macdonald and Jane's, 1973), p. 151.
22 Patterson, *The Other Armada*, pp. 37–9, for an excellent brief discussion; also Mackesy, *War for America*, pp. 190–2.
23 Mackesy, *War for America*, p. 324.

24 G. Lacour-Gayet, *La Marine militaire de la France sous le règne de Louis XVI* (Paris: Honoré Champion, 1905), pp. 19–20; also Raoul Castex, *Les idées militaires de la marine du xviiie siècle, de Ruyter à Suffren* (Paris: L. Fournier, 1911), p. 165.
25 See E. Taillemite, *L'Histoire ignorée de la marine française* (Paris: Librairie Académique Perrin, 1988), pp. 175–6 for a more complete discussion.
26 Ibid., pp. 169, 173.
27 Quoted in Michel Vergé-Franceschi, *La Royal au temps de l'admiral d'Estaing* (Paris: La Pensée Universelle, 1977), p. 44.
28 See John A. Tilley, *The British Navy and the American Revolution* (Columbia: University of South Carolina Press, 1987), p. 150 for the phrase and a general example of failure to grasp French intentions.
29 Henri Doniol, *Histoire de la participation de la France à l'établissement des Etats-Unis d'Amérique: correspondance diplomatique et documents*, 5 vols. (Paris: Imprimerie nationale, 1886–92), vol. 3, pp. 237–52 for summaries of his instructions sent to the French minister to the United States in June 1778 in d'Estaing's own hand. It is simply astonishing that few historians who have heaped so much opprobrium on the admiral have ever referred to his instructions.
30 Dull, *The French Navy*, p. 119.
31 Dull, *The French Navy*, p. 121; also Jenkins, *A History of the French Navy*, pp. 150–2.
32 Taillemite, *L'Histoire ignorée*, pp. 185–6.
33 V.F. Brun, *Guerres maritimes de la France: port de Toulon, ses armements, son administration depuis son origine jusqu'à nos jours*, 2 vols. (Paris: Plon, 1861), vol. 1, pp. 243–4, quoting Admiral René Duguay-Trouin that sea battles cost France infinitely and decided nothing.
34 Jean Tarrade, *Le Commerce coloniale de la France à la fin de l'ancien régime: l'évolution du régime de 'l'Exclusif' de 1763 à 1789*, 2 vols. (Paris: Presses Universitaires de France, 1972), vol. 1, pp. 466–8, esp. note 67.
35 Jenkins, *History of the French Navy*, p. 153 and Dull, *The French Navy*, pp. 123–4.
36 For the best discussion of the campaign in America, see David Syrett, *The Royal Navy in American Waters, 1775–1783* (Aldershot: Scolar Press, 1989), pp. 92–116.
37 Ibid., p. 118.
38 See Dull, *The French Navy*, pp. 126–43; also Murphy, *Vergennes*, pp. 261–79 for the complex diplomacy leading to the convention.
39 Mackesy, *War for America*, pp. 279–80.
40 See Patterson, *The Other Armada*.
41 A.T. Mahan, *The Major Operations of the Navies in the War of Independence* (London: S. Low, Marston, 1913), pp. 101–4; also Mackesy, *War for America*, pp. 231–2.
42 Dull, *The French Navy*, p. 159.
43 See Mahan, *Major Operations*, pp. 105–12 for the best overall account; but see John Creswell, *British Admirals of the Eighteenth Century: Tactics in Battle* (London: George Allen & Unwin, 1972), chapter 9, pp. 132–40 for a more detailed tactical discussion based on the *Barrington Papers* (London: Navy Records Society, 1941).
44 Doniol, *Histoire de la participation*, v. 4, pp. 160–1, Estaing to Gérard, Fort Royal, 9 Mar. 1779.
45 See A.A. Lawrence, *Storm Over Savannah: The Story of Count d'Estaing and the Siege of the Town in 1779* (Athens: University of Georgia Press, 1951); and C.C. Jones Jr., ed., *The Siege of Savannah by the Fleet of Count d'Estaing in 1779* (New York: New York Times [1874], 1968).
46 Doniol, *Histoire de la participation*, vol. 4, p. 295.
47 Quoted in Jenkins, *A History of the French Navy*, p. 158.
48 Mackesy, *War for America*, p. 324.
49 See David Spinney, *Rodney* (London: George Allen & Unwin, 1969), pp. 196–312; and Murphy, *Vergennes*, p. 330.

50 Patrick Villiers, *Marine royal, corsaires et trafic dans l'Atlantique de Louis XIV à Louis XVI*, 2 vols. (Dunkerque: Société Dunkerquoise d'Histoire et d'Archéologie, 1991), vol. 2, pp. 582–3.
51 Taillemite, *L'Histoire ignorée*, p. 204; and Villiers, *Marine royal*, vol. 2, p. 583.
52 See Castex, *Les idées militaires*, pp. 79–97 for a highly critical assessment of Guichen's three battles.
53 Quoted in Mahan, *Major Operations*, p. 141; see also Taillemite, *L'Histoire ignorée*, pp. 200–9 for a recent favorable appreciation of Guichen.
54 See Mahan, *Major Operations*, pp. 128–58 for the classic account of Guichen's and Rodney's campaign; but see also Creswell, *British Admirals*, pp. 141–51 for a different and superior appreciation.
55 Spinney, *Rodney*, pp. 317–44; and also Mahan, *Major Operations*, p. 140.
56 Bouillé's 480-page report on the war in the West Indies, which can be found in Archives des colonies, Série C8A, vol. 82, contains a valuable commentary on the behavior of the navy.
57 Quoted in Tarrade, *Le Commerce colonial*, vol. 1, p. 472, note 82.
58 Quoted in Taillemite, *L'Histoire ignorée*, p. 171.
59 Dull, *The French Navy*, p. 188.
60 See Syrett, *The Royal Navy*, pp. 142, 144–6 for the clearest discussion of Ternay's threat to the British war effort. See Maurice Linyer de La Barbée, *Le Chevalier de Ternay: vie de Charles-Henry-Louis d'Arsac de Ternay, chef d'escadre des armées navales*, 2 vols. (Grenoble: Editions des 4 seigeurs, 1972), vol. 2, pp. 529–642 for a recent account of the French campaign.
61 Dull, *The French Navy*, pp. 197–9.
62 Doniol, *Histoire de la participation*, vol. 4, pp. 544–5.
63 Dull, *The French Navy*, pp. 217–18.
64 Castries, *Le Maréchal de Castries*, p. 89.
65 Doniol, *Histoire de la participation*, vol. 5, pp. 469–70, Castries to Rochambeau, Brest, 21 Mar. 1781.
66 See Murphy, *Vergennes*, pp. 280–8; and Dull, *The French Navy*, pp. 211–16.
67 Ibid., pp. 239–48 for a good summary of the movements of the French forces; but see Mahan, *Major Operations*, pp. 176–8.
68 Mackesy, *War for America*, pp. 394–5.
69 In one of the strangest acts of the war, on 12 February 1781, a small Spanish force captured Fort St. Joseph, near present-day Niles, Michigan, as part of the overall Spanish attack on the British in America. See the proclamation of conquest printed in Joseph L. Peyser, ed. and trans., *Letters from New France: The Upper Country 1686–1783* (Urbana and Chicago: University of Illinois Press, 1992), pp. 220–21.
70 Mahan, *Major Operations*, pp. 227–8.
71 Dull, *The French Navy*, pp. 279–80.
72 Some historians ignore these preliminaries, which were primarily responsible for rendering the British naval victory nugatory; for example, see Creswell, *British Admirals*, pp. 163–5.
73 Creswell, *British Admirals*, p. 163.
74 Villiers, *Marine royal*, vol. 2, p. 603; Dull, *The French Navy*, pp. 283–4.
75 T.H. McGuffie, *The Siege of Gibraltar 1779–1783* (London: Batsford, 1965), pp. 139–67.
76 J.F. Bosher, *French Finances*, pp. 166–82; also Harris, *Necker*, p. 216.

8 Spanish policy and strategy

Thomas E. Chávez

In fulfillment of the Bourbon Family Compact, Spain declared war against Great Britain on 21 June 1779. Spain joined France as an ally and, through France's treaty with Britain's rebelling American colonists, joined the struggle on the side of securing independence for the Americans. France and the American colonies agreed upon Spain's goals as well as the strategy that eventually resulted in victory. Spain's entry into the war was not a surprise so much as a relief. General George Washington observed that Great Britain's failure to agree to Spain's efforts to negotiate a peace, including independence, was "more strongly tinctured with insanity than she has done in the course of this contest." The only excuse for Great Britain's action, he added, was its "obstinacy."[1] Spain, as will be seen, wanted to regain lands that it had lost as a consequence of the Seven Years' War.

Diplomacy and covert aid

Spain began preparing for renewed war as early as the end of the Seven Years' War in 1763. Its field commanders in Spanish Louisiana and Cuba had instructions to prepare for hostilities. The newly appointed and relatively young Bernardo de Gálvez, named governor of Louisiana and commander of all field troops, arrived in New Orleans with instructions to bolster New Orleans' defenses, strengthen the militia, funnel covert funds and supplies upriver through St. Louis to Fort Pitt, and spy on neighboring British settlements, the most important of which were Mobile and Pensacola.

As George Washington knew, Spain began covertly to support the colonists even before the Declaration of Independence was signed in 1776. Spanish supplies entered the aspiring young country directly from Europe, as well as through Havana, Spanish New Orleans and up the Mississippi and the Ohio rivers. Much of the Spanish aid sent directly from Europe was filtered through France.

In August 1777, Spain decided to follow France's lead and send observers to the rebelling colonies. Two of these men were selected and clandestinely sent to the colonies in November and the following January. One of them, Juan de Miralles, would become a confidant of Washington and a close observer of the Continental Congress. He would keep the Americans aware of Spain's efforts on their behalf. When he died in 1780, George Washington presided over his funeral and many members of Congress attended his requiem mass in Philadelphia.[2]

One representative episode of Spain's early covert role in the war involved Captain James Willing of the Continental Army who, in 1778, sailed down the Ohio and the Mississippi rivers with a contingent of soldiers to meet Gálvez in New Orleans. He had a congressional letter to deliver and was to receive supplies to take back upriver. Sailing on an armed boat named *Rattletrap*, Willing and his men successfully surprised and attacked British settlements at Natchez and Concord opposite the mouth of the Arkansas River, and Manchac. In the process, he captured some British boats, including one at the village of Arkansas, which was in Spanish territory. He plundered, took prisoners and left those who escaped vulnerable to Indian attacks. His activities grossly violated Spain's neutrality, and with his arrival in New Orleans he put Gálvez in a difficult position.[3]

While secretly aiding the colonists, Gálvez had the task of maintaining the appearance of Spain's neutrality. Willing's activities had drawn attention to his trip, and he now was camped outside New Orleans. Gálvez ordered Willing to return his plunder, including three slaves and a British vessel. The Spanish governor publicly scolded the American captain, and provided relief for the terrified British subjects he had captured. Gálvez then filled the *Rattletrap* with supplies and ordered Willing and his men out of New Orleans and Spanish territory. The intended recipient of the *Rattletrap*'s Spanish cargo, George Rogers Clark, had been sent into the Ohio River Valley to frustrate Great Britain's aspirations in the West, and he had received supplies from New Orleans more than once. His practice was to go to Spanish St. Louis to requisition matériel and to share information. Upon learning of Willing's conduct, Clarke wrote a letter to Spanish authorities in St. Louis supporting Galvez's position and deploring Willing's "bad conduct ... when plunder is the prevailing passion."[4]

At the diplomatic level, Spain very early encountered Benjamin Franklin, who had been sent to France by the Continental Congress in 1776 to negotiate alliances with European countries. America's most able diplomat was soon working with Spain to get more aid as well as to benefit the American privateers who were attacking and raiding along Great Britain's coast. With France under open criticism for harboring American ships, Franklin learned that Spain had been allowing American ships into its harbors. Franklin asked the Spanish ambassador to France if the practice could continue; he received a favorable reply.[5] After further discussions, Franklin was able to instruct John Paul Jones, among other American naval captains, to replenish and refit in the Spanish port of Bilbao, using the banking firm of Gardoqui e hijos. Diego de Gardoqui, who would become Spain's first ambassador to the United States, became the Americans' point of contact. Through his bank, he cooperatively paid exaggerated prices for seized goods or booty and helped with necessary repairs. The question of how much aid Spain furnished through this Basque banking firm has still to be answered.[6] Unlike the fake firm of Rodriquez & Hartalez in France, which both Spain and France used to funnel money to the colonies, Gardoqui e hijos was a real company.

In using its neutrality to covertly aid the Americans, Spain coordinated its activities with France, and both European governments communicated regularly with the rebelling Americans, especially about negotiating a peace with Great Britain that included American independence. Throughout their period of neutrality, Spain and France were preparing to enter into the war on the side of the Americans. Both countries harbored strong resentments toward Great Britain and saw in the American War of Independence opportunities to recover from their setbacks in the Seven Years' War. As a result of that war, they had lost possessions, experienced weakened economies and suffered continuous British affronts such as illegal settlements and smuggling in the Caribbean and South and Central America, the last of which was called "Goatemala," in the spelling of that day. The chance that colonies breaking away from the mother country, Great Britain, could offer new markets for foreign trade likewise appealed to both the French and Spanish. For all of these reasons, neither country intended to compromise American independence.

As both Spain and France began to appreciate that the rebelling American colonies would remain steadfast, especially after the Continental Army's crucial victory over the British at Saratoga in October 1777, their involvement became increasingly imminent. The development of strategy for that eventuality had begun in earnest after the American Committee of Secret Correspondence, made up of Benjamin Franklin, Arthur Lee and Silas Deane, met with Spain's ambassador to France, the Conde of Aranda, in January 1777. The impetuous Aranda compiled two long letters complete with attachments to his minister of state. Aranda was decidedly pro-American and urged that Spain take advantage of the Revolution. He argued: "Above all, when in centuries will another opportunity arise to bring down England for the afflictions in which she has placed herself?"[7] In a subsequent letter written on the same day, he cautioned that, "while this division lasts, the sights of Spain should be toward the preservation of what is hers, seeking an equilibrium with the other competitors."[8]

His arguments received the attention of his government. At the request of King Carlos III, the minister of state, the Marques de Grimaldi, sought the opinions of a number of influential government officials. He sent out specific questions that had been raised by Aranda. The consensus came back that Spain should not rush into the conflict, nor should France. Both countries needed to take advantage of Great Britain's colonial troubles while negotiating on one hand and preparing for war on the other. The Royal Navy, they understood, was the key to Great Britain's military prowess, but it was not omnipotent. While it remained formidable, the colonial rebellion was taking a toll on the fleet. Many of the Royal Navy's crewmen were impressed American sailors, and still there were not enough men to man the available ships. The American commissioners in Paris made sure to emphasize the point to Aranda, who wrote:

> I have heard Dr. Franklin say that American sailors amounted to 25 or 30 thousand men who in the preceding wars served the British fleets. Since the uprising this third no longer exists, thus England has less men [than those] who in the preceding wars served the British fleets.[9]

With enough preparation, Spain and France could enter the war with a combined naval force that would be larger than that of Great Britain. Nevertheless, they needed time to rebuild the fleets inherited from the previous war. This included modernizing their ships with such things as copper hulls as well as training a new generation of crews. Spain also wanted to prepare its land forces in America.

Spain could use this time to neutralize Great Britain's only European ally, Portugal. Madrid did not want its neighbor in Europe, which possessed rival colonies in the Americas, as an active participant in a war. Realizing this, Aranda pointed out that Great Britain could not afford to interfere if Spain moved against Portuguese and British illegal operations in Spanish America. Carlos III and his ministers agreed with this assessment, and as a result Spain launched a secret, full-scale attack on British and Portuguese establishments along the Rio de la Plata in South America. In what the Spanish strategist Francisco de Saavedra described as "one of the best organized and best provisioned enterprises" ever prepared by Spain, an armada under the command of Pedro de Cevallos embarked from the port of Cádiz on 13 November 1776.[10] The fleet included seven ships-of-the-line, eight frigates, four smaller ships and enough transports to carry 14 infantry brigades and four cavalry squads that amounted to over 9,000 men. Cevallos's fleet was one of the largest fleets to sail to the Americas up to that time.[11]

Spain was gambling that the surprise of such an assertive undertaking, along with Great Britain's preoccupation with its colonies and its desire to avoid war in Europe, would leave Portugal exposed. To make sure, London was informed that any interference in this internal matter would be reason for a declaration of war. Spain, the British were told, was trying to eradicate some illegal merchants and settlements and correct some Portuguese affronts, neither of which had anything to do with Great Britain.[12] The action was bold and calculated, for Carlos III did not want war any more than did the British Parliament. He did, however, want to negate Portugal while making a gesture that indicated Spain's passivity could not be assumed anymore.

While the large fleet of Cevallos sailed into the South Atlantic, another squadron sailed up the Iberian coast to put an exclamation point on Spain's position vis-à-vis Portugal and its pro-English, anti-Spanish minister of state, Sabastiao José de Cerralhoe Mello, the Marques of Pombal. The squadron entered the Tajo River and anchored in front of Lisbon with its guns aimed on the capital. Pombal, who actually ran the Portuguese government, hid his surprise and frustration and did the only thing he could do. He received the Spanish officers with full decorum. The insult had been transmogrified into a fleet visit; the diplomatic point had been made.[13]

Meanwhile, the southern fleet achieved brilliant success. Cevallos's forces moved down the Brazilian coast, smashing British smuggling operations, and taking Uruguay from the Portuguese, thus securing the Rio de la Plata and the city of Buenos Aires. As the ministers of King Carlos had predicted, Great Britain did nothing to oppose the offensive, which, in fact, put the British on the defensive for the first time in a long while. Although none of the Spanish officials in the West Indies would learn of the success of Spain's bold move in South America until the second half of the following year, 1778, they all had been informed of the strategy and action. The success in South America would trigger a renewed enthusiasm for expelling the British from Central America, while the Revolution in North America continued to open options to both France and Spain.

Madrid, under the guidance of José Moniño y Redondo, the Count of Floridablanca, Spain's new minister of state, emphasized negotiation and delay, at least until the return of Cevallo's armada. France, on the other hand, became anxious that the colonies, flush with their victory at Saratoga, would agree to terms with the British. This anxiety, perhaps flamed by Franklin in Paris, resulted in a flurry of diplomatic exchanges between France and Spain. France did not want to lose the opportunity to strike at Great Britain. The French minister of state, the Comte Vergennes, knew the numbers. Great Britain had 66 ships-of-the-line with another 14 ready to sail as soon as crews could be transferred from returning merchantmen. France had 53 ships-of-the-line and Spain added another 50. Together, Spain and France, when combined, had the larger fleet.

Perhaps heeding the advice of his ambassador in Madrid, who clearly understood that France would have to make some concessions, Vergennes asked Floridablanca what Spain needed to assure its cooperation and alliance. Floridablanca's "gigantic demands,"[14] as Vergennes termed them to his king, Louis XVI, included the repossession of Gibraltar and the Mediterranean Island of Minorca, removal of the British from the Gulf of Mexico including the Mississippi River, restoration of Mobile and Pensacola, and removal of the British from the "Bay of Honduras and the Coast of Campeche."[15] No matter Vergennes' reaction, Floridablanca did not share the French minister's impatience. The Spaniard did not believe that the colonies where anywhere near coming to terms with Great Britain. Besides, prudence, if not pragmatism, dictated that he wait for the return of Cevallos' fleet from South America and the arrival of the "treasure ships" from Mexico and the West Indies. Floridablanca postulated that time was needed so that the two countries could determine how their respective fleets could be used to achieve their objectives of defeating Great Britain and aiding the colonies. He saw the two Crowns as protectors who needed to stipulate that the colonies would not be abandoned until they are "recognized as an independent state."[16]

French entry into the war and further diplomacy

Vergennes did not have Floridablanca's patience. He decided to take a risk, and he signed two treaties with the colonies on 6 February 1778. The second treaty included article 13, a secret clause that stipulated that Spain, if it entered the conflict, would come in as a full partner and all the existing agreements would equally apply to the Spanish. The treaties, including full recognition of the United States of America, were an act of war. Hoping to take advantage of timing and surprise, Vergennes simultaneously ordered the Toulon fleet to sail across the Atlantic to surprise and defeat a smaller British squadron at New York, thus stranding 33,756 British troops and ending the war.[17]

On 13 April 1778, Vice Admiral Jean-Baptiste-Charles-Henri-Hector, Comte d'Estaing, embarked with 12 ships-of-the-line with secret orders that he opened while at sea, while France was declaring war, and learned that he was to attack the British fleet at New York. He arrived outside the city to find that nine British ships-of-the-line had secured the port with a blockade at Sandy Hook.[18] Fearing the arrival of British reinforcements, d'Estaing chose not to press action and lost France's advantage of surprise.[19] After resting in New England, the admiral sailed south to protect France's Caribbean Islands. The fleet returned to France a year later.

The Americans were deeply disappointed in the actions of d'Estaing but not as much as Vergennes, who had to inform his king that the plan had failed and that, as a result, France was both at war and in peril. Louis XVI needed to do whatever was possible to entice Spain to come to France's aid, including accepting those demands that suddenly seemed more reasonable; otherwise France would lose the war.[20]

Floridablanca had played his cards perfectly, and he persisted in trying to achieve a diplomatic solution. At first, Spain offered to remain neutral if Great Britain would give up Gibraltar, but when that idea received little response, Floridablanca hardened his stance to the aforesaid position of combining Spain's desires with that of American independence. In essence, Spain suggested that Great Britain could lose the colonies and some of its other possessions through treaty or war. Either way, the result would be the same, while the latter process would be more painful. Some British politicians had tired of war and realized the futility of an armed struggle against Spain joined with France and the Americans. Nonetheless, King George III took a less conciliatory position. He could not believe that Great Britain could not defeat the three potential allies.

The Spanish declaration of war and strategy

In April 1779, Spain gave Great Britain a final ultimatum, and it was quickly refused. London would not even consider allowing Madrid to arbitrate a peace, partly because Spain insisted that the Americans be allowed to sit at the table as equals to Great Britain and France. So King Carlos III of Spain was left with no choice but to prepare a declaration of war. That same month, France and Spain agreed to a treaty that was signed in Aranjuez, south of Madrid. France agreed to the new alliance without consultation with the Americans. Vergennes did not need to confer with them, for the colonists had already agreed to the procedure through their previous treaties with France. The young United States was now committed to Spanish goals, and its leaders were happy to hear the good news of Spain's entry into the war.

The two European countries agreed to a strategy wherein French troops would fight in the rebelling 13 colonies while Spanish forces would concentrate in their own or former territory. Spain feared giving its own colonies any cause for disgruntlement by occupying other colonies; France did not have that problem.[21] On the other hand, the combined navies opened up an opportunity to force Great Britain to make some hard choices. Spain promised to take command of fighting in the Caribbean, which included Central America, the Mexican and Gulf Coasts, and the Mississippi River. France would send a contingent to India in an attempt to win back its possessions, while both countries would cooperate in actions taken on the European front. This last commitment included mounting an immediate siege of Gibraltar followed by an attack on the British-held island of Minorca.

The talk of an actual invasion of the British Isles kept the British anxious for their own safety. All this added up to creating a world war based on the Spanish idea that the two allies, along with the American rebels, had enough resources to stretch the British thin. The British would have to decide what was more important to them: Central America, their West Indies trade, the 13 American colonies, Gibraltar, Minorca, India or, even, defense of the homeland.

Importantly, along with its formal declaration of war on 21 June 1779, Spain agreed not to make peace with Great Britain without France's acquiescence.[22] The latter, of course, had agreed to the goal of American independence by its earlier treaties. Throughout the unfolding of the conflict, Spain consistently recognized that France could not achieve peace until England recognized American independence. Thus without becoming an ally of the rebelling colonies, Spain tied itself to independence. This was the best of all positions for the Spanish regime and as good as could be expected for the Americans, for it prevented defeat and offered victory. American historian Jonathan Dull, an expert on the American War of Independence and France's role, wrote:

> Had the French navy been crushed, Britain could have tightly blockaded the American coast and would have made New York impregnable. Without money and supplies from France the survival of the United States would have been unlikely, and without French military and naval help the expulsion of the British from all their American positions would have been almost impossible.[23]

It was, in fact, the Spanish navy that provided the allies with naval superiority over Great Britain. This advantage would be crucial to the outcome of the war and, specifically, to the decisive Franco-American victory at Yorktown in October 1781. Spain's declaration of war, therefore, introduced something more important then recognition of the struggling colonists: it provided a realistic chance at independence. The totality of Spain's actual involvement in fighting, continued financial support and diplomacy actually proved pivotal for the eventual victory. Spain brought clarity of vision that focused on goals, as well as an understanding of the means for achieving the end. Spain and France had given much thought and preparation to the war. Coordination, especially between the two European countries, was critical for success. It is true that France did indeed provide the troops to fight alongside the Continentals. However, some of their leaders, like the well-known Marquis de Lafayette and the Prussian officer Fredrich von Von Stueben, were direct beneficiaries of Spain's activities. Both men had been transferred to America on Spanish ships.[24]

Spanish wartime actions

Within days of Spain's declaration of war, 14,000 Spanish troops confronted a British garrison of not more than 7,000 men at Gibraltar. With the addition of some French forces, the siege of Gibraltar began on 11 July 1779 and lasted until the end of the war.[25] The siege became the focus of the war in Europe as well as a key component in the strategy that resulted in the independence of the United States. For example, Britain tried to lift the siege on two occasions. In doing so, British naval resources were diverted and the European allies used the openings, not only to inflict some damage on the British navy but also to transfer troops and ships to the Americas unhampered.

One example will suffice to demonstrate the strategy in action. The Admiralty in London recruited one of its famous sea veterans out of retirement to break the allied blockade as well as supply the besieged garrison at Gibraltar. Admiral Sir George Rodney accepted the commission and set sail in late December 1779. En route, he engaged and defeated two out-gunned Spanish attacks. The second of these engagements involved a Spanish squadron of 11 ships-of-the-line and two frigates led by Lieutenant General Juan de Lángara. The Spaniard led his squadron into a confrontation with Rodney's fleet that was more than twice as large, with 22 ships-of-the-line and 14 frigates. The valiant Lángara continued fighting even though his flagship was rendered inoperable. British accounts describe him enduring despite constant fire from four separate ships and his ship's masts being blown away. Not until he was severely wounded and his ship a barely floating wreck did he surrender.[26]

In a carefully written and printed letter under the name of José de Gálvez, who was the minister of the Indies, Carlos III noted that part of the Spanish strategy was to use the season of storms and its own navy to "dearly sell the enemy a victory." So, while Rodney did provide partial relief to the Gibraltar garrison, he could not lift the siege nor stay to help defend the garrison. Lángara's sacrifice, along with bad weather, dismasted one-third of Rodney's ships-of-the-line and scattered most of the rest. Spain reported the additional details that two badly damaged English warships, *navios*, had entered the port of Lisbon but could not be salvaged. Three other ships "without either masts or fixtures, surrendered to the wind's will [and] dashed against the rocks." Others of the smaller ships suffered the same fate.[27] While all this was happening, Spain and France kept their larger fleets in harbor at Brest and Cádiz. They saved their assets while maintaining enough of a defense to divert the British. Both countries were cooperating in a grander scheme. They could maintain the siege of Gibraltar while Spain placated France's desire to concentrate on the Americas.

As a result of Rodney's encounter at Gibraltar, Great Britain had to spend much of 1780 refitting and organizing its American and European fleets. The

British were thus not well prepared to prevent the new emphasis and actions of its European opponents. The first French fleet organized to reinforce the French West Indies embarked with 17 ships-of-the-line and 4,800 troops, while a smaller French force left for India. A Spanish fleet sailed to the West Indies in April with 12 ships-of-the-line and 11,000 troops.

Meanwhile, the Americans suffered defeats at Charleston in May and at Camden, South Carolina, in August. The Continental Army had been reduced to roughly 17,000 men and was facing a force of 30,000. France saw this setback as an opportunity to help the colonies by sending another armada with 8,000 troops under the command of General Jean-Baptiste-Donatien-Vimeur, Comte de Rochambeau, who occupied Newport, Rhode Island, without opposition in July.[28] For their part, in that rather confused summer of 1780, the British attempted to send a huge supply fleet with a weak convoy to their ports in the East and West Indies. Spain learned of the attempt and ordered Lieutenant General Luis de Córdova, who was in command of the fleets at Brest and Cádiz, to intercept the British fleet. Córdova moved accordingly and attacked the unsuspecting fleet, eventually capturing over 60 ships, many civilians, and over 1,800 officers and men of the Royal or East India Company's army. He also captured almost two million pounds' worth of goods.[29]

All these actions on balance served to relieve pressure from the colonies while strengthening all the allies. Great Britain would indeed have to make choices, for Gibraltar remained as before. Now Spain attacked the Mediterranean island of Minorca where, after five months of fighting, Madrid claimed victory. In distant North America, Spanish forces under Bernardo de Gálvez moved aggressively up the Mississippi River to defeat the British at Natchez, Manchac and Baton Rouge. Eventually, the Spanish would be victorious at Mobile, Pensacola and, after Yorktown, the Bahamas. They engaged and defeated British forces in Central America along the Mosquito Coast, the San Juan River and Lake Nicaragua. Spanish St. Louis, with the help of American Continental troops, successfully repulsed a British attack; and a Spanish contingent out of St. Louis traveled upriver, over snow-covered and frozen fields to sack and burn the British Fort St. Joseph in southern Michigan.[30]

The culmination of all this action would come at Yorktown on the Chesapeake Bay, where the British commander, Lieutenant General Lord Charles Cornwallis, moved the bulk of the British land forces in the South after failing to defeat Nathanael Greene's Continental Army in the Carolinas. While Cornwallis was awaiting either reinforcement or evacuation by the Royal Navy, Spain and France created a major diversion in England with a planned invasion in mid-1781. London now faced pressure from a major combined fleet of 66 ships-of-the-line that might attack England. The ministry of Lord North needed to consider homeland defense. The direct result of this conundrum was Britain's decision to not send naval reinforcements at the very time Cornwallis' occupation of Yorktown demonstrated the precariousness of Britain's position in the South, and while it simultaneously was trying to maintain its hold on New York. The distraction of the British navy by the Franco-Spanish fleets thus provided a window of opportunity to trap Cornwallis and his army. The allied formula for success was in place.

The realization of this opportunity required that Generals Washington and Rochambeau move their forces south from New York while the Spanish released the French fleet in the Caribbean to sail north with reinforcements and to blockade the port at Yorktown, Virginia, thereby trapping the British army. Also, enough money needed be raised to pay for the operation. All this needed to be done very quickly.

At Cap Français, then called Guarico, Francisco Saavedra, a Spanish strategist, was working with French Admiral François-Joseph Paul le Comte de Grasse on plans for a combined invasion of British-held Jamaica. When Saavedra and de Grasse received word of Cornwallis' precarious position, both men felt that fate had placed before them an opportunity. France and Spain, they agreed, "could not waste the most decisive opportunity in the whole war."[31] Without waiting for official authority from Europe they, along with Bernardo de Gálvez, who was in command of all the allied forces in the Caribbean, agreed to press forward with Yorktown as the priority. Immediately, Gálvez released de Grasse to sail north with 5,000 French soldiers, and he agreed reciprocally to use the Spanish fleet in the Caribbean to protect French possessions in the area.

The problem of finances became a little more problematic. Saavedra and de Grasse needed to raise 500,000 pesos and, if possible, more. The French admiral posted printed notices requesting money in exchange for bills redeemable at a profitable rate of interest through the Treasury of Paris. The effort secured only 50,000 livres.[32] Spanish Puerto Rico and Santo Domingo provided an additional 100,000 pesos, but that still was not enough. With time pressing, Saavedra took action. He urged de Grasse to embark for the North with all his ships-of-the-line and the troops, along with the money already raised. The French admiral agreed to everything and set sail on 5 August 1781, dispatching in advance a fast frigate to inform Rochambeau in Newport that the game was afoot.

In the meantime, Saavedra used one of the faster frigates available to sail to Havana in an effort to raise the balance of the necessary funds, which would be sent north to de Grasse. After ten days at sea, Saavedra arrived at Havana on 15 July 1781. There he learned that the Spanish government had ordered one million pesos to be paid to the French. Unfortunately, the money, coming from Vera Cruz, Mexico, had not arrived. Saavedra could not wait "because ... the delay ... would put his [Grasse's] fleet in jeopardy."[33] So, understanding the urgency of the situation, the intendant of Havana declared a state of emergency, called together the citizens of Havana, "and in six hours, they collected the required amount, which was put onboard the ship, and at six o'clock in the evening the frigate set sail."[34] All this was done within one day. A few days later, the one million pesos arrived from Mexico. Gálvez, Saavedra and the other Spanish officials resolved to send the additional money north, "forgetting about the part [already] sent to Chesapeake Bay as a new service from Spain to help in our common cause."[35]

In North America, receipt of the news of de Grasse's sortie activated Rochambeau and Washington, and their combined French and American armies began marching to the South for a rendezvous with the French admiral. De Grasse's fleet arrived at Yorktown on 26 August, disembarked 5,000 troops and, in the first days of September, fought a brief engagement with the Royal Navy for local command of the sea. Washington and Rochambeau's forces arrived soon after de Grasse. They used their superior artillery to bombard and intimidate Cornwallis while the French fleet blockaded the port to prevent any hope of aid or evacuation. To preserve his army for another day, Cornwallis scuttled his anchored supply ships and, on 19 October 1781, capitulated with his 8,000-man force.

Post-Yorktown

The Franco-American victory at Yorktown virtually secured the independence of the United States by causing the war ministry in London to resign. It was a key battle won by the strategy delineated by Saavedra, approved by Bernardo de Gálvez and, ultimately, the King of Spain, within the general parameters laid out by Spain before entering the war. The battle was funded by Spain with a line of credit that extended from Mexico through Cuba. De Grasse later wrote that the money that financed the battle of Yorktown truthfully might be regarded as "the bottom dollars" upon which the edifice of American independence was raised.[36]

The global war unfortunately did not end with Yorktown, and fighting continued. Using an American frigate, the state-owned *South Carolina*, as its flagship, a Spanish force took the Bahamas from the British.[37] As negotiations for peace continued, Spain and France organized for an attack on Jamaica, but finally, on 3 September 1783, a treaty was signed in Paris. Benjamin Franklin and the Count of Aranda affixed their signatures to the document that brought victory to both of their countries and independence for the United States.

Notes

1 George Washington to John Jay, 16 Aug. 1779, West Point, in John C. Fitzpatrick, ed., *The Writings of George Washington From the Original Manuscript Sources, 1745–1799*, vol. 16 (Washington, D.C.: United States Government Printing Office, 1931–44), p. 115.
2 For the full story of Miralles, see Vincente Rivas, *Don Juan de Miralles y Independencia de los Estados Unidos* (Valencia: Generalitat Valenciana, 2003).
3 The whole Willing episode is in Thomas E. Chávez, *Spain and the Independence of the United States: An Intrinsic Gift* (Albuquerque: University of New Mexico Press, 2002), pp. 104–6.
4 George Rogers Clark to Fernando Leyba, 6 Nov. 1778, Kaskaskias, in Lawrence Kinard, "Clark-Leyba Papers," *The American Historical Review*, 41, no. 1 (Oct. 1935), pp. 100–1.
5 The Count of Aranda to the Marques de Grimaldi, 13 Jan. 1777, Paris, no. 958, no. 4, legajo 3884, Estado, Archivo Historico Nancional (AHN), Madrid. Grimaldi was about to retire as secretary of state and be replaced by the Count of Floridablanca.
6 For a thorough account of the activities of Gardoqui e hijos, see Reyes Calderón Cuadrado, *Empresarios Españoles en el Proceso de Independencia Norteamericana: La Casa Gardoqui e Hijos de Bilbao* (Madrid: Unión Editorial, S.A., 2004).

7 Aranda to Grimaldi, 13 Jan. 1777, Paris, no. 958, no. 4, legajo 3884, Estado, AHN.
8 Aranda to Grimaldi, 13 Jan. 1777, Paris, no. 939, no. 6, ibid.
9 Ibid.
10 Francisco Saavedra, as quoted in Morales Padrón, in "Editor's Introduction," *Journal of Don Francisco Saavedra de Sangronis During the Commission Which He Had in His Charge From 25 June 1780 Until the 20th of the Same Month in 1783* (Gainesville: University of Florida Press, 1989), p. xxiii.
11 Chávez, *Spain and the Independence*, pp. 43–4.
12 D. Antonio Ballesteros y Beretta, *Historia de España y su influencia en la Historia Universal*, tomo 5 (Barcelona: Sulvat editors, S.A., 1929), pp. 197–203.
13 Ibid., p. 107.
14 See Jonathan Dull, *The French Navy and American Independence: A Study of Arms and Diplomacy, 1774–1787* (Princeton: Princeton University Press, 1975), pp. 127–8. Regarding the French ambassador, Armand-Marc, the Count of Montmorin, see Chávez, *Spain and the Independence*, p. 47.
15 Floridablanca to Aranda, 13 Jan. 1778, legajo 3884, folio 69, Estado, AHN.
16 Ibid.
17 Dull, *The French Navy*, p. 110.
18 Bruce Lancaster, *The American Revolution* (New York: Houghton Mifflin Company, 1985), p. 237.
19 Dull, *The French Navy*, p. 123.
20 The Count of Vergennes to King Louis XVI, 5 Dec. 1778, as quoted in Dull, *The French Navy*, p. 133.
21 Jonathan Dull, *A Diplomatic History of the American Revolution* (New Haven: Yale University Press, 1985), pp. 107–8.
22 The declaration was printed and sent throughout the Spanish empire, France and the United States. See Carmen de Reparz, *Yo Solo: Bernardo de Gálvez y la Toma de Panzacola en 1781* (Barcelona: Ediciones del Serbal, S.A., 1986), pp. 223–34.
23 Dull, *Diplomatic History*, p. 109.
24 This might explain the existence of a Spanish sword in the collections of the U.S. Naval Academy Museum that belonged to George Washington.
25 Histories of the siege of Gibraltar include Tom Henderson McGuffie, *The Siege of Gibraltar, 1779–1783* (London: B.T. Batsford Co., 1965) and Jack Russell, *Gibraltar Besieged, 1779–1783* (London: William Heinemann, Ltd., 1965). Neither of these books used Spanish sources. Eric Beerman, *España y la Independencia de los Estados Unidos* (Madrid: Editorial MAPFRE, S.A., 1992), pp. 261–5, is a history based on Spanish documents and contains a section on the siege of Gibraltar.
26 Sir Charles Petrie, *King Charles III of Spain: An Enlightened Despot* (New York: The John Day Company, 1971), p. 190. The Spanish lost six ships-of-the-line, two of which were destroyed.
27 Dull, *The French Navy*, p. 178; and José de Gálvez to the Governor of Havana, 27 Jan. 1780, leg. 1, Cuba, Archivo General de las Indias (AGI), Seville. The first quotation reads in Spanish, "vender cara a los enemigos una victoria."
28 Dull, *The French Navy*, pp. 190–1.
29 Petrie, *King Charles III*, pp. 191–2.
30 Two detailed overviews of the activities of Spain, listed and very much abbreviated in this chapter are Chávez, *Spain and the Independence* (in English) and Beerman, *España y la Endependencia* (in Spanish).
31 Francisco Saavedra, "Diario inédito," in Carmen de Reparaz, *Yo Solo*, p. 248. In Spanish the words are "...para que no se malgrase el golpe más decisivo de toda la guerra."
32 Saavedra, *Journal*, pp. 204–5, 207–8. One peso equaled forty livres or one dollar. See Chávez, *Spain and the Independence*, p. 224.
33 Saavedra, "Diario inédito," in Reparaz, *Yo Solo*, p. 250; and *Journal*, p. 211.

34 Ibid. The quotation is taken from the *Journal*. While the "Diario" is essentially the same, it gives the time of the frigate's sailing as 8:00 p.m.
35 Saavedra, "Diario inédito," in Reparaz, *Yo Solo*, p. 251.
36 Quoted in Stephen Bonsal, *When the French Were Here* (Garden City: Doubleday & Co., 1945), pp. 119–20.
37 Chávez, *Spain and the Independence*, pp. 205–8. The ship belonged to the South Carolina navy.

9 Dutch maritime strategy

Victor Enthoven

Puffs of white smoke rose above St. Eustatius' crowded roadstead as the cannons of Fort Orange fired their ritual greeting to the *Andrea Doria* on 16 November 1776. The guards inside the Dutch fort had no idea the ship's red and white striped flag represented America's new Continental Congress.[1] The English colonies in America had declared their independence on 4 July 1776. This, at first sight, a rather harmless event, was the beginning of a longstanding Atlantic partnership between the republican kindred spirits: the Dutch Republic and the United States of America. After the colonists had started to revolt, the Dutch desperately tried to remain neutral. The American War of Independence, however, dragged the Dutch into the Fourth Anglo-Dutch War (December 1780–June 1784), a conflict the Dutch had never wanted.

The strategic setting

In a windy and wet northwestern corner of the European Continent lay the United Provinces, also known as the Dutch Republic.[2] In the European context, the Dutch Republic was an anomaly. The primary threats to its existence came from the south (France) and the east (the Holy Roman Empire); its outlook, however, was westward, toward the sea. The economies of the provinces of Holland and Zeeland were maritime-based, the Dutch being the carriers of the world. In 1750, for instance, Lewis Morris, Judge-Commissary of New York, noted that: "[The Dutch] are known to be the cheapest carriers in the world."[3] Furthermore, the Dutch East India Company (VOC) and the Dutch West India Company (WIC) governed overseas possessions in Asia and the Atlantic, respectively.

Dutch continental security policy was rather straightforward. As a small country, its defense lacked depth. To counter this, the Dutch established several defensive lines. The first was a perimeter of two dozen or so forts, fortified towns and strongholds along the border. Most of the standing army was billeted here. The second line of defense was the *Hollandse waterlinie*. In case of an emergency, a large part of the country could be inundated, cutting off Holland from the rest of the country. In 1672 and 1940, for instance, large parts in the middle of the country were intentionally flooded.[4] As a result of the Treaty of

Utrecht (1713), a third line of defense was established, one especially aimed at a French attack. In a separate Barrier Treaty, signed in 1715, the Dutch Republic was allowed to billet garrisons in eight towns in the Austrian Netherlands to guard against the French attack. This became known as the Barrier.[5]

Dutch maritime interests were secured by close ties with Great Britain. They were natural allies, not only against the European powers, but also out of self-interest since both were maritime nations that derived their wealth and power from the sea. With the exception of the Anglo-Dutch Wars of the late seventeenth century, they generally could be expected to collaborate with each other, effectively constituting a single unit on the international scene rather than two separate ones. These natural allies were known as the Maritime Powers, a reputation based on formal treaties between the two countries – above all, those of 1674 and 1678 – the first a commercial agreement, the second a defensive political alliance.[6] The commercial treaty of 1674 established the principle of "free ships, free goods," meaning that when either of the two countries was at war, the cargo in a neutral ship would be considered neutral as well.

During the eighteenth century, Dutch merchant houses gradually lost their once dominant position in world trade through a process of stagnation, contraction and concentration. Dutch merchants could do little about it because of the vulnerable position of the Dutch Republic. It was a small country, lacking raw materials and with a limited internal market, amid larger producing countries protecting their markets with mercantilistic measures. By the time the Americans began their revolt against British rule, Dutch manufacturing and refining industries were dependent on French and British imports. Economically, the Dutch were stuck between the devil and the deep blue sea.

Starting in the 1740s, the position of the Dutch Republic, both domestic and international, began to deteriorate. During the War of the Austrian Succession (1740–48), the Dutch Republic stayed more or less neutral. More important were the events that took place in the Habsburg Netherlands. In 1744, French troops marched into the Austrian Netherlands. They demolished the Barrier. In a 1748 peace treaty between the European powers, the Dutch Republic was the big loser. With the Barrier against France gone, the Dutch were at the mercy of the French. Then a public uprising led to the reinstatement of William IV (1711–51), Prince of Orange, as Stadholder and Captain- and Admiral-General. Four years later, the infant William V (1748–1806) succeeded his father. Now the troubles really began.[7]

The United Provinces were a deeply divided country. The province of Holland, with its large maritime and overseas economic involvements, advocated a strong navy. Powerful Amsterdam, with its large mercantile community, especially supported this policy. The land provinces, on the other hand, wanted a strong army. During the 1770s this debate was known as army augmentation or fleet restoration. Despite many meetings, white papers and decisions, not much was done to strengthen the army or the fleet. Only as late as 1780, as a result of the rising tensions with Britain, did the States General, the highest executive body, allocate for the Admiralty Boards 2,623,590 guilders for a 25-ship building program.[8] Even several of their fellow American republicans were less than impressed by the slow and arduous operations of Dutch institutions.[9]

The controversy over army augmentation versus fleet restoration demonstrates a much deeper rift in Dutch politics: the struggle between the Orangist party, symbolized by the hereditary Stadholder, versus the Patriots. Rather simply put, the Orangists were conservative, pro-army and pro-British, while the Patriots embraced the new ideas of civic liberties, were pro-navy, and anti-British, and eventually became pro-French. Neither of the two parties dominated politics. This paralyzed decision-making, particularly in foreign affairs and security policy.[10]

The American War of Independence and its ideas of civil liberties were embraced by the Patriots. Joan Derk van der Capellen tot den Pol was the author of the pamphlet *Aan het Volk van Nederland* ("To the Dutch People"). On the night of 25 September 1781, the pamphlet surfaced all over the Netherlands, blaming the feeble rule of William V and his clique for the bad state of the country.[11] A year later, the States General recognized the United States of America as an independent nation.

For Dutch foreign policy there was, at the beginning of the American Revolution, only one option, to remain neutral. On foreign policy, the Dutch were in a strategic vise. Compliance with the demands of Britain would eventually involve the Dutch Republic in a land war with France. On the other hand, to choose for the American rebels and their French allies would lead to the disruption of Dutch trade and navigation, and the loss of the empire. To complicate matters further, economically the Dutch were dependent on both France and Britain. The United Provinces did not possess effective sea or land defenses. They were even less prepared for an offensive war, their navy not being strong enough to have the slightest prospect of success in a naval contest with Britain, nor was their army sufficient in numbers, compared with the military forces of the surrounding countries, to assist Great Britain on the continent if the war should spread there.

There was another reason why the United Provinces should keep out of the war. The Dutch were still the most efficient carriers of the world, transmitting the products of Europe to all parts of the Earth, and vice versa, and would remain so as long as they were neutral; but, from the instant they should become involved in the war, their ships would be liable to seizure by the belligerents, and their trade and navigation would decline accordingly. War was, however, all but inevitable.[12]

The road to war

After the American colonists revolted against British colonial rule, the already-cool political relations between Britain and the Dutch Republic deteriorated further. Eventually, the British government had many reasons to declare war on the Dutch, some more important than others. The first was the Scottish Brigade.

The treaty of 1678 between England and the United Provinces stipulated that if one of the countries would be at war on the Continent the other would assist with 6,000 auxiliary troops. In February 1775, Sir Joseph Yorke, the British ambassador to The Hague, presented a memorial to the States General in which he announced that George III was at war. But since England was making war against her own colonies and outside Europe, the 1678 treaty was not applicable and she could not ask for the 6,000 auxiliaries. Instead, William V, as Captain-General, informed the States General of George III's desire to borrow the Scottish Brigade of the Dutch army, which consisted of a dozen or so regiments. In return, George III offered to replace it with an equal number of Hanoverian troops. Most provinces gave their consent to the transfer. Holland, however, accepted England's offer under conditions that made their acceptance equal to refusal: the Brigade should in no case be employed outside Britain's possessions in Europe. For the British, not releasing the Brigade was a violation of the friendly relations between the two governments; for the Dutch, it was an act of neutrality.[13]

A second cause revolved around the concept of *Mare Liberum*: free seas. Since the early days of the Dutch Revolt (1568–1648), the Dutch motto had been "The sea is free." A free ship meant a free cargo; in other words, the cargo of a neutral ship (read a Dutch ship), is free to be shipped to any place in the world.[14] For many a Dutch merchant, the American Revolution meant new business opportunities. After all, the American rebels needed arms and ammunition, and lots of them. And who were better situated than the cheapest carriers in the world to convey them to America? Provided, of course, they stayed neutral.

How and when Dutch merchants started to supply the American rebels is unclear, but as early as August 1774 Sir Joseph Yorke had evidence that military supplies had been shipped from the United Provinces to America. That month, the American vessel *Polly*, out of Nantucket, arrived in Amsterdam and loaded 300,000 pounds of powder. In October, a Rhode Island vessel had loaded assorted firearms and 40 small cannon. On 19 October 1774, the British government expressly prohibited the exportation of warlike stores and ammunition to the American colonies. A few days later, an armed British cutter, *Welles*, appeared before the Texel road, effectively blockading the Rhode Island ship.[15]

The British proclamations prohibiting the exportation of warlike stores and ammunition to the American colonies were followed by a request to the Dutch government in which George III thought it necessary that the rebels should not receive under the pretext of commerce anything that might nourish the insurrection. This request, and the British naval blockade, revived the dormant Anglo-Dutch controversy over the rights of neutrals. The treaty of 1674 again came into the limelight and the principle that "free ships make free goods" became the watchword of the Dutch merchant class. Even the Stadholder and his pro-British faction became increasingly reluctant to endorse measures that would curtail Dutch commercial interests.[16]

Nevertheless, in March 1775, on the pretext of being neutral in the conflict between the English king and his subjects, the States General forbade the exportation of war supplies in British vessels or those flying the British flag. This measure was, of course, aimed at American ships which still flew British colors.

Dutch subjects were also forbidden to export war material without the permission of one of the Admiralty Boards. The Admiralty Boards were instructed to allow such goods to be exported only if the sender should declare under oath that this cargo was not bound, directly or indirectly, for places within the dominion of Britain in America. Failure to comply with the regulations would result in confiscation of the contraband and payment of a 1,000-guilder fine.[17]

At this time the Royal Navy had already imposed a naval blockade upon the rebellious American colonies. During the summer of 1775, 30 Royal Navy ships, including two second-rates, were in North American waters, and in the second half of the year, 20 more sailed for the New World.[18] Direct shipping between the United Provinces and North America came virtually to a standstill.[19] Entrepreneurs, however, are infinitely resourceful at evading regulations and trade obstacles. In this case, they first carried their goods to a French port where the material then passed nominally into the possession of a French intermediary before being shipped to America. Such subventions of the rules were sometimes even performed during voyages, with American and Dutch vessels exchanging their cargoes on the high seas. Annually, hundreds of thousands of pounds of gunpowder were exported in this way. In April 1776, for instance, within two days, 850 barrels (85,000 lbs) of gunpowder were shipped from Amsterdam to France.[20]

Hostilities between Britain and France began in June 1778; this brought serious trouble for the Dutch. There were many complaints about the capture and molestation of Dutch vessels by British men-of-war and privateers. By the end of September, 29 Dutch ships had been taken. By October, the number had risen to 42. For the Dutch, these seizures were in violation of the 1674 treaty. No wonder the pro-British lobby in the Netherlands was rapidly losing ground. The British, though, released the Dutch ships, except those which had naval or warlike stores on board.[21]

During the fall of 1778, merchants from various Dutch ports requested the States General and the Stadholder, as Admiral-General, for protection of their ships. The fear of provoking Great Britain, however, was too great, and in November, the States of Holland refused the employment of armed convoys. The pro-British party had triumphed. For the French government, however, this was a breach of neutrality, and with the secret endorsement of Amsterdam, they let the States General know that Louis XVI would be compelled to suspend the advantages which the United Provinces enjoyed as neutrals. By January 1779, a fleet of around 300 merchantmen with ordinary cargoes bound for France had assembled at the Texel, nine war ships were detailed to take this fleet to its destination. Fifteen vessels were refused this protection because they had naval munitions onboard. Despite the fact that these 15 ships had mingled among the other ships, the fleet passed the English Channel without incident. In return, all of the French edicts against Dutch commerce were repealed, and the sums which the French customs houses had levied above the usual rate were returned to the Dutch merchants. This, however, did not end the matter.[22]

In November 1779, the States General agreed that ships not carrying contraband of war or naval stores should sail under the protection of several men-of-war. One fleet was destined for the West Indies, another for Southern Europe. With the vessels of the combined fleet were intermixed about 20 vessels laden with contraband. The Dutch convoy, with three ships-of-the-line and three frigates under command of Rear Admiral Frederik S. van Bylandt, met off the Isle of Wight six ships-of-the-line and six frigates under British Admiral Charles Fielding. After a short exchange of fire, Fielding took several vessels whose cargo consisted of naval stores from the outnumbered and outgunned Dutch. The convoy was then allowed to continue its voyage. When the news of the incident became known in Holland on 8 January 1780, a great outcry arose. It was thought impossible that Britain, still the friend and ally, should have taken such steps.[23]

It was clear that from this point on the British government would treat the Dutch like all other neutral states not privileged by treaty, and all particular stipulations respecting the freedom of navigation and commerce in time of war contained in the treaties, especially in the commercial treaty of 1674, were revoked. The commanders of the British warships and privateers were ordered

> to seize and detain all ships and vessels belonging to the subjects of the States General when they shall be found to have on board any effects belonging to the enemies of his majesty, or effects which are considered as contraband by the general law of nations.[24]

To no one's surprise, the predominate mood in the United Provinces became anti-British. The result was that, on 24 April 1780, the States General resolved to grant convoy protection to *all* cargoes and adopted a resolution to outfit 52 ships-of-the-line and frigates for the protection of commerce and navigation.

While the Dutch government desperately tried to stay neutral in the conflict between Britain and the colonists, a rather unwelcome guest arrived, and became a third source of tension. On 4 October 1779, Captain John Paul Jones sailed into the Texel. As a captain of the Continental Navy he had commanded the 42-gun *Bonhomme Richard*, a merchant ship rebuilt and given to America by the French shipping magnate Jacques-Donatien Le Ray. Before entering the Texel, Jones had attacked an English convoy. During a fierce firefight, Jones took the *Serapis* and *Countess of Scarborough*, after which *Bonhomme Richard* sank. Jones had come into the Texel with his two prizes, as well as 504 captured English sailors, flying the American flag.[25]

The hybrid squadron – Jones had been joined by two French frigates – soon became an embarrassment. What was the nationality of Jones and his ships? If it were American, Jones could be arrested as a pirate, for the Dutch government had not recognized the American Congress. If Jones, however, had a French commission and flew the French flag, he was entitled to shelter and supplies as a belligerent in distress. Yorke asked for the immediate arrest and imprisonment of Jones, pointing out that the entire world waited to see how the Dutch would treat this "rebel pirate." The French ambassador, P.F. de Quelen, Duc de la Vauguyon, on the other hand, remained silent. The Dutch government, understandably, was anxious to get rid of Jones. William V was, however, of the opinion that American ships coming in with prizes would all have French commissions and colors; after all, the previous year France had joined the war against Britain, and it would therefore be difficult to act against those vessels. The States General would not give shelter to captors and their prizes, other than Dutch, except in emergencies. Jones and his vessels were therefore ordered to leave Dutch waters as soon as they were able to sail. No ammunition or naval stores were to be delivered to him except what he needed for reaching the open sea and the next foreign harbor. A waiting game developed.

By the end of November, the Stadholder, as Admiral-General, in compliance with the States General, urged Jones, politely but firmly, to depart. However, when Captain Van Overmeer arrived on board the *Serapis* to execute the order, he found that the vessel was not commanded by Jones any longer but by a French captain, Cotineau de Corgelin, who held it in the name of the King of France. Such also was the case with the other prize. Jones, now commanding the French ship *Alliance*, was asked to inform the Dutch authorities whether the *Alliance* was to be considered a French or an American vessel. In the first case, Jones would be expected to show his French commission and hoist the French flag and pendant. If it was the other case, Jones was to depart immediately. By the end of December, Dutch navy ships prepared to expel Jones' squadron. Vauguyon let it be known that the squadron now sailed under French colors and that Captain Cotineau was in command. Jones, with the *Alliance*, and flying the American flag, slipped through the British squadron off the Texel and made his way down the Channel into the Atlantic. About his stay in the United Provinces Jones wrote to Dr. Edward Bancroft:

> The only satisfaction I have is that in spite of the diplomats I have used my position here to strain the relations between Holland and England to a point past mending. Nothing now keeps Holland neutral except the influence of the ship owners, who are doing almost the entire commerce of Europe at enormous rates.... But the Dutch people are for us and the war.[26]

The small island of St. Eustatius in the Netherlands Antilles provided a fourth source of tension. In the winter of 1774, two Boston agents were in Amsterdam procuring arms and powder for the rebels. In response, the States General forbade the export of war materials to the rebels. One way to get the ammunition to the Americas was to load it for the coast of Africa and then have the ships go to St. Eustatius where "their cargoes, being the most proper assortments, are instantly bought up by the American agents." From the beginning of the War of Independence, St. Eustatius became the chief point of trade between the Dutch Republic, as well as other European countries, and the American colonies. Regular trade between America and the United Provinces via St. Eustatius was established by 1776. Powder was an especially profitable item, generating exorbitant profits in excess of 120 percent. Dozens of houses were active in the illusive business of arms shipments to the rebels, but three were of particular importance: Crommelin & Soonen, Nicolaas & Jacob van Staphorst and Neufville & Zoon.²⁷ In 1779 alone, over 12,000 hogsheads of tobacco and 1.5 million ounces of indigo were shipped to St. Eustatius from North America in exchange for arms, powder, naval stores and other goods from Europe. In the words of British Admiral Sir George Rodney: "This rock [St. Eustatius] of only six miles in length and three in breadth has done England more harm than all the arms of her most potent enemies and alone supported the infamous American rebellion."²⁸

Tensions over the League of Armed Neutrality constituted a fifth problem between the Dutch Republic and Great Britain. After the Van Bylandt–Fielding incident was reported to the States General, it became crystal clear that maintaining the principle pronounced in the Anglo-Dutch treaty of 1674, that the navigation of neutrals powers should remain as free and unobstructed in time of war as in that of peace, would be impossible. But then two neutral Russian vessels carrying corn were seized in the Mediterranean by the Spaniards, who were trying to keep all provisions from Gibraltar, which they had under siege. To Catherine II, Empress of Russia, it was clear no country owned a navy sufficiently large and effective to cope with the British, and that the only way to again render the seas free and secure was to link the naval forces of the various interested neutral nations.

On 26 February 1780, the Empress sent secretly to various neutral governments a plan to form a coalition. Catherine's declaration of Armed Neutrality stated: that all neutral vessels should be able to navigate freely from one port to another, even upon the coast of the powers of war; that the effects belonging to the subjects of the belligerents should be free in neutral ships, excepting always contraband goods; that naval stores and provisions should not be considered contraband unless belonging to the government of a belligerent (only arms, ammunition and military accouterments should be considered as contraband); that a port should be considered blockaded only if it was guarded so well that no attempt could be made to enter into it without evident danger; and that these principles should serve as a rule when there was a question regarding the legality of prizes.²⁹

In April, the States General was formally invited to join Catherine's crusade for neutral rights. In response, the British government made it perfectly clear to The Hague that such a move might lead to war between Britain and the United Provinces. The threat succeeded for a time in preventing an official Dutch reaction to Russia's proposed convention. Holland, led by Amsterdam, however, continued to make overtures to St. Petersburg through its emissary, De Swart. By the end of October, five of the seven provinces had voted in favor of the Russian plan and it became clear that it was only a matter of time before the Dutch would join the proposed League of Armed Neutrality. For the British, this was unacceptable. The Dutch navy, it is true, was utterly ineffective, but under the protection of this coalition, Dutch commerce could not only do immeasurable damage to Britain's commercial interests, but by the undisturbed furnishing of naval stores to Spain and France, as well as ammunition to the American rebels, the foes of Britain would be considerably strengthened. What the British government needed was compelling evidence of the treacherous nature of the Dutch to convince Parliament that a rupture with the Dutch Republic was the only way to win the war against the American rebels. They needed a smoking gun, and they soon found one in the machinations of American-leaning Dutch entrepreneurs and politicans.[30]

In the early days of the American rebellion, close contacts between the rebels and kindred spirits in the Dutch Republic were forged. In 1775 the Committee of Secret Correspondence, chaired by Benjamin Franklin, appointed Charles W.F. Dumas as its correspondent in The Hague. Franklin had visited the Netherlands in 1766 and probably met Dumas then. Dumas was a great American enthusiast and maintained close contacts with members of the Patriotic party, including Joan Derk van der Capellen tot den Pol and E.F. van Berckel, who was Amsterdam's *pensionaris*, or highest executive officer. These contacts also included Amsterdam tobacco merchant Jean de Neufville, who had traded with North America long before the war. He was appalled by the severance of these trade connections and saw America as threatened with "absolute slavery." He supported the rebels from the start, becoming involved in 1777 in such covert activities as the building of the warship *L'Indien*, which became *South Carolina*, a state-owned frigate.[31]

The next year, De Neufville traveled to Germany to sell tobacco. In Frankfurt, he met William Lee, a brother of Arthur Lee, the American minister in Paris, and his secretary Samuel Witham Stockton, and told them of his hope of re-establishing trade. Upon De Neufville's return to Amsterdam, he received the strongest encouragement from Dumas, Van de Capellen and Van Berckel, and began to draft a treaty of amity and commerce. The burgomasters of Amsterdam endorsed the plan and Van Berckel signed this letter of intent on 4 September 1778, along with William Lee and De Neufville. Dumas sent a copy of the proposed pact to Franklin in Paris, and another to Congress.[32]

A more far-reaching consequence of the Amsterdam treaty initiative was the appointment of Henry Laurens, a South Carolina planter and merchant, who had served as president of the Continental Congress, as the American minister to the United Provinces. He was commissioned to borrow $10,000,000, but it took him almost a year to wrap up his business and set sail for Holland. On 3 September 1780, the packet *Mercury*, bound for the United Provinces from Philadelphia, was intercepted by the Royal Navy frigate *Vestal*. On the approach of *Vestal*'s boarding party, and in full view of her boats' crew, Laurens threw a weighted bag overboard, one that remained afloat long enough to be retrieved. It contained the pending Amsterdam pact of amity and commerce, as well as correspondence between American and Dutch officials concerning financial aid to the colonies.[33]

The Laurens incident was a godsend to Whitehall. By the end of 1780, the position of Britain was becoming extremely critical. She had to depend entirely upon herself in the struggle with France, Spain and her former American colonies. Meanwhile, the United Provinces commercially supported her enemies, and were on the brink of joining the League of Armed Neutrality. Now, a rupture with the Dutch Republic could take place without disclosing the real reason. As the Dutch government had not yet announced its formal accession to the Amsterdam treaty, the Laurens affair would become the excuse for war. An assault upon the Dutch at this time without this pretext would have been difficult to defend in Parliament, and an attack upon the Dutch Republic, openly based upon their accession to the League of Armed Neutrality, would have suggested a hostile attitude toward the other armed neutrals. Britain was anxious not to antagonize them openly because England was almost completely dependent upon Riga and the Northern powers for vital naval stores.[34]

The papers were sent to Yorke in The Hague. This was the right kind of ammunition to curtail the pro-French party, destroy the prestige of Amsterdam, and to elevate the Stadholder and his pro-British followers as the true guardians of Dutch interests. A secret committee of the States General started to investigate the matter and Amsterdam had to account for the action. On 10 November 1780, Yorke asked the States General to formally disavow the secret pact and demanded that De Neufville and Van Berckel be punished. If this was not done immediately, King George III would take such measures as "his own dignity and the essential interests of his people demand." In the midst of these exchanges, a special messenger arrived from St. Petersburg. Catherine requested the immediate accession of the United Provinces to the League. Trying to straddle the diplomatic fence, the States General adopted a resolution disapproving and disavowing the conduct of Amsterdam, and decided at the same time to join the League.

On 16 December 1780, the British government learned of the States General's decision to join the League. For the Cabinet, the Dutch decision was equivalent to entering the war on the side of France and Spain. On 20 December, the ministry of Lord North sent to Yorke a manifesto severing diplomatic relations with the Dutch Republic. It gave five reasons for the Crown's move: the United Provinces had disregarded treaties, withholding the promised succor; they had willingly allowed an American pirate to remain in one of their ports; they had provided protection and warlike supplies to His Majesty's enemies in the West Indies, notably at St. Eustatius; the leading magistrates of Amsterdam had concluded a secret treaty with His Majesty's rebellious colonies, for which they had not been punished; and the States General had refused to answer Yorke's memorials on this subject. This list included not a word on the League of Armed Neutrals. When Benjamin Franklin read the de facto declaration of war he wrote to Dumas: "Surely there never was a more unjust War, it is manifestly such from their own manifesto."[35]

The Fourth Anglo-Dutch War, 1780–84

When war broke out in December 1780 the Dutch were hopelessly divided, unprepared and alone. Even now, in their hour of danger, the United Provinces were torn by inner political and party strife that prevented the mounting of an effective defense. The situation was vividly described by John Adams, the newly appointed American minister plenipotentiary to the United Provinces, in March 1781:

> The nation has indeed been in a violent fermentation and crisis. It is divided in sentiments. There are stadholderians and republicans; there are proprietors in English funds, and persons immediately engaged in commerce; there are enthusiasts for peace and alliance with England; and there are advocates for an alliance with France, Spain, and America; and there are a third sort, who are for adhering in all things to Russia, Sweden, and Denmark. Some are for acknowledging American independence, and entering into treaties of commerce and alliance with her; others start at the idea with horror, as an everlasting impediment to a return to the friendship and alliance with England; some will not augment the navy without increasing the army; others will let the navy be neglected rather than augment the army.
>
> In this perfect chaos of sentiments and systems, principles and interests, it is no wonder there is languor, a weakness, and irresolution that is vastly dangerous in the present circumstances of affairs. The danger lies not more in the hostile designs and exertions of the English than from seditions and commotions among the people, which are every day dreaded and expected. If it were not for a standing army, and troops posted about in several cities, it is probable there would have been popular tumults before now; but everybody that I see appears to me to live in constant fear of mobs, and in a great degree of uncertainty whether they will rise in favor of war or against it; in favor of England or against it; in favor of the prince or of the city of Amsterdam; in favor of America or against.[36]

Like Adams, all of Europe was surprised at the idleness of the Dutch. The Prussian king, for instance, thought the British party and the Duke of Brunswijk responsible for this pusillanimity that thwarted the best intentions of the government.[37]

Dutch security policy was conceived in The Hague. The Raad van State – a Council of State in which all seven provinces were represented – advised the States General on matters of war and peace via a *petitie* and the *staat van oorlog*. The *petitie* was a kind of defense white paper. The *staat van oorlog* was a list of all the necessary troops, weapons and forts needed, and their costs. The Raad van State was also closely involved in the execution of this policy by organizing the logistics of the army and maintaining the garrisons and fortifications. The Stadholder, the highest official of the Union, had to be recognized and appointed by each province. So, the Stadholder was not a sovereign. He was a servant of the Union. He held the title of Captain- and Admiral-General: commander-in-chief of the army and the navy. After the States General had discussed, amended and approved the *petitie* and the *staat van oorlog*, every provincial estate had to consent to the plans. The so-called quote split the cost of war over the seven provinces; Holland's share was almost 60 percent; to be precise, 58.305 percent (see appendix).[38]

The organization of the war at sea was executed completely differently. Representatives from the States General, the Raad van State, the five Admiralty Boards and the Stadholder met during winter in The Hague. At this so-called *Haags besogne* (The Hague palaver), a plan was drawn up for how many ships would be equipped and manned. So, policy was made in The Hague, the execution of it was delegated to five Admiralty Boards, located in different provinces: Zeeland in Middelburg, Maze in Rotterdam, Amsterdam in Amsterdam, Noorderkwartier in Hoorn, and Enkhuizen and Friesland in Harlingen.[39]

From the outset it was clear this would be a maritime conflict. Initially, the British government planned to destroy the Dutch navy and arsenals at home, but Yorke dissuaded them from such a step because of the inaccessibility of the Dutch coast and the shallow and dangerous entrances to the sea. Furthermore, it was to be feared that the British name would be hated in the Dutch Republic for many generations if the war should be carried into the heart of the country. It was much more effective to blockade the Dutch ports, seize their merchant vessels in the open sea and attack their overseas possessions, especially in the West Indies, which figuratively were the gold mines of the age. Yorke recommended the capture of St. Eustatius in order to sever the intercourse between Holland and the American rebels.[40]

The unpreparedness of the Dutch was most evident during the first few months of the war. Besides the Royal Navy, some 500 private ships carrying British *letters of marque* cruised the seas. During the war, 129 Dutch vessels were captured by British privateers. The Royal Navy took another 195. By far, the majority of these ships were taken in European waters during the first three months of the war.[41]

The state of the Dutch navy was deplorable. What was worse was that there was little hope of rebuilding it soon. By 1780 the intention was to have equipped 52 ships and crew them with 14,000 sailors. Five ships were to guard the entrances to the sea, and 47 would protect the merchant marine by doing convoy duty and patrolling. Table 9.1 shows the dispositions of Dutch warships at the start of the conflict.

Table 9.1 Disposition of Dutch navy ships, fall 1780

Region	Ships
North Sea	10
Spain and Portugal	5
Mediterranean	5
West Indies	11
Reserve	5
Unprepared	11
Guard ships	5
Total	52

Source: Project omtrent den dienst der schepen, najaar 1780, NA, Archieven der Admiraliteitscolleges, Aanhangsel XXXII, Van Bleiswijk 10; De Jonge, *Geschiedenis van het Nederlandsche zeewezen*, IV:780.

The Dutch navy could perform only two tasks: homeland defense in conjunction with shore batteries, and protecting economic interests such as the merchant marine and overseas possessions. Other ways of using the fleet were out of the question. First, the Dutch navy had only a few ships-of-the-line. More than half of the ships they did have were armed with 50 guns or less. The Royal Navy had a fleet of some 126 ships, many of them more heavily armed than the Dutch vessels. The Dutch navy was outnumbered as well as outgunned (see Table 9.2).[42] Obviously, any ambition of pursuing some form of sea control by engaging the British battle fleet was chimerical. In addition, power projection from the sea was not an option because the Dutch possessed no expeditionary capability. A plan to create a corps of 6,000 marine commandos was dropped.

Despite the fact that the States General allocated substantial funds for the navy, and most provinces even put up the money (see Appendix 9.1), the prospects for building a fleet that would be a match for the Royal Navy were bleak. First, the Dutch lacked the necessary port infrastructure to harbor ships-of-the-line. The shallowness of the entrances to the sea, especially for Amsterdam and Rotterdam, did not allow the passage of large and heavily armed warships. The only deepwater port was Flushing, but its dock and port facilities were in disarray and it was too small to host a large battle fleet. Second, there was a shortage of shipbuilding materials. The British succeeded in making the North Sea and Baltic so unsafe for Dutch navigation that in 1781 only 11 Dutch ships sailed through the Sound, while in 1780 about 2,058 had passed there.[43] Third, despite all sorts of financial incentives and bonuses, there was a shortage of sailors to man the ships. In several instances the ships were ready, but there were no crews. In April 1781, for instance, the Admiralty Board of Amsterdam was in need of over 1,600 sailors, including 24 officers and 129 petty officers. A month later, in Amsterdam, of 21 ships only six were ready because they were still short 1,340 sailors.[44]

Two years later, in October 1782, the Dutch fleet consisted of 95 large ships and 37 smaller vessels (See Table 9.3). The number of warships capable of serving on the high seas was just over 60. Under these circumstances, the objec-

Table 9.2 Armament of the largest Royal Navy and Dutch navy ships, 1781

Guns	Royal Navy	Dutch navy
100	3	
98	1	
90	10	
84	2	
80	1	
74	48	
70	1	2
68	1	1
64	24	
60	4	4

Source: Missive Admiraal Generaal, 7 October 1782, NA, SG 9252 f. 21.

Table 9.3 Number of Dutch navy ships, October 1782

Guns	Number of ships	Remarks
70 to 76	7	6 under construction
60 to 68	20	8 under construction
50 to 54	13	1 hospital ship
40 to 44	15	2 under construction, 4 guard ships
36	14	
24	15	
Total	95	
Cutters	10	
Gun boats	18	
Small vessels	9	
Total	37	

Source: De Jonge, *Geschiedenis van het Nederlandsche zeewezen*, IV:782.

tives for the Dutch navy were rather limited. The fleet had four tasks: guarding the entrances to the seas; convoying the merchant marine; protecting the overseas settlements; and harming the enemy, if possible, and avenging violated rights and treaties.[45]

Despite the fact that a conflict with a maritime nation such as Britain would be fought at sea, the first action was to strengthen the coastal defenses by sending cavalry, infantry and artillery units to the maritime provinces. There were, however, not enough navy ships to cover the entrances to the sea. By February, the first gunboats were operational. A dozen or so ships, including several capital ships, were stationed in the entrances to the sea for coastal defense.[46] Even though the government supported privateering in many ways – the States General offered premiums for seizing Royal Navy ships and they established an indemnification for ship-owners in the event of a peace treaty being concluded – only 29 Dutch privateers were fitted out during the war. Of the 29 privateers, 15 were commanded by French and American captains. They captured 61 British merchantmen and ransomed 40 British vessels. They also recaptured one French vessel; 16 of the 29 privateers were lost. All in all, not very impressive figures.[47]

In March 1781, the States General wanted to send a convoy of merchant ships to the Baltic. At that moment, not enough warships were available for coastal defense and for convoy duty. Moreover, only eight warships were ready to sail. It was anticipated that, at the end of May, 24 ships would be available. In the meantime, a small squadron under the command of Captain Van Kinsbergen would cruise the North Sea. Due to heavy fog, no English convoys were sighted. Meanwhile, the Admiral-General postponed the departure of the convoy. Only after prolonged insistence from the States General did 71 merchantmen, seven ships-of-the-line, six frigates and several small vessels, all under the command of Rear Admiral Johan Arnold Zoutman, leave the Texel road for the Baltic on 20 July.

The Dutch quickly found themselves embroiled in a global naval war. On 5 August 1781, Zoutman encountered a British convoy of more than 200 merchantmen, ten ships-of-the-line, four frigates and several smaller vessels, all under the command of Vice Admiral Hyde Parker. This resulted in the only major Anglo-Dutch battle of the war. After a firefight of three hours, both sides claimed victory. In any case, Zoutman was not defeated. Considering his lack of firepower, and the generally deplorable state of the navy, the Dutch performance was not too bad. They lost one ship, the *Holland*, and suffered 142 dead and 403 wounded, compared to 104 dead and 339 wounded for the British. There was, however, one major result of the battle. Parker could continue his voyage to Britain safely, while the Dutch merchantmen, including the damaged warships, returned empty-handed to the Netherlands. Despite the fact that the battle was celebrated as a victory, no further naval operations were conducted that year.[48]

In October 1780, Rear Admiral William Crul had left the United Provinces with a squadron of 11 ships bound for the West Indies. They had planned to disperse and sail to different Dutch settlements when they reached the other side of the ocean. Unaware of the breakdown of Anglo-Dutch relations, Crul left an undefended St. Eustatius on 1 February to convoy 23 merchantmen back to the Netherlands. Two days later, an English expeditionary force under Admiral Sir George Rodney and General John Vaughan took the island. Like a swarm of locusts, the British plundered St. Eustatius, taking nearly 200 ships, including the Crul convoy, and goods in the island's warehouses with an estimated value of three million pounds sterling, as well as more than 2,000 American prisoners. The British derived little long-term benefit from their victory. They dispatched the bulk of their spoils for home in a convoy of 34 merchant ships commanded by Commodore William Hotham. Only eight of the merchant vessels, together with the warships, made it to England. A French fleet took the rest. And in November 1781, a French force under Governor Francois-Claude-Amour de Bouillé took St. Eustatius. The island, though, had now lost its importance as a trading post, its place taken by the Danish island of St. Thomas.[49]

After the conquest of St. Eustatius, Rodney sent some ships to the Wild Coast, the shores between the Amazon and the Orinoco rivers. Within two months, the British were in possession of all Dutch Guiana west of Suriname, Essequibo, Demerara and Berbice, and they also took 20 fully laden merchantmen. The British possession of Dutch Guiana was also short-lived. By 15 February 1782, all the former Dutch West Indian colonies, with the exception of Suriname, were in French hands.[50]

On 7 June 1781, Amsterdam ship-owners requested from the States General an armed convoy to Suriname, on the northeastern coast of South America. In September, 17 ships were ready to leave the Texel. The Admiral-General, backed by his admirals, however, was reluctant to furnish the necessary warships. Again and again the promised navy ships were not available. Eventually, on 6 April 1782, 13 merchantmen and two frigates left the Texel. They arrived at Suriname on 11 June, almost 12 months to the day after the initial request. This was the only convoy to Suriname during the war.[51]

In Africa, the Dutch East India Company (VOC) ran a settlement at the Cape of Good Hope, while the Dutch West India Company (WIC) possessed several forts on the Gold Coast in present-day Ghana. In West Africa, the relations between the British Royal Africa Company (RAC) and the WIC had never been very cordial. Their respective headquarters, Dutch Elmina and the British Cape Coast Castle, were only a few miles apart. With the outbreak of war in 1781, several unresolved matters could be settled. In early February 1782, a squadron of four British warships arrived in West Africa. Their aim was to expel the Dutch. An attack on Elmina failed, but in the following months all six Dutch forts east of Elmina were captured.[52]

By 1780, the once small "refreshing" station at the Cape of Good Hope was a thriving settlement, one strategically located between the South Atlantic and the Indian Ocean. As with everywhere else in the Dutch empire, the defenses of this colony were in disarray. On 13 March 1781, a British force of 47 ships and 3,000 troops under the command of Commodore George Johnstone left Spithead for Asia. At the same time, a French fleet of 14 ships had sailed from Brest under Vice Admiral Pierre André de Suffren. On 3 July, the French arrived at the Cape of Good Hope, occupied the colony, and strengthened its defenses with two regiments. When Johnstone arrived, Cape Town was obviously too strong to be attacked. He returned empty-handed to England.[53]

In the East Indies, Anglo-Dutch animosity centered on India and Ceylon. By the 1780s the VOC had lost both the ability and the will to invest in military forces, just when its British and French rivals were not only growing in economic and military power, but showing themselves increasingly willing to use this might against the weakening Indian political structures. In the 1780s, the army of the VOC comprised some 15,000 men, compared to 115,000 British Sepoys.[54] The British at Madras, when learning of the rupture between Britain and the United Provinces, fitted out an expedition against Negapatam, the main Dutch settlement on the Coromandel. There was a danger that the local ruler and the French, with whom he was allied, would make common cause with the Dutch and use Negapatam as a base of operations. All the VOC settlements on the Coromandel coast fell into the hands of the British in June and July 1781. Pulicat, Jaggernaikpurum, Sadraspatnam, Palicol and the other Dutch possessions were taken without any fighting. Negapatman was captured in October. The important harbor of Triconomale on the island of Ceylon (Sri Lanka) fell to the British in January 1782. Suffren recaptured Triconomale on 1 September 1782, but Negapatam remained lost.[55]

By the summer of 1781, it became apparent that the Stadholder and the navy were incapable of protecting the Dutch merchant marine interests, as well as the country's colonial possessions. Ship-owners started to neutralize their vessels on a large scale. The ships destined for the Baltic left the Netherlands in the fall with Swedish papers and under the Swedish flag. Furthermore, in neutral North German and Austrian ports, merchant houses specialized in reflagging ships by providing neutral papers. Over 900 Dutch ships were neutralized in ports like Bremen, Altona and Oostende. This was probably half of the merchant marine of the United Provinces.[56]

Although there was no prospect of a formal alliance between France and the United Provinces – in the Netherlands, the idea of an offensive and defensive alliance with France did have many adherents, especially in the Patriotic party – serious preparations were made for a combined naval action against Britain. In the spring of 1782, the States General asked the Stadholder to confer with the Court of France on such an action. Although the Admiral-General did not consider the fleet strong enough to furnish convoys, defend the coast and fight the enemy at the same time, William V carried out talks. France willingly entered into an agreement, thereby binding the Dutch to its interests. France, however, had made an arrangement with Spain to have the French fleet near Gibraltar, and now kept the Dutch fleet waiting for the promised naval action. Consequently, that year only one naval operation took place, when in July a substantial squadron of 33 ships, including several ships-of-the-line, left port to escort 11 East and West Indiamen outside European waters.

Finally, during the fall, a juncture of the fleets at Brest was arranged between the two powers, but the ten Dutch vessels designated for this purpose refused to sail, declaring that they were not prepared for such an action. This caused a storm of indignation in the United Provinces and violent attacks on the Stadholder. An investigation regarding the condition and idleness of the Dutch navy, and the causes of its inefficiency, was instituted and the Admiral-General had to account for his actions before the States General, but no practical result came from this.[57] Despite this, the States General allocated on 9 January 1783 over 13 million guilders to equip 46 ships-of-the-line, 26 frigates and 59 smaller craft with a complement of 31,000 sailors. But the war was effectively over. Peace negotiations between Great Britain and its four opponents, the American rebels, France, Spain and the Dutch Republic, had started in Paris.

Meanwhile, to replace the imprisoned Henry Laurens, Congress appointed John Adams as the American minister plenipotentiary to the United Provinces in January 1781. He was instructed not only to negotiate a loan, but also to conclude, if possible, a treaty of commerce and amity with the Dutch Republic. Many difficulties had to be overcome, not least the resistance of the Stadholder, before the States General would receive him, which, of course, involved the acknowledgment of the independence of the United States.

One of Adams' principal tasks was to negotiate loans for the impecunious Congress. At first, the Dutch merchant houses seemed to have no inclination at all to risk their money funding the Americans. Several initiatives failed. Only after the news of General Cornwallis' surrender at Yorktown on 19 October 1781 reached the United Provinces did things change. In December, a French loan of five million guilders for the United States was completed, but only a small residual remained available for Congress, most of the sum being expended for advances previously made by France. A few months later, Adams negotiated another loan of five million guilders with W. and J. Willink, N. and J. Van Staphorst, and De la Lande and Fynjé. In the years to come, Amsterdam banking houses invested tens of millions of guilders in the United States.

In December 1781, the first proposals emerged for forming an alliance with the United States, and it was one of many matters of policy and strategy that occupied Dutch leaders for the next year or two. By the summer of 1782, the British party had lost ground completely, with even the Stadholder being compelled to yield to public sentiment that had grown decidedly anti-English. At last, on 8 October 1782, a treaty of amity and commerce, and a convention concerning recaptures, was signed by both parties at The Hague. After its ratification by the two nations, Pieter Johan van Berckel, Burgomaster of Rotterdam and brother of E.F. van Berckel, was appointed minister plenipotentiary of the States General to Congress. He sailed for the United States on 23 June 1783.[58]

In the Netherlands, the idea of an offensive and defensive alliance with France had many adherents. The Stadholder, who still favored Britain, expressed his apprehension that an alliance with France would mean the absolute dependence of the Dutch Republic upon her powerful neighbor. The French Court, on the other hand, was not pleased with the various efforts made for a separate peace between Britain and the United Provinces. During the war, the relations with France were scarcely different from those before the conflict.[59]

Efforts to bring about peace had not been wanting. Since the beginning of the war between Britain and the Dutch Republic, attempts had been made to reconcile the two powers. An initiative of Catherine of Russia, in conjunction with Emperor Joseph II of Austria, failed because the principles adopted by the Dutch and the British regarding the maintenance of the treaty of 1674 were too much in opposition. In the meantime, Britain halfheartedly negotiated with the United Provinces directly in order to satisfy the Whig opposition in Parliament.[60]

The Paris peace

Not having succeeded in concluding a separate peace with the United Provinces, Britain tried to sever France from the rest of her enemies by offering Paris a separate peace. In case this should not be feasible, Britain proposed a general peace. With every option a possibility, in the summer of 1782 preliminary peace negotiations began, the Dutch hoping that France, while negotiating for a general peace, would also defend their interests. The Dutch sought the following: that the Dutch, in confirmation with the principles of the League of Armed Neutrality, would remain "in the full possession and indisputable enjoyment of the rights of the neutral flag and of free navigation"; that naval stores should henceforth be regarded as free merchandise and not contraband; that all Dutch possessions taken by Britain were to be restored to the United Provinces; that losses "unjustly" caused by Britain should be indemnified by the latter; and there would be a restoration to the States General of all Dutch overseas territories in the possession of France at the conclusion of peace.

The negotiations did not proceed as the States General wished. The British flatly rejected the Dutch indemnity claims and free navigation in conformity with the articles of the League of Armed Neutrality. However, Britain was willing to return all Dutch possessions in its hands at the conclusion of peace, except for Triconomale on the island of Ceylon. On 20 January 1783, the preliminary articles of peace were signed by Great Britain, France and Spain, and a cessation of hostilities was arranged. Because of their internal discord, the Dutch were not yet ready to sign the preliminaries, but they were included in the armistice. That France had not delayed the signing of the preliminary treaty until the negotiations had been concluded between the United Provinces and Britain was bitterly resented by the Dutch, who now considered themselves abandoned by the French and delivered to the hatred or mercy of Britain. The belief that France had failed to put pressure upon Britain in favor of the Dutch and would finally conclude a separate peace with London caused great apprehension among the pro-French adherents in the Dutch Republic. The palpable Dutch sense of abandonment and isolation was undoubtedly deepened by the fact that the American commissioners led by Benjamin Franklin had concluded their own separate peace treaty with Great Britain on 30 November 1782, almost two months before the signing of the preliminary articles of peace between Britain, France and Spain.

The definitive treaty of peace between Britain and the United Provinces was finally concluded at Paris on 29 May 1784, and subsequently ratified at the Court of St. James's on 10 June and at The Hague on 15 June. Its principal provisions stated that: the vessels of the Dutch Republic should salute those of Britain; the Dutch would cede to Great Britain the city of Negapatam on the southeastern coast of India; Britain would return to the United Provinces all Dutch possessions conquered in Asia and the New World during the war; British vessels would receive free access to the Dutch East Indies; commissioners should be named to settle the differences between the RAC and the WIC regarding navigation on the coast of West Africa. These submissive stipulations left the British party in the Netherlands "dejected, depressed and divided."[61]

Conclusion

The course of the war made it perfectly clear that the Dutch Republic was a second-rate power not strong enough to successfully defend itself against even one of the three great powers surrounding her: England, France and Prussia. This impotence would necessitate an alliance of the United Provinces with one of these countries, preferably the strongest. This was France. Another option had been joining the League of Armed Neutrality.[62] When war broke out, the States General trusted that the northern countries participating in the League of Armed Neutrality would come to the assistance of the United Provinces. Prompt and efficient help was requested, especially by furnishing armed vessels in excess of the ships which the allies had destined for their common defense. Catherine of Russia, however, excluded the Dutch from the protection which the League would have afforded them if they had remained neutral. She could do nothing with the Dutch as belligerents. By terminating Holland's neutrality, the British declaration of war had pulled the rug from under the Dutch strategic gamble. At the beginning of their war, the United Provinces stood alone.[63]

When the American War of Independence erupted, the Dutch were politically divided, militarily unprepared and diplomatically isolated. During the first phase of the war, until December 1780, the Dutch tried to remain neutral while protecting their economic interests. The issue of the protection of Dutch trade with France and the West Indies, particularly in naval stores, and vigorously championed by Amsterdam, became a matter of great importance to both parties. The menacing attitude of Britain, and its violation of the principal of "free ships, free goods" established in the treaty of 1674, alarmed the merchants. The belief that Dutch neutrality would have to be supplemented by armed escorts marked the turning point in Anglo-Dutch relations and set the stage for an inevitable showdown: London now had either to fight or retreat. The Dutch expansion of their navy marked a defiant refusal to give up the lucrative trade with the American rebels via St. Eustatius. This stance, coupled with the decision to seek admission to the League of Armed Neutrality, made war all but inevitable.

At the start of the Fourth Anglo-Dutch War, the Dutch navy was in a deplorable state. What was worse was that there was little hope of it being rebuilt very soon. The Dutch fleet was outnumbered and outgunned by the Royal Navy; pursuing some form of sea control by engaging the British battle fleet was out of the question. Furthermore, power projection from the sea via an expeditionary operation was impossible. The navy could only be used for homeland defense and protecting the nation's primary economic interests: the merchant marine and the colonies. The limited fleet therefore was called upon to perform four duties: guarding the Dutch entrances to the sea; convoying the merchant marine; protecting the overseas settlements; and harming, when possible, the enemy. In all four tasks, the navy failed. From the start, London had no intention of invading the United Provinces, and the Dutch navy lacked the means to harm Britain. Convoying the merchant marine happened rarely, and British privateers and warships took 324 Dutch vessels. For protection, desperate ship-owners neutralized their vessels. Meanwhile, in the Atlantic, West Africa and Asia, the British took Dutch settlements and possessions almost at will.

Because the United Provinces were deserted by the League of Armed Neutrals during the war, and their erstwhile allies France and Spain during the peace negotiations, Britain could set peace terms to which the Dutch, unable to carry on the war alone, were compelled to submit. The Dutch Republic, by accepting London's conditions, suffered permanent and very painful losses. The possession of Negapatam, together with free navigation among the Dutch East Indies, enabled Britain to establish there a flourishing, interloping trade. In all, the VOC lost over 43 million guilders.[64] St. Eustatius never recovered from Admiral Rodney's plunder, and all six forts east of Elmina on the Gold Coast were lost. The United Provinces, which had proved themselves the benefactors of the United States and France, must be counted among the largest losers of the American War of Independence.

Appendix 9.1 Shipbuilding funds allocated for the Dutch navy, 1771–80

Year	Date	Petitie			Holland	
		Purpose	Allocated amount	Share of 58.31%	Actually paid	Deficit %
Total, 1771–80			20,691,226	12,064,433	11,682,872	–3
1771	19 March	Equipping ships	410,400	239,292	608,682	154
	16 April	Building 24 ships	4,178,508	2,436,363	0	–100
1772	11 August	Equipping ships for Maroc	495,000	288,620	580,533	101
1773	27 May	Equipping 6 ships	745,200	434,504	139,504	–68
	26 July	Equipping 6 ships	388,800	226,698	0	–100
1774					592,788	
1775					492,453	
1776	23 October	Equipping ships	396,000	230,896	982,225	325
			1,521,780	887,304	0	–100
1777	30 April	Equipping 20 ships	2,640,960	1,539,865	1,539,865	0
	30 April	Building materials and spares	1,800,000	1,049,526	1,049,526	0
	24 December	Equipping ships	528,990	308,438	308,438	0
1778	3 November	Half equipment for 32 ships	1,995,840	1,163,714	1,736,864	49
1779	13 April	Hiring additional sailors	221,760	129,302	1,553,184	1101
	14 April	Equipping ships	669,200	390,190	0	–100
	15 April	Guard ships and dispatch yachts	575,198	335,381	0	–100
	16 April	Building materials and spares	1,500,000	874,605	0	–100
1780	25 February	Equipping 25 ships	2,623,590	1,529,737	2,098,810	37

Total, 1781–85			73,689,455	42,966,111	37,611,891	–12
1781	5 January	Building ships	7,342,536	4,281,212	6,991,308	63
	5 January	Equipping ships	5,763,135	3,360,311	0	–100
	5 January	Armament and ammunition	1,500,000	874,605	0	–100
	19 February	Premiums for sailors	462,500	269,670	0	–100
	20 June	Arming ships	1,200,000	699,684	0	–100
	3 October	Building hulks etc.	799,200	465,990	0	–100
	3 October	Building extra ships	9,271,498	5,405,932	0	–100
	31 December	Building 19 ships	8,409,700	4,903,444	0	–100
1782	11 February	Equipping ships	9,429,758	5,498,209	12,490,232	127
	2 April	Support for prisoners in England	100,000	58,307	0	–100
1783	23 January	Armament and ammunition	2,100,000	1,224,447	7,777,170	535
	28 January	Equipping ships	13,956,073	8,137,367	0	–100
	22 September	Support for prisoners in England	50,000	29,154	0	–100
1784	16 January	Equipping ships	2,639,173	1,538,823	6,268,342	307
	16 January	Building quay	2,277,870	1,328,158	0	–100
	4 October	Equipping ships	4,946,413	2,884,105	0	–100
1785	15 April	Buying *hoekers* and spares	3,441,599	2,006,693	4,084,839	104
Total, 1771–85			94,380,681	55,030,544	49,294,763	–10

Source: R. Liesker and W. Fritschy, *Gewestelijke financiën ten tijde van de Republiek der Verenigde Nederlanden. Holland, deel 4, 1572–1795*, Rijks Geschiedkundige Publicatiën, Kleine Serie 100 (The Hague: Instituut voor Nederlandse Geschiedenis, 2004), pp. 416–17.

Notes

1. B.W. Tuchman, *The First Salute* (New York: Knopf, 1988), p. 15.
2. J.I. Israel, *The Dutch Republic: Its Rise, Greatness, and Fall, 1477–1806* (Oxford: Clarendon Press, 1995).
3. C.M. Hough, *Reports of Cases in the Vice-Admiralty of the Province of New York and in the Court of Admiralty of the State of New York, 1715–1788*, Yale Historical Publications Manuscripts and Edited Texts 8 (New Haven: Yale University Press, 1925), pp. 64–5.
4. H. Brand and J. Brand, *De Hollandse Waterlinie* (Utrecht and Antwerp: Veen, 1986); Ch. Will, *Sterk Water: De Hollandse Waterlinie* (Utrecht: Matrijs, 2002).
5. O. Van Nimwegen, *De Republiek der Verenigde Nederlanden als grote mogendheid. Buitenlandse politiek en oorlogvoering in de eerste helft van de achttiende eeuw en in het bijzonder tijdens de Oostenrijkse Successieoorlog, 1740–1748* (Amsterdam: De Bataafsche Leeuw, 2002).
6. H. Dunthorne, *The Maritime Powers: 1721–1740. A Study of Anglo-Dutch Relations in the Age of Walpole* (New York and London: Garland Publishing, 1986), pp. 9–12; R. Pares, *Colonial Blockade and Neutral Rights, 1739–1763* (Philadelphia: Porcupine Press, 1975), p. 298.
7. A. Porta, *Joan en Gerrit Corver. De politieke macht van Amsterdam, 1702–1748* (Amsterdam: Van Gorcum, 1975), pp. 173 ff.; N.A.M. Rodger, "Instigators or Spectator? The British Government and the Restoration of the Stadholderate in 1747," *Tijdschrift voor Geschiedenis* 106 (1993), pp. 496–514; Van Nimwegen, *De Republiek der Verenigde Nederlanden*, passim.
8. J.S. Bartstra, *Vlootherstel en legeraugmentatie, 1770–1780* (Assen: Van Gorcum, 1962).
9. W.H. Riker, "Dutch and American Federalism," *Journal of the History of Ideas* (1957), vol. 18, no. 4, pp. 495–521.
10. S. Schama, *Patriots and Liberators: Revolution in the Netherlands, 1780–1813* (London: Fontana Press, 1977).
11. E.A. van Dijk, "De wekker van de Nederlandse natie: Joan Derk van der Capellen, 1741–1784," *POMflet* 6 (1984), 3:1–12; E.H. Klei, "'A Notre Wilkes.' Het theatraal tegendraadse stijl van optreden van Joan Derk van der Capellen tot den Poll," *Overijsselse Historische Bijdragen* 120 (2005), pp. 104–28.
12. F. Edler, *The Dutch Republic and the American Revolution*, Johns Hopkins University Studies in Historical and Political Science 29/2 (Baltimore: The Johns Hopkins Press, 1911), p. 15.
13. Schama, *Patriots and Liberators*, pp. 57–8; Edler, *The Dutch Republic*, pp. 28–31.
14. H. Grotius, *The Free Seas*, edited and introduced by D. Armitage, *Natural Law and Enlightenment Classics* (Indianapolis: Liberty Fund, 2004); ibid., *Commentary on the Law of Prize and Booty*, edited and introduced by M. Van Ittersum (Indianapolis: Liberty Fund, 2006).
15. D.A. Miller, *Sir Joseph Yorke and Anglo-Dutch Relations, 1774–1780* (The Hague: Mouton, 1970), pp. 30–1, 39.
16. Miller, *Sir Joseph Yorke*, p. 30.
17. Miller, *Sir Joseph Yorke*, p. 40.
18. N. Tracy, *Navies, Deterrence, & American Independence: Britain and Sea Power in the 1760s and 1770s* (Vancouver: University of British Colombia Press, 1988), p. 122; N.A.M. Rodger, *The Command of the Ocean: A Naval History of Britain, 1649–1815* (New York: W.W. Norton, 2005), pp. 333–4.
19. Ships arriving at Amsterdam from North America: 1771 (21), 1772 (25), 1773 (16), 1774 (27), 1775 (8), 1776 (2), 1777 (1), 1778 (3), 1779 (7) and 1780 (14); J. Postma and V. Enthoven, eds., *Riches from Atlantic Commerce: Dutch Transatlantic Trade and Shipping, 1585–1817*, The Atlantic World 1 (Leiden: Brill, 2003), Appendix 14.1.

20 Edler, *The Dutch Republic*, p. 39.
21 Edler, *The Dutch Republic*, pp. 102–6.
22 Miller, *Sir Joseph York*, pp. 91–2; Edler, *The Dutch Republic*, pp. 109–30.
23 Edler, *The Dutch Republic*, pp. 129–31; J.C. de Jonge, *Geschiedenis van het Nederlandsche zeewezen*, 5 vols. (Haarlem: A.C. Kruseman, 1861), IV, pp. 406–16.
24 John Adams to the President of Congress, 13 May 1780. Available on the website of the Library of Congress, American Memory: http://memory.loc.gov.
25 S.E. Morison, *John Paul Jones: A Sailor's Biography* (Annapolis: Naval Institute Press, 1999), pp. 302–13; E. Thomas, *John Paul Jones: Sailor, Hero, Father of the American Navy* (New York: Simon & Schuster, 2003), pp. 199–210; A Return of Prisoners, 4 Nov. 1779, NA Archief C.W.F. Dumas 78.
26 Schama, *Patriots and Liberators*, p. 62; Edler, *The Dutch Republic*, pp. 62–9; Miller, *Sir Joseph Yorke*, pp. 78–87. For biographical details on Edward Bancroft, see John Adams autobiography, par 2, "Travels, and Negotiations," 1777–78, 21 Apr. 1778, available on the Adams Family Papers website: www.masshist.org.
27 Edler, *The Dutch Republic*, pp. 37–56; J.F. Jameson, "St. Eustatius in the American Revolution," *The American Historical Review* (1903), vol. 8, no. 4, p. 687; P.J. van Winter, *Het aandeel van den Amsterdamschen handel aan de opbouw van het Amerikaansche Gemeenebest*, Werken uitgegeven door de Vereeniging het Nederlandsch-Historisch Archief 9, 2 vols. (The Hague: Nijhoff, 1927), passim.
28 Jameson, "St. Eustatius in the American Revolution," p. 695; R. Pares, *Yankees and Creoles: The Trade between North America and the West Indies Before the American Revolution* (London: Longman, 1956); R. Buel, *In Irons: British Naval Supremacy and the American Revolutionary Economy* (New Haven: Yale University Press, 1998), pp. 119–20; Postma and Enthoven, *Riches from Atlantic Commerce*, p. 411.
29 Edler, *The Dutch Republic*, pp. 140–1.
30 I. De Madariage, *Britain, Russia and the Armed Neutrality of 1780: Sir James Harre's Mission to St. Petersburg During the American Revolution* (New Haven: Yale University Press, 1962); Edler, *The Dutch Republic*, pp. 138 ff.; Miller, *Sir Joseph Yorke*, pp. 88 ff.
31 See the Papers of Benjamin Franklin,: www.franklinpapers.org; J.A. Lewis, *Neptune's Militia: The Frigate* South Carolina *During the American Revolution* (Kent: Kent State University Press, 1999); John de Neufville & Son to John Jay, 28 July 1779, Jay Papers 12596: www.columbia.edu.
32 Declaratoir of Pensionaris E.F. van Berckel, Stadsarchief Amsterdam, Archief Burgemeesters 538 (folder Amerika); Van Winter, *Het aandeel van den Amsterdamschen handel*, 1:34–5; Edler, *The Dutch Republic*, pp. 88–91; J.W. Schulte Nordholt, *Voorbeelden in de verte. De invloed van de Amerikaanse revolutie in Nederland* (Baarn: In den Toren, 1979), pp. 61–71.
33 R. Hurst, *The Golden Rock: An Episode of the American War of Independence* (London: Leo Cooper, 1996), p. 55; Edler, *The Dutch Republic*, p. 151; Miller, *Sir Joseph Yorke*, p. 95.
34 Edler, *The Dutch Republic*, p. 157.
35 Edler, *The Dutch Republic*, p. 162; Miller, *Sir Joseph Yorke*, p. 95; Benjamin Franklin to Dumas, 18 Jan. 1780, the Papers of Benjamin Franklin: www.franklinpapers.org.
36 Adams to the President of Congress, 19 Mar. 1781, available on the website of the Library of Congress, American Memory: http://memory.loc.gov.
37 Edler, *The Dutch Republic*, p. 180.
38 H.L. Zwitser, *"De militie van den staat:" het leger van de Republiek der Verenigde Nederlanden* (Amsterdam: Van Soeren, 1991), pp. 62–81.
39 J.R. Bruijn, *The Dutch Navy of the Seventeenth and Eighteenth Centuries*, Studies in Maritime History 15 (Columbia: University of South Carolina Press, 1993), pp. 29–39.
40 Edler, *The Dutch Republic*, p. 181.

41 D.J. Starkey, "British Privateering Against the Dutch in the American Revolutionary Wars, 1780–1783," in H.E.S. Fisher, ed., *Studies in British Privateering, Trading Enterprise and Seamen's Welfare, 1775–1900* (Exeter: University of Exeter Press, 1987), p. 15; D.J. Starkey, *British Privateering Enterprise in the Eighteenth Century*, Exeter Maritime Studies 4 (Exeter: Exeter University Press, 1990), pp. 193 ff.

42 Missive Admiraal Generaal, 7 Oct. 1782, NA, Archieven van de Staten Generaal (SG) 9252 f. 19–22, 41; J. Glete, *Navies and Nations: Warships, Navies and State Building in Europe and America, 1500–1860*, Stockholm Studies in History 48, 2 vols. (Stockholm: Almqvist & Wiksell, 1993), vol. 1, pp. 278–80.

43 Edler, *The Dutch Republic*, p. 181.

44 Missive Admiraal Generaal, 7 Oct. 1782, NA, SG 9252 f. 40, 58; De Jonge, *Geschiedenis van het Nederlandsche zeewezen*, vol. 4, p. 475.

45 Missive Admiraal Generaal, 7 Oct. 1782, NA, SG 9252 f. 31.

46 Missive Admiraal Generaal, 7 Oct. 1782, NA, SG 9252 f. 43; De Jonge, *Geschiedenis van het Nederlandsche zeewezen*, vol. 4, pp. 453–4.

47 J. Van Zijverden, "The Risky Alternative: Dutch Privateering During the Fourth Anglo-Dutch War, 1780–1783," in D.J. Starkey, E.S. van Eijck van Heslinga and J.A. de Moor, eds., *Pirates and Privateers: New Perspectives on the War on Trade in the Eighteenth and Nineteenth Centuries*, Exeter Maritime Studies 9 (Exeter: University of Exeter Press, 1997), pp. 186–205.

48 "Echt en omstandig verhaal van het voorgevallen gevecht tusschen's lands vloot onder den Schout-bij-Nacht Zoutman en die van den Engelschen Admiraal Parker op den 5 augustus 1781," *Marineblad* 60 (1950), pp. 74–80; De Jonge, *Geschiedenis van het Nederlandsche zeewezen*, vol. 4, pp. 514–41.

49 Hurst, *The Golden Rock*, pp. 150 ff.; Jameson, "St. Eustatius in the American Revolution," pp. 700–8; K. Breen, "Sir George Rodney and St. Eustatius in the American War: A Commercial and Naval Distraction, 1775–81," *The Mariner's Mirror* (1998), vol. 84, no. 2, pp. 193–203; Edler, *The Dutch Republic*, pp. 182–5.

50 P.M. Netscher, *Geschiedenis van de kolonien Essequebo, Demerary en Berbice, van de vestiging der Nederlanders aldaar tot op onzen tijd* (The Hague: Martinus Nijhoff, 1988), pp. 264–9; C.Ch. Goslinga, *The Dutch in the Caribbean and in the Guianas, 1680–1791* (Assen: Van Gorcum, 1985), pp. 455–6.

51 N.D.B. Habermehl, "Guillemus Titsingh: een invloedrijk Amsterdams koopman uit de tweede helft van de achttiende eeuw, 1733–1805," *Jaarboek Amstelodamum* (1987), pp. 85–93.

52 A. Van Dantzig, *Forts and Castles of Ghana* (Accra: Sedco Publishing, 1980), p. 63; R. Baesjou, "De *Juffrouw Elisabeth* op de Kust van Guinea ten tijde van de Vierde Engelse Oorlog," in B. Brommer, ed., *Ik ben eigendom van ... Slavenhandel en plantageleven* (Wijk en Allburg: Pictures Publishers, 1993), pp. 51–8.

53 A.B. Smith, "The French Period at the Cape, 1781–1783: A Report on Excavations at Conway Redoubt, Constantia Nek," *Military History Journal* (1981), vol. 5, no. 3, available on the website of The South African Military History Society: http://samilitaryhistory.org/journal.html.

54 R. Callahan, *The East India Company and Army Reform, 1783–1798* (Cambridge: Harvard University Press, 1972), p. 6; S. Alavi, *The Sepoys and the Company: Tradition and Transition in Northern India, 1770–1830* (Delhi: Oxford University Press, 1998).

55 Edler, *The Dutch Republic*, pp. 190 ff.; G.D. Winius and M.P.M. Vink, *The Merchant-Warrior Pacified* (Delhi: Oxford University Press, 1994), pp. 90, 120–1.

56 E.S. van Eijck van Heslinga, "De vlag dekt de lading. De Nederlandse koopvaardij in de Vierde Engelse oorlog," *Tijdschrift voor Zeegeschiedenis* (1982), vol. 2, pp. 102–13; J. Parmentier, "Profit and Neutrality: The Case of Ostend, 1781–1783," in D.J. Starkey, E.S. van Eijck van Heslinga and J.A. de Moor, eds., *Pirates and Privateers: New Perspectives on the War on Trade in the Eighteenth and Nineteenth*

Centuries, Exeter Maritime Studies (Exeter: University of Exeter Press, 1997), vol. 9, pp. 206–26; De Jonge, *Geschiedenis van het Nederlandsche zeewezen*, vol. 4, p. 574.
57 R.B. Prud'homme van Reine, *Jan Hendrik van Kinsbergen, 1735–1819. Admiraal en filantroop* (Amsterdam: De Bataafsche Leeuw, 1990), pp. 154–8; Edler, *The Dutch Republic*, pp. 203–4.
58 Van Winter, *Het aandeel van den Amsterdamschen handel*, vol. 1, pp. 59–87; E. W. Perkins, *American Public Finance and Financial Services, 1700–1815* (Columbus: Ohio State University Press, 1994), passim; J.H. Hutson, "John Adams and the Birth of Dutch–American Friendship, 1780–1782," in J.W. Schulte Nordholt and R.P. Swieringa, eds., *A Bilateral Bicentennial: A History of Dutch–American Relations, 1782–1982* (Amsterdam: Meulenhoff, 1982), pp. 19–32; Edler, *The Dutch Republic*, pp. 205–31.
59 Edler, *The Dutch Republic*, pp. 201–3.
60 Ibid., pp. 193–200.
61 J.H. Rose, "Great Britain and the Dutch Question, 1787–1788," *The American Historical Review* (1909), vol. 14, no. 2, pp. 262–83; Edler, *The Dutch Republic*, pp. 233–45.
62 F.B. Schotanus, *L.P. van de Spiegel, 1737–1800 en de ondergang van de Republiek, deel 1: 1737–1784* (Loenen: Schotanus Boeken, 1995), pp. 203–21.
63 Edler, *The Dutch Republic*, pp. 177–9.
64 J.J. Steur, *Herstel of ondergang. De voorstellen tot redres van de VOC, 1740–1795* (Utrecht: H&S, 1984), p. 155.

10 The League of Armed Neutrality, 1780–83

Leos Müller

In February 1780, the Russian Empress Catherine II issued a proclamation of armed neutrality that became the basis of the 1780–83 League of Armed Neutrality. The declaration was received enthusiastically all around Europe, as well as in the United States. The Scandinavian neutrals, Sweden and Denmark, adhered to it, and later Prussia, Austria, Portugal and the Kingdom of the Two Sicilies joined them. The Empress' statement was primarily understood as a declaration for the liberty of shipping and trade, and directed against British rule of the seas. In a broader sense, the neutrality principles were perceived as a basis of a future international order in which treaties and international law, and not use of domination and violence, were supposed to rule relations between states.

In the United States it was assumed the declaration would lead to prompt recognition of American independence. John Adams believed that a congress of neutral states would meet in St. Petersburg and recognize American independence as one of its first acts.[1] This unrealistic view of the Empress' declaration was also the reason for the first American diplomatic mission to St. Petersburg, that of Francis Dana between 1781 and 1783. The actual significance of the First League of Armed Neutrality proved much more limited, not least in regard to American interests. But the experience of the First League of Armed Neutrality has since played an important role in the practical understanding of neutrality. And, because neutrality was a predominant line of American foreign policy until World War I, the history of the first armed neutrality is especially relevant for American history.[2]

Specifically, armed neutrality from 1780–83 concerned the neutrals' right to conduct trade and shipping under wartime conditions, without being ill-treated by belligerents, the British in particular. Due to the fact that blockades, privateering and the use of naval power against enemy commerce were considered legitimate ways of warfare, the belligerents, or more specifically Britain's enemies, used neutral shipping as the safest way to continue their commerce. French and Spanish maritime trade was conducted under cover of neutral flags, and the neutral powers profitably exploited the situation. Profitable exploitation of neutrality by the Scandinavian neutrals, Sweden and Denmark, was an important, if not the only, hallmark of this agreement. But to put the League in a proper context it is important to look in detail at the diplomatic and political developments in northern Europe between 1776 and 1783, and the early modern concept of neutrality.

The concept of neutrality before 1780

The concept of neutrality is closely connected to the rise of the early modern European state system, usually dated to the Peace of Westphalia of 1648. The concept supposes an international system of power balance resting on a number of more or less equal actors who respect each other's sovereignty and territorial integrity. Such a mutual recognition of sovereignty also entails a possibility of staying neutral in the case of war between other members of the system. This was possible, of course, only when the neutral state was so strong that the belligerents preferred its neutrality to war.[3]

In practice, the concept of neutrality became mainly employed in the context of naval warfare and neutral shipping and trade – belligerents and neutrals had otherwise few practical reasons to meet. The connection between the concept of neutrality and maritime matters also means that neutrality concerned primarily small states with significant maritime interests, such as the Dutch Republic, Denmark, Sweden, Portugal – and, after 1783, the United States; or continental great powers, without significant maritime interests, such as Russia, Prussia and Austria. For the continental great powers, the neutrality declaration was a way of demonstrating their role in the power balance system.

Since the mid-seventeenth century, neutrals, in principle, had the right to carry out commodity trade between belligerents and non-belligerents, with the exception of contraband. This right was broadly accepted as a part of international law and, more explicitly, it was defined in bilateral treaties between early modern states. Disagreements between belligerents and neutrals then concerned differing understandings of treaties and international law. The conflicts arose primarily over the definition of contraband of war and blockade. On the one hand, the most internationally accepted rule of neutrality was that "free ships make free goods," which meant that the nationality, or flag, of a vessel covered the nationality of its cargo. On the other hand, no state allowed the neutral shipping of war contraband to the enemy. In addition, the principle of effective blockade meant that neutrals were not excluded from trade with blockaded ports or coasts if the blockade was ineffective.

The definitions of war contraband and effective blockade were inconsistent, and they varied in different bilateral treaties. For example, the Anglo-Dutch treaty of 1674 rather loosely defined contraband of war. The definition had been a basis of the British benevolent approach toward Dutch neutrality and of the legal foundation for the extensive neutral shipping and trade under the Dutch flag during the eighteenth century.[4] But when the Danes and Swedes attempted to argue for the same benevolent definition of contraband, the British refused.[5]

Due to British dominance of the seas, conflicts over interpretation of the principles of neutrality most frequently concerned the relations between the neutrals and Britain. Britain's enemies – such as France, Spain and, in 1774–83, the rebelling colonies of British North America – on the one hand adhered to the principles of neutrality because they could benefit much more from shipping conducted by a neutral power than the British. On the other hand, the British generally interpreted neutral shipping as enemy trade disguised by a neutral flag.

If neutrality was violated by search and/or seizure of a vessel, a neutral power had a number of possible ways to react. First, it could let a prize court in the belligerent state make a decision. But prize courts were often concerned with the potential international consequences of their decisions and they followed their government's policy. Second, a neutral power could protest against seizing its vessels by diplomatic means. A ship-owner or merchant contacted his country's envoy or consul in the belligerent state and the representative made an official protest. The diplomatic archives of neutral states contain many such protest letters. Courts were supposed to act independently and in agreement with the country's law but, in practice, the international situation and domestic politics might play a decisive role in a court's verdict. The third strategy of a neutral power was convoying. To reduce the risk from privateers and belligerent navies, neutral powers organized convoys of merchantmen protected by naval vessels whose commanders were instructed to prevent any attempt at capture or search. The officer of the convoying naval vessel guaranteed that no vessel under his protection carried contraband of war. This was the proper meaning of armed neutrality. Convoying was a good strategy if the belligerent did not want to risk conflict with the neutral. But it also could rapidly bring the neutral into the war if the belligerent wished.

The armed protection of shipping was the basis of neutral cooperation between Sweden and Denmark beginning in the late seventeenth century. In spite of the fact that the two Scandinavian states were fiery enemies on the northern European scene, they could cooperate as neutrals in the century-long Franco-British conflict. Thus, already in 1691, they established the *Union des Neutres pour la Securité de la Navigation et du Commerce*. There were other attempts at cooperation for neutrality at the beginning of the eighteenth century and in 1756.[6]

From the end of the Great Northern War (1700–21), the two Scandinavian states belonged to the third rank of European powers, dependent on their alliance partners and eager to avoid costly conflicts. At the same time, they were carrying out deliberate economic policies to promote the interests of domestic industries, shipping and trade. They also had very similar commercial interests. In regard to the economics of neutrality, therefore, the League of Armed Neutrality of 1780 was not new. But there were very significant differences between Danish and Swedish security and political interests. Likewise, Russia, the leading power of the League's triangle, had its own unique political position and security interests. The differing strategic situations and concerns of the participants set the stage for assessing the League's proper significance.

The interests of Sweden, Russia and Denmark in the League of Armed Neutrality

The three northern partners of the League of Armed Neutrality entered into the compact with widely differing viewpoints. As mentioned above, Denmark and Sweden had a common interest in the commercial exploitation of neutrality, but they had opposing security and political interests. The major objective of Danish foreign policy was maintaining the territorial integrity of the Danish state and increasing the nation's economic development, views expressed clearly by the Danish foreign minister, Count Andreas Peter Bernstorff, in *Sicherheit und Wohlstand*. The only latent danger that Denmark faced in the 1770s and 1780s was Swedish King Gustav III's plans to occupy Norway, an integral part of the Danish kingdom. The basis of Denmark's security policy was its alliance with Russia, Sweden's primary enemy. This cooperation was strengthened in 1773 by the so-called Eternal Alliance Treaty.[7] Relations with France and Britain were defined by Denmark's economic interests in overseas trade and by the great powers' relations to Sweden and Russia. As regards the British Empire, Denmark principally carried on a pro-British policy; this stance also affected the Danish perception of the American Revolution.

Denmark had a colonial empire, and Copenhagen was the major entrepôt of trade in colonial goods in northern Europe. The Danish West Indian islands were an integrated part of the Atlantic colonial economy. St. Croix, the largest of the Danish islands, produced sugar and imported quantities of food from British North America. Alternatively, the two other Danish islands, St. Thomas and St. Jan, had no colonial production of importance, but they were active in the transit traffic between the West Indies, Europe and British American colonies.

Both the Danish and British authorities were well aware that even after Britain's punitive and restrictive "Coercive Acts" of 1774 there was a frequent illicit trade between the American colonies and the Danish West Indian islands. American vessels regularly arrived from New England, Virginia and the Carolinas with cargoes of timber, rice, tobacco and indigo. This transit trade was lucrative, and the Danish government did very little to stop it. The only clearly defined prohibited trade concerned war contraband, that is, weapons and ammunition.[8] However, the upcoming conflict between the British and Danish authorities did not concern the trade between the West Indian islands and North America, but the Danish-flagged trade between the islands and Denmark.[9] Another area in which the Danish commerce could expect a large wartime boom was the Danish trade with India, in which Britain took a keen interest.

In addition to its colonial trade, Denmark was one of the largest carriers of commodities in Europe; and its vassal, Norway, which was ruled by Denmark until 1814, had a voluminous trade in timber and fish. A large proportion of the Danish–Norwegian trade went to Britain, whereas southern Europe was important as a market for Danish shipping services. Even in regards to the European commodity trade and shipping, the Danes were markedly more pro-British than other neutrals, and the British looked upon Danish trade more favorably than upon, for example, Swedish commerce.

Also, with regard to the struggle of the American colonies against their mother country, Denmark took a pro-British position. The trade with the American colonies was profitable and accepted as necessary for the West Indian islands, but it in no way entailed Danish recognition of the United States. Count Bernstorff saw the Americans as rebels and, consequently, dangerous to all sovereigns.[10] According to a Danish instruction in September 1777, under no circumstances was the American flag to be acknowledged as that of an independent state, and American privateers were not allowed to call in Danish and Norwegian ports.[11]

The situation changed in 1778 when France became involved in the war. In the context of the wider Franco-British conflict, the struggle of the American colonists came to be understood as a part of European politics, and therefore more legitimate. It became, for example, possible for American vessels sailing under French, Spanish or Dutch flags to stay in ports of the Danish kingdom. Yet this did not presage a formal recognition of American independence. After 1778, there were some diplomatic contacts between Benjamin Franklin and the Danish ambassador in Paris, Otto Blome, and at the beginning of 1783 the Americans proposed a Danish–American trade treaty that would even entail recognition of the United States. But the negotiations were unsuccessful.[12]

The results of Swedish policy were very different. The basis of Swedish foreign policy after Gustav III's coup in 1772, in which he made Sweden an absolute monarchy, was close cooperation with France, strengthened by an alliance treaty and substantial subsidies. The friendship with France then influenced Swedish policy toward Britain and its conflict with its American colonies. Similarly to the Danish viewpoint, the struggle in North America was interpreted through the perspective of European great power policy, first as a rebellion of British subjects against their sovereign and, from 1778, as a part of a great power conflict between France and Great Britain – a conflict in which Sweden stayed neutral but was, at the same time, bound to her French ally.

On the northern European scene, Denmark and Russia were Sweden's major enemies. The plan to conquer Norway, which had occupied Gustav III since the beginning of the 1770s, was the most offensive part of his foreign policy.[13] The relationship to Russia was complicated. During some years of the Age of Liberty (1721–72), Sweden was Russia's client state, but Gustav III's coup ended this dependency. Moreover, Gustav III tried, unsuccessfully, to weaken the link between Copenhagen and St. Petersburg, to improve Sweden's prospects in regards to his Norwegian plans.

Sweden's economic interests also played an important role. Sweden had no West Indian colonies, and trade with Asia was limited to that with Canton (Guangzhou) via the chartered Swedish East India Company. But the Swedish authorities clearly saw an opportunity in the weakening of British influence in the West Indies and North America. Moreover, there was the Danish example of successful exploitation of neutrality in the West Indies. The trade with Canton in spite of the fact that Sweden sent only two or three vessels out to China annually, was very profitable. When the other European chartered companies were drawn into the war, the Danish and Swedish companies were left alone as the principal importers of Chinese commodities, and Copenhagen and Gothenburg became large centers for the redistribution of tea, chinaware and silk.[14] Sweden, like Denmark, had a large merchant fleet employed in tramp shipping between southern European ports. Its neutrality in the Franco-British conflict was a large comparative advantage. Already in 1776 and 1777, reports from the Swedish consulates in southern Europe testified to an expanding demand for Swedish shipping capacity.[15] Moreover, demand for Swedish staple commodities increased during wartime.

As third-rank powers, Sweden and Denmark played a limited role within the European system of power balancing. But they had a significant role in European trade, and they were important regional actors. The shipping and commercial interests made them especially interested in the economic exploitation of armed neutrality.

Russia, the third principal member of the League of Armed Neutrality, was the only northern European great power. The Russian interest in the Franco-British conflict was the upholding of the balance of power in western Europe. But, in the long-term, Russia's primary interests were in eastern and southern Europe and centered upon her relations with Austria, Prussia, Poland and the Ottoman Empire. The commercial interests of St. Petersburg were very limited. Russia had an insignificant merchant fleet; Russian exports were carried by British and Dutch ships, which also made Russia more vulnerable to British reactions than the other neutrals.

In contrast to Denmark, Russia had no sea-bound trade in colonial commodities and, in contrast to Sweden, she had no ambitions to acquire such a trade. An American agent, Stephen Sayre, proposed in St. Petersburg to establish a Russian colony on an island near Suriname, which was supposed to function as an entrepôt of illicit trade between the American colonies and Russia, in a way similar to the Dutch or Danish islands. But the proposal came to nothing.[16] In St. Petersburg, a direct American trade with Europe was perceived as a threat, if anything, because North American exports to Europe partly consisted of the same commodities as Russian exports; tentatively, in other words, Russia and North America competed for the same markets.

This short review of Denmark's, Sweden's and Russia's interests before the declaration of the League of Armed Neutrality clearly reveals that the League members entered into cooperation with very different priorities. These dissimilar economic and political agendas also point toward the discrepancy between the perceptions of the declaration and the great expectations of what it would result in, on the one hand, and the declaration's finite results on the other. At least for Denmark and Sweden, the major outcome was the boom in neutral shipping and trade. Any initial dreams that the League would yield a new system of international relations, based not on power but on international law and economic interdependence, were dashed by competing political realities and differing national security interests. In the end, nothing was left of these grand illusions.

The declaration of the League of Armed Neutrality

American privateers in northern waters became, in fact, the issue that made possible the League of northern neutrals. Just after the declaration of war between France and Britain in 1778, the Russian government approached the Danish king with a proposal to organize joint convoys in the waters along Norway's coast. The direct cause of this proposal was the seizure of two British ships sailing from Archangel by an American privateer. A substantial part of Russian exports went on British vessels from Archangel, and the Russians were naturally anxious about the safety of this route. This arrangement also meant that the Russian policy was, at least for the moment, primarily pro-British, with St. Petersburg desiring to protect British shipping between Russia and Britain against American privateers.

The Danish government accepted the Russian proposal of joint convoying, but included in its reply a list of five points defining principles of shipping by neutrals. Then, under Danish–Russian pressure, Britain was supposed to acknowledge the principles. The reply was a part of the Danish ambition to reach an agreement on protection of trade between Russia and Denmark, while excluding Sweden. The five principles were: neutral ships were free to navigate between belligerents' ports and coasts; belligerents' commodities on board neutral ships were free and legal – "free ships make free goods" – with the exception of war contraband; the definition of contraband of war should be explicit, and the British definition should not include any additional commodities different from those delineated by the French; neutrals should respect the blockade of a belligerent's coast only if it were effective; and the mentioned principles should be made public and serve as guidance for privateers. But Catherine II rejected the Danish proposal.

Gustav III of Sweden also attempted to conclude a Swedish–Russian convention on the convoying of neutral vessels; but, in contrast to that of Denmark, Sweden's proposal was directed primarily against Britain. One of the Swedish arguments for such cooperation was the fact that Swedish and Russian exports consisted of naval stores, which the British defined as contraband of war. The Russians refused the proposal for joint convoying. Instead, they suggested to the Swedes the organization of joint protection of the countries' coasts, which would not provide much help to Swedish tramp shipping in southern Europe.[17] The failure of Gustav III's proposal reflected the fundamentally different economic interests of the two countries; Sweden had a very significant interest in the carrying trade, while Russia relied mainly on British bottoms.

Of the three northern powers, Sweden had the most troublesome relationship with Britain. From the summer of 1778, the British authorities applied the most unfavorable definition of war contraband for Sweden, including iron and naval stores, Sweden's main export articles. And, up to March 1779, the British seized 32 Swedish vessels, many of them loaded with cargoes of tar and pitch for French ports.[18] When the attempt to organize combined convoys with Russia failed, Sweden responded by escorting single-handedly. In 1779, Sweden successfully conducted two convoys to Cape Finisterre on the west coast of Spain. A third was hit by a storm in the Channel and many Swedish ships were forced to stay in English ports.[19]

In the course of 1779, relations between Sweden and Britain grew even chillier due to Sweden's reluctance to close Marstrand to French and American vessels. As early as 1775, the Swedish port of Marstrand, north of Gothenburg, was declared a free port, and it became a place where American vessels could acquire desirable Baltic commodities. The port was undoubtedly even used by American privateers.[20] According to the British understanding of the Anglo-Swedish bilateral treaty of 1661, all Swedish ports, including Marstrand, should be closed to enemy vessels. But the Swedish authorities argued that Marstrand was a free port, and thus excluded from the treaty.

Danish–British relations were much better, particularly since, after the Spanish entry into the war, the British government was interested in closer cooperation with Denmark. But, from the Danish point of view, such cooperation also presupposed an alliance with Russia, Denmark's major ally. By late 1779, the countries were negotiating a possible defensive alliance. Count Bernstorff, the strongman of Danish foreign policy, was especially keen to conclude such an alliance. But the Danish crown prince, and State Councillor Ove Høegh Guldberg, linked the alliance with Britain to Russia's participation, and Russia was not prepared to lose her position as an independent power. The Danish attempt to connect Britain to a Danish–Russian alliance failed.

The Russian solution to the international floundering emerged on 19 February 1780, when Catherine II declared her five principles of neutrality. The Empress stated that she could no longer accept violations of the neutral Russian trade, and she ordered her fleet to protect the shipping and trade according to the five Danish principles she had refused the year before. The declaration was forwarded to the belligerent courts in London, Versailles and Madrid, and to the neutral courts in Stockholm, Copenhagen, The Hague and Lisbon. Formally, the proclamation was an answer to Spanish privateering activities around Gibraltar. The Spaniards blockaded British Gibraltar, seized all vessels that might be destined for the enemy and forced them to remain in Spanish ports. The Spanish blockade was brutal and, in regard to Swedish vessels, very efficient. In April 1780, the Swedish consul in Cadiz reported that between September 1779 and April 1780 the Spanish took 32 Swedish vessels to Algeciras, Ceuta and Cadiz.[21]

Catherine II's declaration was a somewhat unexpected step. At first sight the proclamation was seen as a threat against Spain, and consequently as a part of Russia's pro-British policy. Because Catherine II's statement followed the Spanish seizure of a Russian vessel destined for Malaga and Livorno, the British envoy to St. Petersburg, Sir James Harris, took this view.[22] Yet, on a more general level, the declaration possessed a basically anti-British outline. It stressed the rights of neutrals that Britain refused to honor. The conflict over the proper understanding of the Empress' declaration characterized Russia's foreign policy in the coming months, and it reflected the internal political struggle between two protagonists, anti-British Count Nikita Panin, the minister of foreign affairs, and pro-British Grigori Potemkin, the politically very influential lover of Catherine II. Yet the ambiguous meaning of the declaration also caused uncertainty in two other northern courts.

The Danish government, in particular, was pushed into an awkward situation. First, a broad anti-British perception of the declaration was against Denmark's pro-British policy, the same policy that built on the alliance with Russia. Second, the proclamation followed exactly the five principles proposed by the Danes at the beginning of the war; thus the Danes could not speak against it. Third, the proclamation's issuance unveiled the deep discrepancy between Bernstorff's pro-British policy on the one hand, and the more pro-Russian policy of Crown Prince Frederick and his minister, Guldberg, on the other. As a consequence, Denmark carried out a truly dual foreign policy throughout the whole of 1780. Thus, on 9 July 1780, Denmark formally adhered to the League of Armed Neutrality by signing the neutrality convention with Russia – directed against Britain. But at the same time as the Danes were negotiating the specific terms of this neutrality convention, they negotiated in secret with the British government a special amendment to the British–Danish treaty of 1670 relating to a favorable definition of contraband. The contraband declaration concerned Danish exports of provisions and Norwegian timber and was signed on 4 July 1780, a couple of days before the Russo-Danish neutrality convention.[23]

Such a double policy was impossible to maintain in the long term. By autumn the secret contraband amendment became known in Russia and Sweden and, naturally, the reactions were very cold. The Russian response caused the fall of Bernstorff in November and was a triumph for Guldberg's pro-Russian line of offensive neutrality.

Sweden's reaction to the proclamation of the principles of armed neutrality was more favorable, but cautious as well. Catherine II's declaration followed closely Gustav III's pro-French policy, and it suited well his ambitions of rapprochement with Russia. But the King and his advisors could not understand the sudden change in Russia's fundamentally pro-British policy. Therefore, Gustav III delayed his answer and turned to Versailles for advice. Approval by the French ally was necessary for Swedish participation in the League. There also circulated rumors that Catherine II's declaration was, in fact, a result of French pressure on Russia via Berlin. The French did not confirm the rumors; instead, they described the declaration as principally Count Panin's work and recommended that Gustav III join the League.[24] Yet it took additional months before Sweden, on 9 September 1780, signed the convention with Russia.

The central role of Russia in the League of Armed Neutrality was confirmed by the fact that Swedish and Danish participation was first formed in the bilateral Russo-Danish and Russo-Swedish conventions. The League of Armed Neutrality came into effect only when all these mutual declarations were signed.[25] But the relationships between Denmark and Sweden continued to be chilly even after the signatures.

The third state that Catherine II approached was the most important neutral carrier, the Dutch Republic. The northern neutrals were not enthusiastic; the

Danish and Swedish governments saw the Dutch primarily as rivals in shipping. Nonetheless, more important for the latent Dutch participation in the League was the British reaction. Dutch–British relations had been deteriorating in the course of the war, and the British perceived Dutch adherence to the League as potentially the most dangerous development. After Catherine II's proclamation, in April 1780, the British government declared that the special Dutch–British contraband article, included in their treaty of 1674 and the basis of the Dutch neutrality carrying trade, was no longer valid.

The deteriorating relations between Britain and the Dutch Republic also touched the key question of the League's obligations toward its members. Should the League declare war on Britain if one of its members were drawn into a conflict with that power? The Russian standpoint was that the entry of a League member into a war excluded the member from the League. Fortuitously, for the league, the British declared war on the Dutch Republic before The Hague's negotiations with the League of Armed Neutrality were completed. The Dutch delegation did adhere to the League on 4 January 1781, in St. Petersburg; but when they signed the document the Danish diplomats did not know that the Republic had been at war with Britain since 20 December 1780.[26] In the years 1781–83, Prussia, Austria, Portugal and the Kingdom of the Two Sicilies also joined the League, although these neutrals did not participate in the armed cooperation of the three northern neutrals.

The belligerents' reactions followed expectations. France expressed her full support of the declared principles of neutrality. The Spanish reaction was also in line with the declaration, in spite of the fact that Spain's violation of neutral shipping was the cause of the Russian declaration. In fact, the Spanish court explained that British behavior forced Spain to violate the rights of neutrals. As could be expected, London's reaction was chilly, but not completely negative. The British emphasized that they intended to adhere to their treaties with the neutrals.[27]

The American reaction was enthusiastic. News of Catherine II's declaration reached the United States in the summer of 1780. It was interpreted as a pro-American and anti-British measure. Moreover, the American politicians wishfully saw the Russian declaration as a basis of a future international order of free commerce directed against the regulated commerce of the past, a romantic hope that shaped a great deal of U.S. foreign policy up to the War of 1812, and beyond. As mentioned above, the declaration was seen as a sign of the Empress' willingness to recognize the independence of the American colonies. But, as the American historian David M. Griffiths pointed out:

> Congress displayed a total misunderstanding of the aims of the armed neutrality by proclaiming a "leading and capital point" to be the admission of the United States "as a party to the convention of the neutral maritime powers for maintaining the freedom of commerce."[28]

This enthusiastic but unrealistic understanding of Russia's and the other neutrals' interests explains the American steps following the establishment of the

League. The United States formally adhered to the five principles of neutrality; American ships' captains were ordered to observe them, and U.S. envoys abroad were instructed to put their signature under the declaration of neutrality, if possible. Francis Dana's diplomatic mission to St. Petersburg was also a result. Its objectives were Russian recognition of the United States and American participation in the League of Armed Neutrality. Dana was also supposed to promote the development of Russian–American trade and to prepare a trade treaty between the two nations.

In reality, Russia, the leader of the League, was already losing interest in the whole thing in the winter of 1780–81. The attention of Catherine II turned again to Russia's continental policy. Count Nikita Panin, the architect of the Russian policy during the Franco-British conflict, who was deeply engaged in the League of Armed Neutrality, left office in the spring of 1781. Grigori Potemkin, who decisively shaped Catherine II's foreign policy in the coming years, shifted the focus toward southeastern Europe and the struggle against Russia's major enemy, the Ottoman Empire.[29] Russia signed a treaty with Austria. From Russia's geopolitical viewpoint, Britain's favorable neutrality in the Russo-Ottoman conflict was more important than the comparatively insignificant Russian interest in neutral shipping and trade, not to mention its miniscule trade with distant North America.

The weakening of Russian interest in the League meant that plans for building up a combined northern European fleet cooled down and the League lost its odious anti-British character. The disappearance of much of the international political content of the neutrality declaration left the economic aspects rather unscathed, and in its economic contours the League's formulation of neutral cooperation continued to function very well. Danish and Swedish warships convoyed merchantmen, and violation of neutral shipping by the belligerents declined significantly. Moreover, the Dutch entry into the war left the Danish and Swedish merchant marines as the only substantial neutral carriers, and they exploited the situation.

The Danish and Swedish exploitation of neutrality

The opportunities to exploit neutrality between the two countries varied depending on their different economies. The major difference concerned overseas colonial trade. As mentioned, Denmark had a minor colonial empire in the West Indies, India and Africa. The Danish flag increasingly became the only safe means of transportation of colonial commodities to European markets when all the other colonial powers were engaged in the war.

A fine indicator of the rising activity of Danish shipping is the number of sea passports, documents issued for all Danish ships sailing beyond Cape Finisterre in Spain. The number of the passports issued for vessels employed in the West Indian traffic increased from 81 passports in 1780 to 195 in 1782; in tonnage there was an increase from 7,601 to 17,508 lasts (1 Danish commercial last was the equivalent of 2.6 English tons). Copenhagen became the center of the lucrative traffic to the West Indies, with over 50 percent of registered tonnage going to that area.[30] In their endeavor to promote this trade as much as possible, the authorities required Danish-flagged vessels only to touch at some of the Danish West Indian islands and to unload the cargo in one of the Danish ports of Copenhagen, Kristianstad, Glückstadt or Altona.[31]

After the occupation of St. Eustatius, much of the Dutch trade with the United States was transferred to Danish St. Thomas, and American merchants and shipowners found few obstacles when moving to the Danish islands. To protect the shipping, the navy convoyed Danish-flagged vessels going between Danish ports and the West Indies. Naturally, these convoys irritated the British naval officers in the Caribbean because they circumvented the British blockade. The Danish government had to carefully balance between the security interests of the state and economic profits. In the beginning the Danes followed a rather restrictive policy.[32] However, from the winter of 1780–81, as relations with Britain deteriorated, the Danish policy became more relaxed. Nevertheless, the Danes prohibited any direct American shipping to Danish or Norwegian ports.

The Danish trade with India and China was much more limited than that with the West Indies. There was trade with the Danish Indian stations of Tranquebar and Serampore, which was partly organized via the chartered Asiatic Company and partly, since 1772, via private trade. In 1779 both trades entered a wartime boom. The Danish Asiatic Company purchased Indian goods for much better prices and it succeeded in selling profitably its European imports. In addition to traditional Indian commodities such as cottons, the company made money on exports of Indian saltpeter, as long as it could guarantee to the British that the saltpeter was not sold to Britain's enemies.[33]

Private enterprise also expanded during the war. The number of India-bound private vessels from Denmark increased from two in 1779 to four in 1780, nine in 1781, 12 in 1782 and 11 in 1783.[34] The basis of the private Danish trade in Bengal and on the Coromandel Coast was close cooperation with British private trade. The Danish trade with India – both the company's and private trade – was used for transmitting private assets from India to Britain, either through the direct Danish–Indian trade, or through the "country" trade with China. In these rather elaborate transactions the Danes borrowed money from British subjects to finance purchases of Indian or Chinese commodities. After the sale of the Asian cargoes in Copenhagen, these loans were payable by Danish merchant houses. The practice was, of course, a way to evade the East India Company's monopoly. In similarity with the West Indian business, both the Danish and British authorities were aware of what was going on but they did little to stop the transactions. These credit operations increased in importance in the years 1779–83, when over half of the Danish purchases in India were financed with British bills of exchange.[35]

Trade with China was by far the most profitable part of the Danish trade in Asia, and at least two or three Danish vessels annually visited its center, Canton. Also, the Swedish trade with Canton, carried out by the Swedish East India Company, increased significantly. Before the war (1770–77), the Scandinavian companies accounted for 25 percent in volume of the purchases of tea, the most important Chinese commodity. In the years 1778–84, their share increased to 35 percent.[36] The Danish cargoes from Asia were sold at auctions in Copenhagen, while the Swedish cargoes were sold in Gothenburg and re-exports of the Chinese commodities to Europe became a very important part of Scandinavian commerce in the wartime period.

In spite of the fact that Sweden had no colonies and sent out to Asia two or three vessels annually at best, Swedish merchants were heavily engaged in the exploitation of long-distance commerce. The figures for foreign trade testify to a rapid increase in the Swedish re-export trade in colonial commodities. Surging re-exports of the Swedish East India Company increased from 1.6 million rixdollars (Swedish monetary unit) in 1777–78 to 4.1 million rixdollars in 1782, the best year of the wartime boom. In the same year, the total value of Swedish exports, not including re-exports, was 5.3 million, and even that figure was high due to the wartime boom.[37] The Swedish merchants from Gothenburg also attempted to exploit the war in the West Indies, and their exports to those islands increased significantly. The Gothenburg merchant Richard Söderström organized a couple of slave expeditions, and he also proposed to the French to supply slaves for their West Indian islands.[38] Söderström appeared to live in Boston and to organize his triangle trade between Gothenburg, the West Indies and the United States as early as 1780. The same man, in 1783, was appointed Sweden's first consul to the United States. More broadly, the approach of the Swedish authorities to American shipping was more favorable than that of Denmark. As mentioned above, the American vessels were permitted to call at the free port of Marstrand. The data on trade from there shows that North America was a very important destination.[39]

It seems that the exploitation of neutrality in trade in tropical goods was primarily a business of the entrepreneurial Gothenburg merchants; the government in Stockholm and the capital's mercantile elite did not participate in this trade in such a systematic way as their Danish counterparts. The situation in Copenhagen was different. The exploitation of the neutrality boom in colonial trade was methodical, and it was conducted in close cooperation between mercantile and political circles. Thus, during the wartime period, three chartered companies were established in Copenhagen. A typical feature of all these companies was the engagement, or investments, of the leading Danish politicians, such as O.H. Guldberg and H.C. Schimmelmann, and the favorable assistance of the state; for example, in the form of ships and cheap loans. The first of these companies, the West India Trading Company, was established just before the outbreak of the war between France and Britain in 1778, and its supposed domain was the trade in coffee with the West Indies. Another company, the Baltic-Guinea Trading Company, was started in the summer of 1781, aiming to exploit the wartime boom in the trade of Baltic commodities and slaves. The last one was founded as late as in 1782, when the wartime conditions were already waning.

Typical features of the Scandinavian boom in Asian trade included its late start and its rapid decline after the French–British peace. Looking at the number of vessels employed in the Danish Asian trade shows that the largest number of vessels left Denmark in 1782 and 1783, when the most profitable opportunities were already gone. And, typically, almost all of those expeditions entailed losses.[40] The tea trade also declined after 1783. The major chartered companies (the Dutch VOC and English EIC) rapidly returned to the Chinese trade, and especially the EIC greatly enlarged its imports of tea. Moreover, in 1784 Britain reduced excise duties on tea. The Scandinavian trade with India and China had subsisted on artificial conditions of wartime trade and protectionism; it could not survive when the circumstances changed.

The shipping services in European waters were, in the long term, a more stable part of the commercial exploitation of neutrality. The years between 1776 and 1780 were marked by rising demand for neutral shipping capacity and demand for Baltic products. Nonetheless, as long as the Dutch Republic remained neutral, cargo vessels preferred the Dutch flag. The Swedish flag enjoyed an especially low reputation because of the tense relations between Sweden and Great Britain. But, after the declaration of the League of Armed Neutrality, the seizing of neutral vessels declined remarkably. Britain, in spite of the fact that it did not acknowledge the principles of neutral shipping, began to approach the remaining carriers with more respect.

The numbers of issued sea passports again provide a good picture of the increasing Swedish activity.[41] The number of passports issued increased from 222 in 1775 to 282 in 1779, an increase of 27 percent. Between 1779 and 1782 the number of passports increased from 282 to 441. But in 1783 there was a significant decline in Swedish voyages (339 passports). With the exception of two or three East India Company vessels, all these voyages were made to southern Europe. Perhaps there were some Swedes employed in the transatlantic trade, but these vessels are difficult to trace in passport registers.

Also, the Danish data for issued sea passports show a significant increase in shipping beyond Cape Finisterre. The number of passports increased between 1778 and 1782 from 290 to 637, an increase of 120 percent. But after 1782, the number of voyages declined rapidly. There are, however, very important differences between the Swedish and Danish data. The most dynamic part of the Danish shipping was the traffic to the West Indies. The number of passports issued for this destination almost quadrupled, from 57 to 195 between 1778 and 1782. The West Indies, on the other hand, is almost invisible in the Swedish passport registers.

In convoying under the League's umbrella, a division of labor appeared between Denmark and Sweden. Denmark organized convoying to the West Indies. The Danish navy also convoyed the Danish merchant vessels on their return voyages from India and China. Between 1779 and 1780, the convoys were going between the Cape of Good Hope and Denmark, and between 1781 and 1782 the naval vessels sailed as far as Tranquebar in India. In the Indian Ocean the major danger was French privateers operating from Mauritius. These convoys were used even in the protection of Swedish East India ships. For example, in 1781 the Danish ship-of-line *Indfødsretten* convoyed one Swedish

Table 10.1 Scandinavian voyages beyond Cape Finisterre, according to passports issued in 1776–85

Year	Danish voyages to the Mediterranean	Danish voyages to the West Indies	Danish voyages to Asia	Danish voyages in total	Swedish voyages in total
1774					278
1775					222
1776					236
1777					253
1778	219	57	4	290	287
1779	235	71	9	323	282
1780	244	81	8	352	320
1781	371	124	16	550	373
1782	298	195	17	637	441
1783	304	89	24	447	339
1784	351	46	8	416	370
1785	358	68	10	445	389

Source: Danish voyages: Ole Feldbæk, *Dansk neutralitetspolitik under krigen 1778–1783: Studier i regeringens prioritering af politiske og økonomiske interesser* (København, 1971), pp. 205–2; Swedish voyages: Leos Müller, *Consuls, Corsairs, and Commerce: The Swedish Consular Service and Long-Distance Shipping, 1720–1815* (Uppsala, 2004), p. 236.

and two Danish and Indiamen on their voyage to the North Sea.[42] The Swedish convoying, as mentioned above, primarily concerned shipping in the Sound, the strait between Sweden and Denmark, and the most important gateway into the Baltic Sea.

Due to the special conditions of shipping and trade under the neutrality agreement in place between 1780 and 1783, it is difficult to estimate the overall impact on the economies of the Scandinavian states. First, much of the neutrality business concerned such sectors as tramp shipping, re-exports of colonial goods and the illicit commodity trade. Due to the uneasy balance between the states' security interests and economic profits, none of the actors were interested in providing an accurate picture of their wartime trade. Second, the character of the trade, the opinion that it was simply unscrupulous Scandinavian neutrals making bloody money on an awful warfare business, morally colored the analysis. In Denmark, for example, a view that the late eighteenth-century boom in commerce and shipping was "built on sand" prevailed for a long time.[43]

It is also important to consider the different effects of the neutrality boom in different sectors of the national economies. The re-export of colonial goods was probably most dependent upon wartime conditions, and this trade waned as soon as the war was over. Looking at the development of shipping, the impact of the neutrality boom appears more lasting. According to a French report of 1786, just after the end of the American War of Independence, the Danish–Norwegian and Swedish merchant marines were the fourth and fifth largest in Europe, with a combined tonnage near that of the French and far exceeding that of the Dutch.[44] The tonnage per capita in the two Scandinavian kingdoms was in all probability higher than that of Britain. Recent research has also pointed out that the successful development of Scandinavian shipping by the late eighteenth century cannot be explained only by the exploitation of neutrality. There were other underlying factors that made the Danes and the Swedes more successful than other nations, not just other neutrals. For example, Scandinavian wage costs and shipbuilding costs were clearly competitive in comparison with other nations.

When taking this broader perspective, it is clear that the League of Armed Neutrality had a significant impact on the development of Scandinavian shipping by the late eighteenth and early nineteenth centuries. But the successful development of Scandinavian shipping also could be interpreted as a factor in the European and Atlantic economy at large. From such a point of view, the carrying business of the neutrals played an important role in reducing the wartime disturbances of commodity and transport markets, and so neutral shipping played an important role in the development of international trade in the late eighteenth century.

Conclusions

It is apparent that of the three northern neutral powers the leading one, Russia, had the least clear aims in her neutrality policy between 1780 and 1783. Russia had an insignificant economic interest in wartime shipping and trade; Russian exports were primarily destined for the British market, and they also were carried on British bottoms. Thus the primary aim of Catherine II's declaration of the principles of neutrality appears to be Russia's attempt to emphasize her independent status between Britain and France. This turn of Russian policy in February 1780 was unexpected and perhaps not even fully comprehended by its instigator. The declaration and its anti-British outline was principally a product of Panin's foreign policy, and as soon as Panin disappeared, the priorities of Russian policy reverted to its more traditional, continental commitments and ambitions. The declaration did not become more than a declaration. Russia's arbitrary and fluid standpoint also explains why there was so little concrete naval cooperation between the members of the League.

The Danish view of the League of Armed Neutrality was ambiguous. On the one hand, Denmark had strong economic interests in the exploitation of neutrality. However, the Danish objective was not cooperation between neutrals; in particular, Copenhagen did not seek cooperation with Sweden and the Dutch Republic. From the Danish point of view, the most profitable situation was neutrality in isolation, combined with a principally pro-British orientation of its foreign policy. Yet, Denmark's policy was also built on an alliance with Russia. Catherine II's declaration of February 1780 put the Danish politicians in an awkward situation. Balancing Danish security interests between the alliance with Russia and the special relationship with Britain entailed a double foreign policy in the course of 1780. On the one hand, the Danes signed for the general principles of neutrality and for the League with Russia and Sweden; on the other hand, they negotiated in secret a favorable contraband convention with the British.

Such a policy was impossible to maintain in the long run, and it also caused the fall of its master, Count Bernstorff. After Bernstorff, the Danes approached Catherine II with a proposal of a more offensive naval cooperation with Russia. But at that moment the Empress had already lost interest in the whole neutrality League. As a result, in the remaining years of the war Danish policy focused primarily on the economic exploitation of neutrality, and this exploitation proved very successful.

The third northern neutral, Sweden, perhaps benefited most from the League of neutrals. First, the declaration of neutral principles gave Gustav III an opportunity to approach Russia. Second, the League of Armed Neutrality gave Sweden a new place in the system of European powers. It should not be forgotten that during the 1760s Sweden suffered internal political turmoil and that in 1772 Gustav III made Sweden an absolute monarchy. Although Gustav failed to play a bigger European role – his "grand" ambition was to mediate peace between France and Britain – Sweden received a much more secure place in the European state system, without threatening her alliance with France. In fact, in the shape that the League of Armed Neutrality eventually assumed, it enhanced French interests. Moreover, its convoying service provided Sweden with a legitimate reason to restore, rebuild and train its navy. The British reluctance to attack the Swedish convoys during 1780–83, and Sweden's successful naval operations during the Russo-Swedish war in 1788–90, prove that building up the navy through service to the League was a success.

Last but not least, Swedish participation in the League of Armed Neutrality was an economic success. Exports of Swedish commodities expanded, Gothenburg became a large entrepôt for the re-export trade and Swedish shipping became the fifth largest in Europe. As mentioned, it is difficult to assess the economic impact of the neutrality boom on the Swedish economy overall. However, without the profits earned during this time, in all probability Gustav III's expansive economic policy in the 1780s would not have been possible and the financial situation before the war against Russia in 1788–90 would not have been as solid.

At the broadest level, the League of Armed Neutrality of 1780–83 established a significant precedent for future relationships between neutrals and belligerents. In spite of the fact that Catherine II's high-flying declaration did not immediately entail any specific military outcome, its principles were adhered to by all the European powers, with the exception of Britain.

In 1800, Russia, Denmark and Sweden concluded a second league of neutrality, with the same aims and principles. But this time the British were facing Napoleon; and their reaction was immediate and persuasive. The Royal Navy clobbered Copenhagen in 1801, and the Danes were forced to sign a separate peace. The British navy went back to neutral Copenhagen for a repeat performance in 1807, and then they sent the minister who dictated terms to the Danes across to the neutral United States as a warning about the limits of maritime neutrality.

From a legal point of view, the neutrality League of 1780–83 established an important precedent. The Americans in their war of independence embraced its principles instinctively and immediately. The principles of Catherine's declaration were frequently invoked during the nineteenth century, especially by the United States in dealing with wartime Britain and France in the first decade of the century. The ideas of her League were also important in the early twentieth century, in particular during World War I. They weighed heavily in President Woodrow Wilson's interpretations of American neutrality from 1914 to 1917, the failure of which led to the U.S. declaration of war in April 1917. Thereafter, the United States acted more like a great European power than a relatively small number of people struggling for their independence from the world's greatest sea power.

Notes

1. David M. Griffiths, "American Commercial Diplomacy in Russia, 1780 to 1783," *The William and Mary Quarterly* (1970), vol. 27, no. 3, p. 382.
2. Mlada Bukovansky, "American Identity and Neutral Rights from Independence to the War of 1812," *International Organization* (1997), vol. 51, no. 2, pp. 209–43.
3. Mikael af Malmborg, *Neutrality and State-Building in Sweden* (Chippenham: Palgrave, 2001), pp. 15–28.
4. Ole Feldbæk, "Eighteenth-Century Danish Neutrality: Its Diplomacy, Economics and Law," *Scandinavian Journal of History* (1983), vol. 8, p. 5.
5. John B. Hattendorf, ed., *British Naval Documents 1204–1960* (London: Scolar Press for the Navy Records Society, 1993), p. 329.
6. af Malmborg, *Neutrality and State-Building*, pp. 31–5.
7. Ole Feldbæk, *Dansk neutralitetspolitik under krigen 1778–1783. Studier i regeringens prioritering af politiske og økonomiske interesser* (København: Københavns Universitets Fond til Tilvejebringelse af Læremidler, 1971), pp. 14–15.
8. Knud J.V. Jespesen and Ole Feldbæk, *Dansk udenrigspolitiks historie 2, Revanche og neutralitet 1648–1814* (København: Glydendal Leksikon, 2002), p. 374.
9. Feldbæk, *Dansk neutralitetspolitik under krigen 1778–1783*, pp. 21–5.
10. Ibid., p. 160, note 29.
11. Ibid., p. 26.
12. Ibid., p. 28.
13. Lydia Wahlström, *Gustavianska studier* (Stockholm, 1914), pp. 120–58.
14. See Feldbæk, *Dansk neutralitetspolitik under krigen 1778–1783*, pp. 61–5; Leos Müller, "The Swedish East India Trade and International Markets: Re-exports of Teas, 1731–1813," *Scandinavian Economic History Review* (2003), vol. 3, pp. 28–44.
15. Leos Müller, *Consuls, Corsairs, and Commerce: The Swedish Consular Service and Long-Distance Shipping, 1720–1815* (Uppsala: Uppsala Universitet, 2004), p. 112.
16. Griffiths, "American Commercial Diplomacy in Russia," p. 386.
17. Carl August Zachrisson, *Sveriges underhandlingar om beväpnad neutralitet åren 1778–80* (PhD dissertation, Uppsala Universitet, 1863), p. 15.
18. H. Arnold Barton, "Sweden and the War of American Independence," *The William and Mary Quarterly* (July 1966), vol. 3, p. 424. See also notary letters dated 19 Sept. 1778 and 13 Oct. 1778, Diplomatica, Anglica, Swedish National Archives, Stockholm, vol. 442.
19. See the report dated 9 Dec. 1779, from the frigate *af Trolle*, Diplomatica, Anglica, Swedish National Archives, Stockholm, vol. 442.
20. *British Diplomatic Instructions, 1689–1789. vol. v – Sweden, 1727–1789* (London: Royal Historical Society, 1928), pp. 232–3.
21. Müller, *Consuls, Corsairs, and Commerce*, p. 113.

22 Zachrisson, *Sveriges underhandlingar*, p. 25.
23 Jespesen and Feldbæk, *Dansk udenrigspolitiks historie*, p. 359.
24 Zachrisson, *Sveriges underhandlingar*, pp. 30–1.
25 The mutual recognition of Danish and Swedish participation in the League was confirmed by Danish declaration to Sweden (7 Sept. 1780) and Swedish declaration to Denmark (9 Sept. 1780). James Brown Scott, ed., *The Armed Neutralities of 1780 and 1800: A Collection of Official Documents Preceded by the View of Representative Publicists* (New York, 1918), pp. 321–2.
26 Feldbæk, *Dansk neutralitetspolitik under krigen 1778–1783*, p. 90.
27 Zachrisson, *Sveriges underhandlingar*, p. 33.
28 Griffiths, "American Commercial Diplomacy in Russia," p. 383.
29 Ibid., p. 400; and John P. LeDonne, *The Grand Strategy of the Russian Empire, 1650–1831* (Oxford: Oxford University Press, 2004), pp. 116–19.
30 Feldbæk, *Dansk neutralitetspolitik under krigen 1778–1783*, pp. 191, 207.
31 Ibid., p. 115.
32 Ibid., p. 118.
33 Ole Feldbæk, *India Trade Under the Danish Flag 1772–1808* (Lund, 1969), p. 58.
34 Ibid., pp. 248–50.
35 Ibid., p. 244.
36 Louis Dermigny, *La Chine et l'Occident. Le Commerce at Canton au XVIIIe siècle 1719–1833*, tome 1–2 (Paris, 1964), p. 539.
37 Müller, "The Swedish East India Trade," passim.
38 Müller, *Consuls, Corsairs, and Commerce*, pp. 184–5.
39 According to trade statistics, Marstrand's total exports accounted for 116,000 rixdollars in 1782, the American exports for 58,000. See Åke W. Essén, *Johan Liljecrantz som handelspolitiker. Studier i Sveriges yttre handelspolitik 1773–1786* (Lund, 1928), p. 177.
40 Feldbæk, *Dansk neutralitetspolitik under krigen 1778–1783*, pp. 102, 264–5.
41 Müller, *Consuls, Corsairs, and Commerce*, pp. 144–54, 236, Appendix D.
42 Jespesen and Feldbæk, *Dansk udenrigspolitiks historie*, p. 400.
43 For a review, see especially Feldbæk, "Eighteenth-Century Danish Neutrality;" Dan H. Andersen, *The Danish Flag in the Mediterranean: Shipping and Trade, 1747–1807* (PhD dissertation, University of Copenhagen, 2000), vol. 1, pp. 6–7.
44 The French tonnage was estimated at 729,000 tons, the Dutch at 398,000 tons and combined Scandinavian at 555,000 tons (386,000 Danish and 169,000 Swedish). Hans Chr. Johansen, "Scandinavian Shipping in the Late Eighteenth Century in a European Perspective," *Economic History Review* (1992), vol. 3, p. 482.

Select bibliography

Primary sources

Barnes, George. R. and John H. Owen, eds. *The Private Papers of John, Earl of Sandwich, First Lord of the Admiralty 1771–1782*. 4 vols. London: Navy Records Society, 1932–38.

Barrington, Samuel and D. Bonner-Smith. *Barrington Papers*. London: Navy Records Society, 1937–41.

Burgoyne, John. *A State of the Expedition From Canada, As Laid Before the House of Commons*. London: J. Almon, 1780.

Butterfield, Consul Willshire, ed. *Journal of Capt. Jonathan Heart*. Albany: Joel Munsell's Sons, 1885.

Chance, James Frederick and L.G. Wickman Legg. *British Diplomatic Instructions, 1689–1789*. London: Offices of the Society, 1922.

Chase, Philander D., Dorothy Twohig, Frank E. Grizzard and Edward G. Lengel, eds. *The Papers of George Washington, Revolutionary War Series*. 18 vols. Charlottesville and London: University Press of Virginia, 2002.

Cobbett, W., ed. *Parliamentary History of England: 1066–1803*. 36 vols. London: T.C. Hansard, 1806–20.

Collections of the New York Historical Society for the Year 1778. New York: New York Historical Society, 1879.

Fitzpatrick, John C., ed. *The Writings of George Washington From the Original Manuscript Sources, 1745–1799*. 37 vols. Washington, D.C.: United States Government Printing Office, 1931–44.

Fortescue, J.W., ed. *Correspondence of King George the Third: From 1760 to December 1783*. 6 vols. London: Macmillan & Co., 1927–28.

Franklin, Benjamin, Leonard Woods Labaree, William Bradford Wilcox and Barbara Oberg. *The Papers of Benjamin Franklin*. New Haven: Yale University Press, 1959.

Hattendorf, John B., ed. *British Naval Documents, 1204–1960*. London: Scolar Press for the Navy Records Society, 1993.

Lee, Henry. *Memoirs of the War in the Southern Department of the United States*. Robert E. Lee, ed. New York: University Publishing Company, 1869.

Michigan Pioneer and Historical Collections. Lansing: Michigan Historical Commission, 1876–1929.

Peyser, Joseph L., ed. and trans. *Letters from New France: The Upper Country 1686–1783*. Urbana and Chicago: University of Illinois Press, 1992.

Ross, Charles Derek, ed. *Correspondence of Charles, First Marquis Cornwallis*. 3 vols. London: J. Murray, 1859.

Scott, James Brown, ed. *The Armed Neutralities of 1780 and 1800: A Collection of Official Documents Preceded by the View of Representative Publicists*. New York: Oxford University Press, 1918.

Showman, Richard K., Dennis Michael Conrad and Roger N. Parks, eds. *The Papers of Nathanael Greene*. Chapel Hill: University of North Carolina Press, 1976.

Warren–Adams Letters, Being Chiefly a Correspondence Among John Adams, Samuel Adams and James Warren. Boston: The Massachusetts Historical Society, 1917.

Willcox, William B., ed. *The American Rebellion: Sir Henry Clinton's Narrative of His Campaigns, 1775–1782*. New Haven: Yale University Press, 1954.

Secondary sources

Abler, Thomas S. *Chainbreaker: The American Revolutionary Memoirs of Governor Blacksnake*. Lincoln: University of Nebraska Press, 2005.

———. "Scalping, Torture Cannibalism and Rape: An Ethnocultural Analysis of Conflicting Values in War." *Anthropologica*, 34, 1992.

af Malmborg, Mikael. *Neutrality and State-Building in Sweden*. Chippenham: Palgrave, 2001.

Alavi, Seema. *The Sepoys and the Company: Tradition and Transition in Northern India, 1770–1830*. Delhi: Oxford University Press, 1998.

Allen, Robert S. *His Majesty's Indian Allies: British Indian Policy in the Defence of Canada, 1774–1815*. Toronto: Dundurn, 1992.

Andersen, Dan H. *The Danish Flag in the Mediterranean: Shipping and Trade, 1747–1807*. 2 vols. Dissertation, University of Copenhagen, 2000.

Anderson, Fred. *Crucible of War: The Seven Years' War and the Fate of Empire in British North America, 1754–1766*. New York: Knopf, 2000.

———. *A People's Army: Massachusetts Soldiers and Society in the Seven Years' War*. Chapel Hill: University of North Carolina Press for the Institute of Early American History and Culture, 1984.

Anderson, Virginia DeJohn. *Creatures of Empire: How Domestic Animals Transformed Early America*. New York: Oxford University Press, 2004.

Atkinson, James R. *Splendid Land, Splendid People: The Chickasaw Indians to Removal*. Tuscaloosa: University of Alabama Press, 2004.

Baesjou, R. "De *Juffrouw Elisabeth* op de Kust van Guinea ten tijde van de Vierde Engelse Oorlog." *Ik ben eigendom van ... Slavenhandel en plantageleven*. B. Brommer, ed. Wijk en Allburg: Pictures Publishers, 1993.

Ballesteros y Beretta, D. Antonio. *Historia de España y su influencia en la Historia Universal*. tomo 5, Barcelona; Sulvat editors, S.A., 1929.

Banner, Stuart. *How the Indians Lost Their Land: Law and Power on the Frontier*. Cambridge: Harvard University Press, 2005.

Barton, H. Arnold. "Sweden and the War of American Independence." *The William and Mary Quarterly*, 3, July 1966.

Bartstra, Jan S. *Vlootherstel en legeraugmentatie, 1770–1780*. Assen: Van Gorcum, 1962.

Bassford, Christopher. *Clausewitz in English: The Reception of Clausewitz in Britain and America, 1815–1945*. New York and Oxford: Oxford University Press, 1994.

Baugh, Daniel A. "Great Britain's 'Blue-Water' Policy, 1689–1815." *International History Review*, 10, 1988.

———. "The Politics of British Naval Failure, 1775–1777." *The American Neptune*, 52, 1992.

———. "Why Did Britain Lose Command of the Sea During the War for America?" In *The British Navy and the Use of Naval Power in the Eighteenth Century*. Jeremy Black and Philip Woodfine, eds. Leicester: Leicester University Press, 1988.

———. "Withdrawing from Europe: Anglo-French Maritime Geopolitics, 1750–1800." *International History Review*, 20, 1998.

Beach, Edward L. *The United States Navy: 200 Years*. New York: Henry Holt and Company, 1986.

Beerman, Eric. *España y la Independencia de los Estados Unidos*. Madrid: Editorial MAPFRE, S.A., 1992.

Birtle, Andrew J. "The Origins of the Legion of the United States." *Journal of Military History*, 67, 2003.

Black, Jeremy. *The British Seaborne Empire*. New Haven and London: Yale University Press, 2004.

———. *A System of Ambition? British Foreign Policy, 1660–1793*. 2nd edn. Phoenix Mill, Thrupp, Stroud, Gloucestershire: Sutton, 2000.

———. *War for America: The Fight for Independence*. Phoenix Mill, Thrupp, Stroud, Gloucestershire: Wrens Park, 1991.

Boatner, Mark M., III. *Encyclopedia of the American Revolution*. New York: David McKay, 1966.

Bonsal, Stephen. *When the French Were Here*. Garden City: Doubleday & Co., 1945.

Bosher, J.F. *French Finances, 1770–1795: From Business to Bureaucracy*. Cambridge: Cambridge University Press, 1970.

———. *The French Revolution*. New York: W.W. Norton, 1988.

Bowen, Catherine Drinker. *John Adams and the American Revolution*. Boston: Little Brown and Co., 1950.

Bradford, James C. "The Navies of the American Revolution, 1775–1783." In *In Peace and War: Interpretations of American Naval History, 30th Anniversary Edition*. Kenneth J. Hagan and Michael T. McMaster, eds. Westport: Greenwood Press, 2008.

Bradley, James E. "The British Public and the American Revolution: Ideology, Interest and Opinion." In *Britain and the American Revolution*. H.T. Dickinson, ed. London: Longman, 1998.

Brand, H. and J. Brand. *De Hollandse Waterlinie*. Utrecht and Antwerp: Veen, 1986.

Braund, Kathryn E. Holland. *Deerskins and Duffels: The Creek Indian Trade with Anglo-America 1685–1815*. Lincoln: University of Nebraska Press, 1993.

Breen, K. "Sir George Rodney and St. Eustatius in the American War: A Commercial and Naval Distraction, 1775–81." *The Mariner's Mirror*, 84, 1998.

Brooks, Victor and Robert Hohwald. *How America Fought Its Wars: Military Strategy from the American Revolution to the Civil War*. Conshohocken: Combined Books, 1999.

Brown, G.S. *The American Secretary: The Colonial Policy of Lord George Germain, 1775–1778*. Ann Arbor: University of Michigan Press, 1963.

Bruijn, J.R. *The Dutch Navy of the Seventeenth and Eighteenth Centuries*. Studies in Maritime History 15, Columbia: University of South Carolina Press, 1993.

Brumwell, Stephen. *Redcoats: The British Soldier and War in the Americas, 1755–1763*. Cambridge: Cambridge University Press, 2001.

Brun, V.F. *Guerres maritimes de la France: port de Toulon, ses armements, son administration depuis son origine jusqu'à nos jours*. 2 vols. Paris: Plon, 1861, vol. 1.

Buel, Richard, Jr. *In Irons: Britain's Naval Supremacy and the American Revolutionary Economy*. New Haven and London: Yale University Press, 1998.

Bukovansky, Mlada. "American Identity and Neutral Rights from Independence to the War of 1812." *International Organization*, 51, 2, 1997.

Callahan, Raymond. *The East India Company and Army Reform, 1783–1798*. Cambridge: Harvard University Press, 1972.

Calloway, Colin G. *The American Revolution in Indian Country: Crisis and Diversity in Native American Communities*. Cambridge: Cambridge University Press, 1995.

———. *Crown and Calumet: British–Indian Relations, 1783–1815*. Norman: University of Oklahoma Press, 1987.

Campisi, Jack. *The Mashpee Indians: Tribe on Trial*. Syracuse: Syracuse University Press, 1991.

Capps, Michael A. and Steven A. Davis. *Moores Creek National Battlefield: An Administrative History*. National Park Service, Department of the Interior, June 1999. Online, available at: www.nps.gov/history/history/online_books/mocr/adhi_1.htm (accessed 22 Jan. 2007).

Castex, Raoul. *Les idées militaires de la marine du xviiie siècle, de Ruyter à Suffren*. Paris: L. Fournier, 1911.

Chambers, John Whiteclay II, ed. *The Oxford Companion to American Military History*. New York: Oxford University Press, 1999.

Chávez, Thomas E. *Spain and the Independence of the United States: An Intrinsic Gift*. Albuquerque: University of New Mexico Press, 2002.

Christie, Ian. "The Imperial Dimension: British Ministerial Perspectives During the American Revolutionary Crisis, 1763–1776." In *Red, White and True Blue: The Loyalists in the Revolution*. Esmond Wright, ed. New York: AMS Press, 1976.

Clausewitz, Carl von. *On War*. Michael Howard and Peter Paret, ed. and trans. Princeton: Princeton University Press, 1976.

Coleman, Kenneth. *The American Revolution in Georgia, 1763–1789*. Athens: University of Georgia Press, 1958.

Condon, Ann. "Marching to a Different Drummer: The Political Philosophy of the American Loyalists." *Red, White and True Blue: The Loyalists in the Revolution*. Esmond Wright, ed. New York: AMS Press, 1976.

Conway, Stephen. "Britain and the Revolutionary Crisis, 1763–1791." *The Oxford History of the British Empire: The Eighteenth Century*. P.J. Marshall, ed. New York: Oxford University Press, 1998.

———. "British Governments and the Conduct of the American War." *Britain and the American Revolution*. H.T. Dickinson, ed. London: Longman, 1998.

———. "To Subdue America: British Army Officers and the Conduct of the Revolutionary War." *William and Mary Quarterly*, 43, 3, July 1986.

———. *The War for American Independence, 1775–1783*, London: Edward Arnold, 1995.

Corbett, Julian S. *Some Principles of Maritime Strategy*. London: Longmans, Green and Co, 1911; reprint Eric Grove, London: Brassey's, 1988, and Annapolis: Naval Institute Press, 1988.

Corkran, David H. *The Creek Frontier, 1540–1783*. Norman: University of Oklahoma Press, 1967.

Crake, J.E.A. "Roman Politics from 215 to 209 B.C." *Phoenix*, 17, 2, Summer 1963.

Creswell, John. *British Admirals of the Eighteenth Century: Tactics in Battle*. London: George Allen & Unwin, 1972.

Crouzet, Francois. "England and France in the Eighteenth Century: A Comparative Analysis of Two Economic Growths." Reprinted in his *Britain Ascendant: Comparative Studies in Franco-British Economic History*. Cambridge: Cambridge University Press, 1990.

Cuadrado, Reyes Calderón. *Empresarios Españoles en el Proceso de Independencia Norteamericana: La Casa Gardoqui e Hijos de Bilbao.* Madrid: Unión Editorial, S.A., 2004.
Davies, K.G. "The Restoration of Civil Government by the British in the War of Independence." In *Red, White and True Blue: The Loyalists in the Revolution.* Esmond Wright, ed. New York: AMS Press, 1976.
Davis, Andrew McFarland. "The Employment of Indian Auxiliaries in the American War." *English Historical Review,* 2, 1887.
Davis, Ralph. *The Rise of the Atlantic Economies.* London: Methuen, 1973.
de Jeney, Capitaine. *The Partisan: Or, The Art of Making War in Detachment.* J. Berkenhout, trans., London, 1760.
de Jonge, J.C. *Geschiedenis van het Nederlandsche zeewezen.* 5 vols. Haarlem: A.C. Kruseman, 1861.
de La Barbée, Maurice Linyer. *Le Chevalier de Ternay: vie de Charles-Henry-Louis d'Arsac de Ternay, chef d'escadre des armées navales.* 2 vols. Grenoble: Editions des 4 seigeurs, 1972, vol. 2.
de La Croix, René, Duc de Castries. *Le Maréchal de Castries (1727–1800).* Paris: Flammarion, 1956.
de Madariage, Isabel. *Britain, Russia and the Armed Neutrality of 1780: Sir James Harre's Mission to St. Petersburg During the American Revolution.* New Haven: Yale University Press, 1962.
de Reparz, Carmen. *Yo Solo: Bernardo de Gálvez y la Toma de Panzacola en 1781.* Barcelona: Ediciones del Serbal, S.A., 1986.
de Witte, Jehan, ed. *Journal de l'Abbé de Véri.* 2 vols. Paris: Plon, 1933.
Delâge, Denys and Jean-Pierre Sawaya. *Les Traités des sept-feux avec les Britanniques: Droits et pièges d'un héritage colonial au Québec.* Sillery: Septentrion, 2001.
Dermigny, Louis. *La Chine et l'Occident. Le Commerce á Canton au XVIIIe siècle 1719–1833.* Tome 1–2, Paris: 1964.
Derry, John. "Government Policy and the American Crisis, 1760–1776." In *Britain and the American Revolution.* H.T. Dickinson, ed. London: Longman, 1998.
Dickinson, H.T., ed. *Britain and the American Revolution.* London: Longman, 1998.
Dixon, David. *Never Come to Peace Again: Pontiac's Uprising and the Fate of the British Empire in North America.* Norman: University of Oklahoma Press, 2005.
Doniol, Henri. *Histoire de la participation de la France à l'établissement des États-Unis d'Amérique: correspondance diplomatique et documents.* 5 vols. Paris: Imprimerie nationale, 1886–92, vol. 3.
Dowd, Gregory Evans. *A Spirited Resistance: The North American Indian Struggle for Unity, 1745–1815.* Baltimore: The Johns Hopkins University Press, 1992.
Duane, William, ed. *Extracts from the Diary of Christopher Marshall, During the American Revolution.* Albany: Joel Munsell, 1877.
Duffy, M. "The Establishment of the Western Squadron as the Linchpin of British Naval Strategy." *Parameters of British Naval Power, 1650–1850.* M. Duffy, ed. Exeter: University of Exeter Press, 1992.
Dull, Jonathan R. *A Diplomatic History of the American Revolution.* New Haven: Yale University Press, 1985.
———. *The French Navy and American Independence: A Study of Arms and Diplomacy, 1774–1787.* Princeton: Princeton University Press, 1975.
———. "Mahan, Sea Power, and the War for American Independence." *International History Review,* 10, 1, 1988.

Dunthorne, Hugh. *The Maritime Powers, 1721–1740: A Study of Anglo-Dutch Relations in the Age of Walpole*. New York and London: Garland Publishing, 1986.

Eccles, William. J. *France in America*. Rev. edn. Toronto: Fitzhenry & Whiteside, 1990.

Edler, F. *The Dutch Republic and the American Revolution*. Johns Hopkins University Studies in Historical and Political Science 29/2, Baltimore: The Johns Hopkins Press, 1911.

Eid, Leroy V. "American Indian Military Leadership: St. Clair's 1791 Defeat." *Journal of Military History*, 57, 1993.

Egerton, Douglas R. *Death or Liberty: African Americans and Revolutionary America*. Oxford and New York: Oxford University Press, 2009.

Ellis, Joseph J. *His Excellency: George Washington*. New York: Vantage, 2004.

Essén, Åke W. *Johan Liljecrantz som handelspolitiker. Studier i Sveriges yttre handelspolitik 1773–1786*. Lund: 1928.

Faragher, John Mack. *Daniel Boone: The Life and Legend of an American Pioneer*. New York: Henry Holt, 1992.

Feldbæk, Ole. *Dansk neutralitetspolitik under krigen 1778–1783. Studier i regeringens prioritering af politiske og økonomiske interesser*. København: Københavns Universitets Fond til Tilvejebringelse af Læremidler, 1971.

——. "Eighteenth-Century Danish Neutrality: Its Diplomacy, Economics and Law." *Scandinavian Journal of History*, 8, 1983.

——. *India Trade Under the Danish Flag 1772–1808*. Lund: 1969.

Fenn, Elizabeth. *Pox Americana: The Great Smallpox Epidemic of 1775–1782*. New York: Hill & Wang, 2001.

Fenton, William N. *The Great Law and the Longhouse: A Political History of the Iroquois Confederacy*. Norman: University of Oklahoma Press, 1998.

Ferling, John. *Almost a Miracle: The American Victory in the War of Independence*. Oxford: Oxford University Press, 2007.

Fischer, David Hackett. *Washington's Crossing*. New York: Oxford University Press, 2004.

Fischer, Joseph. *A Well-Executed Failure: The Sullivan Campaign Against the Iroquois, July–September 1779*. Columbia: University of South Carolina Press, 1997.

Folts, James. "The 'Wyoming Massacre' Revisited." Paper presented at the 2007 Conference on Iroquois Research, Rensselaerville.

Frazier, Patrick. *The Mohicans of Stockbridge*. Lincoln: University of Nebraska Press, 1992.

Glatthaar, Joseph P. and James Kirby Martin. *Forgotten Allies: The Oneida Indians and the American Revolution*. New York: Hill & Wang, 2006.

Glete, Jan. *Navies and Nations: Warships, Navies and State Building in Europe and America, 1500–1860*. Stockholm Studies in History 48, 2 vols. Stockholm: Almqvist & Wiksell, 1993.

Goslinga, Cornelis Ch. *The Dutch in the Caribbean and in the Guianas, 1680–1791*. Assen: Van Gorcum, 1985.

Graymont, Barbara. *The Iroquois Indians in the American Revolution*. Syracuse: Syracuse University Press, 1972.

——. "New York State Indian Policy After the Revolution." *New York History*, 78, 1997.

Green, Michael D. "The Creek Confederacy in the American Revolution: Cautious Participants." In *Anglo-Spanish Confrontation on the Gulf Coast During the Revolution*. William S. Coker and Robert R. Rea, eds. Pensacola: Gulf Coast History and Humanities Conference, 1982.

———. *The Politics of Indian Removal: Creek Government and Society in Crisis*. Lincoln: University of Nebraska Press, 1982.
Grenier, John. *The First Way of War: American War Making on the Frontier, 1607–1814*. New York: Cambridge University Press, 2005.
Griffiths, David M. "American Commercial Diplomacy in Russia, 1780 to 1783." *The William and Mary Quarterly*, 27, 3, 1970.
———. "An American Contribution to the Armed Neutrality of 1780." *Russian Review*, 30, 2, April 1971.
Grotius, H. *Commentary on the Law of Prize and Booty*. M. Van Ittersum, ed. and intro. Indianapolis: Liberty Fund, 2006.
———. *The Free Seas. Natural Law and Enlightenment Classics*. D. Armitage, ed. and intro. Indianapolis: Liberty Fund, 2004.
Gruber, Ira D. "America's First Battle: Long Island, August 27, 1776." In *America's First Battles*. Charles Heller and William A. Stofft, eds. Lawrence: University of Kansas Press, 1986.
———. "British Strategy: The Theory and Practice of Eighteenth-Century Warfare." In *Reconsiderations on the Revolutionary War*. Don Higginbotham, ed. Westport: Greenwood Press, 1978.
———. *The Howe Brothers and the American Revolution*. Chapel Hill: University of North Carolina Press for the Institute of Early American History and Culture, 1972.
———. "Lord Howe and Lord George Germain: British Politics and the Winning of American Independence." *William and Mary Quarterly*, 22, 2, April 1965.
Habermehl, Nikolaas Dirk Bastiaan. "Guillemus Titsingh: een invloedrijk Amsterdams koopman uit de tweede helft van de achttiende eeuw, 1733–1805." *Jaarboek Amstelodamum*, 1987.
Hagan, Kenneth J. *This People's Navy: The Making of American Sea Power*. New York: The Free Press, 1991.
Hagan, Kenneth J. and Michael T. McMaster, eds. *In Peace and War: Interpretations of American Naval History, 30th Anniversary Edition*. Westport: Greenwood Press, 2008.
Harris, Robert D. *Necker: Reform Statesman of the Ancien Régime*. Berkeley: University of California Press, 1979.
Hart, Sir Basil Henry Liddell. *Strategy*. 2nd edn. New York: Meridian, 1991.
Hatley, M. Thomas. *The Dividing Paths: Cherokees and South Carolinians Through the Era of Revolution*. New York: Oxford University Press, 1993.
Hattendorf, John B. "The Struggle with France, 1689–1815." In *The Oxford Illustrated History of the Royal Navy*. J.R. Hill, ed. Oxford: Oxford University Press, 1995.
Heitman, Francis B. *Historical Register of Officers of the Continental Army During the War of the Revolution, April, 1775 to December, 1783*. Rev. and enl., Washington, D.C.: Rare Book Shop, 1914.
Higginbotham, Don, ed. *Reconsiderations on the Revolutionary War*. Westport: Greenwood, 1978.
———. *The War of American Independence: Military Attitudes, Policies, and Practice, 1763–1789*. New York: Macmillan, 1971.
Hinderaker, Eric. *Elusive Empires: Constructing Colonialism in the Ohio Valley, 1673–1800*. New York: Cambridge University Press, 1997.
Holton, Woody. *Forced Founders, Indians, Debtors, Slaves, and the Making of the American Revolution in Virginia*. Chapel Hill: University of North Carolina Press, 1999.
Horsman, Reginald. *Expansion and American Indian Policy, 1783–1812*. Norman: University of Oklahoma Press, 1992.

228 Select bibliography

Hough, Charles M. *Reports of Cases in the Vice-Admiralty of the Province of New York and in the Court of Admiralty of the State of New York, 1715–1788*. Yale Historical Publications Manuscripts and Edited Texts 8, New Haven: Yale University Press, 1925.

Hull, N.E.H., Peter C. Hoffer and Steven L. Allen. "Choosing Sides: A Quantitative Study of the Personality Determinants of Loyalist and Revolutionary Political Affiliation in New York." *Journal of American History*, 65, 2, September 1978.

Hurst, Ronald. *The Golden Rock: An Episode of the American War of Independence*. London: Leo Cooper, 1996.

Hurt, R. Douglas. *The Ohio Frontier: Crucible of the Old Northwest, 1720–1830*. Bloomington: Indiana University Press, 1996.

Hutson, James H. "John Adams and the Birth of Dutch–American Friendship, 1780–1782." In *A Bilateral Bicentennial: A History of Dutch–American Relations, 1782–1982*. J.W. Schulte Nordholt and R.P. Swierenga, eds. Amsterdam: Meulenhoff, 1982.

Israel, Jonathan I. *The Dutch Republic: Its Rise, Greatness and Fall, 1477–1806*. Oxford: Clarendon Press, 1995.

Jameson, J. Franklin. "St. Eustatius in the American Revolution." *The American Historical Review*, 8, 1903.

Jenkins, Ernest H. *A History of the French Navy*. London: Macdonald and Jane's, 1973.

Jespesen, Knud J.V. and Feldbæk, Ole. *Dansk udenrigspolitiks historie 2, Revanche og neutrlaitet 1648–1814*. København: Glydendal Leksikon, 2002.

Johansen, Hans Chr. "Scandinavian shipping in the late eighteenth century in a European perspective." *Economic History Review*, 3, 1992.

Jones Jr., C.C., ed. *The Siege of Savannah by the Fleet of Count d'Estaing in 1779*. New York: New York Times [1874], 1968.

Kaplan, Roger. "The Hidden War: British Intelligence Operations during the American Revolution." *The William and Mary Quarterly*, 47, 1, January 1990.

Keeley, Lawrence H. *War Before Civilization*. New York: Oxford University Press, 1996.

Keesey, Ruth M. "Loyalism in Bergen County, New Jersey." *The William and Mary Quarterly*, 18, 4, October 1961.

Kelsay, Isabel Thompson. *Joseph Brant 1743–1807: Man of Two Worlds*. Syracuse: Syracuse University Press, 1984.

Kennedy, Paul M. *The Rise and Fall of British Naval Mastery*. London: Allen Lane, 1983; reprint Macmillan, 1985.

——. *The Rise and Fall of the Great Powers: Economic Change and Military Conflict from 1500 to 2000*. New York: Random House, 1987.

Kinard, Lawrence. "Clark-Leyba Papers." *The American Historical Review*, 41, 1, October 1935.

Klei, E.H. "'A Notre Wilkes.' Het theatraal tegendraadse stijl van optreden van Joan Derk van der Capellen tot den Poll." *Overijsselse Historische Bijdragen*, 120, 2005.

Klein, Rachel N. *Unification of a Slave State: The Rise of the Planter Class in the South Carolina Backcountry, 1760–1808*. Chapel Hill: University of North Carolina Press, 1990.

Knox, Dudley W. *A History of the United States Navy*. Rev. edn. New York: G.P. Putnam's Sons, 1948.

Kwasny, Mark V. *Washington's Partisan War, 1775–1783*. Kent: Kent State University Press, 1996.

Labourdette, J.F. *Vergennes, Ministre principal de Louis XVI*. Paris: Editions Desjonquières, 1990.

Lacour-Gayet, G. *La Marine militaire de la France sous le règne de Louis XVI*. Paris: Honoré Champion, 1905.
Lambert, Andrew. *War at Sea in the Age of Sail 1650–1850*. London: Cassell, 2000.
Lancaster, Bruce. *The American Revolution*. New York: Houghton Mifflin Company, 1985.
Lawrence, Alexander A. *Storm Over Savannah: The Story of Count d'Estaing and the Siege of the Town in 1779*. Athens: University of Georgia Press, 1951.
LeDonne, John P. *The Grand Strategy of the Russian Empire, 1650–1831*. Oxford: Oxford University Press, 2004.
Lee, Wayne E. *Crowds and Soldiers in Revolutionary North Carolina: The Culture of Violence in Riot and War*. Gainesville: University Press of Florida, 2001.
——. "Fortify, Fight, or Flee: Tuscarora and Cherokee Defensive Warfare and Military Culture Adaptation." *The Journal of Military History*, 68, July 2004.
Lengel, Edward G. *Washington: A Military Life*. New York: Random House, 2005.
Lewis, James A. *Neptune's Militia: The Frigate* South Carolina *During the American Revolution*. Kent: Kent State University Press, 1999.
McConnell, Michael N. *A Country Between: The Upper Ohio Valley and its Peoples, 1724–1774*. Lincoln: University of Nebraska Press, 1992.
McCrady, Edward. *The History of South Carolina in the Revolution, 1780–1783*. London: Macmillan Company, 1902.
McGuffie, Tom H. *The Siege of Gibraltar 1779–1783*. London: Batsford, 1965.
Mackesy, Piers. "British Strategy in the War of American Independence." *Yale Review*, June 1963.
——. *The War for America, 1775–1783*. Cambridge: Harvard University Press, 1964; reprint Lincoln: University of Nebraska Press, 1993.
Mahan, Alfred T. *The Influence of Sea Power Upon History, 1660–1783*. New York: Hill and Wang, 1957.
——. *The Major Operations of the Navies in the American War of Independence*. Boston: Little, Brown and Co., 1913; reprint New York: Greenwood Press, 1969.
Mahon, John K. "Anglo-American Methods of Indian Warfare, 1676–1794." *Mississippi Valley Historical Review*, 45, 1958.
Malone, Patrick M. *The Skulking Way of War: Technology and Tactics Among the New England Indians*. Baltimore: The Johns Hopkins University Press, 1993.
Maloney, Linda. "The War of 1812: What Role for Sea Power?" In *In Peace and War: Interpretations of American Naval History, 30th Anniversary Edition*. Kenneth J. Hagan and Michael T. McMaster, eds. Westport: Greenwood Press, 2008.
Marshall, George. *Memoir of Brigadier-General John Dagworthy of the Revolutionary War*. Wilmington: Historical Society of Delaware, 1895.
Mason, Keith. "Localism, Evangelicalism, and Loyalism: The Sources of Discontent in the Revolutionary Chesapeake." *Journal of Southern History*, 56, 1, February 1990.
Matloff, Maurice, ed. *American Military History*. Washington, D.C.: Office of the Chief of Military History, United States Army, 1969.
Merrell, James H. "Declarations of Independence." In *The American Revolution: Its Character and Limits*. Jack P. Greene, ed. New York: New York University Press, 1984.
——. *The Indians' New World: Catawbas and Their Neighbors From European Contact Through the Era of Removal*. Chapel Hill: University of North Carolina Press, 1989.
Merritt, Bruce G. "Loyalism and Social Conflict in Revolutionary Deerfield, Massachusetts." *Journal of American History*, 57, 2, September 1970.
Michel, Jacques. *Du Paris de Louis XV à la marine de Louis XVI, l'oeuvre de Monsieur de Sartine*. 2 vols. Paris: Edition de l'Erudit, 1984.

Middlekauff, Robert K. *The Glorious Cause: The American Revolution, 1763–1789*. Rev. and exp. edn. New York: Oxford University Press, 2005.
Middleton, Richard. *Pontiac's War: Its Causes, Course, and Consequences*. New York: Routledge, 2007.
Miller, Daniel A. *Sir Joseph Yorke and Anglo-Dutch Relations, 1774–1780*. The Hague: Mouton, 1970.
Millett, Allan Reed. *Semper Fidelis: The History of the United States Marine Corps*. Rev. and expanded edn. New York: The Free Press, 1991.
Moir, John S., ed. *Character and Circumstance: Essays in Honour of Donald Grant Creighton*. Toronto: Macmillan of Canada, 1970.
Morison, Samuel Eliot. *John Paul Jones: A Sailor's Biography*. Boston: Little, Brown, 1959; Annapolis: Naval Institute Press, 1999.
———. *The Oxford History of the American People*. vol. 1, *Prehistory to 1789*. New York: Meridian, 1994.
Morris, Richard B. *The Peacemakers: The Great Powers & American Independence*. New York: Harper and Row, 1965.
Muhlfeld, Sharon Sauder. "Preserving Independence: Native American Responses to the Revolution in the Ohio Valley." In *Proceedings of the Northeastern Native Peoples & the American Revolutionary Era: 1760–1810 Symposium*. David Naumec, ed. Mashantucket: Mashantucket Pequot Museum & Research Center, 2008.
Müller, Leos. *Consuls, Corsairs, and Commerce: The Swedish Consular Service and Long-Distance Shipping, 1720–1815*. Uppsala: Uppsala Universitet, 2004.
———. "The Swedish East India Trade and International Markets: Re-exports of Teas, 1731–1813." *Scandinavian Economic History Review*, 3, 2003.
Murphy, Orville T. *Charles Gravier, Comte de Vergennes: French Diplomacy in the Age of Revolution, 1719–1787*. Albany: State University of New York Press, 1982.
Nadelhaft, J.J. *The Disorders of War: The Revolution in South Carolina*. Orono: University of Maine at Orono Press, 1981.
Naumec, David. "Connecticut's Native Troops, 1775–1783: Militia, Connecticut Line, and Continental Service." In *Proceedings of the Northeastern Native Peoples & the American Revolutionary Era: 1760–1810 Symposium*. David Naumec, ed. Mashantucket: Mashantucket Pequot Museum & Research Center, 2008.
Naval Historical Center. *Dictionary of American Naval Fighting Ships*. 9 vols. Washington, D.C.: Government Printing Office, 1959–91.
Nelson, Paul David. "British Conduct of the American Revolutionary War: A Review of Interpretations." *Journal of American History*, 65, 3, December 1978.
Nelson, William H. *The American Tory*. London: Oxford University Press, 1961; reprint Boston: Northeastern University Press, 1992.
Nethscher, P.M. *Geschiedenis van de kolonien Essequebo, Demerary en Berbice, van de vestiging der Nederlanders aldaar tot op onzen tijd*. The Hague: Martinus Nijhoff, 1988.
O'Brien, Greg. "The Choctaw Defense of Pensacola in the American Revolution." In *Pre-Removal Choctaw History: Exploring New Paths*. Greg O'Brien, ed. Norman: University of Oklahoma Press, 2008.
———. *The Choctaws in a Revolutionary Age, 1750–1830*. Lincoln: University of Nebraska Press, 2002.
O'Donnell, James. *Southern Indians in the American Revolution*. Knoxville: University of Tennessee Press, 1973.
O'Shaugnessy, Andrew Jackson. *An Empire Divided: The American Revolution and the British Caribbean*. Philadelphia: University of Pennsylvania Press, 2000.

Padrón, Morales. "Editor's Introduction." In *Journal of Don Francisco Saavedra de Sangronis During the Commission Which He Had in His Charge From 25 June 1780 Until the 20th of the Same Month in 1783*. Gainesville: University of Florida Press, 1989.

Pares, Richard. "American Versus Continental Warfare, 1739–63." *English Historical Review*, 51, 1936.

———. *Colonial Blockade and Neutral Rights, 1739–1763*. Philadelphia: Porcupine Press, 1975.

———. *Yankees and Creoles: The Trade Between North America and the West Indies Before the American Revolution*. London: Longman, 1956.

Parmenter, Jon W. "After the 'Mourning Wars': The Iroquois as Allies in Colonial American Campaigns, 1675–1760." *William and Mary Quarterly*, 3rd ser., 64, 2007.

———. "Dragging Canoe (Tsi'yu-gûnsi'ni): Chickamauga Cherokee Patriot." In *The Human Tradition in the American Revolution*. Nancy L. Rhoden and Ian K. Steele, eds. Wilmington: Scholarly Resources, 2000.

Parmentier, Jan. "Profit and Neutrality: The Case of Ostend, 1781–1783." In *Pirates and Privateers: New Perspectives on the War on Trade in the Eighteenth and Nineteenth Centuries*. D.J. Starkey, E.S. van Eijck van Heslinga and J.A. de Moor, eds. Exeter Maritime Studies 9, Exeter: University of Exeter Press, 1997.

Paterson, Thomas G., J. Garry Clifford, Shane J. Maddock, Deborah Kisatsky and Kenneth J. Hagan. *American Foreign Relations, Volume 1: A History to 1920*. 7th edn. Boston: Wadsworth, 2010.

Patterson, A. Temple. *The Other Armada: The Franco-Spanish Attempt to Invade Britain in 1779*. Manchester: Manchester University Press, 1960.

Perdue, Theda. *Cherokee Women: Gender and Culture Change, 1700–1835*. Lincoln: University of Nebraska Press, 1998.

Perkins, Edwin J. *American Public Finance and Financial Services, 1700–1815*. Columbus: Ohio State University Press, 1994.

Perret, Geoffrey. A *Country Made by War: From the Revolution to Vietnam – The Story of America's Rise to Power*. New York: Random House, 1989.

Petrie, Sir Charles. *King Charles III of Spain: An Enlightened Despot*. New York; The John Day Company, 1971.

Peyser, Joseph L., ed. and trans. *Letters from New France: The Upper Country, 1686–1783*. Urbana and Chicago: University of Illinois Press, 1992.

Piecuch, Jim. "Incompatible Allies: Loyalists, Slaves, and Indians in Revolutionary South Carolina." In *War & Society in the American Revolution: Mobilization and Home Fronts*. J.P. Resch and W. Sargent, eds. DeKalb: Northern Illinois University Press, 2007.

Porta, A. *Joan en Gerrit Corver: De politieke macht van Amsterdam, 1702–1748*. Amsterdam: Van Gorcum, 1975.

Postma, Johannes and V. Enthoven, eds. *Riches from Atlantic Commerce: Dutch Transatlantic Trade and Shipping, 1585–1817*. Leiden and Boston: Brill, 2003.

Potter, E.B. and Chester W. Nimitz, eds. *Sea Power: A Naval History*. Englewood Cliffs: Prentice-Hall, Inc., 1960.

Pritchard, James. "French Strategy and the American Revolution: A Reappraisal." *Naval War College Review*, 47, 4, 1994.

Prucha, Francis Paul. *American Indian Policy in the Formative Years: The Indian Trade and Intercourse Acts, 1790–1834*. Lincoln: University of Nebraska Press, 1970.

———. *American Indian Treaties: The History of a Political Anomaly*. Berkeley: University of California Press, 1994.

232 *Select bibliography*

Prud'homme van Reine, R.B. *Jan Hendrik van Kinsbergen, 1735–1819: Admiraal en filantroop*. Amsterdam: De Bataafsche Leeuw, 1990.

Quaife, Milo M. "The Ohio Campaigns of 1782." *Mississippi Valley Historical Review*, 18, 1931.

Richmond, Sir Herbert W. *The Navy in India 1763–1783*. London: Ernest Benn, 1931.

Richter, Daniel K. "Native Peoples of North America and the Eighteenth-Century British Empire." In *The Oxford History of the British Empire*. vol. 3: *The Eighteenth Century*. P.J. Marshall, ed. New York: Oxford University Press, 1998.

——. "War and Culture: The Iroquois Experience." *William and Mary Quarterly*, 3rd ser., 40, 1983.

Riker, William H. "Dutch and American Federalism." *Journal of the History of Ideas*, 18, 1957.

Rivas, Vincente. *Don Juan de Miralles y Independencia de los Estados Unidos*. Valencia: Generalitat Valenciana, 2003.

Robson, Eric. *The American Revolution In its Political and Military Aspects, 1763–1783*. New York: W.W. Norton, 1966.

——. "The Expedition to the Southern Colonies, 1775–1776." *English Historical Review*, 66, 261, October 1951.

Rodger, Nicholas A.M. *The Command of the Ocean: A Naval History of Britain, 1649–1815*. New York: W.W. Norton, 2005.

——. "The Continental Commitment in the Eighteenth Century." In *War, Strategy and International Politics: Essays in Honour of Sir Michael Howard*. L. Freedman, P. Hayes and R. O'Neill, eds. Oxford: Clarendon Press, 1992.

——. *The Insatiable Earl: A Life of John Montagu, Earl of Sandwich, 1718–1792*. London: HarperCollins, 1993.

——. "Instigators or Spectators? The British Government and the Restoration of the Stadholderate in 1747." *Tijdschrift voor Geschiedenis*, 106, 1993.

Rohrbaugh, Malcolm J. *The Trans-Appalachian Frontier*. New York: Oxford University Press, 1978.

Rose, John Holland. "Great Britain and the Dutch Question, 1787–1788." *The American Historical Review*, 14, 1909.

Russell, Jack. *Gibraltar Besieged, 1779–1783*. London: William Heinemann, Ltd., 1965.

Saunt, Claudio. *A New Order of Things: Property, Power, and the Transformation of the Creek Indians, 1733–1816*. New York: Cambridge University Press, 1999.

Schama, Simon. *Citizens: A Chronicle of the French Revolution*. New York: Alfred A. Knopf, 1989.

——. *Patriots and Liberators: Revolution in the Netherlands, 1780–1813*. London: Fontana Press, 1977.

——. *Rough Crossings: Britain, the Slaves, and the American Revolution*. New York: HarperCollins, 2006.

Schotanus, F.B. *L.P. van de Spiegel, 1737–1800 en de ondergang van de Republiek, deel 1: 1737–1784*. Loenen: Schotanus Boeken, 1995.

Schulte Nordholt, J.W. *Voorbeelden in de verte. De invloed van de Amerikaanse revolutie in Nederland*. Baarn: In den Toren, 1979.

Scott, H.M. *British Foreign Policy in the Age of the American Revolution*. Oxford: Oxford University Press, 1990.

Scott, James Brown, ed. *The Armed Neutralities of 1780 and 1800: A Collection of Official Documents Preceded by the View of Representative Publicists*. New York, 1918.

Selby, John. *The Road to Yorktown*. New York: St. Martin's Press, 1976.

Shannon, Timothy J. "War, Diplomacy, and Culture: The Iroquois Experience in the Seven Years' War." In *Cultures in Conflict: The Seven Years' War in North America.* Warren R. Hofstra, ed. Lanham: Rowman & Littlefield, 2007.
Sheidley, Nathaniel. "Hunting and the Politics of Masculinity in Cherokee Treaty-Making, 1763–75." In *Empire and Others: British Encounters with Indigenous Peoples, 1600–1850.* Martin Daunton and Rick Halpern, eds. Philadelphia: University of Pennsylvania Press, 1999.
Shy, John. *A People Numerous and Armed: Reflections on the Military Struggle for American Independence.* Rev. edn. Ann Arbor: University of Michigan Press, 1990.
——. *Toward Lexington: The Role of the British Army in the Coming of the American Revolution.* Princeton: Princeton University Press, 1965.
Skaggs, David Curtis and Larry L. Nelson, eds. *The Sixty Years' War for the Great Lakes, 1754–1814.* East Lansing: Michigan State University Press, 2001.
Sleeper-Smith, Susan. "'Ignorant Bigots and Busy Rebels': The American Revolution in the Western Great Lakes." In *The Sixty Years' War for the Great Lakes, 1754–1814.* David Curtis Skaggs and Larry L. Nelson, eds. East Lansing: Michigan State University Press, 2001.
Smith, A.B. "The French Period at the Cape, 1781–1783: A Report on Excavations at Conway Redoubt, Constantia Nek." *Military History Journal*, 5, 1981.
Smith, Paul H. *Loyalists and Redcoats: A Study in British Revolutionary Policy.* Chapel Hill: University of North Carolina Press for the Institute of Early American History and Culture, 1964.
Snapp, J. Russell. *John Stuart and the Struggle for Empire on the Southern Frontier.* Baton Rouge: Louisiana State University Press, 1996.
Spinney, David. *Rodney.* London: George Allen & Unwin, 1969.
Spring, Matthew H. *With Zeal and With Bayonets Only: The British Army on Campaign in North America, 1775–1783.* Norman: University of Oklahoma Press, 2008.
Starkey, Armstrong. *European and Native American Warfare, 1675–1815.* Norman: University of Oklahoma Press, 1998.
Starkey, David J. "British Privateering Against the Dutch in the American Revolutionary Wars, 1780–1783." In H.E.S. Fisher, ed. *Studies in British Privateering, Trading Enterprise and Seamen's Welfare, 1775–1900.* Exeter: University of Exeter Press, 1987.
——. *British Privateering Enterprise in the Eighteenth Century.* Exeter Maritime Studies, no. 4, Exeter: Exeter University Press, 1990.
Steur, J.J. *Herstel of ondergang. De voorstellen tot redres van de VOC, 1740–1795.* Utrecht: H & S, 1984.
Stevens, Benjamin Franklin. *The Campaign in Virginia: An Exact Reprint of Six Rare Pamphlets on the Clinton–Cornwallis Controversy....* vol. I. London: B.F. Stevens, 1888.
Strachan, Hew. *Clausewitz's On War: A Biography.* New York: Atlantic Monthly Press, 2007.
Sumida, Jon Tetsuro. *Decoding Clausewitz: A New Approach to On War.* Lawrence: University Press of Kansas, 2008.
——. *Inventing Grand Strategy and Teaching Command: The Classic Works of Alfred Thayer Mahan Reconsidered.* Baltimore: Johns Hopkins University Press, 2000.
Sweetman, Jack, ed. *American Naval History: An Illustrated Chronology of the U.S. Navy and Marine Corps, 1775–Present.* 2nd edn. Annapolis: Naval Institute Press, 1991.
Symonds, Craig L. *A Battlefield Atlas of the American Revolution.* Baltimore: Nautical & Aviation Publishing Co., 1986.

Select bibliography

———. *The Naval Institute Historical Atlas of the U.S. Navy*. Annapolis: Naval Institute Press, 1995.

Syrett, David. "Count-Down to the Saintes: a Strategy of Detachments and the Quest for Naval Superiority in the West Indies." *The Mariner's Mirror*, 87, 2001.

———. "The Failure of the British Effort in America, 1777." In *The British Navy and the Use of Naval Power in the Eighteenth Century*. Jeremy Black and Philip Woodfine, eds. Atlantic Highlands: Humanities Press International, 1989.

———. "Home Waters or America? The Dilemma of British Naval Strategy in 1778." *Mariner's Mirror*, 77, 4, 1991.

———. *Neutral Rights and the War in the Narrow Seas, 1778–1782*. Fort Leavenworth: U.S. Army Command and General Staff College, 1985.

———. *The Royal Navy in American Waters, 1775–1783*. Aldershot: Scolar Press, 1989.

———. *The Royal Navy in European Waters during the American Revolutionary War*. Columbia: University of South Carolina Press, 1998.

———. *Shipping and the American War, 1775–83: A Study of British Transport Organisation*. London: The Athlone Press, 1970.

Syrett, Harold C., *et al.*, eds. *The Papers of Alexander Hamilton*. 27 vols. New York and London: Columbia University Press, 1961–87.

Taillemite, E. *L'Histoire ignorée de la marine française*. Paris: Librairie Académique Perrin, 1988.

Tanner, Helen Hornbeck. "Pipesmoke and Muskets: Florida Indian Intrigues of the Revolutionary Era." In *Eighteenth-Century Florida and Its Borderlands*. Samuel Proctor, ed. Gainesville: University Presses of Florida, 1975.

Tarleton, Banastre. *A History of the Campaigns of 1780 and 1781*. New York: New York Times, 1967.

Tarrade, Jean. *Le Commerce coloniale de la France à la fin de l'ancien régime: l'évolution du régime de "l'Exclusif" de 1763 à 1789*. 2 vols. Paris: Presses Universitaires de France, 1972, vol. 1.

Thayer, Theodore. *Nathanael Greene: Strategist of the American Revolution*. New York: Twayne Publishers, 1960.

Thomas, Evan. *John Paul Jones: Sailor, Hero, Father of the American Navy*. New York: Simon & Schuster, 2003.

Tilghman, Tench. *Memoir of Lieut. Col. Tench Tilghman*. New York: New York Times/Arno, 1971 [1876].

Tilley, John A. *The British Navy and the American Revolution*. Columbia: University of South Carolina Press, 1987.

Tillson, Albert H., Jr. "The Localist Roots of Backcountry Loyalism: An Examination of Popular Political Culture in Virginia's New River Valley." *Journal of Southern History*, 54, 3, August 1988.

Tiro, Karim M. "A 'Civil' War? Rethinking Iroquois Participation in the American Revolution." *Explorations in Early American Culture*, 4, 2000.

———. "The Dilemmas of Alliance: The Oneida Indian Nation in the American Revolution." In *War & Society in the American Revolution: Mobilization and Home Fronts*. John Resch and Walter Sargent, eds. DeKalb: Northern Illinois University Press, 2007.

Titus, James. *The Old Dominion at War: Society, Politics and Warfare in Late Colonial Virginia*. Columbia: University of South Carolina Press, 1991.

Townsend, E.D. *Anecdotes of the Civil War in the United States*. New York: D. Appleton and Company, 1884.

Tracy, Nicholas. *Navies, Deterrence and American Independence: Britain and Seapower in the 1760s and 1770s*. Vancouver: University of British Columbia Press, 1988.
Tuchman, Barbara W. *The First Salute*. New York: Knopf, 1988.
Usner, Daniel. *Indians, Settlers, and Slaves in a Frontier Exchange Economy: The Lower Mississippi Before 1783*. Chapel Hill: University of North Carolina Press, 1992.
Valentine, Alan. *Lord George Germain*. Oxford: Clarendon Press, 1962.
van Dantzig, A. *Forts and Castles of Ghana*. Accra: Sedco Publishing, 1980.
van Dijk, E.A. "De wekker van de Nederlandse natie: Joan Derk van der Capellen, 1741–1784." *POMflet*, 6, 1984.
van Eyck van Heslinga, E.S. "De vlag dekt de lading. De Nederlandse koopvaardij in de Vierde Engelse oorlog." *Tijdschrift voor Zeegeschiedenis*, 2, 1982.
van Nimwegen, Olaf. *De Republiek der Verenigde Nederlanden als grote mogendheid. Buitenlandse politiek en oorlogvoering in de eerste helft van de achttiende eeuw en in het bijzonder tijdens de Oostenrijkse Successieoorlog, 1740–1748*. Amsterdam: De Bataafsche Leeuw, 2002.
van Winter, Pieter Jan. *Het aandeel van den Amsterdamschen handel aan de opbouw van het Amerikaansche Gemeenebest*. Werken uitgegeven door de Vereeniging het Nederlandsch-Historisch Archief 9. 2 vols. The Hague: Nijhoff, 1927.
van Zijverden, J. "The Risky Alternative: Dutch Privateering During the Fourth Anglo-Dutch War, 1780–1783." In *Pirates and Privateers: New Perspectives on the War on Trade in the Eighteenth and Nineteenth Centuries*. D.J. Starkey, E.S. van Eijck van Heslinga and J.A. de Moor, eds. Exeter Maritime Studies 9, Exeter: University of Exeter Press, 1997.
Vergé-Franceschi, Michel. *La Royale au temps de l'amiral d'Estaing*. Paris: La Pensée Universelle, 1977.
Villiers, Patrick. *Marine royale, corsaires et trafic dans l'Atlantique de Louis XIV à Louis XVI*. 2 vols. Dunkerque: Société Dunkerquoise d'Histoire et d' Archéologie, 1991.
Wahlström, Lydia. *Gustavianska studier. Historiska utkast från tidevarvet 1772–1809*. Stockholm: Norstedt, 1914.
Wallace, Anthony F.C. *The Death and Rebirth of the Seneca*. New York: Vintage, 1970.
Ward, Harry M. *The War for Independence and the Transformation of American Society*. New York: Routledge, 1999.
Warner, Michael S. "General Josiah Harmar's Campaign Reconsidered: How the Americans Lost the Battle of Kekionga." *Indiana Magazine of History*, 83, 1987.
Weigley, Russell. *The American Way of War: A History of United States Military Strategy and Policy*. New York: Macmillan, 1973.
Wells, Robert V. "Population and Family in Early America." *The Blackwell Encyclopedia of the American Revolution*. Jack P. Greene and J.R. Pole, eds. Cambridge: Blackwell, 1991.
White, Richard. *The Middle Ground: Indians, Empires and Republics in the Great Lakes Region, 1650–1815*. New York: Cambridge University Press, 1991.
Will, Chris. *Sterk Water. De Hollandse Waterlinie*. Utrecht: Matrijs, 2002.
Willcox, William B. "Sir Henry Clinton: Paralysis of Command." In *George Washington's Generals and Opponents: Their Exploits and Leadership*. 2 vols. George A. Billis, ed. New York: Da Capo, 1994.
———. "Too Many Cooks: British Planning Before Saratoga." *Journal of British Studies*, 1962.
Williams, Glenn F. "NOT MERELY OVERRUN BUT DESTROY: George Washington's 1779 Campaign Against the Iroquois." In *Proceedings of the Northeastern Native*

Peoples & the American Revolutionary Era: 1760–1810 Symposium. David Naumec, ed. Mashantucket: Mashantucket Pequot Museum & Research Center, 2008.

Wilson, David K. *The Southern Strategy: Britain's Conquest of South Carolina and Georgia, 1775–1780*. Columbia: University of South Carolina Press, 2005.

Winius, George D. and Marcus P.M. Vink. *The Merchant-Warrior Pacified*. Delhi: Oxford University Press, 1994.

Wise, S.F. "The American Revolution and Indian History." In *Character and Circumstance: Essays in Honour of Donald Grant Creighton*. John S. Moir, ed. Toronto: Macmillan of Canada, 1970.

Wright, J. Leitch. *Creeks & Seminoles: The Destruction and Regeneration of the Muscogulge People*. Lincoln: University of Nebraska Press, 1986.

Wunder, John R. "'Merciless Indian Savages' and the Declaration of Independence: Native Americans Translate the *Ecunnaunuxulgee* Document." *American Indian Law Review*, 25, Spring 2001.

Zachrisson, Carl August. *Sveriges underhandlingar om beväpnad neutralitet åren 1778–80*. PhD dissertation, Uppsala universitet, 1863.

Zwitser, H.L. *"De militie van den staat": het leger van de Republiek der Verenigde Nederlanden*. Amsterdam: Van Soeren, 1991.

Index

"Act for the Government of the Navy of the United States" (1799) 37
Active 44
Adams, John 36, 37, 54, 55, 185–6, 192
Admiralty Board, Netherlands 180, 187, 188
Africa 47, 89, 191
Albany 65–6, 106
Alfred 44, 47
Allen, William 108
Alliance 49–50, 182
Amboy 15
America 50
American Committee of Secret Correspondence 165, 184
Amherst, Jeffery 123
Andrea Doria 176
Anglo–Danish Treaty (1670) 210
Anglo–Dutch Treaty (1674) 183, 203, 211
Anglo–Swedish Bilateral Treaty (1661) 209
Aranda, Conde de 165–6
Arbuthnot, Vice Admiral Marriot 45, 111–12
Arethusa 148
Arnold, Benedict 7, 40–1, 52, 61
Asiatic Company 213
Association of Retaliation 107
Augusta 131
Ax Carrier 128

Bahamas 171
Balfour, Lord Nisbet 28
Baltic 88, 188, 189–90
Baltic-Guinea Trading Company 214
Bancroft, Dr. Edward 182
Barras de Saint Laurent, Comte de 53, 155
Barren Hill, battle of 129
Barrier Treaty (1715) 177
Basking Ridge 16

Baton Rouge 171
Bay of Biscay 78
Bay of Honduras 167
Bayard, John 108
Beach, Captain Edward L. 39
Beaumarchais, Pierre-Augustin Caron 42
Bedford, Duke of 75
Bemis Heights 42
Bernstorff, Count Andreas Peter 205, 209, 210, 218
Bilbao 164
Bird, Captain Henry 131
Black, Jeremy 2, 4, 58–70
Blome, Otto 206
Bolton, Lieutenant Colonel Mason 130
Bombay 78, 91
Bonhomme Richard 48–50, 181
Boston 39–40, 62, 82
Bouillé, Marquis de 150, 153, 156, 157, 190
Boundbrook 16, 17
Bourbon Family Compact 163
Brandywine 17, 42, 65
Breeds Hill 6–7
Brest 85–6, 147, 170
British East India Company 47, 91, 171, 215
British Home Squadron 147
British military strategy 58–70
British naval strategy: case study in global strategy 93–4; defeat in America (1781) 89–91; failure of (1775–7) 81–4; revival of British position/coming of peace (1782–3) 92–3; and Spain/League of Armed Neutrality 86–9; in three dimensions 74–9; war in the Indian Ocean (1781–3) 91–2; war with France and global strategy 84–6; ways of naval war 79–81

British Royal Africa Company 191
British strategy, Loyalists in 100–16
Brooklyn Heights 9
Browne, Montforte 108
Brunswick 15
Brunswijk, Duke of 186
Bunker Hill 6–7, 8, 36
Burgoyne, Major General John 17, 25–6, 41–2, 48, 63–4, 65–6, 82, 84, 108–9, 120
Butler, Major General Benjamin 45
Butler, Major John 128
Byron, Vice Admiral John 85–6

Cabot 38
Cádiz 89, 154–5, 157, 170
Caldwell, Captain William 132
Calloway, Colin 120
Camden 18–19, 22, 26–7, 67, 113, 114, 171
Campbell, Lieutenant Colonel Archibald 111
Canandaigua Treaty (1794) 135
Canton 206–7, 213–14
Cape Breton, Nova Scotia 47
Cape Fear 103
Cape Henry 53
Cape of Good Hope 89, 91, 190–1
Cape St. Vincent 87
Cape Verde Islands 91
Caribbean 47
Carleton, Major General Sir Guy 7, 40–1, 61, 64–5
Carlisle Peace Commission 59
Carlos III, King 165, 166, 168, 170, 173
Castine 44
Castries, Marquis de 155, 156, 157
Catawba Indians 128, 133–4
Catawba River 19, 23
Catherine II, Queen 88, 102, 183, 185, 193, 202, 209–12, 217–18
Caughnawaga Indians 7
Cayuga Indians 127, 129
Cevallos, Pedro de 166–7
Ceylon 91, 191, 194
Chalmers, James 108
Channel Fleet 78, 79, 85–6, 87, 88, 89–90, 92
Charleston 18, 27–8, 38, 44, 45–6, 62, 67, 78, 89, 103–4, 110, 111–12, 171
Charlotte 114
Chatham Turkey 16
Chauncey, Isaac 42
Chávez, Thomas 3, 163–75

Cheraw Hill 22
Cherokee Indians 19, 23, 29, 121, 124, 128, 131, 132
Cherokee War (1776) 126, 127
Chesapeake Bay 38–9, 53, 54–5, 80, 90, 94, 103, 113, 156
Chickamauga Indians 126, 130, 131, 134
Chickasaw Indians 127, 131
China 206–7, 213–14
Choctaw Indians 122, 127, 131, 133
Choiseul, Duc de 143
Claret, Chevalier Charles-Pierre de 147
Clark, George Rogers 132, 164
Clarke, Colonel Elijah 19
Clausewitz, Carl von 5, 24, 40, 68, 74–5, 93
Clinton, General Sir Henry 9, 18, 28, 45, 46, 64, 65, 101, 102–3, 104, 105, 110–12, 113, 115, 151–2
Coast of Campeche 167
Coercive Acts (1774) 60, 205
colonial military strategy: critical shift 11–14; first phase 6–7; founded on weakness and a clear objective 5; nature of war 5–6; second phase 7–10; in the South 18–29; third phase 14–18
colonial naval strategy 35–55
colonial order, decay in 123–4
Columbus 46
Concord 36, 59, 101, 164
Connolly, Lieutenant Colonel John 102
Connyngham, Gustavus 48
Constellation 50–1
Constitution 51
Continental Congress 6–7, 8, 15, 18, 35, 36, 126, 164, 176
Convention of Aranjuez (1779) 149
Cooper River 46
Copenhagen 212–13
Corbett, Sir Julian 55, 74, 79, 93–4, 145
Córdoba, Admiral Don Luis de 156, 171
Cornell, Ezekiel 62
Cornplanter 127
Cornwallis, Lieutenant General Charles 18, 19–20, 22, 24–6, 27, 28, 29, 46, 52–8, 68, 74, 90, 103, 112–15, 156, 171–2, 173
Coromandel Coast 213
Cotineau de Corgelin, Captain 182
Countess of Scarborough 50, 181
Court, General 44
covert aid, Spain 163–7
Cowpens 23, 28, 29, 114–15
Crake, J.E.A. 13

Creek Bridge 103
Creek Indians 121, 125, 127, 131–2
Creswell, John 157
Croix, Charles de la, Marquis de Castries 143
Crul, Rear Admiral William 190
Cuba 88, 155–6, 172

Dan River 24, 29, 115
Dana, Francis 202, 212
Dartmouth, Lord 101, 102, 105
De Lancy, Oliver 108
Deane, Silas 165
Decatur, Stephen 50
Declaration of Independence (1776) 42, 62, 122
Delaware Bay 83
Delaware Indians 124, 130, 132, 133, 135
Denmark: exploitation of neutrality 212–17; interest in League of Armed Neutrality 205–7
Diligent 44
diplomacy, Spain 163–7
Dogger Bank 89
Dominica 150, 157–8
Dragging Canoe 126, 131
Drake 48
Dull, Jonathan 141–2, 169
Dumas, Charles W.F. 184, 185
Dunmore, Lord 38, 124
Dutch East India Company 176, 190–1, 215
Dutch Republic: Fourth Anglo-Dutch War (1780–4) 185–93; as hostile neutral 88–9; Paris Peace Treaty (1784) 193–4; road to war 178–85; strategic setting 176–8
Dutch West India Company 176, 191

England, proposed invasion of 86–7, 110, 146–7, 150, 169
English Channel 48–51, 76, 89, 92–3, 156
Enthoven, Victor 176–97
Estaing, Vice Admiral Charles le Comte de 51–2, 76, 85–6, 87–8, 147–9, 150–2, 155, 168
Eternal Alliance Treaty (1773) 205

Fabian war 11–20, 23, 29–30
Fallen Timbers, battle of 123, 135
Fanning, Edmund 108
Farragut, David G. 50
Ferguson, Major Patrick 113, 114
Fielding, Admiral Charles 181

Fischer, Joseph 130
Flamborough Head 49–50
Floridablanca, Count of 167, 168
Forman, Colonel David 107
Fort Fisher 45
Fort Harmar Treaties (1789) 134–5
Fort McIntosh Treaty (1785) 133
Fort Moultrie 45–6
Fort Niagara 129–30
Fort Ninety-Six 19, 22–3, 27–8, 113
Fort Pitt 163
Fort Pitt Treaty (1778) 130
Fort St. Joseph 171
Fort Stanwix Treaty (1768) 123, 124, 133
Fort Ticonderoga 6–7, 17, 39, 61
Fort Washington 14
Fort Watson 27
Fourth Anglo-Dutch War (1780–4) 185–93
Fox, Henry 90
France: American attacks from 47–51; British war with 84–6; entry into war 167–8
Franco-American Treaty of Alliance (1778) 48, 84, 86
Franklin, Benjamin 42–3, 48, 51, 54, 164, 165, 167, 184, 185, 194, 206
Frederick, Crown Prince 210
Freeman's Farm 42
French strategy 141–59

Gage, General Thomas 101, 102, 105, 128
Galphin, George 122
Gálvez, Bernardo de 163–4, 171, 172, 173
Gardoqui e hijos 164–5
Gaspee 46
Gates, Major General Horatio 18–19, 21, 40, 41, 66, 113–14
George III, King 36, 50, 59, 61, 62, 76, 85, 102, 168, 179, 185
Georgetown 62
Germain, Lord George 62–4, 65, 66, 77, 85, 90, 93, 102–3, 105, 106, 107–9, 111
Germantown 17, 65
Gibraltar 51, 68, 86, 87, 89–90, 92, 152, 158, 167, 168, 169, 170–1, 183, 209
Glasgow 38, 83
global naval strategy, Britain 84–6, 93–4
Gold Coast 191
Governor's Island 9
Grasse, Rear Admiral François J.P. Comte de 52–5, 89–90, 92, 143, 147, 150, 153, 155–6, 157, 172–3
Graves, Rear Admiral Thomas 53, 54–5, 89, 90

Graves, Vice Admiral Samuel 82
Greene, Major General Nathanael 12–14, 16, 19, 20–30, 45, 46, 115, 171
Greenville, Treaty of 123, 135
Grenada 150–1
Griffiths, David M. 211
Grimaldi, Marques de 165
Grove, Eric J. 1–4
Guichen, Comte de 152, 153, 155, 156
Guldberg, Ove Høegh 209, 210, 214
Gulf of Mexico 88, 167
Gustav III; King 205, 206, 208, 210, 218
Guyana 89

Hagan, Kenneth J. 35–55
Halifax, Nova Scotia 39
Hamilton, Alexander 16, 17, 65
Hampden 44
Hancock, John 10
Hannah 39
Hardy, Admiral Sir Charles 49, 87
Harmar, Lieutenant Colonel Josiah 133, 134
Harris, Sir James 209
Harris, Robert 143
Hawke, Admiral Lord 89
Henry, Patrick 6
Herrera, Ricardo A. 3, 100–16
Hillsborough 24–5
Hobkirk's Hill 27, 29
Holland 190
Honduras 86
Hood, Rear Admiral Sir Samuel 53, 54–5, 92, 157
Hopkins, Commodore Esek 38–9, 44, 46, 83
Hotham, Commodore William 190
Howe, General Robert 126
Howe, General Sir William 9, 10, 11, 15, 16–17, 39–40, 41–2, 59, 61–5, 66, 84, 101, 102, 104–5, 106–9
Howe, Vice Admiral Sir Richard 59, 61, 79, 82, 84, 92, 105, 149
Hudson River 7–8, 17, 61, 65–6, 82, 104–5, 108, 112
Hughes, Vice Admiral Sir Edward 51, 91–2
Hull, Isaac 51

India 68, 191, 213–14
Indian Ocean 51, 89; British naval strategy (1781–3) 91–2
Inflexible 41
Infodsretten 215–16

Irish Sea 48–51
Iroquois 121, 122, 128–9
irregular warfare 5–6
Isle of Wight 181

Jamaica 73, 87, 88, 92, 157, 172
Jay, John 54
Jefferson, Governor Thomas 21
Jeney, Capitaine de 15
John 47
Johnson, Colonel Guy 130
Johnson, Sir John 127
Johnson, Sir William 123, 127
Johnstone, Commodore George 191
Jones, John Paul 46–51, 164, 181–2
Jones, Michael W. 3, 5–30
Joseph II; King 193

Kennedy, Paul M. 80, 93, 141, 142
Keppel, Admiral Augustus 79, 85–6
King's American Regiment 108
King's Mountain 19–20, 114
King's Orange Rangers 108
Knox, Colonel Henry 39
Knox, Commodore Dudley W. 50

L'Indien 184
La Belle Poule 148
La Vengeance 49
Lafayette, Marquis de 49, 52, 90, 153, 170
Lake Champlain 17, 40–2, 108
Lake Eerie 39, 42
Lake George 17
Lake Nicaragua 171
Lake Ontario 42
Landais, Pierre 49
Lángara, Lieutenant General Juan de 170
Laurens, Henry 184
Le Cerf 49
Le Duc de Duras 48
Le Ray, Jacques-Donatien 181
League of Armed Neutrality: and British naval strategy 86–9; concept of neutrality before 1780 203–4; Danish and Swedish exploitation of neutrality 212–17; declaration of 208–12; interests of Sweden, Russia and Denmark 205–7; and Netherlands 183, 184–5, 193–4
Lee 39
Lee, Arthur 165
Lee, Colonel Henry 27
Lee, Major General Charles 8
Lee, Wayne 122
Lee, William 184

Leeward Islands 73, 88
Legion of the United States 135
Leslie, Major General Alexander 24, 114
Lexington 36, 59, 101
Liddell Hart, Sir Basil 13, 79
Lincoln, Abraham 67
Lincoln, Major General Benjamin 18, 46, 111
Lisbon 166, 170
Liverpool 49
Lloyd's of London 37
Lochabar Treaty (1770) 124
Long Island 7–8, 9, 10, 11, 109
Louis XVI; King 50, 142–3, 155, 167, 168, 180
Lovell, Brigadier Solomon 44–5
Loyal American Regiment 108
Loyalists in British Strategy 100–16

MacArthur, General Douglas 18
MacDonough, Thomas 42
McKean, Thomas 28
Mackesy, Piers 143, 147
Mahan, Captain Alfred Thayer 35, 43, 51, 54, 55, 145, 152
Manchac 171
Manhattan Island 9, 14
Mare Liberum 179
Marine Committee 37–8
Marion, Brigadier General Francis 20, 27
Maritime Powers 177
Marstrand 209, 214
Martin, Governor Josiah 102, 103
Martinique 86, 89, 150
Maryland Loyalists 108
Massachusetts General Court 44
Maurepas, Comte de 143
Mauritius 91
Mediterranean 51, 85, 156, 183
Mellish 47
Mercury 184
Miami Indians 135
Mifflin, Thomas 14
military strategy: American colonies 5–30; Britain 58–70
Millstone 16
Mingo Indians 127, 132
Minorca 86, 87, 156, 167, 171
Miralles, Juan de 163–4
Mississippi River 47, 88
Mobile 167, 171
Mohawk Indians 127, 129
Monitor 51
Monmouth 17

Montbarey, Comte de 143
Montgomery, Brigadier General Richard 7, 40
Montreal 7
Moore, Colonel John 113
Morgan, Brigadier General Daniel 22, 23, 24, 114
Morris, Lewis 176
Morris, Robert 47
Morristown 16, 17
Mortefontane, Treaty of (1800) 55
Mosquito Coast 171
Müller, Leos 202–19

Nancy 39
Napoleon 2, 81, 135, 145, 146, 218
Nash, Governor Abner 21
Natchez 164, 171
Native Americans: conquest (1783–94) 132–4; decay in colonial order 123–4; fragile neutrality (1775–6) 125–6; mobilization against US (1779–82) 129–32; southern caution/northern destruction 127–9; war in the West (1786–95) 134–5
Naval Committee 36
naval defeat, Britain 89–91
naval operations, Britain 77–9
naval strategy: American states 35–55; Britain 73–94; Dutch Republic 176–97
naval war, ways of 79–81
Necker, Jacques 142–3, 157
Neufville, Jean de 184, 185
neutrality: concept of prior to 1780 203–4; Native Americans 125–6; *see also* League of Armed Neutrality
New Orleans 163, 164
New Providence Island 38, 88
New York City 7–10, 11–15, 17, 52–3, 61–2, 63, 78, 82, 86, 104–5, 106, 109, 149, 168
Newark 16
Newport 52, 53, 154, 155, 171
North Carolina Board of War 20–1
North Sea 49–50, 156, 188, 189
North, Lord 2, 28, 54, 68, 75, 76, 90, 101, 102, 105, 171
Northern states, Native Americans in 127–9

Ohio River 132, 163
Ojibwe Indians 133
Old Smoke 127, 128
"Olive Branch Petition" 36

Oneida Indians 128–9
Orangist party, Netherlands 178
Oriskany, battle of 127, 128–9
Orvilliers, Admiral le Comte de 86, 147–9
Ottawa Indians 133, 135

Pallas 49–50
Palliser, Vice Admiral Sir Hugh 79
Panin, Count Nikita 209–10, 212
Paris Peace Treaty (1783) 123, 133, 146, 158, 193–4
Parker, Commodore Sir Peter 103, 104
Parker, Vice Admiral Hyde 190
Parmenter, Jon 121
partisan warfare 14–15, 20–1
Patriotic party, Netherlands 178, 184
Paulus Hook 9
Pearson, Captain Richard 50
Pelham, Thomas, Duke of Newcastle 79
Pennsylvania Loyalists 108
Penobscot 44
Pensacola 47, 110, 156, 167, 171
Perret, Geoffrey 41
Perry, Oliver Hazard 39, 42
Philadelphia 16, 38, 42, 63–4, 78, 82, 86, 106, 107, 110, 149
Phillips, Major General William 64
Pickens, Andrew 21
Pitt, William (the Elder) 2, 59, 75, 79
Pitt, William (the Younger) 93
Poland 59
Polk, Colonel Thomas 20–1
Polly 179
Pombal, Marques de 166
Pontiac's War (1763–6) 123
Porter, Rear Admiral David Dixon 45
Portugal 166
Potemkin, Grigori 210, 212
Prevost, Brigadier General Augustine 111, 132
Prince of Wales American Regiment 108
Princeton 15, 64, 107
Pritchard, James 141–59
Proclamation (1763) 123
Prohibatory Act (1775) 82–3
Providence 38, 44, 47
Pyle's Massacre 25

Quebec 7, 82
Queen's Rangers 108
Quibbletown 16
Quiberon Bay, France 48, 75

Ranft, Brian 2

Ranger 47, 48, 49
Rattletrap 164
Rawdon, Lord Francis Hastings 19, 26–8, 29
Reeve, John 2, 73–94
Reprisal 47
Revere, Paul 44
Rhode Island 36, 38, 48, 63–4, 86, 106, 110, 151–2, 154, 171
Richelieu River 40–2, 104–5
Rio de la Plata 166–7
Robinson, Beverly 108
Rochambeau, Lieutenant General Comte de 28, 52, 53–4, 90, 152, 154, 155, 171, 172–3
Rockingham, Marquess of 68, 92
Rodger, Nicholas 2, 76, 93
Rodney, Admiral Sir George Brydges 2–3, 54, 68, 76, 79, 87–8, 89–90, 92, 153, 154, 170, 183, 190
Rogers, Robert 108
Roosevelt, Theodore 50
Royal Guides and Pioneers 108
"Rules for the Regulation of the Navy of the United Colonies of North-America" (1775) 37
Russia, and League of Armed Neutrality 205–7

Saavedra, Francisco 166, 172, 173
Sade, Commodore de 153
St. Augustine 103, 110
St. Clair, General Arthur 134
St. Croix 205
St. Domingue 155
St. Eustatius 89, 90, 155, 156, 182–3, 185, 187, 190
St. Helena 91
St. Jan 205
St. Kitts 157
St. Lawrence River 40
St. Leger, Colonel Barry 128–9
St. Louis 163, 171
St. Lucia 86, 110, 111, 150, 151, 153
St. Thomas 190, 205, 213
St. Vincent 150
Saints, battle of 54, 68, 74, 92, 157–8
Saltonstall, Commodore Dudley 44–5, 46
San Juan River 171
Sandusky 132
Sandwich, Earl of 75–6, 78, 84, 85, 90, 93
Saratoga 42, 59, 65, 66, 82, 109, 165
Sartine, Gabriel de 143, 148, 149, 152, 154
Savannah 67, 78, 103, 111

Sayre, Stephen 207
Schimmelmann, H.C. 214
Schuyler, Major General Phillip 7
Ségur, Marquis de 143
Selkirk, Earl of 48
Seminole Indians 127
Seneka Indians 127, 128, 129
Serapis 49–50, 181, 182
Seven Year's War (1756–63) 35–6, 42, 59, 60, 69, 75, 93, 106, 144, 165
Shawnee Indians 121, 122, 124, 127, 130, 132, 133, 134, 135
Shelburne, Earl of 54
Skinner, Cortland 108
Sloat, John 50
Smith, Paul H. 106, 107
Söderström, Richard 214
Solebay 47
South Carolina 173, 184
Southern states: American military strategy in 18–29; Native Americans in 127–9
Spain: declaration of war and strategy 168–70; diplomacy and covert aid 163–7; entry into war 86–9; French entry into war and further diplomacy 167–8; post-Yorktown 173; wartime actions 170–3
Spithead 49
Springfield 16
"Squaw campaign" (1778) 130
Staten Island 15, 17, 61
Stockton, Samuel Witham 184
Stoker, Donald 3, 5–30
strategic context, naval war 75–7
Stuart, John 124, 127
Suffren, Chevalier Pierre André de 51, 89, 151, 155, 157, 191
Sugar Islands 110
Sullivan, Major General John 129–30
Sumter, Brigadier General Thomas 19, 27
Suriname 190
Surprize 48
Sweden: exploitation of neutrality 212–17; and League of Armed Neutrality 205–7
Swedish East India Company 206, 213–14
Sycamore Shoals Treaty (1775) 124
Symonds, Craig 38, 41

Taillemite, Etienne 148
Taitt, David 125
Tarleton, Lieutenant Colonel Banastre 18, 19, 23, 24, 25–6, 113, 114
Ternay, Commodore Chevalier d'Arsac de 154

Thames, battle of 122
Thunderer 40–1
Tilghman, Tench 14, 125
Tiro, Karim M. 120–35
Tobago 155
Touche-Tréville, Admiral Charles-Auguste de la 155
Toulon 85–6, 89
Trade and Intercourse Act (1790) 135
Trenton 15, 64, 107
Trincomalee 91, 191, 194
Truxtun, Thomas 50
Tryon, Governor William 104
Turgot, Anne-Robert-Jacques 142–3, 145
Tyrannicide 44

Union des Neutres pour la Securité de la Navigation et du Commerce (1691) 204
Uruguay 166–7
Ushant 51, 79, 92, 93, 148
Utrecht Treaty (1713) 177

Van Berckel, E.F. 184, 185, 193
Van Bylandt, Rear Admiral Frederik S. 181
van der Capellen tot den Pol, Joan Derk 178, 184
Van Kinsbergen, Captain 189
Van Overmeer, Captain 182
Vaudreuil, Marquis de 157–8
Vaughan, General John 190
Vauguyon, Duc de la 181
Vergennes, Comte de 2, 43, 48, 80–1, 87, 143, 144, 145–9, 151–2, 154, 157, 158, 167–8
Vestal 184
Vietnam 12
Ville de Paris 54
Virginia 51
Virginia Capes 53, 55, 156
von Steuben, Baron Friedrich Wilhelm 21, 170

War of the Austrian Succession (1740–8) 144
War of the Bavarian Succession (1778–9) 67, 69
war, nature of 5–6
Warner, Michael 134
Warren 45
Washington, George 3–4, 5, 6, 7–10, 11, 12–17, 18–19, 20, 28–9, 30, 36, 39–40, 43, 52–4, 61–2, 90, 105, 107, 129–30, 134–5, 155, 163–4, 172–3
Wasp 38

Waxhaws 18, 67
Wayne, General Anthony 131, 135
Welles 179
West India Trading Company 214
West Indies 47, 51–2, 54, 68, 73, 88, 92, 110, 148
Western states, Native Americans in 134–5
Westmoreland, General William 12
Whipple, Commodore Abraham 45, 46
White Eyes 130
Wickes, Lambert 47–8
William IV, King 177
William V, King 177, 178, 179, 182, 192
Williams, Colonel Otho 24
Willing, Captain James 164
Wilmington 25, 115
Wilson, Woodrow 219
Windward Islands 73, 147, 152–3, 157
Winnsboro 114
Wunder, John 122
Wyandot Indians 127, 132, 133, 135
Wyoming Valley 128

Yorke, Sir Joseph 179, 181–2, 185, 187
Yorktown 25–6, 28, 43, 52–3, 55, 59, 68, 70, 90, 132, 142, 156, 169, 171–3

Zeisberger, David 132
Zoutman, Rear Admiral Johan Arnold 189–90

eBooks – at www.eBookstore.tandf.co.uk

A library at your fingertips!

eBooks are electronic versions of printed books. You can store them on your PC/laptop or browse them online.

They have advantages for anyone needing rapid access to a wide variety of published, copyright information.

eBooks can help your research by enabling you to bookmark chapters, annotate text and use instant searches to find specific words or phrases. Several eBook files would fit on even a small laptop or PDA.

NEW: Save money by eSubscribing: cheap, online access to any eBook for as long as you need it.

Annual subscription packages

We now offer special low-cost bulk subscriptions to packages of eBooks in certain subject areas. These are available to libraries or to individuals.

For more information please contact webmaster.ebooks@tandf.co.uk

We're continually developing the eBook concept, so keep up to date by visiting the website.

www.eBookstore.tandf.co.uk